YEATS

An Annual of Critical and Textual Studies

YEATS

An Annual of Critical and Textual Studies

Volume II—1984

EDITED BY

Richard J. Finneran

Cornell University Press

ITHACA AND LONDON

First published 1984 by Cornell University Press.
Published in the United Kingdom by
Cornell University Press Ltd., London.

International Standard Book Number 0-8014-1761-9
Printed in the United States of America

The paper in this book is acid-free and meets the guidelines for permanence and durability of the Committee on Production Guidelines for Book Longevity of the Council on Library Resources.

FOR

F. S. L. LYONS

1923–1983

Contents

Contents

Contents

Editorial Information

We welcome submission of articles, notes, and editions. Unsolicited reviews are not accepted. Although we generally follow the *MLA Handbook for Writers of Research Papers, Theses, and Dissertations,* intending contributors are advised to request a Style Sheet from the editor at Department of English, Newcomb College, New Orleans, Louisiana 70118, U.S.A. Submissions received by May 15th will be assured of consideration for publication in the following year.

The editor is grateful to the Graduate Council on Research, Tulane University, for a grant to aid in the preparation of this volume of *Yeats.* All quotations from Yeats's writings, both published and unpublished, are made with permission of the copyright holders. We are particularly indebted to Michael Yeats; Anne Yeats; A. P. Watt Ltd; Macmillan, London, Ltd; and Macmillan Publishing Co., Inc.

Contributors

GEORGE BORNSTEIN, Professor of English, University of Michigan

DAVID R. CLARK, Professor of English, University of Massachusetts

EDWARD ENGELBERG, Professor of Romance and Comparative Literature, Brandeis University

RICHARD FALLIS, Associate Professor of English, Syracuse University

RICHARD J. FINNERAN, Professor of English, Newcomb College, Tulane University

MARY FITZGERALD, Associate Professor of English, University of New Orleans

GEORGE MILLS HARPER, Professor of English, Florida State University

K. P. S. JOCHUM, Professor of English, Universität Bamberg

JOHN S. KELLY, Senior English Fellow, St. John's College, Oxford University

ELIZABETH BERGMANN LOIZEAUX, Assistant Professor of English, University of Maryland

RICHARD LONDRAVILLE, Professor of English, New York State University College at Potsdam

DEBORAH MARTIN, graduate student in English, Tulane University

JAMES B. MCGUIRE, Professor Emeritus of English, Springfield College

RAEBURN MILLER, Professor of English, University of New Orleans

Contributors

William H. O'Donnell, Associate Professor of English, Pennsylvania State University

James Olney, Professor of English, Louisiana State University

Thomas Parkinson, Professor of English, University of California at Berkeley

Ronald Schuchard, Associate Professor of English, Emory University

Donald E. Stanford, Professor Emeritus of English, Louisiana State University

Mary Helen Thuente, Associate Professor of English, Indiana University–Purdue University at Fort Wayne

Donald T. Torchiana, Professor of English, Northwestern University

Editor's Notes

The essays in this issue by Bornstein, Clark and McGuire, Loizeaux, Olney, and Schuchard are revised versions of their papers presented at the International Yeats Symposium at Winthrop College, Rock Hill, South Carolina, 7–9 April 1983. Organized by Jack W. Weaver and funded in part by the National Endowment for the Humanities, this highly successful conference was attended by most of the leading Yeats scholars in America, as well as representatives from as far away as Australia and, of course, Ireland. The proceedings were also graced by the presence of Anne Yeats and Gráinne Yeats.

K. P. S. Jochum is planning a revised edition of his *Classified Bibliography of Yeats Criticism*. He would be grateful for corrections and additions to the first edition and also to his annual lists, which appear in this publication. He also welcomes offprints and review copies of current work, as well as notices of forthcoming publications. Address: Universität Bamberg, Postfach 1549, D-8600 Bamberg, West Germany.

Work in progress: Colin Smythe continues his work on a new primary bibliography. Readers with corrections or additions to the third edition of the Wade/Alspach *Bibliography of the Writings of W. B. Yeats* are urged to communicate with him at P.O. Box 6, Gerrards Cross, Buckinghamshire SL9 8EF, England. . . . The next volume in the Cornell Yeats will be Sandra Siegel's edition of the manuscripts of *Purgatory*. Nearing completion are editions of the manuscripts of *Mosada* and *The Island of Statues* by George Bornstein and *The Wind Among the Reeds* by Carolyn Holdsworth. . . . With the publication of *The Poems of W. B. Yeats, a New Edition* (to be reviewed in our 1985 issue), the next volume in the Macmillan, London, Collected Edition of the Works is likely to be William H. O'Donnell's *Prefaces and Introductions*.

Abbreviations

The following abbreviations are used throughout the annual, on the model of "(Au 181)" to refer to page 181 of *Autobiographies*. In addition, some of the essays use special abbreviations, as indicated in footnotes. In order to distinguish them from the standard abbreviations, these are italicized (unless an author's name) and followed by a comma and "p." or "pp."

Au	*Autobiographies*. London: Macmillan, 1955.
AV-A	*A Critical Edition of Yeats's* A Vision *(1925)*. Ed. George Mills Harper and Walter Kelly Hood. London: Macmillan, 1978. [Notes and Bibliography cited in italic numerals.]
AV-B	*A Vision*. London: Macmillan, 1962.
E&I	*Essays and Introductions*. London & New York: Macmillan, 1961.
Ex	*Explorations*. Sel. Mrs. W. B. Yeats. London: Macmillan, 1962; New York: Macmillan, 1963.
JSD	*John Sherman and Dhoya*. Ed. Richard J. Finneran. Detroit: Wayne State University Press, 1969.
L	*The Letters of W. B. Yeats*. Ed. Allan Wade. London: Rupert Hart-Davis, 1954; New York: Macmillan, 1955.
LDW	*Letters on Poetry from W. B. Yeats to Dorothy Wellesley*. Intro. Kathleen Raine. London & New York: Oxford University Press, 1964.
LMR	*Ah, Sweet Dancer: W. B. Yeats Margot Ruddock, A Correspondence*. Ed. Roger McHugh. London & New York: Macmillan, 1970.
LNI	*Letters to the New Island*. Ed. Horace Reynolds. Cambridge, Mass.: Harvard University Press, 1934.
LRB	*The Correspondence of Robert Bridges and W. B. Yeats*. Ed. Richard J. Finneran. London: Macmillan, 1977.

Abbreviations

LTSM — *W. B. Yeats and T. Sturge Moore: Their Correspondence, 1901–1937*. Ed. Ursula Bridge. London: Routledge & Kegan Paul; New York: Oxford University Press, 1953.

LTWBY — *Letters to W. B. Yeats*. Ed. Richard J. Finneran, George Mills Harper, and William M. Murphy. London: Macmillan; New York: Columbia University Press, 1977.

Mem — *Memoirs*. Ed. Denis Donoghue. London: Macmillan, 1972; New York: Macmillan, 1973.

Myth — *Mythologies*. London & New York: Macmillan, 1959.

OBMV — *The Oxford Book of Modern Verse, 1892–1935*. Chosen by W. B. Yeats. Oxford: Clarendon Press, 1936.

P — *The Poems of W. B. Yeats, a New Edition*. Ed. Richard J. Finneran. New York: Macmillan, 1983; London: Macmillan, 1984.

SB — *The Speckled Bird, With Variant Versions*. Ed. William H. O'Donnell. Toronto: McClelland and Stewart, 1976 [1977].

SR — *The Secret Rose, Stories by W. B. Yeats: A Variorum Edition*. Ed. Phillip L. Marcus, Warwick Gould, and Michael J. Sidnell. Ithaca & London: Cornell University Press, 1981.

TB — *Theatre Business: The Correspondence of the First Abbey Theatre Directors: William Butler Yeats, Lady Gregory and J. M. Synge*. Ed. Ann Saddlemyer. Gerrards Cross, Bucks.: Colin Smythe; University Park, Pa.: Pennsylvania State University Press, 1982.

UP1 — *Uncollected Prose by W. B. Yeats*. Vol. 1. Ed. John P. Frayne. London: Macmillan; New York: Columbia University Press, 1970.

UP2 — *Uncollected Prose by W. B. Yeats*. Vol. 2. Ed. John P. Frayne and Colton Johnson. London: Macmillan, 1975; New York: Columbia University Press, 1976.

VP — *The Variorum Edition of the Poems of W. B. Yeats*. Ed. Peter Allt and Russell K. Alspach. New York: Macmillan, 1957. [Cited from the corrected third printing (1966) or later printings.]

VPl — *The Variorum Edition of the Plays of W. B. Yeats*. Ed. Russell K. Alspach. London & New York: Macmillan, 1966. [Cited from the corrected second printing (1966) or later printings.]

Wade — Allan Wade, *A Bibliography of the Writings of W. B. Yeats*. 3d ed. Rev. Russell K. Alspach. London: Rupert Hart-Davis, 1968.

YEATS

An Annual of Critical and Textual Studies

The Making of Yeats's Spenser

George Bornstein

When W. B. Yeats recalled the origins of his literary career in *Reveries over Childhood and Youth,* his impulse toward mythic autobiography happily corresponded with accuracy: "I had begun to write poetry in imitation of Shelley and of Edmund Spenser, play after play—for my father exalted dramatic poetry above all other kinds—and I invented fantastic and incoherent plots" (Au 66-67). As that linkage suggests, Yeats's Spenser was always a Romantic, as were the other poets into whose company Yeats sought admission as a brother.[1] Indeed, except for Shelley and Blake, Spenser influenced Yeats perhaps more than did any other English precursor. His impact extended from the plots of Yeats's early verse of the 1880s through the symbolism of the Rose poems of the 1890s to climax in the imagery and themes of some of the great mature lyrics on Lady Gregory and her son Robert. Yeats at first sought simply to imitate Spenser, then to project onto him conflicts from his own career, and finally to adapt Spenser's stance toward aristocratic patrons for his own uses. In so doing he continually revised his image of a Romantic Spenser, first from a poet of fantastic pastoral to one of intense vision of beauty and then from a self-

[1]I mean here not only Yeats's well-known tendency to see himself as a "last romantic," particularly in terms of Blake and Shelley, but also his habit of viewing other poets he admired as in some way Romantic. See, for example, my essays "Yeats's Romantic Dante," *Colby Library Quarterly,* 15 (1979), 93–113, and "Last Romantic or Last Victorian: Yeats, Browning, and Tennyson," *Yeats Annual No. 1* (London: Macmillan, 1982), pp. 114–32. An earlier and shorter version of the present essay appears as the "Yeats" entry in *The Spenser Encyclopedia,* forthcoming from University of Toronto Press.

divided prophet to an impassioned lamenter of necessary defeats by time and death. Throughout, Yeats persistently paired the Renaissance poet with his Romantic admirers Shelley, Keats, or Blake both in published works and in private manuscripts and marginalia, particularly those connected with his 1906 edition of Spenser.

The period of emulation began with several unpublished early plays and with a long, unpublished narrative poem in Spenserian stanzas on the adventures of a medieval knight. The poem struggles confusedly to fulfill the avowal of "Sad love and change" rather than "rime empassioned of envenomed years / Or the embattled earth" in its first and only published stanza.[2] Along the way it mixes Greek, Romance, and Norse elements in the sort of pastoral potpourri that Yeats derived from Keats and Shelley's own redactions of Spenser. The plot is at once "fantastic and incoherent" and yet curiously anticipatory of Yeats's later preoccupations, as a summary will make clear. Like the first hero of Spenser's epic, Yeats's Sir Roland wears a red cross. Singing "a song forlorn about a lady fair / . . . / In iron Norway" (stanza 4), he enters the valley of Lethe, where he encounters another knight. The second knight, "Olaf the Hero dane" (stanza 21), tells of blessedly ruling a peaceful country until a mysterious figure sang him a song about the fair maid Ingeborg in the visionary land of unfading asphodel. Olaf then set out to seek for her by ship with a picked crew, all of whom died and left him still wandering in hopeless quest, upon which Roland seems to join him as the fragment ends. (There are scattered other stanzas which may also belong to the poem, for example those on the Spenserian figures Sansloy and Sansfoy.) Memories of *Alastor, Endymion,* and *Rime of the Ancient Mariner* obviously jostle with elements of *The Faerie Queen* in this early, imitative work. Yet the poem does contain the solitary quest for a visionary woman so important in Yeats's writing over the following two decades.

[2]See Richard Ellmann, *Yeats: The Man and the Masks* (New York: Macmillan, 1948), pp. 28–29. The manuscripts are currently in the collection of Michael Yeats, for whose cooperation I am grateful. Because the manuscripts are confusing, the identification in the text of the two following quotations by stanza number needs a clarification. The stanza 4 containing the first quotation has been renumbered as 5; the stanza 21 containing the second quotation is one of two consecutive stanzas bearing that number.

That theme became more prominent in *The Island of Statues,* Yeats's first major published work (1885) and one more coherent if not less fantastic than the previous unpublished dramas. In *Reveries* he would label it "an Arcadian play in imitation of Edmund Spenser" (Au 92). Imitative elements included characters like the Enchantress and the singing shepherds Thernot and Colin, pastoral settings like Arcadia and the enchanted island, and the rich mellifluence of the verse. Above all, the plot hinged on the noble youth Almintor's quest for the magic flower to win Naschina and its ambivalent resolution.

The early but still superficial emulation of Spenserian questing deepened in the 1890s, when Yeats came to appreciate the Neoplatonic elements in *Fowre Hymns* and elsewhere. The proper object of the Spenserian and Shelleyan plots should have been Intellectual Beauty. In devising his own Rose lyrics around that theme, Yeats looked back to the hymns as much as to the narratives of Shelley and Spenser for literary precedent. Even thirty years later he could find only one distinction between his work and theirs: "I notice upon reading these poems for the first time for several years that the quality symbolised as The Rose differs from the Intellectual Beauty of Shelley and of Spenser in that I have imagined it as suffering with man and not as something pursued and seen from afar" (VP 842). That distinction, as much invented as real, parallels Yeats's desire to move downward upon life after the 1890s. The Rose poems both close and make coherent his period of early devotion.

Yeats's edition of *Poems of Spenser* (1906) for the Golden Poets series marks the middle phase of his interest. The project arose somewhat haphazardly. As he wrote to Lady Gregory in January 1902, "I have had a letter from an Edinburgh publisher asking me to edit a book of selections from Spenser for £ 35. It is good pay and I am writing to ask when it will be wanted. I may do it if I have not to do it at once. I have a good deal to say about Spenser but tremble at the thought of reading his six books" (L 365).[3] Yeats's trembling changed to delight as he made his way through

[3]For a survey of Yeats's letters referring to the edition, see A. G. Stock, "Yeats on Spenser," in *In Excited Reverie: A Centenary Tribute to William Butler Yeats, 1865–1939,* ed. A. Norman Jeffares and K. G. W. Cross (London: Macmillan; New York: St. Martin, 1965), pp. 93–101.

the six books of *The Faerie Queen*. A year later he had finished his task, though the Edinburgh firm of T. C. & E. C. Jack waited three more years to publish the resultant volume. In it Yeats eschewed representation as a principle of selection and instead chose "only those passages from Spenser that I want to remember and carry about with me."[4] The extracts thus offer a fair map of the parts of Spenser that mattered most to Yeats. He began with *An Hymne of Heavenly Beautie,* included *Epithalamion* with extracts from *The Teares of the Muses, Ruines of Time,* and *The Shepherd's Calender,* and cited a few other passages on love, shepherds, or old age. From *The Faerie Queen* he excerpted his favorite sections, including the islands of Phaedria and Acrasia, the Garden of Adonis, and the vision of Scudamour. With perhaps the exception of the strong, elegiac lament for the Earl of Leicester, the passages reflect the aspects of Spenser that underlay Yeats's early adaptations.

The texts themselves and some of the notes for Yeats's edition derive from the controversial J. Payne Collier five-volume *Works of Edmund Spenser* (London: Bell, 1862), which Lady Gregory presented to him. The unpublished but still surviving marginalia to these volumes both reveal Yeats's mind at work as he labored over the edition and provide an intimate glimpse of the way he reacted to Spenser.[5] Sometimes the marginalia simply reveal that charming side of Yeats which he so rigorously excised from his public persona. For instance, worrying over how much of Book 2, Canto 12, of *The Faerie Queen* the publishers will let him include, he finally decides, "give all canto 12 It is most beautiful" (II, 334).

[4]"Introduction" to *Poems of Spenser,* ed. W. B. Yeats (Edinburgh: T. C. & E. C. Jack, 1906), p. xliv. For the reader's convenience, I cite further references to this essay from the more accessible *Essays and Introductions* text, which differs from the 1906 volume in minor ways but not in the passages I cite.

[5]The volumes themselves are part of Yeats's library in the collection of Anne Yeats, whose kindness in helping with the present article as well as other work has been extraordinary. Perhaps the greatest number of markings and marginalia concern problems of selection for Yeats's own edition; I have focused here on more substantive comments instead. The pencil inscription on the flyleaf of volume 1—"W. B. Yeats / March—1892 / A. G."—in Lady Gregory's hand remains something of a mystery owing to the date. Citations of Yeats's marginalia to this edition will be indicated by the volume number in roman numerals followed by the page number in arabic numerals, enclosed within parentheses in the text.

Again, faced with the exasperating complexities of *Muiopotmos,* he replaces a simple question mark with an increasingly desperate series of questions: "Is this poem alegorical. Is it ~~mis~~ Earthly ?talent against divine. reason against instinct. Calculation against genius or what?" (IV, 474). More often, the marginalia reveal three of his chief preoccupations as he read through Spenser's verse—its connection to Ireland, its exaltation of Venus or Intellectual Beauty, and its relation to Romantic poetry. Yeats noted, for example, the comparison of the stones of Alma's castle to Irish marble as the "first sign of Irish influence" (II, 247). He delighted in drawing the astrological sign for Venus [♀] in the margin next to references to the goddess, star, or any other figure he could associate with Intellectual Beauty, and he often threw in the signs for Mars, Earth, and Sun as well. But most often, passages in Spenser reminded him of favorite lines of Romantic poetry. These deserve a closer look.

Comparisons to Romantic poets cluster most frequently in Books 2 and 3 of *The Faerie Queen,* where Yeats paused to jot comments in the margins six times. All concern Shelley, Blake, or Keats. In Book 2 he compares the magic boat in which Phaedria ferries Cymochles over the Idle Lake to the wandering island with "Shelley's boats," perhaps in particular the self-propelled shallop of *Alastor* or the enchanted craft in *The Witch of Atlas* (II, 175). In Book 3 the conception of Belphoebe and Amoret by sunrays which impregnate their supernatural mother resting in rural solitude makes him recall the analogous circumstances of the Witch of Atlas's birth (II, 447). Similarly, Spenser's witch creating the False Florimel out of snow two cantos later suggests to Yeats the hermaphroditic "figure of snow" molded by Shelley's witch to be her companion (II, 486). The two Blake references are more general. When Satyrane encounters the giantess Argante riding with a doleful squire "bounded hand and foote with cords of wire," Yeats remembers that "Blake has chords or nets of wire," as in "The Golden Net"; and Spenser's likening to a discolored snake of the golden threads of the arras in Busyrane's castle where Scudamour languishes reminds Yeats of "Blake's serpent" (II, 477, and III, 52). Those correlations are both supple and acute, striking us with a fine surprise. But none shows Yeats's powers of connection and revision so well as the sole reference to Keats.

When Phaedria conducts Cymochles across the Idle Lake to the island, Spenser writes:

> Thus when shee had his eyes and sences fed
> With false delights, and fild with pleasures vayn,
> Into a shady dale she soft him led,
> And layd him downe upon a grassy playn;
> And her sweete selfe without dread or disdayn
> She sett beside, laying his head disarmd
> In her loose lap, it softly to sustayn,
> Where soone he slumbered fearing not be harmd:
> The whils with a love lay she thus him sweetly charmd.

Coming across this passage, Yeats notes in the margin, "La Belle Dame Sans Merci" (II, 178). The parallels leap out at once: in both poems a supernatural lady misleads a fallible human quester into a hopeless love, entices him to a secluded bower, and charms him asleep with a lovesong, from which he will awaken disillusioned. Yet the differences rate equal attention. The brother of the fiery Pyrochles, Cymochles represents anger; he consorts with Acrasia, who presides over the sensual Bower of Bliss; and he eventually is killed by Arthur while despoiling the knight of Temperance, Guyon. His story may suggest broad psychological or imaginative truth, but also occupies a clear place in the governing Christian allegory of the poem. Keats's knight carries no such Christian connotations. Instead, he stands as a symbol of a mistaken questing for an imaginary ideal wholly separate from the actual. In linking the two stories, Yeats characteristically ignores Spenser's Christian allegory to focus on elements compatible with a Romantic parable of imaginative questing.

The introduction to *Poems of Spenser* writes large the dichotomies of the marginalia. Yeats subsumed the essay into his critical canon by reprinting it under the title "Edmund Spenser" in *The Cutting of an Agate*. Displaying his characteristic fondness for antinomies, he there saw Spenser as divided between a positive, poetically symbolic, aristocratic, and Anglo-French delight in the senses and a negative, prosaically allegorical, middle-class, and Anglo-Saxon allegiance to the emerging State. These antitheses allowed him to admire the Romantic and poetic side of Spenser even while confessing the harshness of *View of the Present State of Ireland,* which troubled his nationalist sympathies. The positive qualities had engendered the later, Romantic poetry of Keats, Shelley, and Blake, whose names dot the essay as they do the marginalia. But even as the Romantics elaborated on Spenser more subtly and more intellectually, they lost the sureness of personal instinct that distinguishes his best work. The result was a retreat from the world and "disintegration of the personal instincts which has given to modern poetry its deep colour for colour's sake, its overflowing pattern, its background of decorative landscape, and its insubordination of detail" (E&I 357). The problem extended even to versification: one had only to compare a stanza from Shelley's *Laon and Cythna* with Spenser's own cadences to conclude that "the rhythm is varied and troubled, and the lines, which are in Spenser like bars of gold thrown ringing one upon another, are broken capriciously. . . . It is bound together by the vaguest suggestion" (E&I 379).

Those defects of excessive attention to detail, troubled rhythms, and vague suggestion sound suspiciously like Yeats's own criticisms of his own early poetry. Indeed, the entire essay—written as Yeats began his movement downward upon life after the aestheticism of the 1890s—reads like a projection of the dangers that he himself feared as he reoriented his own poetry. Would he, like Spenser, forsake the "self-exciting, self-appeasing soul" through trying "to be of his time, or rather of the time that was all but at hand," or would he be able to transform that time "in the mythology of his imagination"? (E&I 370, 358). When Yeats observes "that conflict between the aesthetic and moral interests that was to run through wellnigh all his [Spenser's] works" (E&I 360), we may recall the conflict between aesthetic and occult ones that pervades his own. Just as Yeats's description of the Romantics recapitulates his own recent poetic experience, so does his conception of Spenser's misadventures with Puritan Christianity prefigure the form his own struggles with occult dogmas would henceforth take. "Texts for exposition" were his analogue to Spenserian allegory, and he came to regret even the few that he eventually wrote.

After the Spenser edition Yeats approached his sometime model only with care, as though too close contact with the inspirer of his early islands and escapist paradises would weaken the new strength he sought for his own poetry. But he did turn to Spenser for one of his strongest achievements, the powerful elegiac laments for a lost aristocratic tradition. Much influenced by Castiglione's concept of the courtier, Yeats had included in his edition an excerpt from *Mother Hubbard's Tale,* which was itself a redaction of Castiglione's precepts.[6] With the death of Robert Gregory, Yeats drew upon Spenser to enrich his own allegiance to the Gregory family, particularly in the elegiac mode. Spenser's laments for Sidney in *Astrophel* and for the Earl of Leicester in *The Ruines of Time* lie behind Yeats's own commemorative efforts. In a letter to Lady Gregory on 22 February 1918 he described his first elegy for her son Robert, *Shepherd and Goatherd,* as "in manner like one that Spenser wrote for Sir Philip Sidney" (L 646). The likeness included pastoral shepherds, lament for a young aristocrat dead in a foreign war, and a vision of his continued life as much Neoplatonic or pagan as Christian. The subsequent and more powerful *In Memory of Major Robert Gregory* differs in design and form but still refers to Robert as "Our Sidney and our perfect man" (VP 325).

In the very late *The Municipal Gallery Revisited* (1937) Yeats fittingly turned to Spenser for the last time in a major way, bidding goodbye as much to the progenitor of his favorite literary images as to the painters and friends who had inspired the artistic and personal ones he so loved. Even in the edition of thirty years before he had noticed that Spenser's lament for the Earl of Leicester in *The Ruines of Time* belonged with those passages on men that "seem to express more of personal joy and sorrow than those about women" in his poetry (E&I 359). For Yeats, of course, that situation was often reversed. In his own poem he laments the demise of Lady Gregory's Coole Park in an explicit recollection of the Leicester passage: "And now that end has come I have not wept; / No fox can foul the lair the badger swept— / (An image out of Spenser and the common tongue)" (VP 603). Yet even that explicit echo revises Spenser's image of an unworthy successor as a

[6]I owe this observation to T. McAlindon's generally helpful article "Yeats and the English Renaissance," *PMLA,* 82 (1967), 157–69.

fox creeping into the badger's hole by proscribing the fox from defiling its heritage. It doubtless pleased Yeats that Spenser had in mind his enemy Lord Burleigh, whose Irish policy had been so harsh. Yet his allusion here carries far more than mere national resentment; it carries the full weight of Yeats's mature thought and skill which give his later work its memorable strength. The question and answer he scrawled on a sheet of Lady Gregory's notepaper could just as well be applied to his own work: "Why gentle Spenser? He is rather powerful than gentle."[7]

[7]The notepaper is headed "Coole Park, / Gort, / Co. Galway" and is tucked between pages 386 and 387 of volume 4 of Yeats's copy of Collier's edition. I have replaced Yeats's period with an interrogation mark to clarify the sense.

The Writing of *Sophocles' King Oedipus*

David R. Clark and
James B. McGuire

Yeats Seeks an *Oedipus* to Produce, 1904–1909

That we have W. B. Yeats's version of *Sophocles' King Oedipus* (and therefore also his version of Sophocles' *Oedipus at Colonus*) is a

 We thank them for permission to publish portions of Yeats's unpublished letters and other unpublished manuscripts and in particular we thank them and Macmillan London Limited for permission to publish text and manuscripts of *Sophocles' King Oedipus*. For the letters, thanks are due also to the Delegates of Oxford University Press, to John Kelly, editor of the forthcoming Oxford University Press edition of *The Collected Letters of W. B. Yeats,* to Ronald Schuchard, co-editor of volumes three and four, 1901–1910, and to Mary FitzGerald, co-editor of volume five, 1911–1915. We are also grateful to the estate of Major Richard Gregory (for material by Lady Gregory), Alexander Murray (for material by Gilbert Murray), the National Library of Ireland, the Henry W. and Albert A. Berg Collection, the New York Public Library, Astor, Lenox and Tilden Foundations, the Abbey Theatre, and the Bodleian Library for permission to quote from manuscript material in their possession or charge. We thank the Yeatses, the Macmillan Publishing Company, Inc., New York, Macmillan London Limited, and Rupert Hart-Davis, London, for permission to quote from Yeats's published works. Thanks are due to A. P. Watt Ltd and to Lewis Lusardi and Narayan Hegde of the William Butler Yeats Archives, State University of New York at Stony Brook, for their courtesy. We are grateful for help received from the staffs of the following libraries: Amherst College, the Bodleian, Bucknell University, Cornell University, the Houghton and Pusey libraries of Harvard University, the Incorporated Law Societies, Dublin, Mount Holyoke College, Pearse Street, Dublin, Smith College, State University of New York at Stony Brook, Springfield College, and the University of direct result of the English censorship of the theatre.[1] Yeats's interest in producing *Oedipus the King* recurred off and on during the period 1903–1912. After that it lay dormant until early 1926. Although the book does not mention Yeats, Fowell and Palmer's *Censorship in England* (1913) helps to explain why he was so much impressed when he heard that Sophocles' tragedy of patricide and incest had been successfully produced at Notre Dame University:

> *Oedipus Rex* was for many years regarded as impossible for the English stage. Even when so responsible an actor as Sir Herbert Tree desired to produce it at His Majesty's Theatre, he was prevented. No specific version of the *Oedipus* was in question. Sir Herbert had seen a famous French actor playing in the tragedy in Paris, but when on his instructions the Censor was again asked about the play he was told that it could not be licensed. He gave no specific reason, but stated that the licence had been refused before, and that it was no use submitting the play again.[2]

The reason for the refusal must have been that *Oedipus* deals with incest. This official stupidity aroused the scorn of dramatists

Massachusetts. Thanks are due to Richard Finneran, Mary FitzGerald, Ronald Schuchard, and especially to Carlos Baker and Ann Saddlemyer, for reading the whole essay and making valuable suggestions. We thank also the many other persons who have helped us in our project, including Brother W. P. Allen, Robert Bagg, Damien Boyle, Kevin Boyle, Stephen Brennan, Margaret Byrne, James Carens, Joseph Chadwick, Mary Clapinson, Mary A. Clark, John Dillon, Karen Dorn, Beverly Feldman, John Garvin, Oliver Gogarty, John Kelly, Thomas and Eleanor Kinsella, Helen Langley, Maureen Loughran, Susan Lovènburg, J. B. Lyons, Alf MacLochlainn, Gloria McGuire, Roger McHugh, Brian McInerney, Terry McLaughlin, Liam Miller, Michael O hAodha, D. O'Luannaigh, Brian O'Neill, Christopher Robinson, Colin Smythe, W. B. Stanford, M. J. Stoneburg, Lola L. Szladits, William and Jacqueline VanVoris, Kevin Waldron, Richard and Sigrid Weber, John Reeve Workman, Anne Yeats, and Gráinne Yeats.

The American Council of Learned Societies, the American Philosophical Society, and the University of Massachusetts have helped David Clark, Springfield College has helped James McGuire, and the National Endowment for the Humanities had helped both editors, toward the completion of this research.

[1]The former was first produced at the Abbey Theatre, Dublin, 7 December 1926, and first published in *Sophocles' King Oedipus: A Version for the Modern Stage* (London: Macmillan, 1928). The latter was first produced at the Abbey, 12 September 1927, and first published in *The Collected Plays of W. B. Yeats* (London: Macmillan, 1934).

[2]Frank Fowell and Frank Palmer, *Censorship in England* (London: Frank Palmer, 1913), p. 275; hereafter cited as Fowell and Palmer.

and theatre people. Fowell and Palmer quote (p. 275) a protest from Henry Arthur Jones: "Now, of course, if any considerable body of Englishmen are arranging to marry their mothers, whether by accident or design, it must be stopped at once. But it is not a frequent occurrence in any class of English society. Throughout the course of my life I have not met more than six men who were anxious to do it."

When Yeats heard, during his 1903–1904 American lecture tour, that *Oedipus* had been produced at Notre Dame, the possibility of a performance in Ireland became to him symbolic of the freedom that his new theatre should stand for. His two accounts—long after the event—of how he came to write his own version of the play would lead one to think that he started to do so as soon as he returned from America in 1904. But these accounts are misleading. Although Yeats was interested in producing the play from 1904 on, he did not think of composing his own version until 1912. On 7 January 1912, he wrote to Lady Gregory, "I am making my own version of Oedipus."[3]

It seems best to put before the reader Yeats's two accounts, with their essential truth and with all their inaccuracies of times, places, and persons, and then to reconstruct, from contemporary documents, a demythologized version of the same events. Yeats's first account appeared in the *Irish Weekly and Ulster Examiner* for 12 September 1931, soon after he had read it from the Belfast studio of BBC radio, and shortly before the play itself was broadcast.

> Nearly thirty years ago I was at the Catholic University of Notre Dame at Illinois. I had come there to give a lecture about Irish literature, and stayed for a couple of days. A certain monk, specially appointed, I think, to look after the guests, was the best of companions, and told me a great many exciting things about his monastery, about the Irish in America, and about his own thoughts.
>
> The thing that stayed longest in my memory was that "Oedipus the King" had just been performed under the auspices of his University. "Oedipus the King" was at that time forbidden by the English censor, and I thought that if we could play it at the Abbey Theatre, which was to open on our return, we might make our audience

[3]TLS (typed letter signed), Yeats to Lady Gregory, dictated at the Abbey Theatre "January 7th 1912"; collection of Michael Yeats; photocopy National Library of Ireland MS. 18721.

proud of its liberty, and take a noble view of the stage and its mission.

Some three or four years passed, and I began my version with the help of Mr. Nugent Monk, who was at the time helping us at the Abbey, and has since established a famous theatre in Norwich, and a young Greek scholar, then one of our actors, but now a Circuit Judge; and half a dozen translations. Sometimes I went on to the stage and spoke a sentence to be sure that it was simple enough and resonant enough to be instantaneously felt and understood in every part of the theatre. I did not want to make a new translation for the reader, but something that everybody in the house, scholar and pot-boy, would understand as easily as he understood a political speech or an article in a newspaper. The subject matter might be strange and sometimes difficult, but no word might be strange or difficult, nor must I tire the ear by putting those words in some unnatural order.

I finished my first rough draft and began to look for an actor, but before I had found one the English censorship withdrew its ban, and when the pleasure of mocking it and affirming the freedom of our Irish uncensored stage was taken from me, I lost interest in the play. I put it into the file with my letters and forgot it, and then four or five years ago my wife found it and persuaded me to finish it and put it on to the Abbey Stage.[4]

[4]*The Irish Weekly and Ulster Examiner,* 12 September 1931, 9; hereafter cited as *Irish Weekly*. A working typescript and a final typescript (with the last page missing) are in the collection of Michael Yeats. In the Yeats Archives at the State University of New York at Stony Brook, copies can be found at SB 12.7.113–25 (i.e., pp. 113–25 of volume 7 of the hard-copy derived from reel 12 of the microfilms). Curtis Bradford made a transcription based on these typescripts, a copy of which is in Michael Yeats's collection (SB 12.7.193–98). Bradford added the following note: "Mr. H. W. McMullen, who produced the Yeats programs at Belfast, is now [1954–1955 or 1960] Head of Northern Ireland Programmes for the BBC. He reports that this talk was broadcast at 7:15 P.M. on Tuesday, September 8, 1931. It was billed as follows: 'Mr. W. B. Yeats on his version for the Modern Stage of the Greek play *King Oedipus,* to be broadcast from the Belfast Studio by the Abbey Players on September 14.' This talk, which was broadcast in the Belfast program only, has been transcribed from a typescript" (SB 12.7.193). A transcription of the broadcast (perhaps identical) appears among the Bradford papers at Burling Library, Grinnell College, Grinnell, Iowa. James Lovic Allen and M. M. Liberman, "Transcriptions of Yeats's Unpublished Prose in the Bradford Papers at Grinnell College," *The Serif,* 10 (Spring 1973), 13–27. Allen and Liberman say, contrary to Bradford's note, that it was another program, "Reading of Poems, Belfast," which was aired in the evening, after the talk on Oedipus had been aired that morning. See also Wade 468. Excerpts from the talk were published in "Greek Play over Radio," *Irish Times,* 9 September 1931, p. 4. The article is dated "Belfast, Tuesday"; the correspondent says that the talk was given "tonight" and that the play would be broadcast "next Monday" (14 September).

Yeats's second account appeared in the *New York Times,* 15 January 1933, at the end of his last American lecture tour. By this date he had perhaps learned that Notre Dame is not in Illinois, but he did not chance saying where, in the vast North American continent, it is:

> When I first lectured in America thirty years ago, I heard at the University of Notre Dame that they had played *Oedipus the King.* That play was forbidden by the English censorship on the ground of its immorality; Oedipus commits incest; but if a Catholic university could perform it in America my own theatre could perform it in Ireland. Ireland had no censorship, and a successful performance might make her proud of her freedom, say even, perhaps, "I have an old historical religion moulded to the body of man like an old suit of clothes, and am therefore free."
>
> . . . When I got back to Dublin I found a young Greek scholar who, unlike myself, had not forgotten his Greek, took out of a pigeonhole at the theatre a manuscript translation of *Oedipus* too complicated in its syntax for the stage, bought Jebb's translation and a translation published at a few pence for dishonest schoolboys. Whenever I could not understand the precise thoughts behind the translators' half Latin, half Victorian dignity, I got a bald translation from my Greek scholar. I spoke out every sentence, very often from the stage, with one sole object, that the words should sound natural and fall in their natural order, that every sentence should be a spoken, not a written sentence. Then when I had finished the dialogue in the rough and was still shrinking at the greater labour of the choruses, the English censor withdrew his ban and I lost interest.
>
> About five years ago my wife found the manuscript and set me to work again, and when the dialogue was revised and the choruses written, Lady Gregory and I went through it all, altering every sentence that might not be intelligible on the Blasket Islands.[5]

[5] "Plain Man's *Oedipus,*" *New York Times,* sec. 9, p. 1; rpt. L 537*n,* copyright 1953, 1954 by Anne Butler Yeats. Some remarks of Oliver Gogarty are reported in "Sophocles, Yeats, and Dr. Gogarty" on the same date: "Dr. Gogarty might be said to have been in at the birth of Yeats's version of 'King Oedipus.' It was his copy of Jebb's translation that Yeats borrowed some years ago, ostensibly as a guide in what not to do in making a rendition of some of the lyrics" (*New York Herald Tribune,* 15 January 1933, sec. 7, p. 4). Since Yeats did not translate the choruses until 1926, "some years ago" may refer to that date. He had intended, however, to translate them in 1912. In 1909 he had purchased *The Oedipus Tyrannus of Sophocles: as Performed at Cambridge November 22–26, 1887. With a Translation in Prose by R. C. Jebb, And a Translation of the Songs of the Chorus in Verse adapted to the Music of C. Villiers Stanford, M.A., by A. W. Verrall, M.A.*

Yeats's first mention of his hope is in a 17 March 1903 letter to Gilbert Murray. He suggests the formation of a "Theatre of Beauty," which should produce "Marlowe's Faustus, your translation of the Hippolytus, a translation of Edipus Tyrannus, a play of Congreve's, & contemporary work of Robert Bridges (his 'Return of Ulysses') & myself—." This group became the Masquers Society, founded 28 March 1903. The purpose was to give "plays that have some beauty of staging which shall be of the simplest, and acting which shall be simple too."[6] At the same time Yeats does not seem to have heard that the censor would forbid any performance of Oedipus. In any event the Greek play the Masquers favored producing was Murray's translation of *Hippolytus,* but to everyone's relief the whole project collapsed.[7] Everyone was busy doing other things. In early November 1903, Yeats departed on a four-month lecture tour of the United States.[8]

Yeats did not at this time favor a production of a Greek play by the Irish theatre. On 2 January 1904, he dictated a letter to Lady Gregory from New York: ". . . I hope the company will not adopt Colum's suggestion and play the *Hippolytus*. It is altogether too soon for us to stray away from Irish subjects. Above all, it is too soon for us to put on any non-Irish work of such importance as the *Hippolytus*. It would be playing into the hands of our enemies. On the other hand, if we get through this season keeping our audiences with us and playing a considerable variety of good, new Irish work, we will be able to do as we like." He went on to say that if the *Hippolytus* were to be presented, he wished to be there and to get Charles Ricketts to stage the play. But he wished to do a play by Shaw first (L 420).

(Cambridge: Macmillan & Bowes, 1887), hereafter cited as Jebb. This book is No. 966/L.7.2 in Yeats's library, now at the home of Miss Anne Yeats. Gogarty's Jebb may have been a different edition.

[6]Yeats to Gilbert Murray, from Coole, 17 March 1903, dictated to Lady Gregory and in her hand (even to the signature); Bodleian Library, Oxford.

[7]Murray to Yeats, 12 November 1903 (LTWBY 131). See also *Gilbert Murray: An Unfinished Autobiography,* ed. Jean Smith and Arnold Toynbee (London: George Allen & Unwin, 1960), p. 109.

[8]Joseph Hone, *W. B. Yeats, 1865–1939,* 2d ed. (London: Macmillan, 1962), p. 194; hereafter cited as Hone. According to B. L. Reid in *The Man from New York: John Quinn and His Friends* (New York: Oxford University Press, 1968), p. 17, Yeats arrived in New York on 11 November 1904.

By addressing the question of when it would be strategic to put on *Hippolytus,* Yeats opened himself to suggestion, and when two weeks later, during his lecture-visit to Notre Dame, a priest told him that that Catholic university had produced *Oedipus the King,* the seed was well planted.[9] *Oedipus* had the advantage over *Hippolytus* of having been banned in England.

Yeats apparently kept the idea to himself, however, until the company had got through its first season successfully. He wrote Lady Gregory that he was "entirely delighted by the big merry priests of Notre Dame" (L 422), but his letter does not report his excitement that Notre Dame had produced *Oedipus.* A couple of days later he wrote to Frank Fay about the "really wonderful large tolerant spirit" at Notre Dame, yet he again did not mention *Oedipus.*[10]

In December 1904 Yeats opened his campaign to produce *Oedipus the King*. In the *Samhain* of 1904, along with his announcement of the establishment of the Abbey Theatre, he made the first move in that campaign. He likened Irish people to the Greek chorus. He pointed out the Abbey Theatre's responsibility to stage foreign masterpieces. He exercised himself about the difference between the money morals of the commercial theater and the real morals valued by the Abbey. Then he declared the freedom in Ireland, as in "the great American Catholic University of Notre-Dame," to put on a really moral play like *Oedipus,* hypocritically banned in hated England:

> We are better off so far as the law is concerned than we would be in England. The theatrical law of Ireland was made by the Irish Parliament, and though the patent system, the usual method of the time, has outlived its use and come to an end everywhere but in Ireland, we must be grateful to that ruling caste of free spirits, that being free themselves they left the theatre in freedom. In England there is a Censor, who forbids you to take a subject from the Bible or from politics, or to picture public characters, or certain moral situations

[9]The Notre Dame performance was memorialized in a book with the Greek and English on facing pages: *The Oedipus Tyrannus of Sophocles,* Translated and Presented by the Students of Notre Dame University, Notre Dame, Indiana, May 15, 1899 (University Press).

[10]Letter from New York dated by Wade "[?20 January 1904]" (L 424).

> which are the foundation of some of the greatest plays of the world. When I was at the great American Catholic University of Notre-Dame I heard that the students had given a performance of *Oedipus the King,* and *Oedipus the King* is forbidden in London. A censorship created in the eighteenth century by Walpole, because somebody had written against election bribery, has been distorted by a puritanism which is not the less an English invention for being a pretended hatred of vice and a real hatred of intellect. Nothing has ever suffered so many persecutions as the intellect, though it is never persecuted under its own name. [Ex 131–32]

Thus, without announcing a production of *Oedipus,* Yeats led his audience to desire one.

The Abbey Theatre opened on 27 December 1904. A week earlier Yeats was already busy trying to get Oliver Gogarty to do a translation of *Oedipus* for the Abbey stage. The evidence does not show that Yeats had any intention of writing his own version at this time. As a youth he had recognized that his classics were not good enough to get him into Trinity College (Au 79–80); probably he now considered that he had not enough Greek to be translating *Oedipus.* At any rate, he turned to other poets who did know Greek to provide translations. The most distinguished of these was Gilbert Murray. Murray had already made impressive translations in English rhyming verse of Euripides' *Hippolytus,* of *The Bacchae,* and of Aristophanes' *The Frogs;* and, in 1905, *The Trojan Women* and *Electra* were to follow.[11] Yeats's sprightly invitation to Murray is dated 24 January 1905:

> Will you translate Edipus Rex for us? We can offer you nothing for it but a place in heaven, but if you do, it will be a great event. Our company are excited at the idea. The Fays have read it, and believe we can give a fine performance. There is no censor here to forbid it as it has been forbidden in England. It is much better worth writing for us than for Granville Barker. Nothing has any effect in England,

[11] *Euripides,* translated into English rhyming verse by Gilbert Murray (London: G. Allen, 1902)—this volume included *The Frogs. The Trojan Women,* translated into English rhyming verse with explanatory notes by Gilbert Murray (London: George Allen, 1905). *The Electra,* translated into English rhyming verse with explanatory notes by Gilbert Murray (London: George Allen, 1905).

but here one never knows when one may affect the mind of a whole generation. The country is in its first plastic state, and takes the mark of every strong finger. We have a beautiful little theatre and can stage it well. Do not ask us to play Euripides instead, for Euripides is rapidly becoming a popular English dramatist, and it is upon Sophocles that we have set our imaginations. Besides, I am always trying to persuade Ireland, which does not understand the game, that she is very liberal, abhor censors [,] delights in the freedom of the arts, is prepared for anything. When we have performed Edipus the King, and everybody is proud of having done something which is forbidden in England, even the newspapers will give [up] pretending to be timid. . . .

We can give you plenty of time over Sophocles, for we have so many plays coming on that we can hardly produce the Edipus before our autumn session.[12]

Murray declined Yeats's invitation by return mail (27 January 1905):

O Man,

I will not translate the Oedipus Rex for the Irish Theatre, because it is a play with nothing Irish about it: no religion, not one beautiful action, hardly a stroke of poetry. Even the good things that have to be done in order to make the plot work are done through mere loss of temper. The spiritual tragedy is never faced or understood: all the stress is laid on the mere external uncleanness. Sophocles no doubt did many bad things in his life: I would not try to shield him from just blame. But in this case I am sure, he was in a trance and his body

[12]TLS, Yeats to Gilbert Murray, from the Nassau Hotel, Dublin, 24 January [1905]; Bodleian Library, Oxford. Harley Granville Barker (1877–1946) had successfully produced Murray's translation of *Hippolytus* at the Lyric Theatre, 26 May 1904, and at the Royal Court Theatre, 18 October 1904. The quoted letter seems to show that such assertions as the following are a mistake. "When W. B. Yeats decided to do his own version of King Oedipus he asked Murray to provide him with a literal translation for him to work on. Understandably Murray declined that lowly task": W. B. Stanford, "Gorgeous Greek Tragedies," *Hibernia,* 28 June 1979, p. 19. Similarly, Ulick O'Connor refers to "Murray's refusal to make him [Yeats] a literal translation in 1904": *The Times I've Seen: Oliver St. John Gogarty, a Biography* (New York: Obolensky, 1963), p. 43, hereafter cited as O'Connor. No evidence supports these statements. Yeats was eager to attach Murray publicly to his movement by following his success with Euripides in London with a success with Sophocles in Dublin. He was asking Murray to do a finished translation of his own.

> was possessed by a series of devils—Sardou, the Lord Mayor of London, Aristotle, the Judicious Hooker, and all the Editors of the Spectator from its inception to the present day. It has splendid qualities as an acting play, but all of the most English-French-German sort: it is all construction and no spirit.
>
> I am really distressed that the Censor objected to it. It ought to be played not perhaps at His Majesty's by Tree, but by Irving at the Lyceum, with a lecture before . . . and after. And a public dinner. With speeches. By Cabinet Ministers.
>
> When free from his affliction, Sophocles wrote some very beautiful plays, the Antigone for instance. And Aeschylus has all the great qualities always, though not the second-rate. I shall translate some Aeschylus some day when I feel I can do it, but really I can, as a rule, only work at the people who have got my own religion. And Sophocles hasnt. (The said Religion is not perhaps very visible in the Hippolytus, but it is there. And it is plentiful in the Troades and the Bacchae.) . . .
>
> Seriously, I rather hope that you wont do the Oedipus. It is not the play for you to cast your lot with. Do the Prometheus (Bevan's transln not at all bad: or I might at a pinch attempt it, though I cannot promise without rereading) or even the Persae with a seditious innuendo. Or the Antigone. [LTWBY 145–46][13]

Yeats had also approached Oliver Gogarty. On 20 December 1904, he had written to Lady Gregory, "I mention G., in order to say that he wants to try his hand at translating *Œdipus the King* for us."[14] Nonetheless, although Gogarty was more persuadable than Murray, he did not come up with a translation of which Yeats could approve. In February 1905 Gogarty wrote to his friend G. K. A. Bell, "Item: I am preparing a trans. (verse) of 'Oedipus Rex' for Yeats!"[15] But on 7 April he confesses: "Finally after smoking two

[13]Sir Herbert Beerbohm Tree (1853–1917) had recently been denied a license to perform *Oedipus the King*. Sir Henry Irving (1838–1905) was still active at this time but died suddenly after a performance later that year. Edwyn Robert Bevan had done a verse translation of *Prometheus Bound* in 1902. By "do the Oedipus" Murray means produce it, not translate it.

[14]Lady Gregory, *Our Irish Theatre: A Chapter of Autobiography* (London: G. P. Putnam's Sons; New York: Knickerbocker Press, 1913), p. 44; hereafter cited as *OIT*.

[15]Oliver St. John Gogarty, *Many Lines to Thee: Letters to G. K. A. Bell . . . 1904–1907*, ed. James F. Carens ([Dublin]: Dolmen Press, 1971), p. 73; hereafter cited as Gogarty. Carens dates the letter "February 1905." Since the production of Synge's *The*

of Yeats' cigarettes he condemned my translations not so much for the metre but for the introduction of thou & thee and the want of feeling for the locality—this specially in the chorus. I think its line 196, but it doesn't matter—where Kitharion is addressed. I have retreated and am now studying Yeats' work with interest and respect" (Gogarty, p. 90).

On 11 April Gogarty wrote to Bell, "I have sent for Murray's trans." Murray's *The Trojan Women* of Euripides, translated into English rhyming verse, had been published the previous month. By "Murray's trans." Gogarty must mean *The Trojan Women,* certainly not *Oedipus,* which Murray translated later for publication in 1911. Gogarty goes on to report Murray's 27 January 1905 letter refusing the task which Gogarty himself had accepted: "He wrote to Yeats . . . 'Man, I will not translate Sophocles' 'Fools step in'—" (Gogarty, p. 100).

A 28 April 1905 letter has a good deal about the meaning of *Oedipus* in it and toward the end quotes what may be the only lines of Gogarty's translation to be preserved:

> I have to write a good deal of blank verse before May 30th. . . . How do you like this for my opening of Oe. Rex?
>
> Thebans, my children too, and lateliest born
> Of all those generations which date back
> To Cadmus in the old time King of Thebes
> [Gogarty, p. 112]

Gogarty's lines have movement and vigor, and he might have developed an effective script for the Abbey to perform. By 12

Well of the Saints is mentioned, the letter cannot be earlier than 4 February 1905. On this letter, which he misdates February 1904, Ulick O'Connor (p. 43) bases his conclusion that after Murray's refusal to translate *Oedipus* "the poet turned to his young friend [Gogarty] and asked him to give him a version of the Greek classic, which he could turn into English verse." But when Gogarty says "I am preparing a trans. (verse) of 'Oedipus Rex' for Yeats!" he means "for Yeats to produce," not "for Yeats to rewrite." In his 7 April 1905 letter, Gogarty is clearer when he speaks of mentioning to Yeats "the Sophocles for your theatre" (Gogarty, p. 87). "For Yeats" in the February letter means the same as "for your theatre" in the April letter: "for Yeats to produce at the Abbey." Gogarty was making a verse translation of his own, not a rough draft for Yeats to perfect. We find no evidence that Yeats wished to make his own translation at this date.

October 1905, however, he had abandoned the project: "Personally I have lost interest in the Yeats Theatre. The Art is bad, real bad. And this in spite of Yeats" (Gogarty, p. 125).

A third candidate for making a version of *Oedipus* was William Kirkpatrick Magee ("John Eglinton").[16] It is possibly Magee's version of which Yeats wrote to Annie Horniman from Coole on 17 May 1906: "I should prefer to put Edipus somewhere early in the winter's work, but that will be no use for touring, as the censor wont let it be played in England. I should like to do it early in Dublin as it will be an immense advertisement there among the academical and scholastic people who are most suspicious of us now" (TB 127).

By August, however, the idea of producing *Antigone* was competing with plans for Magee's *Oedipus*. At the end of September 1906, Yeats told Lady Gregory that the Abbey programme for 1907 ought to include "either *Oedipus* or the *Antigone*." He preferred the *Oedipus,* but was worried about Magee's "elaborate style" which might not "prove [to be] vocal," a matter of great moment to one who favored direct and forceful speech. The printed announcement dated 12 October stated that Robert Gregory's translation of the *Antigone* would be offered on 26 January 1907, and the first issue of the Abbey Theatre's new periodical *The Arrow,* 20 October, announced that the *Antigone* would be presented from Saturday, 26 January through Saturday, 2 February.[17] In

[16]Magee (1868–1961), brilliant as a student of classics at Trinity College, was Assistant Librarian of the National Library of Ireland. Yeats's friendly antagonism with "John Eglinton" over what should be the subjects of a national drama? had resulted in the symposium *Literary Ideals in Ireland* (London: T. Fisher Unwin; Dublin: at the Daily Express Office, 1899), to which AE and William Larminie also contributed. See UP2 128. Magee was editor with Frederick Ryan of the magazine *Dana* (1904–1905). In 1905 Yeats had edited *Some Essays and Passages* by Eglinton for the Dun Emer Press. Ann Saddlemyer notes, "After Yeats rejected a draft by Gogarty the preceding year . . . the Directors were now [spring 1906] considering a translation of Sophocles' *Oedipus* by John Eglinton, which was not produced either" (TB 127, n. 3). In answer to our query, Saddlemyer writes that she cannot "say for certain just at what stage Magee provided a complete script" but suspects that "the process was a slow one (Magee was a very tentative person) and went through quite a few drafts." On 18 August 1907, W. G. Fay wrote to Yeats as if the script were still to be supplied: "I hope we will get the Oedipus as well from Eglinton" (LTWBY 187). Perhaps the script was partially done in 1906 and still to be finished or revised in 1907.

[17]On 17 August 1906, Yeats wrote Synge, "Robert Gregory is inclined to translate

the event, it was *The Playboy* that opened on 26 January, precipitating the famous riot. Gregory's version of the *Antigone* was apparently never performed at the Abbey, though in mid-January of 1907 Yeats was still hoping to present it in March.

In spite of the choice of *Antigone, Oedipus* remained an objective. On Thursday, 18 October 1906, Synge expected to attend "this Oedipus dinner with Magee."[18] And in the same issue of *The Arrow* that contains the list announcing *Antigone,* Yeats added, "When this list has run out another will be announced, containing translations of Oedipus the King, from the Greek, of Phedre from the French, and of native plays" (p. 1). On 7 November 1906 Synge promised "I'll bring in Oedipus tomorrow," but whether this refers to Magee's script or some other translation it is impossible to say (TB 159). On 13 December Synge wrote to Lady Gregory, "We are right to do work like the 'Doctor' [Lady Gregory's adaptation of Molière's *The Doctor in Spite of Himself*] and Oedipus because they illuminate our work but for that reason only." A previous draft of his letter read "An occasional foreign play that illustrates our own work should be done, as we have played The Doctor, and are going to play Oedipus. Beyond that I do not think we should go" (TB 178).

In early January 1907 the scales seem to have tipped again to-

---

the Antigone for Miss Allgood" (TB 143). On 29 September, Synge wrote to Lady Gregory that the announcement of the program for the next series should "include, I think, either Oedipus or the Antigone" (TB 147). On 2 October, Yeats wrote to Synge confirming a tentative program announcing "Oedipus or Antigone" for January 1907 (TB 151). Yeats inclined to *Oedipus* rather than to *Antigone*. The next day, 3 October, he wrote to Synge, "Dont put the Antigone but give Edipus as an alternative"; then wrote and canceled "or we may offend Magee. On the other hand it wont do to put Edipus by itself because Magee's elaborate style may not prove vocal." After changing his mind and canceling these words, he continued, "or if you don't like putting the alternatives put Edipus by itself" (TB 152). Perhaps Yeats decided to think better of Magee's powers. In any event, an Abbey Theatre printed announcement dated 12 October 1906 indicated that on 26 January 1907, *The Antigone of Sophocles,* translated by Robert Gregory, would be offered. Berg Collection, New York Public Library, under "Abbey Theatre, Dublin. Programs, 1904–1907." In *The Arrow,* 1, no. 1 (October 20, 1906), p. 6, *Antigone* was again announced for Saturday, 26 January, through Saturday, 2 February 1907.

[18]*Letters to Molly: John Millington Synge to Maire O'Neill, 1906–1909,* ed. Ann Saddlemyer (Cambridge: Belknap Press of Harvard University Press, 1971), p. 38; hereafter cited as *LTM*.

ward *Antigone*. On the 14th, Yeats wrote to Lady Gregory, "Neither you nor Robert would like Miss Darragh for the Antigone and we could not afford to import an actress for one play alone."[19] And the next day, "How about Antigone? I suppose that is for March."[20]

The most momentous event at the Abbey Theatre in 1907 was, of course, the production of *The Playboy of the Western World,* with all its attendant disturbances. This play has often been called a comic version of *Oedipus the King*.[21] It is well to remember, therefore, that during 1906, when Synge was writing the *Playboy,* he was also reading and discussing *Oedipus* with a view to a production. *Oedipus* was one of the plays considered for production, too, by Ben Iden Payne, who was to relieve W. G. Fay—at Miss Horniman's insistence—of responsibility for all but peasant plays (LTWBY 177).[22] Payne, the "new English Manager," had his first interview with Directors Synge and Lady Gregory probably on the day of the second performance of the *Playboy,* 28 January 1907.[23] According to Gerard Fay, there was, during the Payne period, "some question of producing 'Oedipus Rex' with Payne playing the lead but Miss Horniman was against the idea on strictly practical grounds."[24] Lady Gregory wrote to Synge on 4 March: "Payne a treasure, very conscientious & energetic—has too great a craving for 'foreign masterpieces' but the 'Interior' & 'Edipus' must satisfy him for this season—& he is starting on

[19]TLS, Yeats to Lady Gregory, from Woburn Buildings, dictated "Jan 14, 1907"; collection of Michael Yeats; SB 25.9.42–43.

[20]TLS, Yeats to Lady Gregory, from Woburn Buildings, dictated "Jan 15th 1907"; collection of Michael Yeats; SB 25.9.32.

[21]See Susan Solomont, *The Comic Effect of The Playboy of the Western World* (Bangor, Me.: Signalman Press, 1962), pp. 11–23. J. M. Synge, *Plays,* Book II, Vol. IV of *Collected Works,* ed. Ann Saddlemyer (London: Oxford University Press, 1968), pp. 103, 173.

[22]See also Hugh Hunt, *The Abbey: Ireland's National Theatre, 1904–1978* (New York: Columbia University Press, 1979), p. 71; hereafter cited as Hunt. Payne (1881–1976) first appeared with Frank Benson's company in 1898.

[23]*Joseph Holloway's Abbey Theatre: A Selection from His Unpublished Journal, Impressions of a Dublin Playgoer,* ed. Robert Hogan and Michael J. O'Neill (Carbondale: Southern Illinois University Press, 1967), p. 83.

[24]Gerard Fay, *The Abbey Theatre: Cradle of Genius* (Dublin: Clonmore & Reynolds, 1958), p. 122.

Fand" (TB 216). But on 14 March, Miss Horniman wrote to Yeats:

> I shall get the credit if Payne plays Oedipus of putting in an Englishman in Frank Fay's place, so as to spite Willie Fay. This would damage all concerned. It would cause friction and if Payne had to go, a new man would be needed for America if the Company goes there. Could you not let Payne see that taking the part risks his post altogether? . . . I dont think he can realize the circumstances fully—it is not a serious *theatrical* difficulty at all, but a matter in which if he gives Frank Fay's friends (or rather other people's enemies) any cause for complaint he will damage himself severely. [TB 216, n. 1]

Payne was not terribly worried about damaging himself. But he did not do *Oedipus*. He directed the first production of Maeterlinck's *Interior* on 16 March 1907 and of Wilfrid Scawen Blunt's *Fand* on 20 April (Hunt, p. 71), and revivals of *On Baile's Strand, Deirdre,* and *The Hour Glass* (LTM 111n). In May the company set forth on an itinerary including Oxford, Cambridge, and London. At the end of the tour in June, Payne, "feeling he could not find a way of working with the Abbey, left the company," according to Hugh Hunt.[25]

Payne's leaving did not kill the idea of presenting *Oedipus* in Magee's translation. On 18 August 1907, W. G. Fay wrote to Yeats, "I think the translation of [a] Greek play would help us & I hope we will get the Oedipus as well from Eglinton" (LTWBY 187). But by 29 January 1908 they had swung over to *Antigone* again and were picking a translation, and Yeats was proposing to combine the best lines of a number of translations: "'The Antigone' turns out pretty bad so far as the translation goes[.] I shall try

[25]Hunt, p. 77. After his half year at the Abbey, Payne for four years shaped the first repertory theatre in England at Miss Horniman's Gaiety Theatre in Manchester. Later he was a busy Broadway director, then taught theatre at the Carnegie Institute of Technology (until 1934), directed at the Goodman Theatre in Chicago (1934), was general director of the Shakespeare Memorial Theatre at Stratford-upon-Avon (1935–43), and returned to the educational theatre in the United States, especially at the University of Texas, where a theatre is named for him. An amusing account of his work with the Abbey company can be found in *A Life in a Wooden O: Memoirs of the Theatre* (New Haven: Yale University Press, 1977), pp. 63–77.

to make a composite one."[26] Then, by November, they seem to have been expecting to do *Oedipus*. On 29 November 1908, Lady Gregory wrote Synge about a woman very like the one in Joyce's "A Mother" in her eagerness to push her daughter: "I told her the list of plays, which as far as I knew didn't want extra women, and she said yes, her daughter and another could do the Edipus chorus. I said it was a chorus of men, but I dont think even that satisfied her" (TB 295). By the following spring, *Oedipus* and *Antigone* were alternate possibilities, and Yeats hoped that preparations for one of them would enliven the tone of the company: "I suspect that rehearsals [of D. H. Kelleher's *Stephen Grey*] are languid & therefore have to be many. If we start Oedipus or Antigone & Kings Threshold that may set the pace."[27]

[26]ALS (autograph letter signed), Yeats to Lady Gregory, from the Nassau Hotel, Dublin, dated "Wed.," postmarked 29 January 1908 (a Friday); collection of Michael Yeats; SB 25.9.82.

[27]ALS, Yeats to Lady Gregory, from the Nassau Hotel, Dublin, dated "Thursday," postmarked 12 March 1909 (a Friday); collection of Michael Yeats; SB 26.1.269–73. *Stephen Grey* was first performed on 11 March 1909. After Yeats finished *Sophocles' King Oedipus* in 1926, he considered making his own translation of *Antigone* but chose to do *Oedipus at Colonus* instead, as we shall demonstrate later. One chorus, "From the 'Antigone," was written around "Sept 15" [1927], the date on the earliest extant draft, and first appeared in *The Winding Stair* (New York: Fountain Press, 1929). On "Saturday," probably 25 February 1928, Yeats wrote from "Albergo Rapallo" to George Yeats, who had gone to Switzerland for a week to put son Michael in school, "Ezra has written for Cocteau's 'Antigone.' Cocteau has made it into a powerful play for the modern stage & a translation of it for Dublin would complete our Sophoclean trilogy. The chorus does not appear. Some large masks hang upon the back wall, & a voice speaks through them." (Whether Yeats thought of making the translation himself at this time is impossible to say.) ALS, Yeats to George Yeats, from "Albergo Rapallo / Rapallo / Italy," dated "Saturday"; collection of Michael Yeats; SB 24.5.153–55. On Thursday, 23 February 1928, Yeats wrote to Olivia Shakespear from this same address that "George has this very moment started for Switzerland with Michael who is to be left there at school. She returns on Friday week" (L736). See also his letter to Lady Gregory, postmarked 24 February 1928: "George returns next week" (L738). "Saturday," then, is 25 February 1928. It was probably the day before that Pound made his celebrated transposition of lines in "From the 'Antigone.'" See Richard Ellmann, *The Identity of Yeats,* 2d ed. (New York: Oxford University Press, 1954), pp. 131–32; also David R. Clark, *Yeats at Songs and Choruses* (Gerrards Cross: Colin Smythe; Amherst: University of Massachusetts Press, 1983) pp. 211–42.

In Cocteau's *Antigone* "The CHORUS and its leader are concentrated into a single voice which speaks very loudly and quickly as if reading a newspaper article. This voice issues from a hole in the center of the scenery. For a revival in 1927, five monumental plaster heads of young men framed the chorus": Jean Cocteau, *Five Plays* (New York: Hill & Wang, 1961), p. 49.

In November 1909, Yeats and Lady Gregory asserted, "We are about to produce 'Œdipus the King.'"[28] By 22 December, Yeats looked forward to producing *Oedipus* with Murray Carson the following February. He wrote to Lady Gregory that Carson "is now looking at Jebb's translation and Macgee's," "Macgee" being Yeats's misspelling of "Magee."[29]

During all this time, there is no inkling that Yeats had tried to make, or had even thought of making, his own version of *Oedipus*. He had considered making a composite translation of *Antigone* out of several translations, but he had looked to others—to Murray, to Gogarty, to Magee—for an *Oedipus*.

The Carson Period, 1909–1911

When in the summer of 1909 Yeats and Lady Gregory joined battle with the Lord Lieutenant of Ireland over the Abbey's projected performance of Shaw's *The Shewing-Up of Blanco Posnet,* "Yeats decided," as Frederic D. Grab puts it, "further to antagonize governmental stupidity by producing the *Oedipus*."[30] Lady Gregory's journal for Friday, 13 August 1909, reports the Abbey Directors' argument with a government official: "Yeats said we intended to do *Oedipus,* that this also was a censored play [in England], although so unobjectionable to religious minds that it had been performed in the Catholic University of Nôtre Dame" (*OIT,* pp. 150–51). The next day Yeats said to the same official that "if they decided to take away the Patent [to prevent the per-

[28]W. B. Yeats and Lady Gregory, *Paragraphs written in Nov., 1909, with Supplement and Financial Statement* (Dublin 1909), pp. 3–4. Quoted in Liam Miller, *The Noble Drama of W. B. Yeats* (Dublin: Dolmen Press, 1977), p. 146; hereafter cited as Miller.

[29]TLS, Yeats to Lady Gregory, from Woburn Buildings, dictated "December 22, 1909"; collection of Michael Yeats; SB 26.1.93. Murray Carson (1865–1917), London-born actor, manager, and playwright, toured in *The Devil* in 1909 and, as Mr. Brounsall, in *Mr. Preedy and the Countess* in 1910. Besides acting in many popular plays, he played such Shakespearean roles as Hamlet, Othello, and Julius Caesar, as well as parts in other classics (e.g., Bosola in *The Duchess of Malfi*).

[30]Frederic D. Grab, "Yeats's *King Oedipus,*" *Journal of English and Germanic Philology,* 71 (1972), 338; hereafter cited as Grab. It is interesting and an example of the persistence of Yeats's ideas that when *Sophocles' King Oedipus* was first produced, on 7 December 1926, *Blanco Posnet* joined it on the bill.

formance of *Blanco Posnet*], we should put off the production till the beginning of our season, end of September, and produce it with *Oedipus*; then they would have to suppress both together" (*OIT*, pp. 154–55). Yeats's exact words, according to his letter of that date to Miss Horniman, were "to suppress us, not merely for Posnett but because of our performance of the greatest masterpiece of Greek drama."[31] Making Dublin Castle suppress both plays, and at the beginning of the Abbey season, would greatly increase public opposition to the ban. Lady Gregory confirmed this determination in a letter dated 15 August 1909 (*OIT*, p. 158). She and Yeats had no intention of countenancing the automatic application of the English censorship to Ireland. *Blanco Posnet* went on as scheduled, on 25 August, in defiance of the Lord Lieutenant's threats. Yeats wrote to H. J. C. Grierson on 12 October: "We are going to produce *Oedipus the King* early in the New Year with Murray Carson in chief part, as a further precedent of our freedom from the Lord Chamberlain who has forbidden the play" (L 537).

The hope of producing *Oedipus* during the first months of 1910, with Carson in the title role, persisted until February of that year and then faded. A year later Yeats was again considering a date for Carson as Oedipus. There is still no mention of a possible original version by Yeats. Both the Jebb and Whitelaw translations were considered. In a letter postmarked 26 November 1909, Yeats prefers Jebb: "I am going to Cambridge on Wednesday next to see the performance of *The Wasps* with a view to *Oedipus*. I have gone through translations and find Jebb's much the best. I ordered it some days ago. It should have come by this. I ordered an edition used in a performance at Oxford, a performance in Greek I think—2/–[i.e., two shillings a copy]" (L 538–39). Three days later he writes: "I have got the Jebb translation of Oedipus and today before the Museum closes I will compare it with Plumptre, and send a card if it seems the best asking for seven or eight copies. We will have to get leave from Jebb's executors."[32] He obtained the Jebb, and in a letter postmarked 10 December 1909 wrote Lady

[31]TLS, Yeats to Miss Horniman, from Dublin, dated "August 15th 1909"; collection of Michael Yeats; SB 3.9.55.

[32]TLS, Yeats to Lady Gregory, from Woburn Buildings, dated "Nov. 29, 1909"; collection of Michael Yeats; SB 26.2.87.

Gregory that he was seeking copies for the cast: "I will write today to Carson and try to get things settled. I have been trying for more copies of the Jebb but do not yet know if I can get them—1/– copies. There is a metrical version of the choruses given, and the notes state that Stanford has done music, but I suppose we had better stick to O'Brien. If we do, it makes it desirable that he should justify himself by making it as good speech as he can or he will hardly beat Stanford as a musician" (L 542–43).[33] By 22 December, he has talked personally with Carson and estimates that on:

> [t]he 20th February . . . Oedipus will be only just through. I saw Murray Carson last night, he agrees to our producing the play in the middle of February and says he will come at the end of January to start rehearsing. He cannot put it later than the middle of February for his Spring tour begins then. I shall have to go to Dublin a week or so before he arrives and start rehearsing the Company. He will start letter perfect. He is now looking at Jebb's translation and Macgee's [Magee's]. He is very enthusiastic about the project.[34]

Frederic Grab is probably right that the edition of Jebb's translation referred to in both these letters is that for the Cambridge performance of 22–26 November 1887.[35] This edition gives the English and the Greek on facing pages. A much-used copy exists in Yeats's library today.[36] The front paper cover is missing and the signatures have come loose from the binding. The cuts and annotations in this copy, however, date from a later time, as we shall see.

The stage scenery of Edward Gordon Craig had increasingly

[33]"Incidental Music to the 'Oedipus Tyrannus,'" opus 29 of the Dublin-born composer Sir Charles Villiers Stanford (1852–1924), was created for the 1887 Cambridge performance. Vincent O'Brien (1870–1948), Dublin organist and composer, was appointed musical director of the Pro-cathedral Palestrina Choir in 1902. John MacCormack and, briefly, James Joyce were his students; Edward Martyn befriended, encouraged, and endowed him. Apparently he was to do both words and music of the choruses for the *Oedipus* projected in 1909.

[34]TLS, Yeats to Lady Gregory, from Woburn Buildings, dated "December 22, 1909"; collection of Michael Yeats; SB 26.1.93.

[35]Grab, p. 339, n. 8.

[36]No. 966 / L.7.2. as catalogued in Anne Yeats's collection.

interested Yeats since he had discovered it in the spring of 1901. In 1911 the Abbey Theatre would become the first theater to adopt Craig's methods and thereafter the only theatre to use them for an extended period (Miller, pp. 49–50). It is natural then that Yeats hoped to use Craig scenery in *Oedipus*. On 31 December 1909, he wrote at length to Lady Gregory about the advantages of the Craig screens:

> Craigs invention will be valuable for plays rather out of Time & space. It would be perfect for Oedipus. I doubt its being of much special advantage for out of doors & I said this to him. He says I must see it in his studio before I judge. It gives you elaborate built up scenes which can be changed in a moment. It could suit "Oedipus" "Kings Threshold" "Countess Kathleen" "Interior" (I think) "Bailes Strand" Your "Diarmuid & Grania" perhaps. Its point is that it is a convention of a majestic sort. It looks like great blocks of stone, in all the scenes Craig has shown me photographs of.[37]

Craig, however, discouraged this hope, as Yeats explained to Lady Gregory in a letter postmarked 8 January 1910: "Craig dined with me last night. . . . I asked if we would get his scene in time for *Oedipus* but he wants us to play about with his model first and master its effects" (L 546). Yeats then proceeded with his own plans for scenery. On 16 January, he wrote from Gogarty's house, Fairfield, that he was rehearsing "[indecipherable] and will start the Oedipus after that. We shall play Oedipus against a great purple curtain and take away the front rows of the stalls to make room for chorus."[38]

Carson proved unavailable until late in the spring of 1910. Moreover, he chose a translation—Whitelaw's—that was almost certainly one of those Yeats had already found inferior to Jebb's (L

[37]ALS, Yeats at Woburn Buildings to Lady Gregory at Coole, dated "Friday," postmarked 31 December 1909; collection of Michael Yeats; SB 26.1.195–201. Maurice Maeterlinck's *Interior* (*Intérieur*) was first produced at the Abbey by Ben Iden Payne, 23 March 1907.

[38]Quoted in A. Norman Jeffares and A. S. Knowland, *A Commentary on the Collected Plays of W. B. Yeats* (Stanford: Stanford University Press, 1975), p. 179, where it is wrongly used as evidence that Yeats was himself translating *Oedipus* at this time; hereafter cited as *Commentary*.

538–39). In a letter to Lady Gregory, postmarked 6 February 1910, Yeats reported the situation: "Carson writes—letter came today—saying that he is ready for Oedipus any time after April but [Secretary] Henderson says there won't be time in May with our tours eating into both ends of the month so I suppose he must be put off until Autumn. I will look at the dates again, however. He has chosen Whitelaw's translation."[39]

Carson was put off until autumn, and he was still being put off a year later. But first let us examine Grab's statement (p. 339) that "[b]y the end of 1910 . . . Yeats had lost interest in the project [of producing *Oedipus*], since the English censor withdrew his ban on the play late that year." Grab bases this conclusion on a 9 December 1910 letter from Gilbert Murray to Harley Granville Barker stating that the poet Herbert Trench had been successful in getting the Lord Chamberlain's license to produce Murray's version of *Oedipus*.[40]

Yeats knew of the projected production. He wrote to Lady Gregory on 10 December: "Last night Trench told me that sometime next Spring he hopes to play 'Oedipus' in a new translation by Gilbert Murray. So you were right. Should I see Murray Carson? They will do it better than we will—alas."[41] This sounds as if he were thinking of dropping *Oedipus,* not because the ban had been lifted, but because of the greater resources Trench had. But Carson reassured him. On 19 December, Yeats wrote:

> I saw Murray Carson last night. He has heard that Tree also is planning to do Oedipus. He thinks, however, that both Tree and

[39]ALS, Yeats to Lady Gregory postmarked 6 February 1910; collection of Michael Yeats; transcribed from photocopy in National Library of Ireland MS. 18714.

[40]Murray wrote to Barker on 6 August 1910 that he had "just finished a first draft of *Oedipus.*" On 1 December Barker wrote to Murray about the possibility of the Trench-Frederick Harrison management doing Oedipus. On 9 December Murray wrote Barker that the license had been obtained. C. B. Purdom, *Harley Granville Barker* (London: Rockliff, 1955), pp. 112, 115, 116.

[41]Collection of Michael Yeats; quoted from a typed transcription in National Library of Ireland MS. 18689. We are grateful to Joseph Chadwick for calling this to our attention. In a letter dated "Tuesday" and postmarked 13 December 1910, Yeats wrote further, "Murray Carson is to see me this evening & I wrote to Iden[?] Payne about Manchester & now we have this contract trouble. . . . I will write when I have seen Carson. I shall have more time to think about all these things": ALS, Yeats to Lady Gregory, from London; collection of Michael Yeats; SB 25.3.120.

> Trench would take a good long time getting ready. He is prepared to come to Ireland on the 7th of February and start playing on Monday the 13th, if that will suit us. He will arrive knowing his part. But he is anxious that we should make our experiment in the best season for Dublin. This date would suit him best, he is prepared to keep any later date we name open for it. He cannot come before February 7th for until then he is playing in a music hall. He is certainly in earnest about the whole thing and says he looks upon it as the crowning event in his life as an actor. He points out that now the bar of the censorship has been withdrawn we can tour the play if sufficiently successful. This may be an advantage or an embarrassment.[42]

He is still hesitant in a 2 January 1911 letter to Lady Gregory, and the lifting of the ban is not one of the negative considerations mentioned: "I shall write in a few minutes to Murray Carson with whom I have not yet arranged, but I will ask him if he can give me a few days longer as I would really rather like to have a talk with you and Robinson, especially in the light of recent disturbances, before fixing the Oedipus date. We might have to work up new work if Miss Allgood went away for a time."[43]

Neither the Trench production nor the one considered by Sir Herbert Beerbohm Tree occurred, and although Yeats's letter of 2 January is the last we hear of Murray Carson's doing *Oedipus* at the Abbey, the year 1911, far from ending Yeats's interest in the play, saw a resurgence of it. In February Yeats went to Norwich to see *The Countess Cathleen* staged by Nugent Monck and began an increasingly close association with Monck, which resulted in new efforts in 1911 to stage *Oedipus* at the Abbey and, in 1912, in Yeats's writing his own version. The Lord Chamberlain's willingness to license *Oedipus* in 1910, then, did not stop Yeats from

[42]TLS, Yeats to Lady Gregory, from Woburn Buildings, dictated "December 19, 1910"; collection of Michael Yeats; SB 25.3.97.

[43]TLS, Yeats to Lady Gregory, from Woburn Buildings, dictated "2nd January 1911"; collection of Michael Yeats; photocopy National Library of Ireland MS. 18716. "Recent disturbances" may refer to Miss Horniman's legal dispute with the Directors as she brought her subsidy to an end or to conflicts among the players. "Miss Allgood" sounds like Sara, the elder sister. There was uncertainty as to whether Sara Allgood would stay with the company; if she did not, it would be necessary to replace with new work the plays in which she starred. As a result there would be less time to get *Oedipus* ready. On the other hand, "Miss Allgood" might refer to Molly, who left to get married in 1911, but promised to return to the company when needed.

writing his *Oedipus,* which, in fact, he had not yet begun. Grab takes too literally Yeats's account of losing interest when the Lord Chamberlain raised his ban. It was not until months after the opening of Max Reinhardt's 1912 production of Gilbert Murray's *Oedipus* that Yeats gave up the play.

Monck's Jebb

Yeats recognized from the start the talent of Nugent Monck (1878–1958), who founded the Norwich Players in 1911 and directed the Maddermarket Theatre from 1921 to 1952.[44] Yeats saw Monck's 22 February 1911 production of *The Countess Cathleen* and returned to Norwich between 16 and 25 March to see The Book of Job as a play.[45] By summer it had been arranged for Monck to come to the Abbey and to produce plays with the second company and to direct a school of acting while the first company was on tour in the United States during the autumn and winter. On Saturday, 22 July [1911], Yeats wrote Monck from Coole: "I want you for (say) three months and am to give you £5 a week. . . . You can come (say) for Oct. Nov and December. You will take charge of pupils and if they mature produce some plays and help me with some work with Craig screens. It is all rather vague but we may be able to do some interesting work."[46]

Monck was greatly interested in Craig's work, and Yeats wanted to use the Craig scenery for *Oedipus.* Monck and Yeats had discussed a production before Monck's arrival in Dublin. On 25 August, Yeats wrote to Lady Gregory: "Monck dined with me

[44]Obituary, *The Times* (London), 23 October 1958, p. 17.

[45]Two ALS, Yeats to Lady Gregory, from Woburn Buildings, postmarked 16 March 1911 and 25 March 1911; collection of Michael Yeats; transcribed from photocopies in National Library of Ireland MS. 18717.

[46]One of a group of typed copies in the possession of Ann Saddlemyer "of letters from Yeats and Lady Gregory to Monck, courtesy of a colleague who got xeroxes from a former student who got them from those in charge of Monck's estate" (letter from Saddlemyer). Under these circumstances neither she nor we can guarantee the accuracy of the copies. Dates in square brackets, for these letters only, have been supplied by Professor Saddlemyer.

last night—is anxious to produce Oedipus and thinks he can get a man for principal part for about £10."[47] Accordingly, Yeats announced in a letter to the *Irish Times* on 8 September 1911 that Monck was about to "give certain productions at the Abbey Theatre—perhaps a classical play."[48]

On 10 September, Yeats explained to Monck that because Maire O'Neill [Molly Allgood] was ill and unable to go to the United States, Lady Gregory had to go over, in order to coach new players in Molly's roles, so that Monck would have neither Yeats nor Lady Gregory to greet him when he started in Dublin:

> You will do nothing about a production of a decisive kind until I am back, but you might begin working with them at Oedipus. You will find a number of copies of Jebb's translation in the office. . . . As you are giving a production in Norwich on the 4th you had better open in Dublin I suppose on Monday the 9th. I will try to be back from America before you have been many days at work. Please also work out your scheme for Edipus with Seaghan Barlow, anything which can be made in the building Seaghan might begin, or any Hessian could be dyed or painted in the building itself.[49]

Yeats was abroad from about 13 September to middle or late October, but when he returned, his letters to Lady Gregory, who was still in the United States, were full of Monck and his activities. *Oedipus* was tackled immediately. The text was without doubt the edition of Jebb mentioned earlier, *The Oedipus Tyrannus of Sophocles as Performed at Cambridge*. . . . The dilapidated copy of this volume in Yeats's library is full of substantial cuts and of stage directions in what is unmistakably Nugent Monck's hand. Speaking of his own further work on the play in a 7 January 1912 letter to Lady Gregory, Yeats wrote: "Monck had already made his cuts." When Monck made the cuts Yeats does not say, but pre-

[47]Dictated typescript dated "25th August, 1911"; collection of Michael Yeats; transcribed from a photocopy in National Library of Ireland MS. 18720.

[48]Quoted in Donald T. Torchiana and Glenn O'Malley, "Some New Letters from W. B. Yeats to Lady Gregory," *Review of English Literature*, 4 (July 1963), 11.

[49]From a copy in the possession of Ann Saddlemyer (see note 46). Seaghan Barlow was the stage carpenter and scene painter at the Abbey Theatre.

sumably it was when he first started rehearsing the play at the Abbey in October 1911.[50]

A production of *Oedipus* was underway by 28 October, when Yeats wrote to Lady Gregory from Dublin: "I saw a rehearsal of the chorus of Eodipus [sic] last night, an immense chorus, certainly very well managed, but till I see the individual players I won't know what acting power he [Monck] has found; I am going to take a class each night as there are too many for one to teach and may try to get over Miss [Maire] O'Neill. . . . We have been working out a scene for Oedipus, but have not got it yet; it is a question of getting the chorus on different levels."[51] Two days later he wrote again: "I am anxious to let the work develop rather than to force it, especially now as we shall have longer. 'Oedipus' will not come on until after Christmas."[52] In these two letters Yeats appears more concerned with the staging than with the words, and it seems definite that the Jebb translation, as cut and annotated by Monck, was the text used.

In December, plans were renewed for after-Christmas production. In a letter that we date 13 December 1911, he wrote to Lady Gregory from the Abbey Theatre: "We will carry the school on—Monck will take charge till return of company. . . . We shall separate for two weeks from next Monday & then I hope produce Oedipus and Building Fund & after that the cycle of religious plays."[53] A couple of days later he wrote again: "I go back to London for two weeks on Monday—Monck is worn out & must rest. When he returns I think we will play Oedipus with a pupil as Oedipus—it may just have the effect of finally making an actor."[54]

[50]TLS, Yeats to Lady Gregory, from the Abbey Theatre, dictated "January 7th 1912"; collection of Michael Yeats; transcribed from a photocopy in National Library of Ireland MS. 18721.

[51]TLS, Yeats to Lady Gregory, from the Nassau Hotel, Dublin, dictated "October 28th 1911"; collection of Michael Yeats; transcribed from a photocopy in National Library of Ireland MS. 18720.

[52]TLS, Yeats to Lady Gregory, from the Abbey Theatre, dictated "30th October 1911"; collection of Michael Yeats; transcribed from a photocopy in National Library of Ireland MS. 18720.

[53]ALS, Yeats to Lady Gregory, from the Abbey Theatre, dated "Wednesday"; collection of Michael Yeats; transcribed from a photocopy in National Library of Ireland MS. 18718.

[54]ALS, Yeats to Lady Gregory, from the Abbey Theatre, dated "Friday Dec 19 [1911]"; collection of Michael Yeats; photocopy National Library of Ireland MS. 18718.

The following week, writing from London, Yeats announces a specific date: "Monday I spent in the Theatre with Monck & his dress maker showing the Craig screens. We had in a man with a magic lantern & made all sorts of experiments. . . . I am also getting costumes for Oedipus which will do for any Greek play. . . . Jan 18 we play Oedipus & Building Fund. Then there is a blank week—theatre is let for part of that week & Monck has to look after his Norwich pageant."[55] On 2 January 1912, Yeats mentioned a Miss Moore, who "is making the costumes for Oedipus and for Canavans."[56] In none of these letters is there any hint that he was making his own version of the play. As 18 January neared, however, he started improving the speakable qualities of Jebb and thus began the evolution of his own version of *Oedipus*.

In a letter to Lady Gregory dated "Saturday" (probably 6 January 1912), Yeats first mentioned his own involvement in making a text for the *Oedipus* production: "I am much better but must go to Monck's when I am & dictate a revision of Jebb's Oedipus from the point of view of speech. I am taking out the 'Thou's.'" In this same letter, Yeats mentioned Dr. Rex Rynd for the first time. The Reverend Rex Rynd, Preceptor of Norwich Cathedral, had been a fellow student of Monck's at the Royal Academy and first brought Monck to Norwich in January 1909.[57] Yeats reported that a "clergyman friend of Monck's is over & full of wonder at the acting—nothing like it can be done with amateurs in England."[58]

Joseph Hone's statement, that "Dr Rynd of the Norwich Cathedral Chapter, who was on a visit to Dublin, stood over him [Yeats] with the Greek text while he turned Jebb into speakable English with rough unrhymed verse for Chorus" (Hone, pp. 274–

Since 19 December 1911 was a Tuesday, this letter is misdated; 15 December 1911, a Friday, seems probable. It was certainly not Friday, 19 December 1913, when Yeats was at Stone Cottage with Ezra Pound.

[55]ALS, Yeats to Lady Gregory, from Woburn Buildings, postmarked 21 December 1911; collection of Michael Yeats; photocopy National Library of Ireland MS. 18720. "Monday" would have been 18 December 1911, before he left for London.

[56]TLS, Yeats to Lady Gregory, from Woburn Buildings, dictated "Jan. 2, 1912"; collection of Michael Yeats; photocopy National Library of Ireland MS. 18721.

[57]Monck's obituary, *The Times* (London), 23 October 1958, p. 17.

[58]ALS, Yeats to Lady Gregory, from the Abbey Theatre, dated "Saturday"; collection of Michael Yeats; photocopy National Library of Ireland MS. 18721. The letter is wrongly paired with an envelope postmarked 2 January 1912, a Tuesday. Yeats must have returned to Ireland between 2 and 6 January.

75), is probably based on Yeats's letter to Lady Gregory of 7 January 1912. In this letter, Yeats saw himself not merely "taking out the 'Thou's'" of Jebb, but rather making his own version:

> Rynd, a friend of Monck's, a clergyman from Norwich Cathedral saw the rehersal [of *McDaragh's Wife*]. . . . I am making my own version of Oedipus, I have done about 350 lines. I take Jebb and turn him into simple speakable English dictating the result. Yesterday I had Rynd's help he took the Greek text and looked up the literal meaning of passages for me. The choruses I am putting into rough unrhymed verse. I am of course making it very simple in fact turning it into an Abbey play. Monck had already made his cuts. The costumes will cost us £10 or £11, so there is little chance of the performance paying but they will go for any Greek play. They are made to go with the screens. . . . I am to give a lecture to fill up the gap after Oedipus. . . .[59]

Yeats wrote to A. H. Bullen on the same day that he intended to "produce Oedipus here in about 10 days." He was "merely putting the dialogue into prose and the choruses into rough unrhymed verse" and "not trying to make a serious work of it, I haven't the time for that but something had to be done for the existing translations won't speak."[60]

It is significant that the earliest actual pages we have of a draft of *Oedipus* by Yeats are consistent with Yeats's description in his letters of how he dictated the new version in the Abbey office.

Yeats Writes His Own Version

Beginnings (1912): Rex 1

According to Yeats's 7 January 1912 letter to Lady Gregory, quoted above, he had "done about 350 lines' by that date. We believe that the typescript he was working on, the first stage after

[59]TLS, Yeats to Lady Gregory, from the Abbey Theatre, dictated "January 7th 1912"; collection of Michael Yeats; photocopy National Library of Ireland MS. 18721.

[60]TLS, Yeats to A. H. Bullen, from the Abbey Theatre, dictated "January 7th 1912"; University of Kansas Library. Slightly edited in Frank C. Nelick, "Yeats, Bullen, and the Irish Drama," *Modern Drama,* 1 (1958), 202.

Jebb, is represented by what we have called "Rex 1." (There exist five typescripts that predate the published play. We have arranged them in order of composition, as determined by internal evidence, and have named them Rex 1, 2, 3, 4, and 5. Four different typewriters are involved. Description here will be limited to what is essential to the story of Yeats's writing the play.)

Since Yeats's translation is in prose, the "350 lines" must refer to the Greek and would bring us into the Teiresias episode. Line 350 begins the speech in which Teiresias startles Oedipus with the news that "*Thou* art the accursed defiler of this land."[61] There is no break here in Yeats's typescript, and perhaps there is no reason that there should be, since he went on dictating day by day. But lines 151–202, the first stasimon, are indeed translated into "rough unrhymed verse" and are found on pages 4 and 5 of Rex 1. (This is the only chorus that Yeats attempted in 1912. He simply left indications in his typescript of where the others were to be inserted.)

Four days after the letter of 7 January 1912, a week before the planned performance, *Oedipus* was put off to a new date. On 11 January, Yeats wrote to Lady Gregory from Dublin giving the program of performances "right up to the return of the Company." The last item was "Feb 29th, Oedipus with some revival. We had to put off Oedipus as the rivalry for the chief part was causing the first serious trouble in the School,[.] Monck may have to do it himself."[62]

We can date the completion of that portion of the writing represented by Rex 1 as somewhere around 21 January 1912. Rex 1 is incomplete, breaking off on page 39 with line 1252 of the Greek (Jebb, p. 103), the Second Messenger's speech about Jocasta: "and how after that she died I do not know, for Oedipus with a shriek burst in. . . .[63] This break accords with Yeats's account of the writing. On 18 January, he described his schedule: "I have been working very hard. I do my poetry in the mornings, for the last 7 or 8 days I have been working at a lyric which I finished to-day

[61]Jebb, pp. 28–29. "Accursed" is canceled by Monck or Yeats. In Rex 1, p. 10, Yeats also gets rid of the "*Thou*": "You are the defiler of this land."

[62]TLS, Yeats to Lady Gregory, from the Abbey Theatre, dictated "January 11th 1912"; collection of Michael Yeats; photocopy National Library of Ireland MS. 18721.

[63]Rex 1, p. 39. Jebb (p. 38) has "and how thereafter she perished, is more than I know. For with a shriek Oedipus burst in. . . ."

then I go down to the Theatre and dictate letters, then I generally work at Oedipus for an hour and after that often come out to Miss Byrne for more letters. At 1/2 past six we begin rehearsals and when I am here I always take some of them.[64] Three days later he wrote that he was to go to London "where I give two lectures on my ghost theory. . . . I am to work on [*The Land of Heart's Desire*] and the Oedipus choruses while I am away."[65] We can probably associate this hiatus with the point when Yeats had completed the thirty-nine pages represented by Rex 1. When first examined in the Abbey Theatre by James McGuire in 1968, Rex 1 consisted of three carbon copies of these thirty-nine pages, copies probably made for the actors.[66]

It is evident that in dictating Rex 1, Yeats was working from Jebb as cut by Monck, but also that he followed or departed from Monck as his own judgment directed. He made some of Monck's changes but ignored others, kept in some material that Monck cut, cut some material that Monck left in, and put in some of Monck's stage directions but not others.

Rex 2

Rex 2 is a very complicated corrected typescript, dating from 1912 but containing extensive alterations and additions made in early 1926.[67] The first thirty-nine pages are the ribbon copy of which Rex 1 is the carbon copy. Added to these are seven pages, numbered 1–7, black carbon copies, made on the same typewriter, typewriter A, as pages 1–39. These seven pages are the only additions made in 1912. They were completed sometime between 15 February, when Yeats was back in Dublin and hard at work on the

[64]TLS, Yeats to Lady Gregory, from the Abbey Theatre, dictated "January 18th 1912"; collection of Michael Yeats; photocopy National Library of Ireland MS. 18721. "Miss Byrne" may be Nell Byrne, who played in several of Monck's productions at the Abbey in 1911–1912.

[65]TLS, Yeats to Lady Gregory, from the Abbey Theatre, dictated "January 21st 1912"; collection of Michael Yeats; photocopy National Library of Ireland MS. 18721.

[66]Rex 1 is now in National Library of Ireland MS. 21497(i), the three copies being reduced to one.

[67]In the collection of Michael Yeats (catalogued as 426*); SB 21.1.155–209.

play, and 22 February, when he had finished all but the choruses. On the first sheet of Rex 2, in Monck's hand, appears "Oedipus / Nugent Monck / Prompt Copy." This could have been written there either when the first thirty-nine pages were completed or after the final seven pages were added.

On 15 February Yeats declared: "Another days work—if I can't finish to-day—will finish the dialogue of Oedipus, I will then take a week over the choruses. The play will be done the 1st week of March."[68] But in a letter dated simply "Thursday," which can have been written only on 22 February 1912, he told Lady Gregory that *Oedipus* would not be performed until after Monck had left the Abbey for the year and the first company had returned from America, although Yeats had successfully completed the dialogue: "We have put off Oedipus—I thought Monck was getting ill from overwork. We will do it if you will with both companies say Donovan as Oedipus. I shall have to stage manage it myself—though I shall be very clumsy compared to Monck. I have made a fine version. I have finished all but the choruses. Next week Moncks last week, we shall revive a lot of mystery plays and do one new one."[69]

[68]TLS, Yeats to Lady Gregory, from the Abbey Theatre, dictated "February 15th 1912"; collection of Michael Yeats; photocopy National Library of Ireland MS. 18721.

[69]ALS, Yeats to Lady Gregory, dated "Thursday"; collection of Michael Yeats; photocopy National Library of Ireland MS. 18720. The letter was written while Yeats was staying "at Margate with a Mr. & Mrs Tucker." It is with an envelope postmarked 2 November 1911 at Boston, England, which cannot be the correct envelope. A letter written at Margate is unlikely to be posted at Boston. The contents of the letter show that its date is Thursday, 22 February 1912. "Monck's last week" would be the week of 26 February–2 March 1912. On 5 March 1912 Yeats wrote to J. B. Yeats, "It is a moment of transition with us here. Nugent Monck—who has been the teacher of the School—has gone, and I am in charge until the Company arrives, which should be next week" (L567). On the same day, a tribute to Monck on his departure, written by Joseph Holloway, appeared in *The Evening Telegraph* (Dublin): James W. Flannery, *W. B. Yeats and the Idea of a Theatre: The Early Abbey Theatre in Theory and Practice* (New Haven: Yale University Press, 1976), p. 275, n. 11. Monck returned in the autumn, but as of 18 March his return was not certain: in a letter of that date to Lady Gregory, Yeats used the phrase "if Monck comes back in the Autumn" (TLS, Yeats to Lady Gregory, from the Abbey Theatre, dictated "March 18th 1912"; collection of Michael Yeats).

The plays scheduled for "next week Moncks last week" are consistent with the dates 26 February–2 March 1912: "we shall revive a lot of mystery plays and do one new one." The new mystery play was *The Worlde and the Chylde*, a fifteenth-century play produced by Monck at the Abbey on 29 February 1912. The revivals must be some of

On 18 March 1912, Yeats wrote to Monck from the Abbey: "I am very sorry about Oedipus. . . . I suppose you couldn't have come over early in May for Oedipus? Number one Company goes on tour at the end of April, so you would have had the place to yourself again. . . . Number one has come back and the two companies meditate upon each other from different Green Rooms like fighting cocks. We all miss you."[70]

Although Monck had returned by the autumn, this is, so far as we know, Yeats's last mention of the idea of producing *Oedipus* for fourteen years. The completed choruses are inserted in Rex 2, and manuscript revisions are made in the dialogue, but these additions were not made until 1926.

Yeats Loses Interest

Yeats's explanations in the 1930s of why he abandoned the play are only approximately correct. It is time now to take a closer look at those two accounts. In general the pattern of events that we have deduced from the contemporary documents accords fairly well with Yeats's own recollections, although some of his allusions remain unexplained:

> I began my version with the help of Mr. Nugent Monk [sic], who was at the time helping us at the Abbey, and has since established a famous theatre in Norwich, and a young Greek scholar, then one of our actors, but now a Circuit Judge; and half a dozen translations. [*Irish Weekly*, p. 9]

> . . . I found a young Greek scholar who, unlike myself, had not forgotten his Greek, took out of a pigeonhole at the theatre a manuscript translation of *Oedipus* too complicated in its syntax for the stage, bought Jebb's translation and a translation published at a few pence for dishonest schoolboys. Whenever I could not understand

the mystery plays already produced by Monck in 1911–1912. The date of this letter certainly cannot be 2 November 1911; 6–11 November 1911 was hardly "Monck's last week." The correct date is 22 February 1912. "Donovan" is Fred O'Donovan, a leading player at the Abbey, 1908–1918.

[70]From a copy in the possession of Ann Saddlemyer (see note 46).

the precise thoughts behind the translators' half Latin, half Victorian dignity, I got a bald translation from my Greek scholar. [L 537*n*]

The young Greek scholar and Abbey actor, later a circuit judge, was probably Charles Stewart Power (1892–19??), son of John Wyse Power (who contributed to the character of Myles Crawford in *Ulysses* and whose name appears in "Gas from a Burner"). Charles Power was a student of junior sophister standing at Trinity College in October 1910 when he was admitted as a student of law. He was engaged in his law studies for the next two years. Power had been involved in the Abbey acting class under Lennox Robinson before Monck arrived.[71] While the first company of the Abbey was on tour in America from September 1911 to March 1912, Power played in six productions under Monck. After the first company's return, Power played in eight productions under Robinson between April 1912 and October 1913. In October he was admitted to the degree of Barrister-at-Law in the Inns of Court in Ireland. He was indeed young, as Yeats says, being nineteen going on twenty in January 1912 when, while playing Gabriel in Monck's production of *The Annunciation,* he probably appeared as a harbinger of Yeats's own version of *Oedipus*.[72] We say "prob-

[71]John Wyse Power contributed to Myles Crawford, the Aeolus of *Ulysses,* the expression "He can kiss my royal Irish arse.": James Joyce, *Ulysses* (New York: Modern Library, 1961), p. 147; Richard Ellmann, *James Joyce* (New York: Oxford University Press, 1959), p. 298. Documents in the Four Courts record the particulars of Charles Power's law-student days. On 15 September [1911] Lady Gregory wrote to Monck about the possibility of his directing a production of *The Workhouse Ward* for Marie Tempest's company in London, using Abbey actors including "a young fellow, Power, who had been working at the play at the class at the Abbey and Robinson had thought very promising." Copy in the possession of Ann Saddlemyer (see note 46). The "young Greek scholar" has been incorrectly identified as Oliver Gogarty, "in whose house, 'Fairfield,' in County Dublin, Yeats wrote some of his version [of *Oedipus*]" (*Commentary,* p. 178). The date, 1910, is too early, and Gogarty never was a circuit judge.

[72]Power acted at first for Edward Martyn's Theatre of Ireland, in Molesworth Hall. He played John in Charles Macklin's eighteenth-century comedy *The True Born Irishman,* 18 February 1910; Hugh Deely in Seumas O'Kelly's *The Homecoming,* 28 March 1910; and a bit part in J. O'E.'s *The Spurious Sovereign, or Nailed to the Counter,* 28 March 1910. In *Sinn Féin* (Easter Week, 1910), p. 1, Arthur Griffith wrote that in *The Homecoming* Power "played with great restraint and feeling": quoted in Robert Hogan, Richard Burnham, and Daniel P. Poteet, *The Modern Irish Drama, IV: The Rise of the Realists* (Dublin: Dolmen Press; Atlantic Highland, N.J.: Humanities Press, 1979), pp.

ably," because although Power is the only person who fits Yeats's description, being a circuit judge in 1931 and an Abbey actor in 1911–1912, we cannot establish that he knew Greek. His records at

---

79–80; hereafter cited as *Realists*. After the first Abbey company left for America on 12 September 1911, classes for dramatic training were given by Nugent Monck, opening on 10 October 1911. Power joined the school. Among first productions at the Abbey, Power played Pride in *The Interlude of Youth: An Old Morality* and Martin in Lady Gregory's translation of Douglas Hyde's *The Marriage*, 16 November 1911; Michael Flanagan, the younger, in Rutherford Mayne's *Red Turf*, 7 December 1911; Gabriel in *The Annunciation*, and Gabriel in *The Flight into Egypt*, 4 January 1912; and Perseverance in *The Worlde and the Chylde*, 29 February 1912. Power also played the First Demon in Yeats's *The Countess Cathleen*, 14–16 December 1911; A Wandering Songmaker in Lady Gregory's *Dervorgilla*, 18 and 20 January 1912; The Gatekeeper in her *The Gaol Gate*; James Ryan in her *Spreading the News*; Captain Headley in her *The Canavans*; and Shawn Bruin in Yeats's *The Land of Heart's Desire*; all in February 1912. *The Gaol Gate, Spreading the News*, and *The Land of Heart's Desire* were repeated in March. A fellow actor in the Acting School "told Yeats that Monck had helped to make . . . Charles Power . . . into a more effective actor: simple and unpretentious, what he used not to be" (*Realists*, p. 174).

One less positive report appears after the return of the first company when Lennox Robinson had taken over. Miss Byrne wrote to Yeats on 15 April 1912 about Power's portrayal of Willie Sullivan in Robinson's *Patriots* on 11 April 1912: "the only blot on it was poor Power, in one bit I liked him, but in most of it he was so very much Power, full of artificiality and tricks, though honestly I believe many of his tricks are natural to him, for the other morning I was writing for Mr. Robinson in his room, when Power came in and his manner was very much the same, he can never forget himself, and it is not a pleasant self!" (*Realists*, p. 186). In other first productions under Robinson, Power played Father John in Joseph Campbell's *Judgment*, 15 April 1912; His Grace the Duke of Ormond in G. Sidney Paternoster's *The Dean of St. Patrick's*, 23 January 1913; A Policeman in S. R. Day and G. D. Cummin's *Broken Faith*, and Jaymony Shanahan in George Fitzmaurice's *The Magic Glasses*, 24 April 1913; Doctor in Rabindranath Tagore's *The Post Office*, 17 May 1913; David, son of Charles O'Donnell, in T. C. Murray's *Sovereign Love*, 11 September 1913; and Burnett, president of the Geological Society, in Joseph Connolly's *The Mine Land*, 2 October 1913. Of *The Dean of St. Patrick's*, a review in *The Irish Citizen*, 1 March 1913, p. 325, said that the minor characters such as Power's "supercilious Oxford . . . came nearer the scope of regular Abbey drama" than did the overambitious major ones (*Realists*, p. 245). We find no record of Power's playing after he became a barrister in October 1913 until he played Son in an Abbey production of Richard Brinsley Sheridan's *The Critic*, 26 December 1914. A review in *The Irish Times*, 28 December 1914, p. 7, singled out Power, "who was very cleverly inane—his faint was . . . charmingly wooden" (*Realists*, p. 346). Finally he appeared in Edward Martyn's *The Privilege of Place*, back with the Irish Theatre, now in the Hardwicke Street Hall, 8 November 1915. A review in *The Evening Mail*, 9 November 1915, p. 5, said that "The part of Mark Bodkin, described as an experimentalist in life, was efficiently played by Mr. Charles Power" (*Realists*, p. 400).

We get just a glimpse of Power, before and after the war, from a fellow member of

St. Mary's Christian Brothers School and at Trinity College show no formal study of that language.

Yeats says that he had the help not only of Monck and the young Greek scholar but also of "half a dozen translations." We cannot be certain what the "half a dozen translations" were. We have seen that he knew of Whitelaw.[73] There remains in his library the Lewis Campbell verse translation.[74] And in fact the Gilbert Murray translation of 1911, a copy of which is in Yeats's library, was out in time to influence Yeats's 1912 version.[75] The "translation published at a few pence for dishonest schoolboys" is still in Yeats's library. It is Roscoe Mongan's translation in the "Kelly's Keys to the Classics" series.[76] None of these shows the heavy use that the Jebb does, nor does internal evidence show much influence. The "manuscript translation of *Oedipus* too complicated in its syntax for the stage" has disappeared, although perhaps it is the one completed by W. K. Magee between 17 May and 22 December 1909.[77] Yeats feared, as we have seen, that "Magees elaborate style may not prove vocal" (TB 152, n. 1).

We saw from Yeats's 18 January 1912 letter, describing his daily schedule, that he did much of his work on *Oedipus* while in the

---

Monck's school, the comic peasant actor Michael Conniffe, in an interview conducted by Robert Hogan: "I was in the Magic Glasses, by George Fitzmaurice. And Charlie Power was in it. Charlie Power, he's dead. He became Judge Wyse Power at the turn of the Government. His mother, God rest her, she had a restaurant down in Henry Street" (*Realists*, p. 437).

Thanks are due to Registrar Kevin Waldron of the High Court and Counselor Oliver Gogarty, Four Courts, Dublin, for helping us to identify Charles Stewart Power.

[73]A possible edition would be *Sophocles*, translated into English verse by Robert Whitelaw, 2d ed. (London: Longmans, Green, 1897).

[74]Sophocles, *The Seven Plays in English Verse*, translated into English verse by Lewis Campbell, new ed., rev., World's Classics (London: Oxford University Press, 1906). No. 963 / L.7.2. in Yeats's library. There are no marks or annotations on *Oedipus the King*.

[75]Sophocles, *Oedipus King of Thebes*, translated into English Rhyming Verse with Explanatory Notes by Gilbert Murray (London: George Allen & Sons, 1911). No. 967A / L.7.2. in Yeats's library.

[76]Sophocles, *Oedipus Tyrannus*, Literally translated by Roscoe Mongan, Kelly's Keys to the Classics (London: James Cornish & Sons, n.d.). No. 967/L.7.2 in Yeats's library. All the pages are cut, but there are no marks in the book.

[77]See LTWBY 186 for the editors' suggestion that the manuscript translation may be Magee's.

theatre. His later comments give us a fuller picture of what he was doing:

> Sometimes I went on to the stage and spoke a sentence to be sure that it was simple enough and resonant enough to be instantaneously felt and understood in every part of the theatre. [*Irish Weekly,* p. 9].

> I spoke out every sentence, very often from the stage, with one sole object, that the words should sound natural and fall in their natural order, that every sentence should be a spoken, not a written sentence. [L 537n]

But Yeats's explanation of his motivation in failing to produce *Oedipus* in 1912 is inexact. He bases it completely on the withdrawal of the English censor's ban on the play, and the facts simply do not bear him out:

> I finished my first rough draft and began to look for an actor, but before I had found one the English censorship withdrew its ban, and when the pleasure of mocking it and affirming the freedom of our Irish uncensored stage was taken from me, I lost interest in the play. [*Irish Weekly,* p. 9]

> Then when I had finished the dialogue in the rough and was still shrinking at the greater labour of the choruses, the English censor withdrew his ban and I lost interest. [L 537n]

Yeats's "loss of interest" did not happen as suddenly as he claimed. The censorship was indeed lifted. Fowell and Palmer report (p. 275) that "[i]n time the Censor slowly followed public opinion, and the *Oedipus* was performed at Covent Garden in 1912 for twenty-six performances, with the most unstinted public approval." This was Max Reinhardt's production of Gilbert Murray's *Oedipus Rex,* which had opened in London on 15 January with Martin Harvey and Lillah McCarthy. (Reinhardt had already produced Hugo von Hofmannsthal's version in Germany with great success.[78]) In a letter postmarked 31 January 1912, Yeats

[78]Reinhardt's *Oedipus Rex* opened in Vienna in October 1910; in Budapest, with Hungarian players, October 1910; in the Zirkus Schumann, Berlin, 7 November 1910; in Covent Garden, London, with Martin Harvey and English players, 15 January 1912;

praises Reinhardt's production in the highest terms: "I saw Oedipus last week—not well acted but a most wonderful production. I quite surrender—Reinhardt is a great man. He used sounds in the most emotional way—a gong, a single flute, inarticulate cries & expressed that horror of the people at the death of Jocasta by making people run in and out of the palace in an aimless way. It was the most imaginative production of a play I have ever seen."[79]

But the facts, contrary to his explanations in the 1930s, are that Yeats continued to work on his own *Oedipus* after seeing Reinhardt's. His letter of 15 February 1912 projects that "[t]he play will be done the first week of March," and the letter we have dated 22 February, though it says *Oedipus* has been put off indefinitely, looks forward to doing it "with both companies" and with "Donovan as Oedipus." In his 18 March letter to Monck, Yeats notes the possibility of doing the play in May with the second company. However, a "Petition to the King," dated 11 June 1912 and signed by over sixty dramatists, shows that Reinhardt's triumph had made the censorship look silly and had thus accomplished very thoroughly what Yeats was aiming at. The dramatists resolved

> That the Lord Chamberlain's Department by working on custom and not on ascertainable results has been grossly unjust to managers, authors, and the public, and has cast discredit on the administration of the Department by its treatment of classical plays, and of plays in which Scriptural characters appear, as may be instanced by the repeated refusals to many managers of a license for Sophocles' great play *OEdipus Rex,* which now, at last permitted, has been produced with every indication of public approval. [Fowell and Palmer, p. 375]

Perhaps it was finally borne in upon Yeats that since the censorship had been lifted for such a spectacular success as Reinhardt's *Oedipus Rex,* an Abbey production might be an anticlimax. We hear no more of Yeats's *Oedipus* for many years.

---

in St. Petersburg, Moscow, Riga, Warsaw, Kiev, Odessa, and Stockholm, winter 1912: *Max Reinhardt and His Theatre,* ed. Oliver M. Sayler (New York: Brentano's, 1924), pp. 356–58. It was a world success.

[79]ALS, Yeats to Lady Gregory, from Woburn Buildings, dated "Wednesday," postmarked 31 January 1912; collection of Michael Yeats; photocopy National Library of Ireland MS. 18721.

David R. Clark and James B. McGuire

Completion (1926–1928): Rex 2 Continued

How Yeats came to take up his *Oedipus* again fourteen years later is also told in the 1930 commentaries, although there is little mention of it in his correspondence. "I put [*Oedipus*] into the file with my letters and forgot it, and then four or five years ago my wife found it and persuaded me to finish it and put it on to the Abbey stage" (*Irish Weekly*, p. 9). "About five years ago my wife found the manuscript and set me to work again" (L 537n). Rex 2 shows four stages of work. In 1912, as we have said, Yeats wrote first pages 1–39, then finished the play with the additional pages numbered 1–7. These forty-six pages, held together by a brass fastener that pierced all the pages in the top left corner, were what Mrs. Yeats found in the file.

In 1926, as a first step, Yeats completed the choruses. Although he uses the words "when the dialogue was revised and the choruses written," implying a sequence, Rex 2 shows that the choruses had been written before the dialogue was revised. He was "still shrinking at the greater labour of the choruses" (L 537n) when he put the play away, and the choruses were the first thing he did when he took the play out again. The holograph versions of the choruses date from about 21 February 1926, when he wrote to Herbert Grierson that he was working on one: "I have been writing the material [metrical?] version of a chorus for a version of *Oedipus* intended for the stage and my faculties have gone to the deuce" (L 710). When completed, the choruses were typed out in a distinctive typeface, typewriter B, and on distinctive paper—this typewriter and this paper not being used elsewhere in Rex 2. The choruses were then slipped in individually and paper-clipped to the nearest page without disturbing the brass paper-fastener that bound all other pages together.

The fourth stage of work on Rex 2 was the revision of the whole. Rex 2 is covered with corrections and revisions in Yeats's hand, all in the same blue-black ink, whether they appear on pages 1–39, on the final seven pages, or on the added choruses. The manuscript corrections were probably all made at the same time—the manuscript has that look—and subsequent to the completion of the metrical versions of the choruses. The conclusion of the play written on the verso of the final page is in that same ink. (This conclusion Yeats treated as a choral ode and thus had probably left it uncompleted, like the other odes, in 1912.)

Rex 3

Next we have Rex 3,[80] a fair copy, made on typewriter C, incorporating the revisions and additions found in Rex 2. This typing was probably done to provide a script for the first performance, 7 December 1926. A number of parts copied from this typing exist, and Rex 3, the ribbon copy, contains stage directions in the hand of Lennox Robinson, who directed the performance. Speaking of the first performance, Yeats wrote to Olivia Shakespear:

> My version of *Oedipus* comes on to-night. I think my shaping of the speech will prove powerful on the stage, for I have made it bare, hard and natural like a saga, and that it will be well, though not greatly, acted—it is all too new to our people. I am more anxious about the audience, who will have to sustain an hour and a half of tension. The actor who plays Oedipus felt the strain at dress rehearsal so much that he could hardly act in the last great moments—a good audience will give him life, but how will the Catholics take it? In rehearsal I had but one overwhelming emotion, a sense as of the actual presence in a terrible sacrament of the god. But I have got that always, though never before so strongly, from Greek Drama. [Then, on the envelope, he added:] *Oedipus* great success. Critics and audience enthusiastic.[81]

[80]National Library of Ireland MS. 21497(ii). There is no copy at Stony Brook.

[81]L 720. *Oedipus the King* (so titled on the programme) by Sophocles, prose version by W. B. Yeats, was produced at the Abbey Theatre by Lennox Robinson on Tuesday evening, 7 December 1926. The cast was as follows: Oedipus, F. J. McCormick; Jocasta, Eileen Crowe; Creon, Barry Fitzgerald; Priest, Eric Gorman; Tiresias, Michael J. Dolan; Boy, D. Breen; First Messenger, Arthur Shields; Herdsman, Gabriel J. Fallon; Second Messenger, P. J. Carolan; Nurse, May Craig; Children (Antigone and Ismene), Raymond and Edna Fardy; Servants, Tony Quinn, Michael Scott, C. Haughton; Leader of the Chorus, J. Stephenson; Chorus, Peter Nolan, Walter Dillon, T. Moran, M. Finn, D. Williams. Lennox Robinson composed the music for the choruses (included in the 1928 edition) and mounted the set, two square pillars against a curtained background. A photograph appears in *Theatre Arts Monthly*, 11 (January 1927), 216. Yeats's satisfaction

The next day he wrote to Lady Gregory: "Oedipus I think a very great success with papers & the audience enthusiastic. . . . At 3 MacCormack & Lennox come to make cuts in Oedipus."[82] Lady Gregory replied on 9 December: "I am delighted that Edipus has been such a success—for you & for the Abbey—I wish I could have seen it but I suppose it will be on again."[83] In a letter dated "Dec 13" but postmarked 12 December 1926, Yeats comments on the entire week: "Oedipus was a very great success—packed houses towards the end—but there was little or no profit as Oedipus & [?] both require emmense [sic] casts & of course Monday was the Gaelic players. MacCormac has now established himself in the minds of our audience as a great tragedian. He had certain magnificent moments."[84]

The excitement of success stirred Yeats with an ambition to make versions of all three of Sophocles' Theban plays. On 18 December, he wrote to Lady Gregory:

> I have begun Oedipus at Colonus—done about 10 pages—but hesitate between it & the Antigone. I feel that these three closely united plays put into simple speakable prose may be my contribution to the

---

was shared by as disengaged a critic as Joseph Holloway, not always impressed by Yeats's triumphs:

"*Tuesday, December 7.* The word great would be fairly employed to describe the first performance at the Abbey of W. B. Yeats's prose version of *Oedipus the King* by Sophocles with F. J. McCormick as the king. . . . The Greek play was simply and effectively set and dressed. The chorus sang or chanted too vocally, but, when J. Stephenson as "Leader of the Chorus" spoke, his words came very clearly. McCormick was very dignified in bearing and impressive of speech in the opening episodes; his sudden change when blind at the end might be considered too pronounced, and his voice too whiningly pitched, though his episode with the children was moving in the extreme; on the whole, however, his impersonation had the quality of greatness in it, and at the end of the tragedy he got four enthusiastic curtains. . . . Yeats's version of *Oedipus the King* was very clear in meaning and actable": *Joseph Holloway's Irish Theatre, Volume One—1926-1931,* ed. Robert Hogan and Michael J. O'Neill (Dixon, Calif.: Proscenium Press, 1968), p. 20.

[82]ALS, Yeats to Lady Gregory, from 82 Merrion Square, dated "Dec 8"; collection of Michael Yeats; SB 3.7.159–60. "MacCormack" is F. J. McCormick (Peter Judge, 1889–1947), who played Oedipus.

[83]ALS, Lady Gregory to Yeats, from Coole, dated "Thursday Dec 9"; collection of Michael Yeats; photocopy National Library of Ireland MS. 18683.

[84]ALS, Yeats to Lady Gregory, from 82 Merrion Square, dated "Dec 13," postmarked 12 December 1926; collection of Michael Yeats; SB 3.7.171–74.

> Abbey Repertory. Oedipus at Colonus is magnificent but might not be the sure [or, same?] immediate success as the "Antigone," though that lacks a great part for MaCormac who is now quite certainly a great tragedian. Saturday night, which I missed I was there on Friday night as well as on Tuesday and Thursday, was I am told the most stirring ever known at the Abbey.[85]

And on 29 December, he continued, without further mention of *Antigone*:

> I am more than half through "Oedipus at Colonus." Another week should finish the dialogue & then I need a fortnight for the rhymed chorus. I think it should play as well as "Oedipus the King." I shall be much more content with my work for the Abbey when this play is finished. I shall have done my part in creating a repertory, & without going outside my professed work in life. It will play an hour & three quarters.[86]

A letter that Yeats mistakenly dated "Dec 6" (to which Wade, also mistakenly, adds the year 1926), but which we date 6 January 1927, comes in best at this point. Yeats wrote to Olivia Shakespear: "My work on *Oedipus at Colonus* has made me bolder and when I look at *King Oedipus* I am shocked at my moderation. I want to be less literal and more idiomatic and modern. I shall finish tonight all the dialogue for *Oedipus at Colonus* and then will come six weeks' work at the lyrical choruses, two of which are very famous" (L 721).[87] It was approximately 6 January and not 6

---

[85]ALS, Yeats to Lady Gregory, from 82 Merrion Square, dated "Dec 18"; collection of Michael Yeats; SB 3.7.175–76.

[86]ALS, Yeats to Lady Gregory, from 82 Merrion Square, postmarked 29 December 1926; collection of Michael Yeats; SB 3.7.166–68.

[87]We are convinced that Yeats wrote "Dec" in error for January. The likely date is 6 January 1927. If it were 6 December 1926, Yeats would almost certainly have betrayed some concern about the opening of Oedipus on the next evening. In his 7 December 1926 letter he does express such concern. Moroever, that letter begins "I have not written as life has been rather broken since I returned . . ." (L 719). If he had written on 6 December, why would he say a day later that he had not written? A 6 January 1927 date accords well with the contents. Yeats goes on, "I shall be in England before I have finished. They are playing my *Baile's Strand* at Cambridge from Jan 31 to Feb 5. . . ." If six weeks from date includes 31 January, then the date is more likely 6 January than 6 December. Yeats says that he has almost finished the dialogue for *Oedipus at Colonus,*

December that Yeats was finishing the dialogue of *Oedipus at Colonus* in a first draft and thinking of starting on the choruses. It was then, too—not before or immediately after the "very great success" of the first performance of 7 December—that he was shocked at his moderation in *King Oedipus* and determined to be "less literal and more idiomatic and modern." This desire affected not only his writing of *Oedipus at Colonus* but also the revision of *King Oedipus* that he carried on early in 1927. Rex 4 represents this revision.

Rex 4

The Rex 4 typescript[88] is a carbon copy, Rex 3 being the ribbon copy. But Rex 4 is covered with revisions in Yeats's hand, which advances it far beyond Rex 3. Some of these revisions may be referred to in Yeats's 6 January 1927 letter to Olivia Shakespear, in which he wrote: "I won't send you *Oedipus* yet, I have only one complete copy—beside the prompt copy—and that I keep by me to alter in odd moments" (L 721); the complete copy that he kept by him was Rex 4, and the prompt copy was Rex 2.[89] Rex 2, as we have seen, has on it the words "Prompt Copy," written in 1912 by Nugent Monck. It could still have been used as a prompt copy in 1926, since it is revised in Yeats's hand.

---

yet on 18 December 1926 he writes that he has done only ten pages (see above). A 5 January 1927 letter to Lady Gregory says, "Tomorrow or to-night should finish the first draft of *Oedipus at Colonus* (the dialogue for no chorus is yet begun)" (ALS, Yeats to Lady Gregory, dated "Jan 5," postmarked 5 January 1927; collection of Michael Yeats; photocopy National Library of Ireland MS. 18745). The letter we date 6 January 1927 says the same thing to Olivia Shakespear the next day. Forced to choose between the conclusion that Yeats momentarily forgot what month it was and the conclusion that he did not know where he was in writing the dialogue of his play, we unhesitatingly prefer the former. That Wade was disturbed by the problem in dating is shown by his placing this supposedly 6 December letter *after* the 7 December letter to Olivia Shakespear (L 719–22).

[88]National Library of Ireland MS. 8765; SB 28.1.9–82.

[89]Rex 4 remained at Mrs. W. B. Yeats's home until she gave it to the National Library of Ireland. Rex 2 is still in the collection of Michael Yeats. Rex 1, 3, and 5 were all at the Abbey Theatre. Rex 4 shows revision in Yeats's hand in black ink, blue-black ink, pencil, and brown crayon consistent with his altering it "in odd moments" with whatever writing instrument was at hand.

Many of the revisions on Rex 4, however, must represent Yeats's work on the play with Lady Gregory in February 1927. In his 1933 *New York Times* essay he notes: "When the dialogue was revised and the choruses written [i.e. after, in fact, the play had received its first performance], Lady Gregory and I went through it all, altering every sentence that might not be intelligible on the Blasket Islands." In a journal entry of 2 February 1927, Lady Gregory wrote: "I helped Yeats yesterday & this morning in his revision of his Edipus—comparing it with a French translation—& getting some more direct speech & better sound." On 4 February she added, "Working still on Edipus," and on 6 February, in a passage hard to decipher, "We have finished going through Edipus to King. I've been reading the 'Colonus' in the French version—it is less tragic than the other, having the triumph at the end of burial off to gods—as with Moses and Elijah—." We take these entries to mean that Lady Gregory worked on *King Oedipus* with Yeats and then went on to read *Oedipus at Colonus* on her own. On 11 February she noted that Yeats had said to her, "With your help I have made the Edipus a masterpiece of English prose." And on 22 February she recorded, "We finished work at Edipus yesterday. Yeats thanked me—said my help had made a great difference in getting it into natural speech."[90] It may be that by "Edipus" and "it" Lady Gregory referred to both plays, but it seems certain that at least *King Oedipus* was revised at this time with her help and that Rex 4 records the revisions.

In Yeats's library today we still find the two volumes of Sophocles translated into French by Paul Masqueray that Yeats and Lady Gregory pored over.[91] Tome I, in which *Oedipe-Roi* is found, is dated 1922, and Tome II, which contains *Oedipe à Colone*, is dated

[90]Henry W. and Albert A. Berg Collection, New York Public Library, Astor, Lenox and Tilden Foundations. We thank Ann Saddlemyer for making us transcriptions of difficult passages.

[91]Sophocle, Tome I, *Ajax—Antigone—Oedipe-Roi—Electre,* texte établi et traduit par Paul Masqueray (Paris: Société d'Édition "Les Belles Lettres," 1922). No. 964 / L.7.2 in Yeats's library. The pages are cut for all the plays but not for most of the introductory commentary on each of them. We are grateful for the late Glenn O'Malley's comments on the cards he made in cataloguing the library. Also in the library is Sophocle, Tome II, *Les Trachiniennes—Philoctète—Oedipe à Colone / Les Limiers,* texte établi et traduit par Paul Masqueray (Paris: Société d'Édition "Les Belles Lettres," 1924) in which only the pages of the translation of *Oedipe à Colone* are cut.

1924. In Tome I the pages containing introductory material, pages i—xxv, 1–10, 129–32, and 135–38 are all unopened (i.e., uncut). Only pages 139–97 containing the play itself are cut. The effect of Masqueray on Yeats's version can be demonstrated. On page 154 Yeats has penciled in a translation of Teiresias' "C'est toi, malheureux, que me fais ces reproches, que tous sans exception te feront bientôt": "It is you wretched [indecipherable] who fling insults at me that will soon be flung at yourself by all—". Jebb had translated the Greek of lines 372–73: "Aye, and thou art a poor wretch to utter taunts which every man here will soon hurl at thee" (Jebb, p. 30). Monck cut the speech out. Yeats restored it as "You are but a poor wretch speaking taunts that in a little while everyone here shall speak of you," which is found in the first typing (Rex 1 and Rex 2) and the second typing (Rex 3 and Rex 4). But in Rex 4 Yeats crossed out "speaking" and wrote in "flinging," crossed out "here" and "speak of" and wrote in "fling at," making the line read, "You are but a poor wretch flinging taunts that in a little while everyone shall fling at you." That is how the line reads in all published versions (VPl 819). "To fling insults" is not a literal translation of "faire ces reproches," but the French has freed Yeats to use idiomatic English. These alterations, clearly based on Masqueray, are in black ink, and it may be that that ink identifies (at least tentatively) the work done on the manuscript with Lady Gregory's help. But this is a very dubious point.

On 13 March 1927, Yeats wrote to Olivia Shakespear, showing satisfaction with the version, and mentioning a cut that we find in Rex 4: "You speak of the long speech in *Oedipus the King* as being unactable. It is so on our stage but I cut all of it out but a few lines" (L 722). Whatever speech Yeats means, it must have been retained in rehearsals and perhaps in first performance for him to find out that it was unactable "on our stage." Then, later, it must have been abridged. Such a speech is found in Rex 4, translating ll. 1369–1415 of the Greek (Jebb, pp. 110–13), and ending up as ll. 1082–1111 of Yeats's printed text (VPl 847–48). It is Oedipus' answer to the chorus's horrified response to his blinding: "You were better dead than blind" (l. 1081). Oedipus' answer runs from pages 61 to 63 of Rex 3 and Rex 4. On Rex 3 Yeats scratches out four passages, of fifty-eight, thirty-nine, six, and thirteen words, in this speech. It is Rex 4, however, in which Yeats "has cut all of it out but a few lines." In Rex 4 he scratched out most of page 62 and broke up what was left of the speech by writing in two speeches by the chorus that are not in Sophocles. Rex 4 brings this "unactable" speech essentially to what we have in the published version. All things considered, then, we are probably safe in assigning Rex 4 to January and February of 1927.

Rex 5

Probably at the end of February 1927, a new typing on typewriter D incorporated the revisions on Rex 4. What we call "Rex 5" is a ribbon copy, probably prepared in the spring of 1927 with a view to publication and as a corrected text for further performances.[92] On 2 (or 4) October [Postmark 1927] Yeats wrote to Olivia Shakespear that "[t]wo typed copies sent to the publisher have [gone] astray in the post and that has held up publication for months" (L 729). These may have been copies of Rex 5 or further typescripts based on it. *Sophocles' King Oedipus* was published on 27 March 1928. There were performances of both *Sophocles' King Oedipus* and *Sophocles' Oedipus at Colonus* in early September 1927. (The reviewers ignored Yeats's extensive revisions of *King Oedipus*.) Yeats wrote on 7 September (postmarked 1927): "We are back from Ballylee for *Oedipus*—the *King* this week and *Colonus* next" (L 728). Rex 5 contains stage directions in Lennox Robinson's hand. Acting parts were typed from it, and some of the parts from Rex 3 were revised to fit Rex 5. Probably Rex 5 is the text of the September 1927 performance.

The story of Yeats's writing of *Sophocles' King Oedipus* is a long and complex one but worth studying, not only for the high quality

[92]Rex 5 was examined by David Clark in the Abbey Theatre in 1969. Since that time a number of scripts have been moved from the Abbey to the National Library of Ireland. Rex 5 is not one of these, however. In the spring of 1981, on asking to examine the typescript again, in order to make a bibliographical description, Clark was told at the Abbey that it was no longer there. So its whereabouts is a mystery. Clark had made a photocopy of the typescript in 1969, and a copy of that copy has been made for the National Library collection. There is no copy of this typescript at Stony Brook.

of the achievement, but also for the principles observable in the process. *King Oedipus* is important not only in Yeats's development as a dramatist, but equally in his development as a poet. It was published in the same year as his greatest volume, *The Tower*. Attention to the manuscripts of *Sophocles' King Oedipus* will put the reader in possession of some of the reasons for Yeats's mature power and mastery.

Aesthete among the Athletes: Yeats's Contributions to *The Gael*

John S. Kelly

That W. B. Yeats, who was soon to become known for his floppy bow ties and carefully cultivated aesthetic pose, should have made some of his earliest literary contributions to a magazine founded for, and predominantly read by, beefy athletes of the Gaelic Athletic Association has always been a pleasing anomaly. It would have been even more pleasing if it had not been tantalizing, for with only one number of the magazine surviving it has been difficult to ascertain what he wrote in its pages or to tell with accuracy what contribution it made to the Irish literary revival. Football players and hurlers do not save up back numbers of their journals in the way that literary young men do; once the latest scores have been marked and the accounts of the matches digested, the sporting paper is tossed aside. Thus Roger McHugh and Allan Wade, when preparing their editions of Yeats's letters, found many references to *The Gael* but only one extant copy, which—as luck would have it—contained nothing by Yeats. This was frustrating, since it became evident that the magazine had published an early essay on Finn Mac Cumhaill, a long review of Katharine Tynan's *Shamrocks,* and a number of poems, including one he called "Lug-na-Gall"; and it was likely that *Dhoya* had first appeared in a Christmas number. All these works date from 1887, when Yeats was in his twenty-second and twenty-third years, and would thus illuminate that period in his development when, as he tells us in a later essay, he began to hammer his thoughts into unity and to seek in the crossways of his inspiration a definitely Irish path for his poetry.

It would be a happy thing to say that the tantalizing days were over and that a full file of *The Gael* had come to light, buried under a fading bundle of jerseys in the attic of some descendant of a Gaelic Athletic pioneer. Perhaps such a file does exist, but if so it still rests under its sporting shroud. There are, however, odd pages and fragments of the magazine dispersed in libraries in Belfast, in Dublin, and in Carbondale, Illinois.[1] They are like pieces of an incomplete jigsaw puzzle, but from them—and from unpublished letters of Douglas Hyde, Ellen O'Leary, and Katharine Tynan—we can gain at least some sense of the literary policy of the magazine and of Yeats's association with it. Together these fragmentary sources provide us with a sizable portion of Yeats's essay on Finn Mac Cumhaill—including his rhymed adaptation of a translated poem; the full text of his review of *Shamrocks*; and a long missing

[1]The largest collection of extracts from *The Gael* is at the Belfast Public Library and forms part of the Crone Papers. These items probably originated with John O'Leary and came to J. S. Crone through D. J. O'Donoghue. A copy of Yeats's review of *Shamrocks* is to be found at the Morris Library of Southern Illinois University at Carbondale, and I am grateful to Louisa Bowen for her help in making a copy available to me. More recently, a second example of this review has come to light among the papers of Katharine Tynan's daughter, Pamela Hinkson, in Dublin. Mr. Peter van de Kamp, who made this discovery, is now cataloguing this extensive archive, and his work will be an important tool for future research into Anglo-Irish literature. The National Library of Ireland owns a complete number of *The Gael,* that for 7 January 1888; and the collection of Michael Yeats has a stray page of the issue for 16 April 1887, announcing that the article on Finn Mac Cumhaill has been postponed for a week.

 Thanks are due to them for permission to publish portions of unpublished manuscripts and letters, as well as to the officers of Oxford University Press and to the editors of the various volumes in the forthcoming edition of Yeats's letters.

Quotations from the letters of Ellen O'Leary are made with the kind permission of the Belfast Public Library. My search for the executors of her estate has not yet been successful, and I would be grateful for any information which might lead to their discovery.

All quotations from unpublished and published sources are presented uncorrected, including letters by W. B. Yeats, which have been retranscribed from his originals. For convenience, however, these are cited in the text with the pagination of Wade's edition of *Letters*. In this essay, unattributed quotations by Yeats are taken from *The Gael* extracts given below.

and hitherto unrecorded poem variously entitled "Lug-na-Gall" and "The Protestants' Leap."

The connection between Yeats and *The Gael,* as between Yeats and many aspects of Irish life at this time, was John O'Leary. As a young man, O'Leary had been deeply influenced by the literary propaganda of Thomas Davis and *The Nation,* so that when he became editor of the Fenian newspaper *The Irish People,* he was particularly assiduous in publishing literary contributions. Imprisonment and exile put an end to this early work, but on his return to Ireland in 1885 he busied himself at once with the cultural and intellectual education of his countrymen, going far and wide to give his lectures "How Irishmen Should Feel" and "What Irishmen Should Know," the latter being published in *The Gael* on 6 and 13 August 1887. His library, his knowledge of Anglo-Irish literature, his sponsorship of various Young Ireland societies, and—above all—his example were to have an important formative effect on Yeats, who was quick to acknowledge that "[w]e of the younger generation owe a great deal to Mr. O'Leary and his sister. What nationality is in the present literary movement in Ireland is largely owing to their influence . . . . He, more clearly than any one, has seen that there is no fine nationality without literature, and seen the converse also, that there is no fine literature without nationality" (LNI 75–76). O'Leary dedicated himself to putting forward this gospel at every opportunity, and so it is less remarkable than it might appear at first sight that the man who had attempted to give Fenianism a literary dimension would also try the same policy on the Gaelic Athletic Association.

The G.A.A., as it was known for short, had been founded by Michael Cusack at Thurles, County Tipperary, on 1 November 1884, with the purpose of popularizing and codifying the rules of native Irish games in opposition to English sports. From the beginning the movement had connections with the extreme wing of Irish nationalism, and at least four of the seven men who attended the inaugural meeting were Fenians—a relationship further cemented in 1886 when John O'Leary was invited to become a patron. Cusack, who appears as the Citizen in Joyce's *Ulysses,* a man of rancorous mind and vociferous speech, soon fell out with the society he had founded, and after only twenty months, in July

1886, he was forced to resign from it. He went with an ill grace, and to make as public as possible his antipathy to the way in which the association was now being conducted he founded in January 1887 *The Celtic Times,* through whose columns he aimed a non-stop barrage of criticism and abuse at the G.A.A., his particular targets being Pat T. Hoctor, its vice-president, and John Boyle O'Reilly, who had replaced him as honorary secretary. Faced with this onslaught and in response to plaintive resolutions passed by the county conventions, the executive of the G.A.A. decided to set up *The Gael* as the quasi-official mouthpiece of the association: Hoctor was appointed editor and John O'Leary literary editor, but the magazine was supposed to be self-financing and no demands were made on the funds of the association. *The Gael* was published weekly, cost one penny, and consisted of eight pages on the average. In the first issue, which probably appeared on 9 April 1887, it announced its intention of being "Kindly Irish of the Irish, neither Saxon nor Italian." The tilt against England was to be expected in such a periodical, but the implied dissociation from the Catholic church reflected the anticlerical attitude of the Fenians on the executive, an attitude that was in large part to cause the downfall of the magazine. For during 1887 the influence of the Irish Republican Brotherhood in the association grew and culminated in an attempt to have P. N. Fitzgerald, a well-known Fenian suspect, elected chairman of the annual convention at Thurles in November. This led to a schism in the meeting, and troubled reverberations rumbled on through the following weeks, bringing down the wrath of Archbishop Croke and *The Freeman's Journal* on the unrepentant executive. A special convention was summoned at Thurles on 4 January 1888, as a result of which the Fenians were shorn of much of their power, and very shortly afterward a newly elected executive ordered *The Gael* to suspend publication. The only complete surviving number of the magazine is dated 7 January 1888, and this may well have been the final issue.[2] Certainly it was

[2]This is the issue in the National Library of Ireland. It contains outraged denunciations of the second, extraordinary, Thurles Convention of the G. A. A., and a three-page article by Douglas Hyde on popular ballads of Ireland, "Some Words About Unpublished Literature." It is number 38 of volume 1 of the magazine and is addressed to G. Coffey, Esq., that is, George Coffey (1857–1916), archaeologist and antiquarian.

defunct by 2 February 1888, for Douglas Hyde wrote to commiserate with Ellen O'Leary on its disappearance and told her that Cusack's *Celtic Times,* whose leading articles reminded him of *The Eatanswill Gazette* in *The Pickwick Papers,* had ceased coming in the last three weeks and was apparently also dead.[3]

The Gael, then, occupies a brief, curious, and not wholly uncontentious place in modern Irish cultural history. On the one side, it conducted a fiery polemic against Cusack and those of his persuasion, so that amid the announcements of games to come and reports of those already played, we find ringing denunciations of inoffensive-sounding but apparently rabidly heretical organizations such as the Grocers' Assistants Athletic Club, the proscription and banning of various other teams, and a no-holds-barred battle between warring factions in the correspondence columns. On the other side, the magazine found itself under attack for its Fenian connections. *The Union,* a weekly of unswerving loyalist views, denounced the G.A.A. as "an institution for drilling and preparing the manhood of Ireland for insurrectionary purposes," and pointed to O'Leary's involvement with *The Gael* as proof of this.[4]

Amid such controversies, the literary pages must have seemed an oasis of peace. They were also the most distinguished of any then running in an Irish periodical. As the acknowledged doyen of the new literary generation, O'Leary could call upon the talents of Yeats, Douglas Hyde, Katharine Tynan, John Todhunter, T. W. Rolleston, and his own sister Ellen. It is clear that his editorship of the magazine was part of a conscious attempt to imitate the literary revival begun by Thomas Davis and the Young Irelanders, and he lost no opportunity of pointing out the connection—praising, for instance, Hyde's poem "Marching Song of the Gaelic Athletes," which appeared on 8 October 1887, for having "something of the old patriotic fire that ran through the old *Nation.*"[5] There is, too,

[3]This unpublished letter was among the Hyde papers sold at Christie's (London) on 20 July 1983 and is now apparently in private hands.

[4]*The Union,* 9 July 1887, p. 1.

[5]*The Gael,* 8 October 1887, page number cropped (Belfast Public Library). Hyde's poem was reprinted in *Poems and Ballads of Young Ireland* (Dublin: M. H. Gill and Son, 1888), pp. 77–78.

overwhelming evidence that much of the verse in the anthology of the new generation, *Poems and Ballads of Young Ireland,* published in May 1888, first appeared in *The Gael;* thus, this collection bears the same relationship to *The Gael* as its influential model, *The Spirit of the Nation,* had to *The Nation*. Indeed, the very title of the later book makes explicit the connection between the young poets of the 1880s and the Young Irelanders of the 1840s. O'Leary revered the Young Irelanders because he felt that they had heightened the national consciousness, and he saw that it was above all through their immensely popular poetry that they had effected this change. In his lecture "What Irishmen Should Know," he declared that "though Young Ireland did much for us in prose as well as verse, indeed, much in nearly all the realms of thought and action—still it was by song mainly that the young Irelanders, as one of them has proudly boasted, 'Brought a soul into Eire.'" In a decade of parliamentary political rhetoric, of which he disapproved, and of agrarian agitation, which he denounced even more strongly, O'Leary considered it his duty to save and enrich the Irish soul through literature and especially poetry. In his lecture he insisted "that the more we any of us know, or can know, about Irish poetry, the better it will be for us and Ireland," and concluded by urging his listeners to "read as much poetry, Irish and other, as you can; but above all, seek in the poetry that is more specially Irish the fitting food for the soul that is within you."[6] It is this sense of program and of mission that distinguishes the literary pages of *The Gael* and makes its contribution to modern Irish literature significant.

For Yeats, *The Gael* not only provided a welcome vehicle for his writing, but also seemed to promise the audience he wanted at this stage in his career. Only five months before the foundation of the magazine, he had rounded off an article on the poetry of Sir Samuel Ferguson with a rousing but discriminating appeal: "I do not appeal to the professorial classes, who, in Ireland, at least, appear at no time to have thought of the affairs of their country till they

[6] *The Gael,* 13 August 1887, p. 7 (Belfast Public Library). The lecture had been delivered on numerous occasions before its publication in *The Gael.*

first feared for their emoluments—nor do I appeal to the shoddy society of 'West Britonism,'—but to those young men clustered here and there throughout our land, whom the emotion of Patriotism has lifted into that world of selfless passion in which heroic deeds are possible and heroic poetry credible" (UP1 104). And one place where such young men might be expected to be clustered was in the Gaelic Athletic Association. The theme of Yeats's article had been to extol Ferguson's bardic qualities and to insist upon the crucial importance of mythology to the literature and consciousness of a nation. "Of all the many things the past bequeaths to the future," he had written, "the greatest are great legends; they are the mothers of nations"; and he went on to insist that it was the duty of every Irish reader to study the legends of his own country "till they are familiar as his own hands, for in them is the Celtic heart" (UP1 104). Little wonder, then, that his first contribution to the new weekly should be an article on Finn Mac Cumhaill, one of the greatest of bardic heroes. This was to have appeared in the second number, on 16 April 1887, shortly after he and his family had left Dublin for London, but a single page of this issue, preserved in the collection of Michael Yeats, contains a note "To Our Readers" regretting that pressure of athletic news had crowded out "Finn Mac Cumhaill" and hoping it would be published the following week. And so it was, but because Yeats was changing addresses in London, a copy of the 23 April 1887 issue did not reach him until late May, by which time he had already sent in further contributions in the form of two ballads and a long review of *Shamrocks*.

There were many reasons why Yeats would have been attracted to the stories associated with Finn. In the first place, Finn was a major figure in Irish mythology, and, as we have seen from the article on Ferguson, Yeats believed these myths to be central to any understanding and articulation of the national consciousness, a matter of growing importance to him as he came to see, under O'Leary's tutelage, that it was from Ireland that he must draw his themes. His reading of Standish James O'Grady's *History of Ireland: Critical and Philosophical,* with its evangelical insistence upon the part played by mythology in the continuing race memory and its messianic prophecies that the Gaelic legends held proof of "the great future of this race and land," had also clearly excited him.[7] Yeats's view, as expressed in the Finn Mac Cumhaill essay given in the following pages, that a "nation's history is not in what it does . . . the elements or destiny decides all that; but what a nation imagines that is its history, there is its heart; than its legends, a nation owns nothing more precious," unmistakably echoes O'Grady's insistence that "[a] nation's history is made for it by circumstances, and the irresistible progress of events; but their legends they make for themselves" and that "legends represent the imagination of the country; they are that kind of history which a nation desires to possess."[8] Although these ideas came to Yeats early, they remained with him as deep and persistent convictions: indeed, the notion that "[w]ithout her possible mythical siege of Troy, perhaps, Greece would never have had her real Thermopylae" was to become the underlying theme of his poem "The Statues" as late as 1938. Perhaps even more important, bardic literature seemed to offer not only national but also personal salvation in presenting an escape "from that leprosy of the modern—tepid emotions and many aims" (UP1 104). It would, he believed, save him from the sophistication, isolation, and even solipsism of the late Romantic tradition by providing him with a more ancient and a more profound inheritance "appealing to all natures alike, to the great concourse of the people, for it has gone deeper than knowledge or fancy, deeper than the intelligence which knows of difference . . . to the universal emotions that have not heard of aristocracies" (UP1 101).

These views would have held true of Irish mythology in general, but Finn was particularly attractive because he had been largely ignored by previous poets and writers such as Ferguson, Aubrey de Vere, R. D. Joyce, and Standish James O'Grady, who had all been more interested in the Red Branch cycle. Finn thus offered an untilled field to the new generation, a field that Yeats and his close friend Katharine Tynan had already begun to plow; he was still at

[7]Standish James O'Grady, *History of Ireland: Critical and Philosophical* (London: Sampson Low; Dublin: E. Ponsonby, 1881), I, 58.

[8]Standish James O' Grady, *History of Ireland* (London: Sampson Low; London: Searle, Marston, & Rivington; Dublin: E. Ponsonby, 1878–80), I, 22.

work on "The Wanderings of Oisin" (whose plot he alludes to in the article) and he had undoubtedly read in manuscript Tynan's most ambitious poem to date, "The Pursuit of Diarmuid and Grainne," part of which had appeared in the first number of *The Gael*. In this sense, the article is also an exercise in what was then known as "laying pipe" for his own and his friend's work.

There is a further reason why his interest in Finn was strong at that point but became less pronounced later, and it is one that rested on misapprehension. Yeats erroneously supposed the Fenian stories to be of a later date than those of the Red Branch and was persuaded that they were therefore the product of a different consciousness.[9] Thus he was led to believe that Finn and his warriors "sought to be that which Cuchulin and his followers were without seeking—men of nature. They were chivalrous; the primeval men were heroic." He saw them as direct precursors of Arthur and his knights and, in this aspect, they appealed to the medieval predilections of his Pre-Raphaelite enthusiasms. What is more, in their deliberate choice to be men of nature at a time when others were settling down to kingdoms and organized societies, they consciously chose, as he might have later put it, their appropriate mask in a process of self-creation. Their choice was not dissimilar to that which presented itself to Yeats as he pondered whether to find a niche in the artistic life of metropolitan London or to seek out a more primitive muse amid the scenery of rural Ireland.

By the time he came to write the introduction to *Gods and Fighting Men*, Lady Gregory's translations from the *Fianaigheacht*, Yeats had realized his historical mistake and knew that Finn came before Cuchulain. Indeed, the hostile reception of his and George Moore's play *Diarmuid and Grania* had led him in the autumn of 1901 into considerable research on Finn. In that play the Fenians are presented as aristocrats, arrogant toward the common people who look back with a forlorn satisfaction on the popular uprising led by Cairbre Cathead. One detects in the play the beginnings of that conflict between aristocratic attitudes and popular feeling that was to be the theme of *Responsibilities* and to which he was to give

[9]He had almost certainly taken this idea from *History of Ireland: Critical and Philosophical*, I, 336–39, where O'Grady argues that the Fenians lived long after Cuchulain and the other Red Branch figures.

dramatic expression in the figures of the Fool and the Blind Man in *On Baile's Strand*. The hero of this latter play, of course, is Cuchulain, not Finn or Diarmuid: after the turn of the century, as Yeats's poetry and drama changed in style and theme toward something harder and more definite, he found that Finn would no longer answer his purpose and turned to the more coherent tales of the Red Branch, peopled by more firmly delineated characters with unimpeachable pedigrees. Cuchulain, in his confrontations with Conchubar, his relationships with women, and his heroic distance, provided the mature Yeats with a fitting hero and anti-self. The stories of the Red Branch had not devolved into popular folklore as had those of Finn, and therefore they retained an Apollonian and mythological character more suited to Yeats's new manner. The Fenian stories are of the people (Whitley Stokes had, as Yeats discovered, even alleged that "the Fenians were all servile tribes"[10]), and in his introduction to *Gods and Fighting Men,* using astrological imagery to overlay Nietzschean categories, he explained that they were the product of a "lunar influence" as were all thoughts and emotions created by the common people (Ex 24). Although he was to argue that great art must be a marriage of the sun and moon, it was the Apollonian solar influence that was to dominate Yeats's imagination in the years after 1900.

In 1887 this change of direction was obviously unforeseeable. His immediate task, as he saw it, was to heighten the imagination of Ireland by making her legends available to the younger generation of writers, and indeed, although his *Gael* article could not be said to have had a direct influence, his judgment that Finn would have an animating force in Irish literature was sound enough, for the Fenian stories were to provide themes for modern Irish writers as diverse as Austin Clarke, Lady Gregory, Flann O'Brien, James Stephens, Alice Milligan, Standish James O'Grady, Padraic Fallon, Stephen Gwynn, and of course James Joyce—in *Finnegans Wake.*

[10]Cited by Yeats in an unpublished letter of [26 November 1901] to Lady Gregory (collection of Michael Yeats). The elements that were to make Finn less attractive to Yeats in later years—the popularity of the tales and their consequently democratic flavor—were precisely the features that appealed to him in 1887 as he strove to make his own poetry "popular" and so escape the exclusiveness of the coterie. In Finn, mythology and folklore seemed to coalesce.

Confining ourselves to Yeats's own work, we can detect sources or echoes in the *Gael* article of "A Faery Song," "King Goll," "The Valley of the Black Pig," "The Secret Rose," "The Wanderings of Oisin," *Diarmuid and Grania,* "The Statues," and "The Black Tower."

For the raw material of his article Yeats went to a variety of sources: Eugene O'Curry, Standish Hayes O'Grady, and John O'Daly, but above all to "The Boyish Exploits of Finn Mac Cumhaill," translated by John O'Donovan and published in Volume IV of the *Transactions of the Ossianic Society.*[11] As this was printed immediately following Bryan O'Looney's translation of Michael Comyn's "Lay of Oisin in the Land of Youth," Yeats presumably stumbled across it at the same time as he discovered the source of what was to become his first long narrative poem. Because he follows O'Donovan very closely in the first portion of what remains of the article, we can, by going back to this source, supply a good deal of what is missing. That anything of the article remains at all is purely fortuitous, since the fragment, which is among the Crone Papers at the Belfast Public Library, has clearly been preserved not for Yeats's article but for Part II of Ellen O'Leary's story "Courting in Lent to Marry at Easter," and this happens to begin on page 5, immediately after Yeats's essay, which extends over the first three and a half columns.

The Finn Mac Cumhaill Essay

The original Irish narrative that Yeats summarizes in this essay is, as he points out, awkward and poorly constructed. It was transcribed into the Psalter of Cashel in 1453 by John Boy O'Clery and others from a twelfth-century original at Potterlath in Kilkenny for Edmond Butler, head of the sept of Mac Richard, later Earls of Ormonde. It was this Edmond, and not a "brother Edmund," that the scribe wished home earlier from the meeting. In planning his article, Yeats probably would have begun by discussing the place

[11] *Fenian Poems,* ed. John O'Daly, *Transactions of the Ossianic Society,* 4 (1859), 281–304..

of Finn in Irish mythology, before turning to an account of his early adventures paraphrased from O'Donovan's translation. This translation, and also presumably Yeats's version, begins with an account of the Battle of Cnucha fought between Cumhall (Finn's father) and Uirgrenn for the chieftainship of the Fianna, in which Cumhall is slain by Goll, a son of Morna, a killing that is to lead to continuous feud between the two clans. At his death, Cumhall's wife Muirenn is with child, and upon the birth of her son, whom she names Deimne but who is subsequently to be known as Finn, she asks two aged druidesses to rear him secretly, as she fears for his safety at the hands of the sons of Morna. The two wise women sequester him in the woods of Sliabh Bladma (Slieve Bloom), and after six years his mother, now pregnant by her second husband, makes a clandestine and perilous journey to see him. Finding him asleep in a forest hut, she composes a tender lullaby over him, and before leaving, she asks the women if they will continue to foster him until he is of age and able to hunt. They evidently agree to this, for the narrative moves on to his first hunting kill: "The boy came forth alone on a certain day, and saw the ducks upon the lake. He made a shot at them, and cut off her feathers and wings, so that she died, and afterwards took her to the hunting booth: and this was Finn's first chase."[12] It is at this point that the preserved fragment of Yeats's article in *The Gael* begins, and by reference to the translation it is possible to guess at the words missing because of a tear in the page. These appear in brackets below.[13]

[Finn Mac Cumhaill]

. . . nt to return to the boy in his forest. [His] first exploit is the killing of a wild [duck] with an arrow; later on he aston[ishes] his two old nurses by dragging a [wil]d deer to them by the horns; but the budding hero does not long use so innocently his boyish strength.

[12] *Transactions*, 4 (1859), 295.

[13] Throughout this essay, items from *The Gael* are reproduced as they appear, with spelling and punctuation uncorrected. Such errors are not normally noted, but clearly in the following article "millitia" should read "militia," "Arthirian" should read "Arthurian," "Edmund" should read "Edmond," and the spelling of "Cuchulin" should be standardized.

While roving about, he had made the acquaintance of a large party of boys, and played hurley against them, and beaten them. Then he played singlehanded against a fourth, then a third, then all of their number, and won. All this they told to the master of a neighbouring fort, who answered "kill him." They tried, and failed. Some time afterwards, while wandering in the forest, he came upon a place where the boys were bathing, and being full of rage, he sprang in and drowned nine of them. Now, having come to his strength, it was needful that he should acquire the second power of an ancient warrior, that of poetry. Accordingly, we find him living seven years on the banks of the Boyne, with an old bard called Fin-eyes,[14] who sought the salmon of wisdom. At last the famous salmon is taken. "Have you eaten of it?" says the bard. "No, but it's burnt my finger, and I put my finger in my mouth." "Then you have tasted it, and you are the Fin of whom they prophesied and not I." Ever after, if Fin wished to know anything that was going on in the world, he had only to put his finger in his mouth. He was now admitted into the order of Fenians—the Irish "Table Round"—and to prove his mastery of verse, composed a poem to May Day, the day, perhaps, of his initiation, which has come down to us. I give here a somewhat hasty, though fairly literal version of it, in rhyme:—

How beautiful thy colours are, oh marvellous morn of May,
The black-birds pour their copious lays; would Leigha were here,
The cuckoos sing unceasingly; how welcome day by day
The gay and noble seasons; the summer swallows shear
The streams beside the branchy wood, the horses seek the pool,
The heather spreads her long loose hair; the frail marsh-cottons grow,
The far bewildered planets pour on all an influence cool,
And seas are lulled in quietness, and lavish blossoms blow.[15]

[14]This name appears as "Finn-eges" in *Transactions,* 4 (1859), 301.

[15]O'Donovan's translation of this poem (*Transactions,* 4 [1859], 303) reads as follows: "May-day delightful time! how beautiful the color!/The blackbirds sing their full lay, would that Laighaig were here/The cuckoos sing in constant strains, how welcome is the noble/Brilliance of the seasons ever; on the margin of the branchy woods/The summer suaill skim the stream, the swift horses seek the pool,/The heath spreads out its long hair, the weak fair bog-down grows./Sudden consternation attacks the signs, the planets in their courses running exert an influence:/The sea is lulled to rest, flowers cover the earth." Although "somewhat hasty," Yeats's version is a distinct improvement upon the original translation. When the new edition of *The Poems* is revised, it will be placed between the present A10 and A11.

The book, translated by the Ossianic Society, from which the early adventures of Fin are taken, was copied by some medieval monk from an older MS., and being much wearied by it all, he probably shortened and marred it. Ah, poor monk, what a bore you found; ah, this heathen world! "Oh, Virgin Mary, what a long time till brother Edmund comes home from the meeting," he wrote in gaelic on the margin, and there it is still.[16]

Fin was now a member of the Fenians or Fiani. Hard trials had each competitor for membership to undergo. He was first chased through a wood, with the odds of a single tree, by men with spears, and he failed if they reached him, if his arms trembled in his hands, if his plaited hair was unloosed by the boughs, if his feet broke a withered branch. He had to leap as high as his forehead, stoop under a branch as high as his knees, and pluck a thorn out of his heel without stopping in his course. When this trial was over, standing in a trench to his knees, a willow wand in one hand, a shield in the other, he defended himself against nine of the Fenians, casting their spears all together. If they touched him he failed. Succeeding in all these, he had to prove his proficiency in the many sorts of poetry. This over, he swore many things; never to receive a portion with a wife, but choose her only for herself; never to refuse anything to him who has asked; never to fly from less than nine champions. Henceforth he shall have no home, his food he shall cook by laying it, wrapt in rushes, in a hole dug in the earth, and strewing red hot stones above.[17]

These Fenians, of whom before long Fin became the chief, having around him Ossian, Oscar, Dermot, Caolte, and many more, were the Millitia of Ireland; their duties, the defence of the country against Albian[18] and African Pirates, the protection of the Ardrigh, at this time the famous *Cormac Mac Art,* in whose reign Tara was at its greatest splendour; but far from this luxury in the vast forests, the Fenians lived rudely and simply as Cuchullin of old; while those around them sought to be architects of kingdoms, of armies, of splendour, they longed only to be the architects of themselves, to be braver than any, and generous beyond dreams. Homeless, in winter they were quartered on the people; in summer they slept on the earth

[16] *Transactions,* 4 (1859), 300–301, n. 4.

[17] Yeats takes many of these details from Nicholas O'Kearney's introduction to *The Battle of Gabhra, Transactions of the Ossianic Society,* 1 (1854), 41–46.

[18] That is, Alban or Scottish.

they loved—that earth they were ever won't to kneel down and kiss before they entered the battle.

They sought to be that which Cuchulin and his followers were without seeking—men of nature. They were chivalrous; the primeval men were heroic. History knows of nothing more important than this brotherhood, for the wave of their influence swept on through Wales with her Arthirian Knights, on over Britain, over Europe, till joining with the worship of the Virgin, surging in from the east, it became mediaeval chivalry, that dim seeking for a light departed in the morning of the world.

Not till he is old, with his sons, and his sons' sons about him, does Fin do his greatest deeds. First he challenges the demons. It is a fine scene from the epic of those times,[19] the now old Fin on the grey peak of Sleive Cullun defying the demons of the earth. Henceforth he has dealings without end with men and phantoms; at Ventry he repels the invasion of the "King of the world." For a year the battle rages with such frenzy, that a young prince who has done most brave deeds, goes mad in the battle, and rushing away, screams and chatters in a far off valley, where, says the old story, all the madmen of Ireland would congregate if loose.[20]

Like Conor, the pursuer of Deirdre in the previous cycle, this old man, full of the solitude and weariness of age, has an implacable love. He pursues the wise and beautiful Grania and her lover Dermot, over the whole of Ireland; they escape through the friendship of the Fenians; at last Dermot is wounded mortally by a boar. Fin can cure him by giving him a drink from his enchanted hands; he will not, and the lover dies foretelling the battle in which shall fall the hosts of Fin. The Fenians are gathered apart, muttering and planning, yet still obedient. Suddenly they see Fin and Grania approaching. Yes, even she, fascinated by that imperious, fatal, and scarce human existence on which she leant. Strangest of love stories. Mysterious tragedy of a soul. From the whole ranks of the Fini there goes a single shout of laughter.[21]

[19]*Fenian Poems, Second Series,* ed. John O'Daly, *Transactions of the Ossianic Society,* 6 (1861), 3–19. "The Chase of Sliabh Guilleann [Cuillin]" tells how Finn is enchanted into a decrepit old man, but is finally restored to vigor, except for his hair, which remains grey.

[20]The legend provided Yeats with the story for "The Madness of King Goll" (P 16–18).

[21]This incident occurs near the end of *The Pursuit After Diarmuid O'Duibhne, and Grainne the Daughter of Cormac Mac Art,* ed. Standish Hayes O'Grady, *Transactions of the*

Scorning everyone who was not daring as themselves; imposing on the whole country such terrible game laws, that no one, according to Mr. O'Grady, would venture to pick up a hare even if he found it dead on his path;[22] they had raised up innumerable enemies, who, under Cairby of the Liffy, gave them battle at Gabra. They kill Cairby, and his people they scatter to the winds. But their power is broken; three alone of the heroes remain: Fin, Caolte, and Ossian. In the battle they find Oscar dying, the blood pouring from his mail. He dies. They sit on the ground beside him heeding nothing, says the old tale, till, through the dim air of morning shone his masterless banner, and the red berries of the quicken trees. They make him a great Tomb. Soon after, his wife, Aideen, dies, and they bury her under the cromlech at Howth:—

> They heaved the stone; they heaped the cairn;
> Said Ossian, in a queenly grave
> We leave her 'mong the fields of fern,
> Between the cliff and wave.
>
> The cliff behind stands clear and bare,
> And bare, above the heathery steep,
> Scales the clear heaven's expanse, to where
> The Danaan Druids sleep.[23]

Fin is killed. How? Rumour has confused voices; and now he sleeps in the centre of a mountain in Donegal, his hound and his steed

---

Ossianic Society, 3 (1857), 1–211, as follows: "After that Fionn and Grainne went their ways, and no tidings are told of them until they reached the Fenians of Erin; and when they saw Fionn and Grainne [coming] towards them in that guise they gave one shout of derision and mocking at her, so that Grainne bowed her head through shame" (p. 209). This version of the end of the story occurs in only two eighteenth-century manuscripts: the one used by O'Grady and not since identified, the other in the Royal Irish Academy. The two oldest of the forty-one extant manuscripts of the tale show Grainne seeking revenge against Finn (P 620). Significantly, Yeats and George Moore chose to use the ending found in O'Grady for their play *Diarmuid and Grania* (VPl 1168–1222).

22O'Grady, *History of Ireland: Critical and Philosophical*, I, 333: "No person dares to take any salmon, fawn, or smaller game, even though he found them dead on his path at the end of every ridge, except a person belonging to the ranks of the Fianna Eireen." O'Grady does not specifically mention a hare.

23The opening stanzas of the poem "Aideen's Grave" by Sir Samuel Ferguson, published in *Lays of the Western Gael and Other Poems* (London: Bell and Daldy, 1865), pp. 60–69.

beside him, awaiting, like another Barbarossa, the time of his country's greatest need, when he will awake and sound his dreadful horn. And Ossian? He passed away to the island of Hy-Brazil, till longing after three hundred years to see Fin once more, he returned; but the moment his feet touched an earthly shore, his three hundred years fell on him, and his beard swept the ground, and his form bent double, and his eyes became blind. Patrick and his saints kept him with them, and tried hard to make him think of heaven, but the burthen of his cry was ever, "better Hell with the Fini, than Heaven without them." And, what of the unconquerable Caolte? He stormed the palaces of the Gods at Ossory; and lives there in immortal youth.[24]

Under all these old legends there is, without doubt, much fact, though, I confess, I care but little whether there be or not. A nation's history is not in what it does, this invader or that other; the elements or destiny decides all that; but what a nation imagines that is its history, there is its heart; than its legends, a nation owns nothing more precious. Without her possible mythical siege of Troy, perhaps, Greece would never have had her real Thermopylæ. Learn those of your own country, let the young love them. I wish I could recommend you some poem concerning these events, but there is none of any importance. About the previous cycle there are plenty, by Ferguson, and Joyce, and De Vere.

Miss Tynan, however, will soon publish a "Dermot and Grania." A fragment descriptive of the peace that followed the long flight, and preceded the death of Dermot, appeared in the last GAEL.

W. B. Yeats.

The Tynan Review

The last sentence of the Finn Mac Cumhaill article clearly looks forward to Yeats's review of Katharine Tynan's second book of verse, *Shamrocks* (1887). Although the book was not to be published until 31 May, the astute Tynan was circulating a set of proofs among her reviewer friends, obviously in the hope that it would be greeted immediately upon publication with a clutch of admiring notices, a stratagem in which she was remarkably successful. Yeats had already undertaken a review for *The Gael* and

[24]See ll. 16–18 of "The Secret Rose" (P 69–70).

was to publish a second in *The Irish Fireside* and a third in *Truth*. As if this were not enough, he also persuaded T. W. Rolleston to notice the book in *The Academy* (L 35), passed on the proofs he had used to James Granville Legge (L 35), and doubtless spoke of it with Montgomery Ranking (L 41), a London critic and friend of Tynan's who was to publish three enthusiastic reviews.

Yeats began his article for *The Gael* on 27 April and took nearly three weeks over it, for it was not sent off to O'Leary until the middle of May. One of the reasons it took so long to write was that Yeats's health had been impaired by his move to London and by a strict but nutritionally deficient vegetarian diet that he had set himself. The resulting coughs, colds, and nervous headaches "wrought ill for the review," he confessed to Tynan, adding that she "would be astonished at the number of petulant pages against this man or that other I have chopped out of it." The adverse conditions under which he had labored made him diffident about his work, and he warned her defensively that "now, as it stands, it is a calm though not very brilliant exposition of your book" (L 36). His apology was, however, unnecessary since, as Ellen O'Leary told him on 29 May, Tynan, who had helped correct the proofs (rather incompetently, as we shall see), "was delighted with your article which she says is splendid."[25] The article actually appeared thirteen days later on 11 June.

Yeats's diffidence is explicable on grounds other than his being merely out of sorts. All his literary articles to date had been about people who were safely dead; this article, however, was reviewing the work of someone not only still living but also a close personal friend, someone who had, moreover, given a friendly notice to *Mosada,* as yet his only published book. Tynan had, in addition, the more securely established reputation of the two: she had first published her poetry as long ago as 1875 ("Dreamland" in *Young Ireland*), and thereafter contributed very frequently to English and Irish periodicals, including *United Ireland, The Graphic, The Spectator, The Irish Monthly,* and *Merry England.* In 1885 her friend Wilfrid Meynell arranged for Kegan Paul to publish her first book

[25]Unpublished letter from Ellen O'Leary to Yeats, 29 May [1887] (Belfast Public Library).

of verse, *Louise de la Vallière,* at her father's expense. To Paul's surprise the volume was a success, going into a second edition and eliciting letters of commendation from Cardinals Newman and Manning, Sir Samuel Ferguson, and leading members of the Irish Parliamentary Party. Critics identified the influence of Rossetti in her verse, although she claimed that she had known nothing of him before her first trip to England in 1884. While her subsequent poetry owes a debt to both Dante Gabriel and Christina Rossetti, the style and themes of *Louise de la Vallière* derive more directly from Adelaide Proctor, whom she had read at school, and Henry Wadsworth Longfellow, whose influence persisted until scotched by Yeats's disparagement.

She met Yeats for the first time in June 1885, when C. H. Oldham brought him to her home in Clondalkin to discuss plans for the *Dublin University Review.* Writing to a friend soon after this meeting, she described him as "very interesting, he has the saddest, most poetical, face I ever saw,"[26] and from then until his departure for London in April 1887 the two poets saw each other regularly. Under the influence of John O'Leary, they encouraged each other to take up Irish subjects. *Shamrocks,* drawing its themes from Gaelic legends and from its author's Catholicism, was, as its title suggests, the first fruit of this new inspiration, and thus an achievement about which Yeats could not hope to be indifferent. Yet, since he had boldly announced only a few months before that Irish critics had consistently failed in their duty by becoming men of tact rather than men of conviction (UP1 88), this personal involvement put him in a delicate position. In the review, he meets his difficulty head on by declaring his interest at once. He writes, he confesses, "somewhat uncritically—as fellow-worker of fellow-worker—having my hands on the same plough—lacking altogether the needful aloofness of the critic." This is a shrewd beginning, for it gives his friendship license to overpraise if he wishes without thereby compromising the impartial standards that he wished to inculcate in Irish critics and reviewers. Nor was this merely a general consideration: the irascible O'Leary would have

[26]Letter to Mrs. James Pritchard, 30 June 1885, in Geoffrey Barrow, "Katharine Tynan Letters 1884–5," *Apex One,* 1 (1973), 23.

castigated him, as he well knew, for special pleading or insincere praise. Yet even here, Yeats's disclaimer worked: in a headnote to the review, O'Leary acknowledged that "Mr. Yeates does not pretend to that judical frame of mind, which is generally assumed by the critic, and we do not know that his review is any the worse for its absence."[27]

Shamrocks contains thirty-nine poems, but as we might expect from the sentiments he had already expressed in his articles on Ferguson, R. D. Joyce, and Finn Mac Cumhaill, Yeats directed his

[27]O'Leary's headnote is worth quoting in full: "We are happy to be able to give our readers, this week, an early and full notice of Miss Tynan's new book, or rather, more properly, of the more definitely Irish portion of it. Mr. Yeates does not pretend to that judical frame of mind, which is generally assumed by the critic, and we do not know that his review is any the worse for its absence. Towards a poem or any other work of genius, the proper primary attitude is always one of admiration; criticism, involving more or less of censure, or at least limitation of praise, may easily enough come after, and, indeed, such is human nature, and especially critical human nature, such censure is sure to come quite soon enough, and sharply enough too. But fame fights always on the side of the poet. Who knows, or, knowing, cares now about the once famous "this will never do" of Jeffrey's Review of the Excursion. Wordsworth has been found to have done, if not the very best, at least some of the very best work of his generation, and Jeffrey's criticisms have been long since relegated to the limbo of mere literary curiosities. We must, however, mark our dissent from Mr. Yeates, and from "probably the highest judge of sacred verse now living," whoever that may be, as to the value, poetical or other, of Miss Tynan's devotional verses. While admiring greatly "St. Francis to the Birds," and in a lesser degree some of the other religious poems, we are very far, indeed, from thinking that "Miss Tynan's very highest note is a religious one." We merely put in our protest in this matter, having neither time nor inclination to motive our opinion just now; besides, our views on this point matter probably little to the world at large, and need matter less to Miss Tynan herself, while she has Mr. Yeates, "the possibly highest judge," and, no doubt, many others on her side.

"We give no original poetry in the present number, partly because we desire to be economical in that article, being necessarily never sure of anything like an adequate supply, partly because our readers ought to find sufficient food for this once in the extracts from Miss Tynan, and partly, perhaps, because we may not be too anxious to bring our other poetical contributors into too direct competition with that brilliant young lady. Not that there is not room, and that we do not hope to find place, for all sorts and conditions of poetry, reserving, however, naturally, the far larger portion of our space for such poetry as is essentially Irish, either in subject or treatment. Next week, for instance, and in shortly succeeding ones, we mean to give our readers some more fresh, strong, and intensely Irish verse from the pen of AN CHRAOIBHIN AOIBHININ [*An Chraoibhín Aoibhinn,* pen-name of Douglas Hyde]."

Though I have called this a "headnote," the *Gael* compositor in fact saw fit to interpose between it and Yeats's review a paragraph headed "Goals, Points, and Forfeits," arguing that the goal umpires for football and hurling matches should adopt a system of green, red, and white flags.

attention in the review almost exclusively to the three Irish legendary works and especially to the seven-part retelling of the Diarmuid and Grania story, which takes up over a quarter of the book. In treating such themes, Katharine Tynan had taken her place in that tradition of Anglo-Irish poetry that all his critical articles had been striving to reveal: the line of poets who, in drawing upon Gaelic mythological sources, had transcended the limitations of modern poetry and whose work might be characterized by Spenser's words, "barbarous truth" (UP1 87).[28] Thus, although Yeats claims a friend's right to praise, there is, in fact, little evaluative criticism in his article; he is far more concerned to stir the imagination of his readers by retelling the plots of the main poems, illustrated by quotations. Nonetheless, a critical problem obtrudes itself intermittently throughout the review, for in dealing with a living poet Yeats is brought up against the question of the relationship of tradition to the individual talent, a question forced upon his attention by T. W. Rolleston.

As we have noted, Yeats persuaded Rolleston to write on *Shamrocks* for *The Academy*. But while he was engaged in writing his own review, he learned that Rolleston was not being quite so fulsome as he could have wished. As Yeats reported in some alarm to Tynan, Rolleston did not like the religious poems and thought "'Dermot and Grania' not like Fergusson which is true and therefore . . . not as good as it might be which is not true for all imitation is barren" (L 35). It is this point that he tries to meet in his own notice, and in so doing attempts to identify the peculiar qualities and limitations of Tynan's poetic gift: her voice is "individual," it is "a new voice—a strong voice—a passionate voice," but it is less rugged than that of Ferguson. A critical touchstone is her handling of the end of the Diarmuid and Grania story, for as we have seen in his article on Finn Mac Cumhaill, Yeats had been fascinated by the psychological and emotional paradox, that "[m]ysterious tragedy of a soul" that had led Grania after Diarmuid's death back to Finn and to the scornful laughter of the Fenians. This episode is entirely missing in the *Shamrocks* version,

[28]Misidentified in UP1, but given correctly on the errata page on UP2 as a quotation from the *Faerie Queene* (I.vi.2).

which concludes with Grania's distributing Diarmuid's armor among their sons like a dutiful wife, and with Diarmuid's being borne away to the god Angus by four golden eagles. In not using Ferguson's ending, Tynan had missed something of the barbaric "bitterness" of the story, Yeats finds, and—as he goes on to suggest in a curiously disjointed and ambiguous paragraph in which he seems to be thinking aloud—she has been content merely to float upon the surface of the mystery that underlies all myth. In this she is not, finally, to blame, for she is playing to her strength: "It would need a longer and more subtly dramatic method, and her genius is, in the main, lyrical and passionate, rather than dramatic. Limitations are as needful as aught else; they are the dam that contains the stream." It is for its romantic passion, lyricism, and luxuriant life that Yeats praises her verse, and these attributes are seen to better effect in "The Story of Aibhric," where, picking up a casual reference from the legend of the Children of Lir, she retells the tale through the narrative of the emotionally engaged King Aibhric and tells it, according to Yeats, with "winning melancholy and delicate word finesse." The term "melancholy" hints that Tynan is to be regarded as mediating the legends through a "Celtic" rather than a "Gaelic" sensibility, that the forceful vigor of Ferguson's impulse has been transformed in a consciousness influenced, whether knowingly or not, by categories derived from Arnold's lectures on Celtic poetry into something more plangent and indefinite. This is certainly the case with the poem "The Fate of King Feargus," which, although based on the same source as Ferguson's "Fergus Wry-Mouth,"—the Brehon law that no one with a physical disability could hold kingship—is utterly different in tone and treatment. In Ferguson's poem the hero is stricken with his disability in a heroic if foolhardy quest against a water-monster that he subsequently kills in an epic encounter. In Tynan's poem, as in Yeats's later story "The Wisdom of the King," the imperfection is congenital and the crisis is brought about by unrequited romantic love rather than heroic anger.[29] Comparing the two, Yeats prefers Tynan's version, and yet one detects in the paragraph of jerky prose in which he makes this judgment a linger-

[29] "The Wisdom of the King" (SR 25–33) first appeared as "Wisdom" in *The New Review*, September 1895, pp. 285–89.

ing regret for the loss of Ferguson's bardic power: "Heretofore it was treated by Ferguson with that Homeric definiteness of his, and hardness of outline that seem to the conventional or the sophisticated, baldness. Altogether too delicate a flower for that mountain atmosphere. It needed a more lyrical mind."

Although Yeats had undertaken to review the poems inspired by Irish legend, he turns at the end of his article to a brief consideration of her shorter poems and of her religious verse in particular. Once again, we see him moving to counter Rolleston's as yet unpublished review, for he knows that Rolleston intends to disparage the religious poems. This puts him once more into a critical quandary, because he himself has reservations about some of these poems, and yet to confess as much outright would be to compound the error he had already committed in helping to commission Rolleston's notice. He arrives at a cunning solution to his dilemma by summoning the unnamed Christina Rossetti to his aid. She, portentously invoked as "possibly the highest judge of sacred verse now living," enables him to dissolve whatever dislike he feels in an awed diffidence, and at the same time to remind his readers of Tynan's international reputation. Meanwhile, he can unfeignedly commend the religious poetry of which he does approve, and so triumphantly pronounce that "Miss Tynan's very highest note is a religious one." Thus, in a carefully contrived pincer-movement, is Rolleston's adverse criticism preempted and disarmed.

By the time we come to the end of the review, we realize that Yeats has not placed Tynan quite where he and we might have supposed. He begins with a roll call of the bardic school of modern Irish poets, but it is soon apparent that Tynan, with her lyricism and romanticism, is not so securely of this band as he would have us believe. He spends five-sixths of the review praising her for her treatment of Irish legendary material, and then astonishes us by concluding that her "very highest note is a religious one" and that her popularity will probably lie in her shorter poems. Her present and future success appears to owe less to Irish mythology, and still less to its "barbarous truth," than to her "delight in those things that are common to all classes and all ages." Her virtues turn out to be homely rather than Homeric, romantic rather than barbaric, lyrical rather than epic, Christian rather than pagan.

This judgment raises serious questions that go beyond Tynan's individual poetic achievement to the very heart of his campaign to restore Irish poetry to its tradition. The propaganda and polemic of his essays on Ferguson and Joyce had been unequivocal: now, in dealing with a living poet, he is obliged to acknowledge, albeit obliquely, that the late Romantic sensibility cannot perhaps so easily appropriate bardic simplicities or unself-conscious heroic energies. We even detect a more exacting second look at those poets who had adopted such an approach: Ferguson, it seems, can be too bald and rugged; Joyce lacks poetic intensity; and de Vere appears "somewhat monkish." And yet Yeats remains convinced that the future greatness of Irish poetry is intimately bound up with the exploitation of its mythological inheritance. Moreover, only through such an inspiration can it escape the limitations of the coterie that otherwise seems the inevitable fate of modern verse. Yeats will spend many years pondering these problems, and in working at his own "The Wanderings of Oisin" during the following year, he will discover that symbolism offers a possibility of negotiating the interstices between what he had described in his article on Joyce as "bardic" and "obscure" poetry (UP1 105). To arrive at this discovery took him far beyond Tynan's superficial treatment, and he had to learn that he must no longer be content to luxuriate like the "footless frigate birds" on the surface of myth but instead should plunge into its mysterious depths. With Max Müller, Andrew Lang, Standish James O'Grady, Sir John Rhys, and Alfred Nutt as guides, he began to attend to the great intellectual debates among comparative mythologists and anthropologists as to the symbolic significance of legend and its sources.

The Celtic Romances in Miss Tynan's New Book

Frankly, in what follows I write somewhat uncritically—as fellow-worker of fellow-worker—having my hands on the same plough—lacking altogether the needful aloofness of the critic.[30] The leaders of the Irish legendary and barbaric school have long been

[30]Errors in Yeats's quotations from Tynan's poems are corrected in the notes. An extract from this review was discovered in *The Irish Monthly,* 16 (February 1888), 110–15, by Taketosh Furomoto, and was printed as "W. B. Yeats's Missing Review," *Times Literary Supplement,* 4 January 1974, p. 12.

Ferguson, De Vere; and Joyce. Ferguson easily best. De Vere, though not surpassed in the notes of minor passion—witness the bard, Ehell—withall somewhat monkish; like the old nobleman in the play "no thronging presence but a ceremonious chapel filled with music,"[31] and Joyce, a gallant story teller, lacking the poetic intensity of either.[32] To this band Miss Tynan joins herself with the story of Dermot and Grainne (ancient), with the story of Fergus (half her own), and the story of Aibric (her own). "Dermot and Grainne," the biggest. Argosy she has yet sent forth on the troubled waters of song, I shall do my best to describe, letting Miss Tynan, as often as may be, speak for herself.

At Tara, in the halls of Cormac Mac Art, there was much feasting, for his daughter, Grainne, was to wed with Fionn Mac Cumhaill—"June's red rose with snow."

> This was the bridegroom, Fionn, the king of Eire:[33]
> Gnarled like an oak, his face like lichened stone;[34]
> Sullen and fierce, his red eyes sunk and weary,
> Towered o'er all men that giant frame alone.
>
> Like an old tiger that hath lonely lasted
> Years after all his kin be turned to clay;
> Like a huge tree, the thunderbolt hath blasted,[35]
> Black and accurst it stains the face of day.[36]
> Yet a great hero—famed in many a story,
> Victor on many a bloody field of fight;[37]
> But drunk with blood and war, and blind with glory,
> And as men deemed, too old for lovers delight.[38]

[31]Quotation not yet traced.

[32]Sir Samuel Ferguson (1810–1886), poet and antiquarian, about whom Yeats had already written two enthusiastic articles. Aubrey de Vere (1814–1902), poet, Catholic convert, and friend of Tynan; "The Bard Ethell," in which a fiercely pious Irish poet of the thirteenth century recollects his life and times, occurs in part one of de Vere's "Inisfail," a lyrical chronicle of Ireland, in *The Sisters and Inisfail* (London: Longmans, 1867). Robert Dwyer Joyce (1830–1883), poet and doctor, was a friend of O'Leary's; Yeats had written two articles on his work for *The Irish Fireside,* 27 November and 4 December 1886. All three poets mentioned here had been singled out for praise by O'Leary in his lecture "What Irishmen Should Know."

[33]*Shamrocks:* "King" (p. 1).

[34]*Shamrocks:* "stone," (p. 1).

[35]*Shamrocks:* "tree the" (p. 2).

[36]*Shamrocks:* "accursed, it" (p. 2).

[37]*Shamrocks:* "fight," (p. 2).

[38]*Shamrocks:* "And, as . . . love's" (p. 2).

In Grainne there are no smiles, though her maidens laugh around her, nor does she care that her name be named among the toasts. Little does she prosper among these rubies and silks and ambers, these diamonds that lighten "like the sea's floor when summer moons are white."[39] Ah! how evade this old man, whom armies follow, whom omens encircle?

To her side comes Daire, the high priest, and commences naming and describing all that assembled bright host. Little does she heed him. Oh! that she were beyond the "pleasant plains" and "wide grey seas," afar in *Tir N'an Oge.* There are no old men there.

> Then she woke up from dreams, and sighed full drear,
> And heard the old voice crooning in her ear[40]
> Of this and that fair deed of many a one;
> And so she turned her weary sense to hear.

He over there is Ossian "whose song might wake dead world's again."[41] Beside him his son, Oscar, but who, she asks, is that bronzed warrior "freckled with many a noon sun's heat".[42]

> The stateliest man of all the world of men,
> Yon with the great hound's head upon his knee.[43]

Ah, that is Diarmuid.

> Oh! the warm flash rose up from chin to hair;[44]
> And down amid the great feasts song and glare[45]
> All in a stillness and a sudden pause,
> Diarmuid, the knight, looked up and found her fair.

She whispers to one of her maidens, who goes, and returns with a silver goblet studded with gems, lurid like a serpent's eyes. From feaster to feaster it is sent; all sink into a deep drugged slumber save

[39] *Shamrocks:* "summer noons" (p. 3).
[40] *Shamrocks:* "at her" (p. 8).
[41] *Shamrocks:* "worlds" (p. 9).
[42] *Shamrocks:* "noon-sun's" (p. 9).
[43] *Shamrocks:* "knee," (p. 9).
[44] *Shamrocks:* "warm flush" (p. 10).
[45] *Shamrocks:* "feast's" (p. 10).

Oscar, Ossian and Diarmuid, to whom the wine was not given. Unto the three, passing among the sleepers, with drooping head, goes Grainne. Unto the fated Diarmuid she tells her love, and places him under Gesa, those mysterious bonds no Fenian might break.

"One golden summer hour,[46]
Through the blue windows of my maiden bower,
At the great games, I saw thee victor crowned,[47]
And my heart gave to thee its rose-red flower.[48]

Who knew thee not, nor how they named thy name,[49]
Until this night; now by thy knightly fame[50]
Take me." Her heavy hair was on the ground,[51]
And o'er his hands and feet. His eyes 'gan flame,

And flamed and lightened all his dusky face,
Who leaned to her, and for a minutes space[52]
Looked on her, thinking how all loss were gain,[53]
To kiss the lovely eyelids in their place;

Yet forced his gaze from her, and loyally
Urged his allegiance to the king, but she,[54]
"Your bonds—your bonds, my knight," like silver rain,[55]
Rang through her tears, her laughter, suddenly[56]

Then he bent down and swung her from her knee,
And kissed her long, and kissed her passionately,
Held to his heart her face so still and chill;
"Sweet thou and I together till death," said he.[57]

[46]*Shamrocks:* "one" (p. 13).
[47]*Shamrocks:* "games I" (p. 13).
[48]*Shamrocks:* "flower," (p. 13).
[49]*Shamrocks:* "'Who . . . name" (p. 13).
[50]*Shamrocks:* "night. Now, by" (p. 13).
[51]*Shamrocks:* "ground" (p. 13).
[52]*Shamrocks:* "her and . . . minute's" (p. 13).
[53]*Shamrocks:* "gain" (p. 13).
[54]*Shamrocks:* "King. But" (p. 13).
[55]*Shamrocks:* "knight! Like" (p. 13).
[56]*Shamrocks:* "tears her laughter suddenly." (p. 13). Yeats omits the stanza that follows this, in which Oscar tells Diarmuid that he is under *gesa* and must elope with Grainne (*Shamrocks,* p. 14).
[57]*Shamrocks:* "'Sweet, thou . . . death!'" (p. 14).

They fly. Omens are about the palace of Tara. The corpse lights dance on the heath—all night the banshee cries.

Away they go, into the forests, the faithful Oscar and Ossian speeding them on their way. Out into the entangled forest, no more for him the battle Standard—the Council of his Peers no more, only the entangled forests. No more for her the dance and the brightening of eyes, nor dear companionships for ever; but year after year, life shall wax and wane in flight and in hiding below the interlacing boughs. They have no illusions; Fionn never forgives, alike implacable in hatred and in love. Youth, with all its weakness, with all its generosity has long gone by and left him steel and fire. His sons and his sons' sons have many a day been warriors about him. On this supernatural existence even time fawns.

Before the morning, the great hound, Bran—sent by Oscar and Ossian—warns them by thrusting his head against the breast of Diarmuid.

Then Diarmuid woke, and kissed his love in her sleeping,[58]
    "Waken, heart of my heart, for the king is here,[59]
And his wrath is only for me; thou art safe in his keeping."
    "With thee I live or I die," was her answer clear.
She bathed her face in a brooklet, singing and sunny;
    She plaited her wealth of hair to a crown for her head;
She cheered the gloom from his heart with her words like honey,
    And fed his lips with the wine and the good white bread.

With the gathering of the followers of Fionn about them, finish the first three parts. Heretofore the manner has been passionate and lyrical, now it becomes, as is needful for the rendering of an intricate story more purely narrative, though still changing the metre every canto to the end. A Druid, from whose fingers flows the mist, befriends them, and would carry them away beneath his cloak, but Diarmuid sending Grainne, remains himself, for he will not fly from the face of his enemy in secret now or at any time.

"Silken-foot as a thief that flieth by night"[60]

[58]*Shamrocks:* "sleeping." (p. 21).

[59]*Shamrocks:* "King" (p. 21).

[60]This line occurs earlier in the poem (*Shamrocks,* p. 16). The Druid is in fact the god Aengus, Diarmuid's foster-father.

He has built a fort of wattles, with seven doors; at every door are the Fenians; from door to door he passes; they tell him they are friends, he may go free and they will not harm him.

"Not he, for all his hundred fights shall hurt a single hair."[61]

Well he knows how terrible for them would be the rage of Fionn, and passes on; at the seventh door is Fionn himself, To him blithely—

By the door at which thou keepeth watch,[62]
I win my way to freedom."

And through them he escapes and comes where Grainne waits him by the Lower Shannon, in a cave, where a boar hangs roasting before a wood fire. There that night they slept, and in the grey of the morning, while the old moon waned in the air, the Druid Angus roused them and sent them on their way, warning—

"Before I go, my lovers, this warning take from me—
Seek refuge not, nor shelter in, a single trunked tree,[63]
With but a single opening, or a cave with but one door,
Or an island of the sea with single channel;[64]
Wherever you shall cook your meal you shall not stay to eat,
Nor sleep where you have eaten, but still with tireless feet,[65]
Lie down afar and rise afar from the place you slept before."[66]

Nay, not all the forests of the world piled above their heads would hide them secure from Fionn. They visited in their flight, says the old tradition, every corner of Ireland. Of the quaint old narrative which Miss Tynan had to draw upon, I will give one fragment. For a time, a great, gentle giant, called Muadhan, became their servant, and their fisher; and thus is his fishing described:—

[61] *Shamrocks:* "his thousand fights, shall" (p. 26).
[62] *Shamrocks:* "'By . . . *thou* keepest watch" (p. 27).
[63] *Shamrocks:* "not nor shelter in a single-trunkèd tree" (p. 29).
[64] *Shamrocks:* "channel:" (p. 29). This line is indented.
[65] *Shamrocks:* "feet" (p. 29).
[66] *Shamrocks:* "wake afar" (p. 29).

"He betook himself to a neighbouring wood, and, plucking the straight, long rod of a quicken tree, made fast upon the rod a hair and a hook, and put a holly berry upon the hook, and went and stood over the stream, and took a fish that cast. He put up the second berry, and killed the third fish. Then, putting the hook and the hair under his girdle, and the rod into the earth, he took his three fish with him where Diarmuid and Grainne waited, and laid the fish upon spits. When it was broiled, Muadhan said—"I give the dividing of this fish to thee, Diarmuid." "I had rather that thou shouldst divide it thyself," said Diarmuid. "Then," said Muadhan, "I give the dividing of this fish to thee, O Grainne." "It suffices me that thou divide it," said Grainne. "Now, hadst thou divided the fish, O Diarmuid," said Muadhan, "thou wouldst have given the largest share to Grainne; and had it been Grainne that divided it, it is to thee she would have given the largest share; and since it is I that am dividing it, have thou the largest fish, O Diarmuid, and let Grainne have the second largest fish, and let me have the smallest fish.' "[67]

It would take me a long while to tell their other adventures with sufficient detail for interest. Suffice it to say, they are narrated in this poem with full and picturesque utterance. Peace at last is made with Fionn; for many years they are happy. The beautiful lines descriptive of their life, you read, doubtless, in the initial GAEL. When was sumptuous leisure and victorious love more beautifully described?—

They loved as in that hour's surprise,
    When, with a sudden flush and quiver,
Each looked to meet the other's eyes,[68]
    And knew they loved for ever![69]

They loved as in those days of old[70]
    When death was with them night and morning;[71]

[67]Although Muadhan is briefly mentioned in part four of Tynan's poem (*Shamrocks*, p. 29), this incident does not occur. Yeats slightly misquotes O'Grady's translation in *Transactions*, 3 (1857), 79–81.

[68]*Shamrocks:* "eyes" (p. 43).

[69]*Shamrocks:* "ever." (p. 43).

[70]*Shamrocks:* "old," (p. 43).

[71]*Shamrocks:* "Death . . . morning—" (p. 43).

Upon their eyes his breathings cold—
Within their ears, his warning![72]

Diarmuid was killed at last by the enchanted boar of Benbulben, roused from his lair treacherously for this slaying, by Fionn. Fionn might have saved him, but he would not and Angus, the Druid, came on the wind,

"And shrieked three times, so that the shriek did fill[73]
The waste world of the clouds, and the wild heaven,
And the sea islands, and the greenwood seas;
And valley and forest, and the highest hill[74]
Reeled at that sound that rung from morn to even,
Blown on all airs, and borne on every breeze.[75]

"I cannot give thee life, son, whispered he;[76]
But I will heal thy gaping wounds, and bear thee[77]
To my bright house, and on a golden bed
Thou'lt lie, and every day I'll breathe on thee,[78]
Life for an hour; thou'lt speak, and I shall hear thee,[79]
We two together till the world is dead."

Through the dusk glooming came a golden bier[80]
Borne by four eagles whose wide wings were golden,
And hovering, lit the startled evening grey,[81]
And took the good knight with crossed sword and spear,
And sailed away, and never of man beholden[82]
Was Angus or my Diarmuid from that day.

[72]*Shamrocks:* "ears his warning." (p. 43). The lovers' married life is described in part six of the poem (pp. 40–43). Yeats is quoting the antepenultimate and penultimate stanzas of this part.

[73]*Shamrocks:* "And" (p. 53). In these three stanzas, the third and sixth lines are indented further to the right than the second and fourth lines.

[74]*Shamrocks:* "valley," (p. 54).

[75]*Shamrocks:* "airs and" (p. 54).

[76]*Shamrocks:* "son,'" (p. 54).

[77]*Shamrocks:* "'But" (p. 54).

[78]*Shamrocks:* "thee" (p. 54).

[79]*Shamrocks:* "thee—" (p. 54).

[80]*Shamrocks:* "dusk gloaming . . . bier," (p. 54).

[81]*Shamrocks:* "hovering lit . . . grey;" (p. 54).

[82]*Shamrocks:* "away;" (p. 54).

Here Miss Tynan's poem ends, and few, I fear,[83] will miss that laugh from the assembled Feni that greeted Grainne leaning on the neck of Fion. Grainne whose lamentations once were heard "in the clouds of the heaven and the wastes of the firmament." Ideal love! Long years of devotion! Failure and laughter inextinguishable! A vast and bitter poem, no dreamy operatic idyl this; we pause, remembering this little deed and that other. Were they only as they seemed a pretty wilfulness or rather some inbred frailty of the nature subtly pourtrayed. Mystery—sea at all times flowing beneath great books. Our spirits float forth like footless frigate birds, nor long to plunge there in. The luxury of the great deep is upon them.

This is a digression; but then, quoth Sir Walter Raleigh. "We digress all the days of our life."[84] In not treating this latter episode, Miss Tynan was right. It would need a longer and more subtly dramatic method, and her genius is, in the main, lyrical and passionate, rather than dramatic. Limitations are as needful as aught else; they are the dam that contains the stream. I notice in this poem its luxuriant life, like the greater number of Miss Tynan's poems it is very positive. You will not read it with indifference; At once you will either like or dislike. And yet, it were advisable to begin with the *story of Aibhric,* [85] if it be for those greenwood adventures of the lovers ye lack some needful sympathy, say a fountain of childlike wonder, since from the winning melancholy and delicate word finesse of Aibhric, ye cannot turn. Aibhric, the king, rode a hunting through the reeds of the river bed.

> We had been hunting since out of, in the eastern skies,[86]
> The dawn fires began;
> The stag was king of the head—he was fearless and wise,[87]
> Thrice the age of a man.

On rode Aibhric until evening, when he looked round him, and he was alone.

[83]Since Yeats preferred the alternate ending, he had perhaps written—or meant to write—"and a few, I fear."

[84]Quotation not yet traced.

[85]"The Story of Aibhric" (*Shamrocks,* pp. 71–81).

[86]*Shamrocks:* "since out in the eastern skies" (p. 72).

[87]*Shamrocks:* "the herd" (p. 72).

Lord and lady were gone.[88]
Back to the lighted board in the palace huts—[89]
I was riding alone.[90]

The stag had vanished;—a long gold gleam in the West;[91]
The grey pools mirrored all chill,
And the shrieking water-fowl flew up from the nest;[92]
The wind in the reeds sobbed shrill.[93]

Dreary, dreary seemed the place and strange;[94]
The moon was barred with drifts,[95]
And great cloud-mountains rose stormily, range after range,
And broke into rifts;
An eagle sailed overhead with a flapping wing,[96]
And a wild, long cry.
I stayed my horse, and I mused with much questioning,
In what strange country was I.

The hounds looked up in my face, and shivered with dread,[97]
Then cowered, and were still;[98]
Only the moon's wild face, like the face of the dead,
Looked up from each marsh-pool chill.[99]

From the air falls a "strange song, subtle and slow." The voice of one of the children of Lir changed into a swan, with still a human voice, by evil enchantment, long ago. Year after year he follows; a hundred winters go by; she sang his manhood away—

[88]*Shamrocks:* "gone" (p. 72).
[89]*Shamrocks:* "palace hall" (p. 72).
[90]*Shamrocks:* "alone:" (p. 72).
[91]*Shamrocks:* "long, gold . . . west" (p. 73).
[92]*Shamrocks:* "nest," (p. 73).
[93]A conscious or subconscious memory of this line may have suggested to Yeats the title for his *The Wind Among the Reeds* (1899).
[94]*Shamrocks:* "strange," (p. 73).
[95]*Shamrocks:* "with the drifts," (p. 73).
[96]*Shamrocks:* "wing" (p. 73).
[97]*Shamrocks:* "face and" (p. 73).
[98]*Shamrocks:* "cowered and" (p. 73).
[99]*Shamrocks:* "chill;" (p. 73).

I am old and weary—the lost years vanished apace while I
wandered alone,
Forgotten of men, and another reigned in my place on my
father's throne.[100]

At the sound of the first saint's bell, they fall, with broken wings, those nurselings of heathendom.

Then he to whom God had spoken bent in his place, and
laid on each brow[101]
The life-giving waters;

and they lay there, four dying, human creatures; and she whom Aibhric loved, died at his feet, wrapt in her bright hair, turning on him her eyes for a moment—

Oh! sweet is her sleep in the earth that the saint hath blest,
there she shall not hear[102]
The cruel waves; but the birds will sing her to rest, and the
voices of children dear;
And the wind will chant overhead, and the grasses wave, all
for her sake.[103]
When I die—I am old—I shall sleep by her side in the
grave, and I shall not desire to wake.[104]

Complimenting this poem of *Aibhric,* I have received a note from a hand not altogether unknown in Irish literature—complimenting this, and, in appearance, blaming Dermot and Grainne, because it is not "Fergussonish."[105] Surely imitation is ever barren? They are all

[100]These lines have been conflated, probably by the compositor. "While I wandered alone" and "On my father's throne" are separate lines (*Shamrocks,* p. 78).

[101]"And laid on each brow" is a separate line (*Shamrocks,* p. 80).

[102]*Shamrocks:* "Saint . . . / Where" (p. 80).

[103]*Shamrocks:* "overhead and the grasses wave / All for her sake" (p. 81).

[104]*Shamrocks:* "And shall not" (p. 81). The lines in the stanza have been conflated, probably by the compositor. New lines should begin at "Where she shall," "And the voices," "All for her sake," and "And shall not."

[105]The note was from T. W. Rolleston (1857–1920), poet, scholar, and man of letters (L 35). For Rolleston's criticism of *Shamrocks,* see above. Tynan was less concerned by

individual, these legendary poems; a new voice—a strong voice—a passionate voice.

In a book rich in stories, the most fantastically dreamy and beautiful, is the tale of *Fergus.*[106] Heretofore it was treated by Ferguson[107] with that Homeric definiteness of his, and hardness of outline that seem to the conventional or the sophisticated, baldness. Altogether too delicate a flower for that mountain atmosphere. It needed a more lyrical mind. Indeed the story is well nigh Miss Tynan's own, so much has she added to the ancient hints in the introductory portion of the Brehon laws.

Once reigned, as she tells the tale, a wise and in every way desirable king; well, one fine day his enemies abolished him. After his death there was born unto him a son with a most foul face, some witch's power had marred the whole of his body. But through his eye there looked a soul uncorrupted by all witch spells whatsoever. In that beauty worshipping land there was a law that all its kings should be of stateliest make. Surely he cannot reign, this boy. The Druid High Priest has a vision, this deformed one is the gift of the high Gods, there should be none like him in wisdom.

As he ceased his, face grew shadowed, for some pain he groaned
aloud,[108]
Unheard of all the crowd;
And thrice he touched the piteous babe and shook his hoary head,[109]
To his own heart whispered—[110]

He has seen another vision dimly, one of sadness beyond measure.

Thereafter is proclamation made, maugre his marred beauty and the law he shall be king. Twenty years go by. Never in this land was there so wise a king. The father of his people; "a brother to his knights in arms."

---

his views than was Yeats, and told Father Matthew Russell in an unpublished letter of 12 May 1887 that "Mr. Yeats is suddenly afraid of Rolleston's review: I am not" (*Archivae Provincia Hibernia*). Rolleston was a friend and disciple of O'Leary's and contributed a number of poems to *The Gael.*

[106]"The Fate of King Feargus" (*Shamrocks,* pp. 100–111).

[107]Ferguson's poem "Fergus Wry-Mouth" first appeared in his *Poems* (Dublin: William McGee; London: George Bell & Sons, 1880), pp. 44–47.

[108]*Shamrocks:* "his face grew shadowed;" (p. 104).

[109]*Shamrocks:* "babe, and" (p. 104).

[110]*Shamrocks:* "whisperèd—" (p. 104). Lines 2 and 4 of this passage are indented.

And well the people loved him—on sea shore or the street[111]
Would fall to kiss his feet;
And the women sang his praises to the children on their knees,[112]
For their babies lullabies.[113]

But all these years he knows not of his own foul face. The great High Priest, fearing that in his justice he would obey the law and reign not, had issued an edict, and the secret slept.

Would a damsel busk her bravely then for feasting in the hall,[114]
For the dearest knight of all,
She might out unto the lake side, and when no ripples are,[115]
See her own face like a star.[116]

These were no days of mirrors, and the king was guarded well,[117]
From knowledge of the secret no mortal tongue dare tell;[118]
So he took his youth's day brightly, chased the deer and cast the
ball.[119]

But sometimes when he rides along the woodland path, turning with cheerfull words to some peasant mother at the wayside, he saddens vaguely, seeing her baby weep and spring away from him. At last he falls in love, as even the gift of the high Gods will do, and she whom he loved,

She shrank as sore afraid,[120]
When he would urge his wooing, and she fled him with a cry
Whenever he came nigh.[121]

[111]*Shamrocks:* "on the sea-shore" (p. 107).
[112]*Shamrocks:* "at their" (p. 107).
[113]*Shamrocks:* "babies'" (p. 107). Lines 2 and 4 of this passage are indented.
[114]*Shamrocks:* "then, for" (p. 108).
[115]*Shamrocks:* "lakeside, and where no" (p. 108).
[116]*Shamrocks:* "face, like" (p. 108).
[117]*Shamrocks:* "King . . . well" (p. 108).
[118]*Shamrocks:* "From the knowledge" (p. 108).
[119]*Shamrocks:* "deer, and . . . ball," (p. 108). These seven lines just quoted form a single stanza, with lines 2, 4, and 7 indented.
[120]*Shamrocks:* "she . . . afraid" (p. 109). The line begins "But she."
[121]Lines 1 and 3 of this passage are indented.

Finally, one evil day he sees in her eyes a shrinking hate,[122] and turning away his head goes forth in silence, and taking his steed from stall, rides furiously—

By dead forest paths unknown to men, by many a tangled brook[123]
And haunted mound, and fairy rath, and eerie pool and lake.[124]

At the setting of the sun he finds a little mere. He will slake his thirst and rest his weary limbs. The water mirrors his stooping form. With a cry he casts himself "down to meet the face that was his own."

"His steed came home at day-break, and they sought him far and
near,[125]
Through many a hopeless year;
Though the birds sang out his story, and the wood sprite cried in
vain,[126]
And the spirit of the rain;
And the maids of mist and mountain knew the grey pool where he lay,
And sometimes was his wild cry heard at dawn or close of day,[127]
But they never knew his people, who in war and famine drear,[128]
Prayed the gods to give them back their king again."[129]

The story is beautifully told. I do not believe the choice of the peculiar Gaelic stanza was equally fortunate—a stanza whose ultimate line is so far from its rhiming fellow is surely more fitted for poems with a resonant burden, like "the fair hills of holy Ireland," than flowing narrative.[130]

I have now fulfilled my bond, which was the reviewing of the Celtic romances only, but cannot finish without concerning myself

[122]*Shamrocks:* "a look of shrinking hate" (p. 109).

[123]*Shamrocks:* "forest-paths . . . tangled brake," (p. 110).

[124]*Shamrocks:* "lake," (p. 110).

[125]*Shamrocks:* "daybreak" (p. 111).

[126]*Shamrocks:* "the story, . . . wood-sprite" (p. 111).

[127]*Shamrocks:* "day;" (p. 111).

[128]*Shamrocks:* "knew, his . . . drear" (p. 111).

[129]*Shamrocks:* "Gods . . . King" (p. 111). In this passage, lines 2, 4, and 7 are indented.

[130]Ferguson's poem "The Fair Hills of Ireland" first appeared in *Lays of the Western Gael* (pp. 225–226). It has two refrains: "*Uileacan dubh O!*" and "On the fair hills of holy Ireland." Yeats's remarks are of interest given his own use of the refrain.

somewhat with the shorter poems that in future anthologies will, many of them, delight thousands of simple people, whom the longer poems, in their more expensive form, may never reach. In the earlier volume "*Louise de la Valeare,*"[131] there was much youthful ardour—some garish colour, and a somewhat over display of lyrical vehemence. In the best of these is the old fervour subdued into a far nobler music—for do not "the gods approve the depth and not the tumult of the soul."[132] In the romances there are things I would gladly see changed, for no one spends a week with the best of friends, or the best of books, without sometimes differing, but all in "a child's day," and "The Heart of a Mother," and "St. Francis to the Birds" seems very right.[133] Truly in their sadness there are tears in their happiness a brightening of the eye and a jubilant step. Miss Tynan's very highest note is a religious one, as in "the Heart of a Mother" and some few lines in "Death and the Man," and here and there in other places, but besides these dealing with the here and the hereafter there are others of the hereafter and the spiritual world, more exclusively such as "Sanctuary."[134] Poems full of the passionate and sensuous religion of Italy and the South. In caring less for these I do so diffidently, knowing how much in the matter of one of them, I differ thereby from possibly the highest judge of sacred verse now living.[135] Other good things are there I have found no space to mention. Verses that already have gone hither and thither solacing many a weary heart. I have heard of a peasant woman from the west crying over one of them as she read it to her gossip. Here is a lyric that I find most solemn and musical.[136]

In September,[137]
The land grows gold with miles of waving wheat;[138]

[131]*Louise de la Vallière* (London: Kegan Paul, 1885).

[132]From Wordsworth's poem "Laodamia" (I.74).

[133]*Shamrocks:* "A Child's Day" (pp. 55–58); "The Heart of a Mother" (pp. 64–66); "St. Francis to the Birds" (pp. 116–119). The last was chosen by Yeats for publication in *A Book of Irish Verse* (1895).

[134]*Shamrocks:* "Death and the Man" (pp. 126–129); "Sanctuary!" (pp. 82–85).

[135]This was Christina Rossetti (1830–1894), poet and sister of Dante Gabriel Rossetti (L 38). Tynan had met her in 1885 and corresponded with her thereafter. On 1 January 1886, Christina Rossetti wrote praising "Sanctuary!", which she said "has a very touching feeling, and may easily go to the reader's heart because I *think* it comes from the writer's" (unpublished letter, Morris Library, Southern Illinois University, Carbondale).

[136]"Autumnal" (*Shamrocks,* pp. 112–113).

[137]*Shamrocks:* "September" (p. 112). The comma is omitted throughout the poem.

[138]*Shamrocks:* "wheat:" (p. 112). The second line of each stanza ends with a colon.

Sad heart! dost thou remember[139]
How tall and fair the green spears stood in May?
Alack! the merry morn that might not stay;
'Tis sunset now, and night comes grey and fleet.[140]

In September,
Droopeth the red fruit in the orchard close;
Sad heart! dost thou remember
How the boughs bloomed auroral in the May;[141]
Waxed paler, flushed rose-redder day by day?
For these, we shall have winter, with his snows.[142]

In September,
Chirps the bright robin, with his breast afire;[143]
Sad heart! dost thou remember
How the thrush trilled his love-song in the May,[144]
And the bold blackbird sang when eve was grey?
Silence hath fallen on all the tuneful choir.

In September,
Redly the trees, like wind-blown cressets, burn;[145]
Sad heart! dost thou remember
How the leaves gleamed transparent in the May,
And danced against the sky in happy play?
The hearth grows cold, the fires to ashes turn.

In September,
The green, young world is waxen old and sere;[146]
Sad heart! dost thou remember
The golden breath the cowslips had in May;
How the breeze waved each scented hawthorn spray?
Our year goes out, and we go with the year.

139 *Shamrocks:* "heart, dost" (p. 112). This error is repeated throughout the quotation.
140 *Shamrocks:* "comes, grey" (p. 112).
141 *Shamrocks:* "May," (p. 112).
142 *Shamrocks:* "these we . . . Winter with" (p. 112).
143 *Shamrocks:* "robin with . . . a-fire" (p. 112).
144 *Shamrocks:* "her love-song" (p. 113).
145 *Shamrocks:* "trees like . . . cressets burn" (p. 113).
146 *Shamrocks:* "green young" (p. 113).

I find this book a garden, where here and there a bough needs pruning, and here and there a blosson has grown astray; and yet with all, boscage and verdure enough for many a score of common gardens—a book, in every way, an advance on all hitherto coming from the same hand. I find, also, no imitation—a rare spontaneity, once or twice marred by an over-weighting of picturesque detail, an originality without caprice or any pride of strangeness—a delight in whatever man's heart has dwelt on from the beginning, in birds and fields, in the reaping of the reapers, in hounds and horses. Grainne stroked their raven-dark necks; and

They knew the hands that every day to the manger
Brought them the ruddy apples, so crisp and sweet;[147]
In their true-hearts they guessed at her need and her danger,[148]
And whinnied low, and stamped with their eager feet.

A delight in those things that are common to all classes and all ages. Wishing for an external standard I open the volume of another deservedly noted poetess of our days, and find a sequestered nature of abnormal likings, singing for the leisured and the well read. Besides an ever increasing number of leisurely and well read people, Miss Tynan has, for hearers many simple folk in many lands, and provided the mind of an author be too watchful to grow careless, there is no better audience, year after year it will draw forth whatever belongs to humanity, and leave to wither whatever belongs to a coterie.

W. B. Yeats.

This review was not, however, Yeats's last word on *Shamrocks,* for, faithful friend that he was, he undertook two further notices, both short and hardly more than afterwords. The first, for *The Irish Fireside* (UP1 120-22), appeared on 9 July 1887 and contrasted the "pre-Raphaelite mannerism and alien methods of thought" of *Louise de la Vallière* with the fidelity to nationality and to "things themselves" of the later book, once again praising "St. Francis to

[147]*Shamrocks:* "apples so" (p. 18).
[148]*Shamrocks:* "true hearts . . . and danger," (p. 18).

the Birds" and "The Heart of a Mother." His third notice appeared in the London weekly *Truth,* in the regular column "Letters on Books."[149] Although this feature was signed by Barry O'Brien, he collected reviews for it from a variety of hands, including that of the literary editor of the magazine, Richard Ashe King. On 3 August, Katharine Tynan wrote to Father Matthew Russell: "Mr. Yeats has written a bit about my book to go in Mr. King's *Truth* letter. Mr. K. wanted me to do it myself!!!!"[150] The notice duly appeared on 11 August 1887, finding *Shamrocks* "full of gorgeous colour and rich music. Miss Tynan is an Irish Jean Ingelow, neither very subtle nor very thoughtful, but, what is perhaps better, fervid and passionately direct."[151]

The Ballad

Long before this, however, Yeats's interest in *The Gael* had taken a new turn, for he began to submit poetry to the magazine. Writing to Tynan on 27 April 1887 to tell her that he was just about to begin the review of *Shamrocks,* he also announced that he had "written a couple of Ballads which will probably appear in the 'Gael' " (L 34). He must have sent these poems to Dublin with his completed review in mid-May, because on 18 May 1887 he confided to her that "one I expect O'Leary will like one not" (L 36). As it happened, he erred on the side of optimism: on 29 May, Ellen O'Leary cheerfully informed him: "John says your ballads are Irish in nothing but the name. He thinks them abnormal. I like the Normandy legend better than either of those though I think the Sligo one treated highly poetically though sad and painful. I like you better when you give "Earth Touches" as you say your-

[149]Yeats's authorship of this unsigned review was first suggested by Roger McHugh in his edition of *W. B. Yeats: Letters to Katharine Tynan* (New York: McMullen Books, 1953), p. 158. In a comprehensive study of the Yeats-Tynan relationship, " 'Shelley Plain': Yeats and Katharine Tynan," *Yeats Annual,* 2 (1983), 59–92, Carolyn Holdsworth supports McHugh's attribution and reprints the paragraph in question (p. 63).

[150]Unpublished letter to Father Matthew Russell, 3 August 1887 (*Archivae Provincia Hibernia*).

[151]P. 247. Jean Ingelow (1820–1895), English poet and novelist.

self."[152] On receipt of this disappointing news, Yeats wrote at once to Tynan, asking her to send the rejected poems to Father Russell, the benign and tolerant editor of *The Irish Monthly* (L 39). Owing to O'Leary's carelessness, however, they probably never reached him. Meanwhile, Yeats was evidently brooding over their rejection, and on 13 June he wrote once more to O'Leary, confessing his sins and offering a new contribution:

> one of the ballads is certainly morbid (the woman about whom it is, is now in the Sligo madhouse or was there some while since). However I do not think the Howth one morbid though now on thinking it over I quite agree with you that neither are suitable for a newspaper. I enclose a ballad on another Sligo story something like Douglas Hide though not suggested by him for I have long had it in my mind. [L 37–38]

Even this did not set his mind at rest, and it took him two postscripts to resolve what was obviously a vexing problem:

> PS1 On second thoughts the Sligo ballad of the mad woman was I fear not only morbid in subject but a little so in the treatment. It was a mere experiment.
>
> PS2 The ballad I enclose I believe to be good. The copy I send you has many corrections my own has not, so please return it if you cannot make use of it . . . If enclosed ballad is suitable I will add a short note giving the story & saying where it took place. In one point you see it differs from Hides—in mine the rebel goes over the cliff. [L 38–39]

We are dealing here, then, with three poems, none of them mentioned by name. The latest contribution, the ballad similar in theme to Hyde's "A Ballad of '98," is readily identified as the poem known variously as "Lug-na-Gall" or "The Protestants' Leap," which was based on an episode that would also furnish Yeats with the plot of his story "The Curse of the Fires and of the Shadows" (SR 40–47). Of the other two ballads, the "morbid"

[152] Unpublished letter from Ellen O'Leary to Yeats, 29 May [1887] (Belfast Public Library).

one about a Sligo madwoman is now lost; "the Howth one" was presumably "The Ballad of Moll Magee," the story of which Yeats took "from a sermon preached in the Chapel at Howth if I remember rightly" (P 618).[153] In 1908 Tynan told Allan Wade that she thought "The Ballad of Moll Magee" had appeared in *The Gael* (Wade 22), but if so, it did not appear until after 20 November 1887, because on that day Ellen O'Leary wrote to Yeats, "we shall do nothing to Mollie Magee until you tell us."[154] One of the reasons for such a long delay in publishing two of the poems and for the disappearance of the other seems to be that O'Leary had carelessly lost all three soon after receiving them. By mid-July 1887 Yeats had heard nothing about "Lug-na-Gall" and begged him to "kindly let me have the two poems you did not care for back as *I did not keep a copy of either*" (L 45). O'Leary evidently told him what had happened, because at the beginning of August, Yeats wrote that he had "a copy though an imperfect one of my poem" and asked if he should send this or "will we wait to see if the old copy turns up" (L 47). The evidence is that he did wait for a few weeks to see if the original version would be found, and when it was not, rewrote the poem from his imperfect copy. At the same time he probably recomposed "The Ballad of Moll Magee," of which he had not even an imperfect copy, and with O'Leary's criticism in mind, perhaps even made the new version less sentimental. In any event, O'Leary may have printed it. Even if O'Leary had not mislaid the other poem, "The Protestants' Leap," it is likely that he would have delayed publishing it for some weeks, since the theme was very close to that of Hyde's "A Ballad of '98," which had evidently appeared in *The Gael* in mid-June 1887.[155]

While this confusion about his poems was still in progress, Yeats took the opportunity to improve his position with O'Leary by

[153]But see LNI 200–201, where Yeats recounts the story of a Howth mother who returns from the dead to comfort her neglected children.

[154]Unpublished letter from Ellen O'Leary to Yeats, 20 November [1887] (Belfast Public Library).

[155]See O'Leary's headnote to Yeats's review, above (n. 27). In an unpublished letter to Yeats on 29 May [1887], Ellen O'Leary told him that "Douglas Hyde sent back his 98 ballad improved and shortened also the little Irish one which you like so well, John O'Mahoney's Death Lament and a new one" (Belfast Public Library).

adapting for *The Gael* a poem derived from a poet O'Leary had praised for "possessing in a supreme degree the great qualities of simplicity and pathos."[156] This was "Love Song," which Yeats rewrote from Edward Walsh's translation of a stanza from "Edmund of the Hill" by Edmund O'Ryan. He had found it in the introduction of Walsh's *Irish Popular Songs* and later said of it that he knew "nothing more impossibly romantic and Celtic" (UP1 153). Walsh's translation, stiff and slightly rhetorical, reads:

> My hope, my love, we will proceed
> Into the woods, scattering the dews,
> Where we will behold the salmon, and the ousel in its nest,
> The deer and the roe-buck calling,
> The sweetest bird on the branches warbling,
> The cuckoo on the summit of the green hill;
> And death shall never approach us
> In the bosom of the fragrant wood.[157]

Yeats rendered this more simply and more lyrically:

> My love, we will go, we will go, I and you,
> And away in the woods we will scatter the dew;
> And the salmon behold, and the ousel too,
> My love, we will hear, I and you, we will hear,
> The calling afar of the doe and the deer,
> And the bird in the branches will cry for us clear,
> And the cuckoo unseen in his festival mood;
> And death, oh my fair one, will never come near
> In the bosom afar of the fragrant wood.
>
> [VP 717]

The poem was exactly what O'Leary had been looking for, and he thought it was "one of the best" that Yeats had ever written.[158] Given this, it is almost certain that it was published in *The Gael*

[156]"What Irishmen Should Know," *The Gael,* 13 August 1887, p. 7 (Belfast Public Library).

[157]Edward Walsh, *Irish Popular Songs,* 2d ed. (Dublin: John O'Daly, 1883), p. 18.

[158]Quoted in an unpublished letter from Ellen O'Leary to Katharine Tynan [early 1888?] (Belfast Public Library). The poem was published in *Poems and Ballads of Young Ireland,* p. 80.

before its appearance in *Poems and Ballads of Young Ireland*. In sending O'Leary this poem, Yeats also spoke of "an article on the stocks for the Gael," which he had laid aside for the present (L 48), but since he shortly afterward left London for Sligo, we may suspect that this essay was never completed.

Since he spent much of his time in Sligo collecting folklore and writing his short prose tale "Dhoya," Yeats perhaps sent little more to the magazine during the autumn. Probably his next appearance, then, was "The Protestants' Leap" on 19 November 1887. The status of the printed version of this poem is uncertain, as we have seen. It is unlikely to have been the original composition that O'Leary had lost in June; more probably it was a new version reconstituted from the "imperfect copy" that Yeats retained, in which case it may well have differed from the version he first sent to O'Leary. Whether the "imperfect copy," which still survives in the collection of Michael Yeats, was closer to the original than to the redrafted version must be a matter for conjecture, but certainly it gives a sense of what the poem as first conceived was like.[159]

The most striking difference between the "imperfect copy" and the redrafted version, however, is the ending: in the rough draft it is clear that the guide is a demon, something only hinted in *The Gael* printing; and far from finishing with a chastened Cromwellian contemplating a brooding eagle, the narrator of the earlier version has returned to rebel hunting with renewed zeal. Since O'Leary disapproved of Yeats's interest in the occult (L 125), he may have suggested between receiving the two versions that the supernatural element should go. Or perhaps Yeats may have felt the continuation of the story beyond the immediate action into the Cromwellian's later deeds detracted from the unity of the poem.

Whether it was O'Leary's criticism or authorial second thoughts, Yeats must have prepared a second fair copy for *The Gael,* using his "imperfect copy" as the basis but altering as he went along. As it happens, three and one-half stanzas of such a fair copy remain in Michael Yeats's collection, and these correspond very closely to stanzas one, two, three, and half of stanza five in the published

[159]Transcriptions of all the manuscripts of "The Protestants' Leap" will be included in the second of the two volumes of early poetic manuscripts being edited by George Bornstein for the Cornell Yeats.

version. In making this copy, Yeats evidently wrote out half of stanza five as four before he realized his error, whereupon he put this manuscript aside and began a new one, which he completed and sent to O'Leary. The remaining fragment, however, helps us to correct the compositor's errors in this part of the poem.

In sending his adaptation of "Love Song" to *The Gael* in early August 1887, Yeats availed himself of the lesson his prose articles had taught him and begged to "see a proof as a missprint in a short lyric is quite ruinous & I am always especially unfortunate in that way" (L 47). In the case of "The Protestants' Leap," his ill fortune not only persisted but intensified, and he obviously saw no proof. The poem appeared, as the two versions printed below make clear, with errors of transcription and punctuation extraordinary even given Yeats's bad luck and worse handwriting. Ellen O'Leary, suitably mortified, lost no time in dashing off a letter of apology and explanation to him: "To my great annoyance and Johns they put in your poem in "The Gael" without letting us know, deeming it better without consulting John to leave out some article. In they stick the ballad with all its misprints. Tis too bad and this has been going on this long time owing to pigheadnesses with regard to things those in the office know nothing of. . . . I am very sorry about your poem but tis not my fault in the least."[160] Yeats, inured by now to the worst that compositors could do, decided to adopt a lofty and ironic stance, and in its issue of 26 November 1887, *The Gael,* which apparently apologized for "imperfect editorial supervision of the proofs," printed his letter:

> DEAR SIR—I write to correct a mistake. The curious poem in your issue on 19th inst. was not by me, but by the compositor, who is evidently an imitator of Browning. I congratulate him on the exquisite tact with which he has caught some of the confusion of his master. I take an interest in the matter, having myself a poem of the same name as yet unpublished.
> Yours faithfully
> W B Yeats [L 55–56][161]

[160]Unpublished letter from Ellen O'Leary to Yeats, 20 November 1887 (Belfast Public Library).

[161]No copy of *The Gael* containing this letter has yet come to light. Wade took his text from *The Irish Monthly* of July 1891, where it had been reprinted to illustrate Yeats's bad luck with compositors.

The poem that had provoked this retort was printed as follows:

THE PROTESTANTS' LEAP[162]
(Lug-na-Gal, Sligo).
THE CROMWELLIAN SPEAKS.

Mat formed our guide as from a failing tribe
Hurried and starved as suits earth crazy rust,
Tiller of sordid cliffs, the strong man's jibe,
All over grey from sitting in the dust.

On his pale eyes and forehead moist with hair,
Hanging like red iron drippings down a rock,
Fell from his pine wood torch a smoky flare,
Fifty and twain by many a mountainous block.

Clotted in clay and on the hill's edge laid,
With horses breathing heavily, we wound
Skyward along a path turf cutters made,
Sound from four hundred hoofs from us no sound.

Rolled over us the clouds in grisly smoke,
When moonless, starless, stood we on the height,
Gazing, and vaguely through the darkness broke,
From a low dusky pool, a palid light.

Above, the bats went shrilling to and fro,
The bubbles from the ebbs arose, and slipped
Poolward dull frogs luxurious in the slow;
Water his flame the grey guide, whispering, dipped.

He had one shoulder low, one shoulder high,
And he was lame, we might have known him then,
No minor minion, Belial, Molock, aye,
Or Satan murmuring in his favourite den.

To the grey slime. Thus he "along the brown
Mould follow me, nor hold ye silence deep,
The rebels when I lead ye, laid them down,
Weary, and they are very fast asleep."

[162]When the new edition of *The Poems* is revised, this poem will appear between the present A13 and A14.

John S. Kelly

Awhile the heavens touching dew bright mould,
    Round us, who in our saddles spurring bent,
Lay level as, neath God's imminent finger rolled,
    Our fifty hearts brimmed over with content.

Then down a dipping way we spurred together,
    The grey guide rose a form of flying mist,
As over mountain laurel, over heather,
    The grey guide leading ever on more swift

Went we, and loosed the sword in the long sheath,
    For near the idolators we surely came,
The flashing of the flint fires underneath,
    Our hoofs made an interminable flame.

The ground sloped ever steeper and more steep,
    More headlong we our raiment in the wind
Beyond our shoulders' gan to roar and leap,
    And bellowed all the blue bare world behind.

* * * *

Senseless, for many moments, I lay still,
    Then I arose, on knees and fingers propped;
My weary horse had fallen, with a will
    He the spare dew bright grasses near me cropped.

I thrust one foot forth, and found emptiness—
    It swung over an abyss before my gaze;
Blackness, a thousand feet down, more or less,
    And a waste water's few, far tranquil rays.

As from a lidless eye, and here and there
    A sound of torrents in the invisible woods,
Else silence. Once a meteor's fickle flare,
    That slanted, slipping from the starry broods,

Showed the mild mountains, mournful in their shrouds;
    Showed the dim river, like a wandering spark;
Showed where the ash wood on the pine wood crowds;
    Showed a far eagle brooding on the dark.

W. B. Yeates.

Lug-na-Gal is a very grey cliff overlooking that Glen-car lake, where Dermot and Grania had once a cranoque (whereof the remnants were found some years back.) Concerning this cliff are two legends, or rather two versions of a legend. This the protestant and ascendancy one. Certain papists, at their old massacreing habit again, did hurl at dead of night, by main force, upon the stones beneath, many mild martyrs who were protestants. This the authentic and peasant one! Certain Cromwellian protestants, at their old massacreing habit again, rode forth at dead of night, priest and rebel hunting, and being met, below the mountains, by a peasant who volunteered as guide, were lead into space, all save one, over this precipice of Lug-na-Gal which, interpreted, means the Protestant's Leap.[163] Beneath, in the debris, some years ago, were found old rusty sabres.

It was not so long since Spencer had written of the people—"Out of every corner of the woods and glyns they came creeping forth upon their hands, for their legs could not bear them; they looked like anatomies of death, they spake like ghosts crying out of their graves: They did eat the dead carrions, happy where they could find them; yea, and one another soon after: insomuch as the very carcases they spared not to scrape out of their graves."[164] And during the interval, England had not ceased this planting—as the "Times" would have phrased it—the "institutions of that more civilized country" instead of our "slovenly barbarism." Therefore I have made the guide one whose incorruptable heart moved in a body corrupted by generations of famine, suffering, fear, and foiled projects. One of those whose fruitless lives have saved Ireland at any rate from the modern worship of success.—ED. GAEL.

Although ascribed to "ED. GAEL," this note is clearly by Yeats himself and is the one he had promised to send O'Leary in June, "giving the story & saying where it took place." This wrong attribution was far from the compositor's only error, and a more authoritative text for the poem can be established by comparing the *Gael* version with drafts in Michael Yeats's collection. In these, the early stanzas are all that remain of what was apparently an

[163]In fact *Lug na Gal* means "the hollow of the strangers." In SR 47 Yeats calls it "the Steep Place of the Strangers."

[164]A quotation from Edmund Spenser's *A View of the Present State of Ireland*. Although put into modern spelling, Yeats's transcription is accurate. See *Spenser's Prose Works*, ed. Rudolf Gottfried (Baltimore: Johns Hopkins University Press, 1949), p. 158.

attempt at a fair copy. Among other things, they banish "Mat" from the poem:

Lug-na-Gall
The Cromwellian speaks

Malformed he seemed as from a failing tribe
　　Harried and starved as suits earth's crazy rust,
Tiller of sordid cliffs, the strong man's jibe
　　All grey from sitting in the scorching dust

On his pale eyes & forehead moist with hair
　Hanging like red-iron-drippings down a rock
Fell from his pinewood torch a smoky flare.
　Fifty and twain by many a mountainous block

Clotted in clay and on the hill's edge laid
　With horses breathing heavily we wound
Skyward along a path turf cutters made
　Sound from four hundred hooves, from us no sound

~~Above the bats went shrilling to and fro~~
　~~Poolward dull frogs luxurious in the slow~~
~~Water his flame~~

Above the bats went shrilling to and fro
　The bubbles from the [word omitted by WBY] arose, and slipped
Poolward dull frogs luxurious, in the slow
　Water his flame the grey guide whispering dipped

At this point Yeats seems to have abandoned this copy and probably began another, which he presumably sent on to O'Leary.

Five other separate drafts survive in Michael Yeats's collection. Four of these remaining versions are attempts to get the opening stanzas right, but one of them, although on separate sheets, seems to go with a rough draft of the rest of the poem, so that the two parts constitute what is perhaps the "imperfect copy" mentioned by Yeats in his letter to O'Leary. This version has the demonic ending, reveals that the Cromwellian is more of a zealot than his companions, and shows that the bubbles of stanza five are produced by "eels" rather than "ebbs" (even in the wilds of Sligo, mountain pools are not tidal!). I give this copy entire with Yeats's corrections and variant readings:

Loquiter the Cromwellian

1

Over our grey fell
~~On our~~ guide forehead ~~shone~~ the flair
heaven road we
—As ~~round~~ ward round the mountain shoulder
From his pine torch his forehead moist with hair
Hanging like red iron drippings on a boulder
As rode we on the path turf cutter made
My horse breathed heavily for all that day
chased
Gods torch Id ~~sought~~ the idolaters while stayed
lounging
My comrades ~~lounge~~ there dull hours away

2

grisly smoke
rolled greasy cloak
Now over us the clouds a gleam
starless
As moonless ~~starles~~ stood we on the hight
Gazing wile vaguely through the darkness broke
from a low dusky pool a pallid light
Above the bats went shrilly two and frow
The bubles from the eals arose and liped
Pool ward
~~By us~~ the frogs luxurious there below
His ~~haf~~ his flame the grey guide whispering dipped

3

He had one shoulder low one shoulder high
[deletion] ~~intend~~
And he was lame we might have ~~known him then~~
Moloch
~~We were~~ no minor minion—Belial—Aye
in favourite den
Or satan murmuring among his populace bad
To the grey slime the he
Then Spake follow on this pleasant down
Follow me now
Swiftly no need for silence deep
The rebels where I leed ye laid them down
of time and
Weary and they are very fast a sleep

4

Down the far slope we golloped on togeather
fluttering flying
The grey guide seemed a form of pallid mist
As over mountain laurels over heather
ever on more
The grey guide leeding rode on swift
We rode
burning of the
We rode the flint fires under neath
Our hooves
Made an interminable flame
[went
~~We rode~~ &
~~leaning an~~ loosed the sword in the long sheath
near surely
For ~~surely nigh~~ the idolators we came

5

more steep
The ground sloped even steeper and
More headlong we our raimint in the wind
beyond
~~beyond over~~ our shoulder 'gan lour and leap
duly
world
And bellowed all the blue bare earth behind

Now stunned five ~~flattened~~ I lay still
~~I laid~~
~~A Darkness! Some five moments had~~ gone by
I lay still

When I arose on knees and finger propped
~~with a will~~
with a will
My weary horse had fallen ~~now anigh~~
near me
He the spare dew bright grasses slowly cropt
Senseless for many moments I lay still

6

I thrust on foot forth and found nothiness
It swang on an abyss before my gaze
~~Blackness and a guide~~
a thousand feet down more or less
waste
And a ~~great~~ water few far tranquil rays
and
As from a lidless eye ~~sent~~ here and there
A sound of torrents of the invisible woods
~~fifty~~
Else silence ~~gone the whole troop~~ do they tare
now ~~naked~~ with flames rolled on their brows for
there flesh with coals for shoes and flames for hoods?

~~Or was this dying penalty enough~~
Or did the mere death penalty sufice
for slackness? in mid while of their descent
The demon wings like those of flitter mice
Fell wide and bore him to his element
sin gaze
boasting with all the souls he won that night

8

but I now full of zeal did slay and chase
~~copse~~ so my soul Light
I burnt nine heathen in a wood therefore my light
~~flames~~ still ineffible
Shines on before the still eternal face

In writing this poem, Yeats was consciously trying to please O'Leary and to address a specifically nationalist audience. His ballads about mad mothers in Howth and Sligo, although perhaps rooted in authentic personal concerns—his mother's nervous breakdown was not far off—had proved unsuitable. What clearly were more appropriate to *The Gael* were the political poems that Douglas Hyde had been publishing there, poems such as the "Death Lament of John O'Mahony," the elegy for those who fell at Kinsale, and, of course, "A Ballad of '98," to which Yeats had referred in sending the poem to O'Leary. (Ellen O'Leary had written enthusiastically to Yeats about it on 29 May, only a couple of weeks before he sent his own poem to *The Gael*.[165]) In writing ballads he was following the example of Davis and the Young Irelanders, but even when his enthusiasm for them was at its height—and his enthusiasm was never to be higher than it was at this point—he could not disguise from himself the fact that their inspiration was not his. "Moll Magee" and the ballads of the Old Foxhunter and Father O'Hart, though drawn from Irish sources, have closer affinities to Wordsworth than to Davis. "The Protestants' Leap," inspired by an incident of religious and national strife, would appear to be more obviously in line with the Young Ireland tradition, and yet in treatment and in feeling even this topic—permeated as it is with religious and racial hatred—is far less politically charged than one might have anticipated. Certainly it is far less so than Hyde's rendering of the same subject: Hyde transposes the story to the time of the 1798 rebellion, dispenses with the supernatural elements, and writes from the point of view of the rebel guide, who having seen his house burned and his wife and children slaughtered, is intent upon the uncomplicated satisfactions of personal and patriotic revenge.[166] The political significance of Yeats's poem, on the other hand, is marginalized into the accompanying note, where the "peasant" version of the legend is apparently authenticated, and the unflattering depiction of the native Irish justified by a literary reference to Spenser. This note, in fact, was itself an afterthought prompted by Yeats's fear that the O'Learys suspected him of taking the Protestant and antinational side. On hearing of their doubt, he had written at once to reassure them: "You have not said wheather you care for

[165]See above, n. 155.

[166]Hyde's poem was collected in *Poems and Ballads of Young Ireland*, pp. 64–67.

"Lug na Gall" . . . . Miss O'Leary speaks of it as from the other side than Hides. Of course that is not so, the Cromwellian being used dramatically alone. My note will state the old legend and point out the place of its happening" (L 45). O'Leary's suspicious silence, together with his assertion that the other ballads had been "Irish in nothing but the name," was evidently a cause of great apprehension, because it seemed to call into question the sincerity of Yeats's new-found nationalist aspirations, and it is significant that he goes to some lengths to give two versions of the story. This may be no more than an early example of his lifelong inclination to apprehend experience in terms of contraries, but the Protestant version as set out in his note seems singularly lacking in circumstantial detail, and one wonders whether Yeats hadn't simply invented it to convince O'Leary that his own treatment was far less biased in comparison. Certainly the most likely source for his poem, W. B. Wood-Martin's *History of Sligo,* gives no hint of a Protestant version, although Wood-Martin was a Protestant himself:

> Cope's mountain, with its fearful precipices (bordering the valley of Glencar) is the scene of the alleged "Protestant leap." The legend connected with it is as follows:—A detachment of Colonel Hamilton's troops (garrisoned in Manorhamilton during the war of 1641) was making a raid into Sligo, and obtained a guide, who stipulated, in return for a certain sum of money, to enable the party to fall on the Irish unawares, at the close of the evening. "Accordingly he led them up the mountain, directing them to halt a little short of the precipice, of the existence of which they had not the most remote idea, while he himself moved forward to ascertain if all was favourable among the Irish, in which case he was to give them a signal, by dropping his cloak, to rush on to the work of havoc. The cloak was dropped, on perceiving which, rushing forward with eager haste, they reached the verge of the precipice, where, unable to check themselves, the rear pressing on the front rank, every man of the detachment was hurled down that fearful abyss. . . . Their deceitful guide had dropped the cloak just on the edge of the abyss, towards which they accordingly rushed, and he, stepping aside, either made his way down the mountain again, or remained to gloat over the destruction of his victims."[167]

[167]W. G. Wood-Martin, *History of Sligo, County and Town* (Dublin: Hodges, Figgis, 1882–92), III, 384–385; the ellipsis is in the original. I am grateful to Mr. J. C. McTernan, Sligo County Librarian, for his help in tracing this passage.

Wood-Martin loses no time in discounting the whole story, but Yeats—once again prizing myth above mere history—did not allow this skepticism to curb the play of his imagination: "It is almost needless to add that there does not appear to be the slightest substratum of truth in the legend, particularly if it be remembered that many of Hamilton's troopers were men who had escaped from Sligo, and were well acquainted with its environs."[168]

Although Yeats's poem is closer to the received "peasant" version of the tale than the alleged "Protestant" version that he provides, O'Leary's doubts were not altogether unfounded. Given the fact of his nationalist intentions, it is curious that Yeats should have wanted to mediate this incident through the consciousness of a Protestant trooper, but perhaps not so curious if we consider his background and the place of this poem in his development. It was written at the time when he first resolved "that I should never go for the scenery of a poem to any country but my own" (VP 844), but the easy proprietorship that this aspiration implies was in reality less secure than it seemed. Born in Dublin and reared for long periods in London, Yeats could be sure of neither the geographical nor the psychological hinterland of Ireland, despite his claims. Even in Sligo his interest centered mainly on the sea, and his fascination was rather more for boats than for people. In this poem, the Irish landscape composes itself into dark woods, bare featureless mountains, and sudden precipices. To traverse such gloomy and uncertain terrain, lit by the lurid glares of fitful meteors, one is dependent apparently upon an ambivalent native guide who is following by the light of a smoky torch the alien tracery of turf-cutters' paths. The guide may have been inspired by Spenser, as Yeats suggests, but he is also an image of the native Irish seen through Anglo-Irish, Protestant, middle-class eyes—through the eyes of those who peopled Yeats's Sligo childhood, where as he tells us "Every one I knew well . . . despised Nationalists and Catholics" (Au 33–34). The guide, abject and yet dangerous, has affinities with those who during time of famine had obliged William Yeats, Rector of Drumcliff, to dine with his curtains drawn, and with those who, like the "idolators" the Cromwellians

[168]Wood-Martin, III, 385.

are pursuing, might perhaps be found adding prayer to shivering prayer. Moreover, for all Yeats's claim in his note that this guide represents "the incorruptable heart" of Ireland, he is described in satanic terms both in the printed version:

> No minor minion, Belial, Molock, aye,
> Or Satan murmuring in his favourite den

and in the rough draft:

> . . . in mid while of their descent
> The demon wings like those of flitter mice
> Fell wide and bore him to his element
> boasting with all the souls he won that night.

Indeed, shorn of its interpretive note, the poem is surprisingly ambiguous. Only the intermittent ironies of the author hint that the troopers are mistaken: they appear as pious men to whom biblical language comes naturally; unlike the guide, they are associated with heavenly light; and they ride, lacking any suspicion of irony, confident of divine sanction. It is significant that this more ironic and ambiguous stanza appears to have been a later addition.

> Awhile the heavens touching dew bright mould,
> Round us, who in our saddles spurring bent,
> Lay level as, neath God's imminent finger rolled,
> Our fifty hearts brimmed over with content.

In his arch letter to *The Gael,* Yeats purports to suppose that the compositor is an imitator of Robert Browning. There is more truth in this than he perhaps intended: had the compositor been only slightly more competent at reading poetry than at setting type, it would have been of Browning that he first thought when looking over the poem. Yeats's Irish guide, "one shoulder low, one shoulder high, / And he was lame," owes an obvious debt to the "Hoary cripple, with malicious eye" of Browning's "Childe Roland to the Dark Tower Came." And yet, precociously enough, Yeats had already produced his Childe Roland poem with "The Seeker," published in *The Dublin University Review* in September

1885 and written before he had come under O'Leary's influence. O'Leary, in giving him a nationalist dimension for his poetry, had provided him with a way out of the self-enclosure of the Romantic quest that "The Seeker" represents, but it was a way no less beset by imaginative doubts and temperamental complexities. We have seen how fond Yeats was of reciting O'Leary's catechistic doctrine that "there is no fine nationality without literature, and . . . no fine literature without nationality," and yet although this might for a time satisfy his waking critical mind, its seesawing simplicity could not contain the deeper tensions of his imaginative drives. For Yeats to enter into Irish national life was as difficult as for Joyce to escape it: in neither case was the choice merely one of straightforward intellectual predilection, but of painful emotional reorientation. Yeats's childhood had been made unhappy, as he tells us, by his brooding sense of guilt and remorse, in which his Pollexfen grandfather, who read only two books—one of them the Bible—appeared in the likeness of the Old Testament God. His first experiences of poetry had been the partisan rhymes of an Orange stableboy, and he imagined that when he grew up he would fight on the loyalist and Unionist side against the Fenian nationalists (Au 14). Now he was choosing to leave the house of his fathers and throw in his lot with the "idolators" of the Catholic-Celtic tradition, those whom he had been taught by his uncles and aunts to look upon with scorn and suspicion. Little wonder, then, that nationalism is a dangerous commodity in his poems of this period: the grey-haired youth of "The Two Titans" remains a prisoner with only failure for his glory; Ferencz Renyi gives up kith and kin and love for his nation, and runs mad; the narrator of "The Protestants' Leap," in following a native Irish guide, loses his way and a troop of friends. The Cromwellian's demon takes on the aspect of Yeats's own daimon, an ambivalent, shape-changing image out of the hidden Ireland, a "form of flying mist" that spurs him on to take a leap into the dark as he deracinates and declasses himself. In "The Wanderings of Oisin," which he was just about to finish when he wrote this poem, he exchanges the doomed Puritan militia for the Fenians, a doomed pagan militia, and the Irish myth provides him with a structure through which to explore his private and public concerns. In his final heroic affirmation, Oisin rejects both clerical asceticism and fairy escapism to plunge fighting into hell itself. "The Protestants' Leap" holds back at the very brink. Far above, the lidless eye of a brooding eagle gazes into an abyss to be met by the glint of the lidless eye of a river; somewhere in between, prostrate on the edge of a precipice, Yeats's now uncertain hero uncertainly waits.

Our knowledge of what more Yeats may have written for *The Gael* awaits the discovery of further fragments or even, to be more optimistic, a complete run of the magazine. We may be sure, however, that even if the contributions published in the present article were all that he submitted to it, its suppression in early 1888 by the purged G.A.A. executive must have been a grievous blow to his aspirations to find an Irish audience—especially since two other Dublin periodicals for which he wrote had also recently folded, *The Irish Fireside* in October, and *North & South* in December. The difference that these closures made to him can be gauged by the fact that in 1887 he published at least twelve articles or poems in Irish magazines, whereas in the following year he published only one. The disappearance of *The Gael* was certainly the most serious loss: *The Irish Fireside* had been rather juvenile, *North & South* rather erratic, while *The Irish Monthly,* although it continued publication, proved to be too Catholic and printed no more of his work. What *The Gael* had given him, and these could not, was a distinguished company of contributors and a small but defined readership. More than this, with the literary editorship in the hands of O'Leary, the magazine provided him with an opportunity of testing his writings against the determined, even obstinate judgment of the very man whose ideas had done most to give them their theoretical occasion.

The challenge was not, as we have seen, an easy one for Yeats to meet, given the complexities of his poetic sensibility and psychological processes. For, if one of O'Leary's watchwords was nationalism, another was simplicity. In "What Irishmen Should Know," a lecture that we may regard as setting out the precepts upon which his editorship was founded, he had praised in particular certain nineteenth-century Irish poets for possessing "in a supreme degree the great qualities of simplicity and pathos" and went on to argue that there was now "more need to draw attention to the simpler sort of poetry, seeing that a new school of poetry seems to be springing up amongst us which is anything rather than simple, and, I think, partly as a consequence, scarcely Irish in other than name."[169] It was a doctrine that Yeats tried desperately to endorse, and it clearly lies behind the distinction he draws in his essay "The Poetry of R. D. Joyce" (UP1 104–14) between coterie poets and bards. Yeats's poetic precursors were the great Romantics, but under O'Leary's influence he disparages Coleridge, Shelley, and Wordsworth because they "investigate what is obscure in emotion, and appeal to what is abnormal in man" and, in a bizarre contortion, attempts to praise the soon-to-be-despised Hugo, Burns, and Scott (UP1 105). In a similar quest for simplicity, he schooled himself to write ballads, but in this, as we have seen, he even failed to convince O'Leary, who found those he had submitted to *The Gael* "morbid" and "Irish in nothing but the name," judgments that echo the very words he had used to denounce the "new school." It is significant that few of the ballads Yeats wrote at this time found their way into the *Collected Poems,* and even in those that did he later found a sentimentality that came from an imitation "not natural to me" (VP 851).

He was left with another resource, that of mythology. In his lecture, O'Leary had been cagey on this topic: it was, he argued, "hardly a thing for many Irishmen to know, or at least, not until some have more fully investigated and elucidated the matter."[170] Investigation and elucidation were just what Yeats's essay on Finn Mac Cumhaill was about. At the same time he was making room for himself artistically by redefining O'Leary's injunctions with the aid of Standish James O'Grady's Carlylean assertions. Of all the things that Irishmen should know, O'Leary insisted that Irish history was the most important. Yeats, with O'Grady's sanction, could turn from the dry and academic history books that O'Leary recommended, those of W. E. H. Lecky, Barry O'Brien, and Thomas Davis, to urge the claims of a more essential, if less exact, history that had been mediated through the imagination: "what a

[169] *The Gael,* 13 August 1887, p. 7 (Belfast Public Library).
[170] *The Gael,* 6 August 1887, p. 6 (Belfast Public Library).

nation imagines that is its history, there is its heart." Here, then, was a potent literary source for Irish writers, but, as the qualifications and paradoxes in his review of *Shamrocks* reveal, he still had to negotiate the problem of how mythological themes were to be rendered by the late-nineteenth-century sensibility and what forms and genres were suitable for their articulation.

To sum up, we find in the surviving pages of *The Gael* a process that is to be repeated throughout Yeats's creative life: working by the light of an apparently straightforward idea, or cluster of ideas, he is time and again brought up against unforeseen complications that arise from an attempt to impose ready-made formulas on the refractory intricacies of experience and the restless energies of his own creativity. In the end, creativity and felt experience win—the theory is revised to accommodate their inconvenient demands—and the story of their victories is the story of Yeats's artistic ripening. At this time and in this place, the animating ideas derived predominantly from O'Leary and centered upon the importance of nationalist feeling, Irish history, and simplicity of expression. What O'Leary preferred in Yeats's verse were what his sister Ellen described as "Earth Touches,"[171] and since one of Yeats's abiding ambitions was to think like a wise man but express himself in the speech of the common people, this preference was far from eccentric. Nevertheless, what the O'Learys regarded as simple may appear in terms of Yeats's development merely simplistic, and it was inevitable that while always stimulated by their criticism, he should move beyond their influence. In his articles and poems in *The Gael,* as well as in his correspondence about those writings, we detect the first stirrings of that movement. O'Leary's prescriptions will not quite satisfy the problems that he encounters, and indeed, many of the questions that Yeats addresses here—the relationship of the poet to a popular audience, the significance of mythology, the place of the ballad in modern poetry, the conflict between nationalist sentiment and personal authenticity—were to trouble him fruitfully through a lifetime.

O'Leary's contribution was to direct Yeats's muse at an important formative stage in his career—"It was through the old Fenian

[171]She is, of course, quoting Yeats himself.

leader John O'Leary I found my theme" (E&I 510)—and to provide him, for as long as he could, with an outlet for his work. Outspoken in his critical opinions he might have been, but he was never patronizing, and submitting work to his stern editorial eye helped Yeats to define his own artistic position. Brought up in the school of Thomas Davis, O'Leary managed to preserve an openness and balance in his literary judgments not always given to other disciples of the Young Irelanders. As two examples from *The Gael* illustrate, he never confused propaganda with literature: he publicly rebuked Hyde for using the stock and facile racial slur "creeping" as an epithet for "Saxon" in "Marching Song of the Gaelic Athletes,"[172] and he printed "The Protestants' Leap" despite the reservations he may have had about its political viewpoint.

Above all, O'Leary believed in Yeats, recognizing in this young man, so unlike himself in temperament and background, a poet of genius. In "What Irishmen Should Know" he said he regretted that it was "one among the many misfortunes of Ireland that she has never yet produced a great poet" but went on to hope "that God has yet in store for us that great gift."[173] In Yeats he found the promise of that gift. No longer in a position after January 1888 to publish Yeats's work himself, he gave some of the hours set free from editorial work to drumming up "almost all" (Au 212) the subscribers for *The Wanderings of Oisin,* and it is unlikely that the book would ever have been published without his help. *The Wanderings of Oisin* brought Yeats's poetry before his Irish readers in book form for the first time. Ironically, given Yeats's attempts to be popular and his criticism of "obscure" coterie poets, the Dublin reviewers found in the collection an "obscurity" and a "sense of unreality, of remoteness from life" that they deprecated.[174] Perhaps partly because of this, the book failed to sell widely, and it was not until the fall of Parnell had persuaded the Parnellite weekly, *United Ireland,* in 1891 to take up the role of Davis' *Nation* that

[172]*The Gael,* 8 October 1887, page number cropped: "We can hardly agree with our poet in the epithet creeping, as applied to 'The Saxon.' The Saxon has more of the lion than the snail in his composition" (Belfast Public Library).

[173]*The Gael,* 13 August 1887, p. 7 (Belfast Public Library).

[174]See, for example, *The Freeman's Journal,* 1 February 1889, p. 2; and *The Nation,* 25 May 1889, p. 8.

Yeats once again found, for a few years, a regular way of getting his poetry and ideas across to the Irish public.

What advantages might have accrued to Yeats's development had *The Gael* continued publication must be a matter for surmise. It would probably have accelerated the maturing process it had helped to begin by obliging him to formulate his ideas more carefully as he went on exposing them to O'Leary's criticism and to a homogenous Irish readership. What is more certain is that O'Leary's attempt to turn an athletic journal into a vehicle for cultural regeneration was by no means as ridiculous or misguided as might at first sight appear. Even from the few fragments that remain and from passing references in letters it is possible to compile a checklist that gives some indication of its vigorous literary life:

1887

9 April	"The Pursuit of Diarmuid and Grainne: Part VI, Their Happy Wedded Life." A poem by Katharine Tynan.
20 April	"Courting in Lent to Marry at Easter: Part I." A story by Ellen O'Leary.
27 April	"Finn Mac Cumhaill." An article by W. B. Yeats.
	"Courting in Lent to Marry at Easter: Part II."
4 May	"Courting in Lent to Marry at Easter: Part III."
11 June	"The Celtic Romances in Miss Tynan's New Book." A review of Katharine Tynan's *Shamrocks* by W. B. Yeats.
18 June?	"A Ballad of '98," "Death Lament for John O'Mahony," and, probably, "Oh were you on the mountain." Poems by Douglas Hyde.[175]
6 August	"The Lament of Aidheen" and "A Dear Dead Hand." Poems by John Todhunter.
	"What Irishmen Should Know: Part I." A lecture by John O'Leary.
13 August	"What Irishmen Should Know: Part II."
late August?	"Love Song." A poem by W. B. Yeats.

[175]See above, n. 152, for an unpublished letter of 29 May [1887] in which Ellen O'Leary told Yeats that Hyde had sent these poems to O'Leary. From the final comment in his headnote of 11 June (see n. 27), it seems likely that O'Leary printed them in the following week or weeks.

3 September	"A Modern Greek War Song." A poem by William Smith O'Brien.
	"Aghadoe." A poem by John Todhunter.
8 October	"Marching Song of the Gaelic Athletes." A poem by Douglas Hyde.
? October	A poem about Fermoy by T. W. Rolleston.[176]
19 November	"The Protestants' Leap." A poem by W. B. Yeats.
	A review of Charlotte Grace O'Brien's *Lyrics* by Ellen O'Leary.
26 November	A letter to the editor by W. B. Yeats.
? December	"The Ballad of Moll Magee." A poem by W. B. Yeats.
24 December	"How Ferencz Renyi Kept Silent." A poem by W. B. Yeats.
	A poem (probably "Dying in the Backwoods") by Ellen O'Leary.[177]
	Possibly "Dhoya." A story by W. B. Yeats.[178]

1888

7 January	"For Irish Hearts." A poem by "C."
	"Some Words About Unpublished Literature." An unsigned article by Douglas Hyde.[179]

Even if most copies of the magazine itself are lost forever, *The Gael*'s memorial remains in *Poems and Ballads of Young Ireland,* a

[176]In an unpublished letter, undated but written early in 1888, Ellen O'Leary asked Douglas Hyde: "Did you like that poem of Mr. Rolleston's on Fermoy, twas in the Gael some months since. John thought highly of it" (National Library of Ireland).

[177]In an unpublished letter, undated but written in December 1887, Ellen O'Leary told an American friend, Mrs. Luby, that she had "a grand piece of news. I have just got £2 from 'The Boston Pilot' for a ballad. We've reprinted it in Dublin in 'The Gale.' Mr. Yeats got 3£ for his which we also reprint in our Xmas number and Rose Kavanagh 3£ for a long one 'In Exile. Theirs were longer, perhaps better" (Belfast Public Library). *The Boston Pilot* published "How Ferencz Renyi Kept Silent" on 6 June 1887 (p. 1); Rose Kavanagh's "In Exile" on 1 October 1887 (p. 1); and Ellen O'Leary's "Dying in the Backwoods" on 3 December 1887 (p. 5).

[178]On 13 December 1887 Yeats wrote to O'Leary: "I see by the paper the 'Gael' will come out as an Xmas number. I repent me of the idea of sending Dhoya elsewhere and send it to you hoping it may suit for the Xmas number for some number anyway" (L 56).

[179]Identified in pencil as by Hyde in the National Library of Ireland copy. A further copy of the article apparently survives among Hyde papers in private hands.

seminal anthology that drew largely from its pages and that, according to M. J. MacManus, initiated the Irish Literary Revival.[180] Certainly it introduced a new generation of poets to the world and signaled that, after many years of decay, Irish poetry was putting forth lively shoots. In this O'Leary had achieved at least one of his aims.

APPENDIX

A corrected and repunctuated version of "The Protestants' Leap" might read as follows:

THE PROTESTANTS' LEAP
(Lug-na-Gall, Sligo).
THE CROMWELLIAN SPEAKS.

Malformed our guide as from a failing tribe,
Harried and starved as suits earth's crazy rust,
Tiller of sordid cliffs, the strong man's jibe,
All over grey from sitting in the dust.

On his pale eyes and forehead moist with hair,
Hanging like red iron drippings down a rock,
Fell from his pinewood torch a smoky flare.
Fifty and twain by many a mountainous block.

Clotted in clay and on the hill's edge laid,
With horses breathing heavily, we wound
Skyward along a path turf-cutters made,
Sound from four hundred hoofs, from us no sound.

Rolled over us the clouds in grisly smoke,
When moonless, starless, stood we on the height
Gazing, and vaguely through the darkness broke,
From a low dusky pool, a pallid light.

[180]Quoted in *Adventures of an Irish Bookman*, ed. Francis MacManus (Dublin: Talbot Press, 1952), p. 21.

John S. Kelly

Above, the bats went shrilling to and fro,
The bubbles from the eels arose,and slipped
Poolward dull frogs luxurious; in the slow
Water his flame the grey guide, whispering, dipped.

He had one shoulder low, one shoulder high,
And he was lame. We might have known him then,
No minor minion: Belial, Molock, aye,
Or Satan murmuring in his favourite den

To the grey slime. Thus he, "Along the brown
Mould follow me, nor hold ye silence deep,
The rebels where I lead ye laid them down
Weary, and they are very fast asleep."

Awhile the heavens touching dew-bright mould,
Round us, who in our saddles spurring bent,
Lay level as, neath God's imminent finger rolled,
Our fifty hearts brimmed over with content.

Then down a dipping way we spurred together,
The grey guide rose a form of flying mist,
As over mountain laurel, over heather,
The grey guide leading ever on more swift,

Went we, and loosed the sword in the long sheath,
For near the idolators we surely came.
The flashing of the flint fires underneath
Our hoofs made an interminable flame,

The ground sloped ever steeper and more steep.
More headlong we, our raiment in the wind
Beyond our shoulders 'gan to roar and leap,
And bellowed all the blue bare world behind.

* * * *

Senseless, for many moments, I lay still,
Then I arose, on knees and fingers propped;
My weary horse had fallen; with a will
He the spare dew-bright grasses near me cropped.

I thrust one foot forth, and found emptiness—
It swung over an abyss before my gaze;

Blackness, a thousand feet down, more or less,
    And a waste water's few, far tranquil rays

As from a lidless eye, and here and there
    A sound of torrents in the invisible woods,
Else silence. Once a meteor's fickle flare,
    That slanted, slipping from the starry broods,

Showed the misty mountains, mournful in their shrouds;
    Showed the dim river, like a wandering spark;
Showed where the ash wood on the pine wood crowds;
    Showed a far eagle brooding on the dark.
W. B. Yeats

Most of the mistakes in the *Gael* printing arise from faulty punctuation. One has some sympathy with the compositor in this, since Yeats's syntax is unusual and sometimes confusing. The three obvious verbal errors, "Mat formed" for "Malformed," "ebbs" for "eels," and "mild" for "misty," result from an understandable misreading the original manuscript. Since it is unlikely, however, that the compositor would have missed out "scorching" completely in line four of the first stanza, we must assume that Yeats changed the line in the course of his final transcription, probably because he had not mentioned that the guide had been sitting by a wood fire (a detail given in "The Curse of the Fires and of the Shadows" [SR 45–46]), and consequently felt that the adjective might be puzzling.

As I have argued above, the poem has considerable interest for anyone tracing the development of Yeats's response to his new Irish themes; but technically it is the work of a young poet, and its faults stand out clearly. Some of the irregularities in word order are caused by an inexperienced poet inverting simply for the sake of rhythm and rhyme, but they are also part of an attempt to make the monologue more dramatically convincing by mimicking seventeenth-century syntax and vocabulary. Thus anachronisms such as "twain," "raiment," and "no minor minion" have a historical justification, although the "meteor's fickle flare" and "the starry brood" owe more to Pre-Raphaelitism than to Milton. Valid though Yeats's attempt to find a Cromwellian register of language may be, it is far from a complete success, and lines such as "slipped

/ Poolward dull frogs luxurious" and "And he the spare dew-bright grasses near me cropped" sound like awkward translations from another tongue.

A further sign of immaturity is the too insistent use of alliteration, although in combination with metrical dexterity this is not without effect, as in "The flashing of the flint fires underneath / Our hoofs" and "bellowed all the blue bare world behind" at the end of the first part, where the pattern of labials helps to mark the climactic moment and the heavy stresses in the second part of the line slow the rhythm sufficiently to hint at an elegiac gesture toward the doomed horsemen's lost world. Throughout the poem Yeats is striving for atmospheric effects mainly through adjectives, and some details are nicely caught: the horse, oblivious to the recent catastrophe, cropping the grass (not unlike Auden's back-scratching horse in "Musée des Beaux Arts"); the river reflecting fitful light "like a wandering spark"; and the final image, the "far eagle brooding on the dark," a symbol of inscrutable fate and a cousin, no doubt, of the "two old eagles, full of ancient pride" whose "dim minds were with the ancient things" in "The Wanderings of Oisin" (VP 34).

The only image that Yeats retained when converting this poem into a story was the simile of the guide's moist hair "Hanging like red iron drippings down a rock" (see SR 46), although the guide himself is made into a more active and sidhe-like figure than the miserable creature in "The Protestants' Leap." Indeed, "The Curse of the Fires and of the Shadows" has more historical and geographical detail. It is clear that Yeats has reread Wood-Martin, for he makes his troopers local men and identifies them as the bodyguards of Sir Frederick Hamilton. He thins their ranks, too, from "Fifty and twain," to five—a sensible reduction since it is improbable that at least the back-markers in a troop of fifty-two would not have had time to pull up or swerve aside before going over the cliff. The lessening of the number also gives the story dramatic tension, for these are the very five soldiers who led the murderous attack on the White Friars in Sligo and were specifically cursed by the dying abbot. The curse not only opens the way for a gothic treatment of chilling supernatural effects, but also allows Yeats to weave the light and dark images of the poem into the fabric of the narrative as thematic structuring devices, for the abbot damns his murderers to "wander among shadows, and among fires!" (SR 41–42). Indeed, the curse is the integrating element in the story, giving a motive for the subsequent action which is lacking in the poem. Thus, although there are more incidents in "The Curse of the Fires and of the Shadows," and although it lacks the restraints of the poem's iambic pentameters and rhyme, it has a more satisfying shape and a more cogent theme. The source material is more amenable to a prose treatment, and it is an evidence of Yeats's growing artistic maturity that when he came to look at the legend again he recognized this and decided upon a recasting rather than a revision.

Yeats's Early Landscapes

ELIZABETH BERGMANN LOIZEAUX

In 1913, when trying to sort out his poetic practice, Yeats wrote his famous letter to J. B. Yeats characterizing his early verse as poetry of vision: "meaning by vision," he said, "the intense realization of a state of ecstatic emotion symbolized in a definite imagined region" (L 583). He contrasted his early work to the poetry he now wished to write in which there would be "more self portraiture" (L 583).

Both the emphasis on vision as the predominant sense to which poetry appeals (and from which, at times, it comes) and the use of the term from painting—self portraiture—to describe his future poetic endeavors indicate that Yeats had thought and continued to think of his poetry as analogous to the visual arts. He himself made that point in 1910, when he explained in the second of three lectures on poetry, "Last time I was speaking here I used a great deal of analogies from painting, and I shall begin again with an analogy from painting. I began my own life as an art student and I am a painter's son, so it is natural to me to see such analogies."[1] In his early efforts to coax his abstractions into "picture and dramatization" (Au 188), Yeats found the analogies helpful and frequently turned to painting as model. In an early unpublished poem he

[1]Robert O'Driscoll, "Yeats on Personality: Three Unpublished Lectures," in *Yeats and the Theatre,* ed. Robert O'Driscoll and Lorna Reynolds (Toronto: Macmillan, 1975), pp. 26–27.

declared that a "song should be / A painted and be [-] pictured argosy,"[2] implying that the painter's craft and work could serve as guidelines for the poet.

All the terms in Yeats's definition of poetry of vision provide ways of approaching the relationships between that poetry and the visual arts. I would like to focus here on the "definite imagined region." The connections between the two arts implied in Yeats's concept of the poem as region can be explored by adopting his own method, analogy. Selecting those works of art which particularly interested Yeats and examining their relation to the "regions" of his poems suggest how his poetry and the visual arts are allied. This approach also illuminates some of the aesthetic problems with which Yeats struggled as he worked toward his own style.

By conceiving of poetry as "region," an idea he first formulated in 1889, Yeats violated the distinction Gotthold Lessing had drawn—in the *Laokoon,* the classic argument for the necessary separation of the arts—between the visual arts as conveying their ideas and emotions in a single moment, and literature as conveying them over time.[3] Responding in part to the overabundance of descriptive poetry and the lavish praise it received, Lessing had argued that the arrangement of objects in space (which descriptive poetry tried to reproduce) belongs to the province of painting and sculpture, the relation of events in time (narrative) to the province of literature.[4] Such arguments can be, and have been, refuted on a number of grounds.[5] Yeats implicitly attacked them on one, when

[2]Quoted in Richard Ellmann, *Yeats: The Man and the Masks* (New York: Macmillan, 1948), p. 29; hereafter cited as *MM.*

[3]*Laokoon,* published in German in 1766, was first translated into English in 1836 (Ian Jack, *Keats and the Mirror of Art* [Oxford: Clarendon Press, 1967], p. 281), and was well known in the latter half of the nineteenth century (for a discussion of Arnold and Lessing, see Alan Roper, *Arnold's Poetic Landscapes* [Baltimore: Johns Hopkins University Press, 1969], pp. 23–29). Although Yeats probably did not read it, he was most likely familiar with its stance on the arts.

[4]*Laocoon: An Essay upon the Limits of Painting and Poetry,* tr. Ellen Frothingham (New York: Noonday, 1957), section xvi, pp. 91–92.

[5]For an excellent recent rebuttal to Lessing, see W. J. T. Mitchell, "Spatial Form in Literature: Toward a General Theory," in *The Language of Images,* ed. W. J. T. Mitchell (Chicago: University of Chicago Press, 1980), pp. 271–99.

in conceiving of his poems as regions he claimed for poetry a spatial quality.

Yeats rarely recognized explicitly the theoretical questions such concepts of poetry raised, but he grappled with them instinctively. If not in such terms, he understood that there was an important difference between the poem as spatial and the poem as temporal (or narrative). The distinction was on his mind when he first explained his notion of the poem as region in an 1889 letter to Katharine Tynan: "'Oisin' is an incident or series of incidents; the 'Island of Statues' a region" (L 106). Although Yeats here prefers the narrative of his most recent achievement, *The Wanderings of Oisin,* to the region of *The Island of Statues,* both *Oisin* itself and future theory and practice show Yeats choosing the spatial over the temporal.

From his earliest poems on, "region" meant to Yeats a geographic place. Nearly all the poems of the 1880s and 1890s are set in, or evoke through metaphor and simile, a landscape. There are the islands of *Oisin* and *The Island of Statues,* Colooney and the salley gardens, Innisfree and Fergus's woods, to name a few. Yeats clearly did not advocate a return to the loco-descriptive poetry of the eighteenth century which had been so closely tied to painting and which Lessing had deplored. He seems to have been unfamiliar with the work of Cowper and Thomson, as Frayne implies (UP1 30); and, as part of his revolt against Victorianism, he vociferously rejected "irrelevant descriptions of nature" (OBMV ix), not because they infringed on the painter's territory, but because no art should ever be merely mimetic. Yeats renounced descriptive poets for the same reasons he hated the Impressionists and ignored Constable. They shared the sin of Wordsworth with whom, Yeats said, "poetry gave up the right to consider all things in the world as a dictionary of types and symbols and began to call itself a critic of life and an interpreter of things as they are" (E&I 192). Yeats, then, set out to correct Wordsworth's error. He wanted his landscapes to be far from daily life, from "things as they are": "a long poem should be . . . a region into which one should wander from the cares of life," he explained (L 106). His "definite imagined region" was to be not an "interpreter of things as they are," but a symbol of "a state of ecstatic emotion." Yeats attributed his belief in the symbolic potential of landscape to painting: "It is a natural conviction for a painter's son," he said, "to believe that there may be a landscape that is symbolical of some spiritual condition and awakens a hunger such as cats feel for valerian" (Au 74).

Yeats could hardly have avoided landscape art, the most prominent form of painting in England in the eighteenth and nineteenth centuries. Although he rarely mentioned Ruskin,[6] Ruskin's writings on landscape painting had helped make it a much-discussed subject, and his ideas were part of the intellectual climate in which Yeats lived. Yeats had first learned about landscape, however, through J. B. Yeats. His father's friends included the landscapist George Wilson, whom Yeats knew and whose works his sisters acquired (Au 46). J. B. Yeats himself, in 1876, had suddenly become ambitious to improve his landscape technique and hurried to England for that purpose. Once installed, he sent for his son[7] who years later remembered when "my father and I and a group of landscape-painters lodged at Burnham Beeches" (Au 28). Although J. B. Yeats was primarily a portraitist (and W. B. Yeats's desire for landscape seems at some level a repudiation of his father's art), he had taught his son that mere mimesis would never do, and he had introduced him to Blake. In Blake's works and in those of his followers Samuel Palmer and Edward Calvert, Yeats found landscape symbolic of a spiritual condition. They provided him, as critics often note,[8] with visual precedents for the experiments in symbolic landscape he carried out in the 1890s.

But Yeats's notions of symbolic landscape were not firmly fixed in either theory or practice when he began his poetic career. Just as

[6]Ruskin appeared in Yeats's thought early in his life as the author of *Unto This Last,* which he read in defiance of his father, and late in his life as the man who threw from a window "a tempting demon in the form of a cat," the subject of a lengthy debate with T. Sturge Moore (Mem 19; LTSM 63–114).

[7]William M. Murphy, *Prodigal Father: The Life of John Butler Yeats (1839–1922)* (Ithaca: Cornell University Press, 1978), p. 110; hereafter cited as Murphy.

[8]George Mills Harper mentions Palmer, Calvert, AE, Robert Gregory, and Jack B. Yeats as visual influences ("Yeats's Quest for Eden," *The Dolmen Press Yeats Centenary Papers MCMLXV,* ed. Liam Miller [Dublin: Dolmen Press, 1968], p. 295; hereafter cited as Harper). See also D. J. Gordon and Ian Fletcher, *W. B. Yeats: Images of a Poet* (Manchester: Manchester University Press, 1961), pp. 103–7, hereafter cited as *Images;* and Raymond Lister, "Beulah to Byzantium: Parallels in the Works of Yeats, Blake, Palmer and Calvert," in *The Dolmen Press Yeats Centenary Papers,* pp. 29–68.

the symbolic landscapes of Blake, Palmer, and Calvert historically developed out of the ideal landscapes of Claude Lorrain and his followers,[9] so in Yeats's work symbolic followed ideal. Most of Yeats's earliest experiments in poetic regions were idealized pastoral landscapes. Although they convey a mood and a belief in the realm of beauty, they are not explicitly symbolic. Yeats owes his pastorals directly to a poet, Spenser, but his instinctive interest in the form is part of his impulse to link poetry to the visual arts. Landscape painting as a genre derived from Virgil. In Virgil's "delicate suggestions of scenery" and his "myth of ideal rusticity," Kenneth Clark tells us, the first painters of landscape as such found their inspiration (Clark, p. 54). When Yeats wrote most of his pastorals in the mid-1880s, he knew of Blake's direct treatment of Virgil in the illustrations for Robert Thornton's school edition,[10] but there is no evidence that he particularly admired them. He did, however, admire and praise Turner's depiction of a scene from the *Aeneid, The Golden Bough* (Fig. 1), whose visual ancestry can be traced back through Claude and a long line of ideal landscape painters to those whom Virgil first inspired.

The Island of Statues, Yeats's most ambitious experiment in the genre, can serve as an example of his pastoral landscapes. He completed this verse play in August 1884[11] while he was enrolled in the Metropolitan School of Art[12] and his longing for nonmimetic art—specifically as represented by *The Golden Bough*—was especially intense. "I . . . returned again and again to our National Gallery to gaze at Turner's *Golden Bough,*" he recalled (Au 81). *The Island of Statues* was the first work that Yeats explicitly called a "region" (L 106). The poem shows clearly what he meant by the term: most of its approximately 1600 lines describe in rich detail the landscape through which the characters wander. The play opens with the shepherds Colin and Thernot contending for the

[9]Kenneth Clark, *Landscape into Art* (1949; rpt. Boston: Beacon, 1961), pp. 71–73; hereafter cited as Clark.

[10]Yeats had read Alexander Gilchrist's *Life of William Blake, "Pictor Ignotus"* (London: Macmillan, 1863), which contains a short chapter on the illustrations (pp. 270–75) and reprints three of the designs (p. 271).

[11]A fair copy of the poem in nearly final form appears in a notebook dated August 1884, although Yeats subsequently made minor changes, particularly in the last scene. I am grateful to Professor George Bornstein for providing this information.

[12]Yeats was enrolled in the art school from May 1884 to April 1886 (Murphy, p. 139).

love of the shepherdess Naschina by singing songs which compete in the extravagance of their natural description:

Colin. Come forth: the morn is fair; as from the pyre
Of sad Queen Dido shone the lapping fire
Unto the wanderer's ships, or as day fills
The brazen sky, so blaze the daffodills;
As Argive Clytemnestra saw out-burn
The flagrant signal of her lord's return,
Afar, clear-shining on the herald hills,
In vale and dell so blaze the daffodills;
As when upon her cloud-o'er-muffled steep
Oenone saw the fires of Troia leap,
And laugh'd, so, so along the bubbling rills
In lemon-tinted lines, so blaze the daffodills.
Come forth, come forth, my music flows for thee,
A quenchless grieving of love melody.
[*Raises his lute.*]
Thernot. [*Sings*] Now her sheep all browsing meet
By the singing waters' edge,
Tread and tread their cloven feet
On the ruddy river sedge,
For the dawn the foliage fingereth,
And the waves are leaping white,
She alone, my lady, lingereth
While the world is roll'd in light.

[VP 645–46]

This is, as Ellmann has observed, "a picture play with Spenserian shepherds" (*MM*, p. 36). While having some fun with his contending shepherds, Yeats piled up the visual details, trying to avoid abstraction and produce a picture. As in Turner's *Golden Bough,* whose subject is brought to mind by Colin's reference to the *Aeneid,* the landscape created by the shepherds' descriptions is ideal. In Yeats's terms, it is a "definite imagined region." "Definite" for Yeats never connotes "realistic," although he knew from Pre-Raphaelite painting that realistic details could serve imaginative art. Both Yeats's and Turner's regions are places with names: Yeats's, the subtitle tells us, is Arcady; Turner's, we know from Virgil is the Sibyl's grove near Lake Avernus. But neither presents an identifiable landscape. The sheep in Thernot's song browse by

1. J. M. W. Turner, *The Golden Bough* (first exhibited 1834). By permission of The Tate Gallery, London.

the water, their feet are cloven and the river sedge is ruddy, but these are not particular sheep, nor is the river a particular one. As in Turner's painting, the landscape is definite, but generalized.

Both Yeats and Turner elevate the general to the ideal through the transforming powers of light. The action of *The Island of Statues* takes place at dawn and dusk. Whereas in later poems Yeats exploits the symbolic significance of the half-light, here he seems most interested in the golden glow the rising sun casts over his scene. For one hundred lines Colin and Thernot describe a world "roll'd in light." The "blaze" of the daffodills in vale and dell, Colin tells us, reflects the "brazen sky," suffusing the landscape with the same golden light that Turner used to convey the ideality of his pastoral scene in *The Golden Bough*. There light softens the forms of jagged hills and hard stones, removing the harsh edge of ordinary experience.

The landscapes of both poem and painting are ideal—depictions of the Golden Age—but neither is free of the stamp of human history and imperfection. Yeats's Arcady "has experienced Clytemnestra, the 'fires of Troia,' and Dido," as Edward Engelberg has pointed out.[13] The sleepers Naschina frees at the end of the poem awaken into a world of change and death, a world with which she has already reckoned. While the moon casts the shadows of Almintor and the sleepers "*far across the grass*" at the play's close, Naschina stands "*shadowless*" (VP 679). Similarly, Turner's celebrants dance amid the ruins of previous civilizations, and beside the tree in the foreground a fox plays with a snake. Naschina's lack of shadow, the painting's ruins and snake, in their indication that even the Golden Age came after the Fall, suggest a symbolic impulse in poet and painter. For Turner, the impulse led to the "rich enigmas"[14] of his late paintings; for Yeats it led to the symbolic landscapes of his early verse.

[13]"'He Too Was in Arcadia': Yeats and the Paradox of the Fortunate Fall," in *In Excited Reverie: A Centenary Tribute to William Butler Yeats, 1865–1939*, ed. A. Norman Jeffares and K. G. W. Cross (London: Macmillan; New York: St. Martin, 1965), p. 80; hereafter cited as Engelberg.

[14]John Gage, "Turner and Stourhead: The Making of a Classicist?" *Art Quarterly*, 37 (1974), 75. For its overview of critical discussions of *The Golden Bough*, I am indebted to Martin Butlin and Evelyn Joll's *The Paintings of J. M. W. Turner* (New Haven: Yale University Press, 1977), I, 186.

In the epilogue to his poem, Yeats acknowledges that "the woods of Arcady are dead" (VP 64), leaving the poet only one recourse, as Engelberg (p. 85) has remarked: to keep the Golden Age "alive through poetry." Turner faced the same challenge in art, yet his depiction of the Golden Age differs from Yeats's in a way that suggests that he believed, as Yeats could not despite his efforts, that Arcady could be so preserved for men. Unlike *The Golden Bough,* Yeats's landscape in *The Island of Statues* does not achieve that quality which made the Claudian tradition famous: a sense of depth. Using Claude's formula, Turner placed the vanishing point in the center of the picture, framed the foreground with trees and ruins, and blended the mid-ground into the background, creating for the viewer the illusion of looking out over a vast expanse. The view, the painting implies, is limited only by the human eye's inability to see farther. Turner's use of perspective also gives the viewer the sense that he can step into the picture. Its space extends into his, making the painting's world and the viewer's world seem coextensive. The painting implies that modern man might easily enter the better world the Golden Age represents.

Yeats's early landscapes never give this sense of depth. In *The Island of Statues,* the relationships among the elements of the landscape are so vague that the reader cannot locate them in space. They give us a two-dimensional, not a three-dimensional, view. We know, for example, that "Over the lake the water-flowers / Drift and float" (VP 647), so we can place the flowers above the lake, but we do not know where the lake is in relation to Thernot, who describes it. Is it far away, or is it close by? Is it to the left or right of the shepherds, or behind them? When we do get a spatial word which suggests a third dimension, as in the "afar" in Colin's speech above, it describes where Clytemnestra saw the "signal of her lord's return," not the landscape Colin actually sees. The simile, of course, suggests that "vale and dell" are also "afar," but the vague sense of space that word conveys is made even more nebulous by its secondhand application to the present scene. Because we cannot place the details of the landscape with any sureness in space, they tend to sit vaguely next to each other, almost on a flat surface, instead of assuming their proper places in a world with depth as well as height and breadth.

This spatial vagueness, in addition to other features of *The Island of Statues,* denies the reader "access" to the ideal world of the poem. Its space is discontinous with his, and he cannot easily enter into its region. In Romantic and Victorian landscape poetry, there is frequently a speaker, an "I," with whom the reader stands or walks through the landscape, creating a sense of depth and giving the reader an entree into the poetic scene. The young Yeats rarely gives the reader such a guide.

The reader's exclusion from the ideal world of the poem betrays Yeats's often-noted uneasiness with man's potential for reclaiming the Golden Age (for example, Harper, p. 299). Turner's ideal world is at least a possibility for man; Yeats's never is, not even as a place of escape from the daily world. He might want his poem to be a region into which one can wander from the cares of life, but the poem itself undermines the goal.

Yeats's response to this difficulty determined one part of his poetic program for the 1890s. In an important letter to Katharine Tynan written in 1888, Yeats criticized her ballad on Kinsale and in the process revealed the direction his own poetic landscapes were to take: "We should make poems," he advised, "on the familiar landscapes we love, not the strange and rare and glittering scenes we wonder at" (L 99). Yeats sensed that his earlier landscapes offered worlds separate from both poet and reader—they were strange and inspired wonder, not love—and he sought to overcome the distance by turning to the more familiar, to Ireland. "When I first wrote," he recalled in 1908, "I went here and there for my subjects as my reading led me, and preferred to all other countries Arcadia and the India of romance, but presently I convinced myself . . . that I should never go for the scenery of a poem to any country but my own" (VP 843–44). The poems after *The Wanderings of Oisin* are often set in a specific Irish place, as in "The Lake Isle of Innisfree," the exemplary poem with which Yeats closed his letter of advice to Katharine Tynan. The cold, gray light of Sligo and the Rosses replaced the blazing gold Turner had brought from Italy.[15] Instead of the unfamiliar warmth and

[15]Gold was also one of the colors Yeats thought Shelley had brought from Italy: "when I found my verses too full of the reds and yellows Shelley gathered in Italy, I thought for two days of setting things right . . . by eating little and sleeping upon a board" (E&I 5).

lushness of a southern landscape, Yeats cultivated, he said, "an impression as of cold light and tumbling clouds" (Au 74). He did not mean his landscapes to record "things as they are," but he did want his readers to "wander from the cares of life" in an Irish region.

As the Irish scene localized the poems, its symbolic use universalized them, creating that tension between the particular and its large meaning that found perfection in such later poems as "The Tower." Despite the new specificity of place, the elements within Yeats's landscapes of the 1890s are strangely general and chosen for their symbolic significance. Whereas in *The Island of Statues* Yeats gave heightened meaning to the generalized landscape by casting the golden glow over all, here he composed his landscapes by selecting features which already, in themselves, possessed special significance. His occult studies and the collaboration with Edwin Ellis on an edition and explanation of Blake's works encouraged his growing belief in the symbol and taught him that the basic elements of the landscape—earth, water, air, and fire—carried inherent symbolic power.[16] He thus found he could use them and the various forms in which they appear—sea, wind, hills, stars, and so on—to compose a landscape whose features would individually and collectively resonate with meaning.

Symbolism created a more significant and more enduring connection between Yeats's poetry and the visual arts than the similarity of visual appearance that characterizes the relation of *The Island of Statues* and *The Golden Bough*. The essays of the 1890s bear out the implication of Yeats's statement "It is a natural conviction for a painter's son to believe that there may be a landscape that is symbolical of some spiritual condition"—that his ideas about the symbol in poetry were bound to its use in the visual arts. A surge of expressed interest in artists whose work was considered symbolic accompanied his major exploration of the symbol in a series of essays written between 1896 and 1900.[17] In addition to Blake

[16]See Richard Ellmann, *The Identity of Yeats*, 2d ed. (New York: Oxford University Press, 1964), pp. 26–37, and Allen R. Grossman, *Poetic Knowledge in the Early Yeats: A Study of The Wind Among the Reeds* (Charlottesville: University Press of Virginia, 1969), *passim*.

[17]"William Blake and His Illustrations to the *Divine Comedy*" (1896), which summarizes Blake's theory of the symbol—already puzzled out with Ellis's help in "The Symbolic System" in Volume I of *The Works of William Blake*—as background to

and the Pre-Raphaelites, Giotto, Orcagna, Tintoretto, Michelangelo, Beardsley, Whistler, Ricketts, Shannon, and Calvert all make an appearance. Yeats used their art to illustrate his ideas about symbol. More important, the essays make clear that Yeats's observations of the visual arts helped him formulate concepts of symbolic effects that he applied to poetry. In "Symbolism in Painting" (1898), he offered the following explanation of how the combination of personal and traditional symbols affected the viewer of Rossetti's paintings:

> If you paint a beautiful woman and fill her face, as Rossetti filled so many faces, with an infinite love, a perfected love, 'one's eyes meet no mortal thing when they meet the light of her peaceful eyes,' as Michelangelo said of Vittoria Colonna; but one's thoughts stray to mortal things, and ask, maybe, 'Has her lover gone from her, or is he coming?' or 'What predestinated unhappiness has made the shadow in her eyes?' If you paint the same face, and set a winged rose or a rose of gold somewhere about her, one's thoughts are of her immortal sisters, Piety and Jealousy, and of her mother, Ancestral Beauty, and of her high kinsmen, the Holy Orders, whose swords make a continual music before her face. [E&I 150]

Two years later, Yeats argued in "The Symbolism of Poetry" (1900) that intellectual and emotional symbols in a poem produced this result: "If I say 'white' or 'purple' in an ordinary line of poetry, they evoke emotions so exclusively that I cannot say why they move me; but if I bring them into the same sentence with such obvious intellectual symbols as a cross or a crown of thorns, I think of purity and sovereignty" (E&I 161). Just as the rose helped focus the symbolism of beautiful women in Rossetti's paintings, so the cross or crown of thorns would help the symbolism of colors in poetry.

The visual arts feature so prominently in Yeats's discussions of symbol in part because the perspective offered by another art facilitated the understanding of his own, and in part because the symbol

understanding his illustrations to Dante; "A Symbolic Artist and the Coming of Symbolic Art" (1898), which praises the work of the artist Althea Gyles; "Symbolism in Painting" (1898), which focuses on the Pre-Raphaelites and in its original form served as the introduction to the visionary artist W. T. Horton's *A Book of Images;* and, finally, "The Symbolism of Poetry" (1900), which addresses the problem in his own art.

naturally provided for the intersection of poetry and the visual arts. As an "object," the symbol, even when used in poetry, retains its attachment to the physical world. Yeats conceived of its physical nature as explicitly visual: "it entangles, in complex colours and forms," he wrote in 1898, "a part of the Divine Essence" (E&I 148). As critics of modern painting and poetry frequently note, the advent of symbolism historically effected a closer alliance between those two arts, a point Yeats implicitly asserted when he claimed in his discussion of the "coming of symbolic art," "I cannot separate art and literature in this" (UP2 134).

The symbol provided a meeting ground for poetry and the visual arts in two ways: first, the poet and painter could follow the same symbolic method even if the pictures produced differed; second, because symbols could be transferred from one medium to the other without losing power, poet and painter could use each other's motifs. While Yeats never "followed" any one artist or work of art, and drew his material and methods from a wide range of sources, the symbolic regions of the 1890s owe much to the visual arts he admired in both method and motif. Blake's woodcuts for Thornton's Virgil and the work of Samuel Palmer and Edward Calvert that they inspired, in particular, provided Yeats with the visual precedents for his new symbolic landscapes. Calvert especially interested Yeats, and a comparison of his early engraving *The Bride* (Fig. 2) and Yeats's "The Song of Wandering Aengus" can reveal some of the elements of Yeats's symbolic regions and the ways they are connected to the visual arts.

Edward Calvert and Samuel Palmer, who had been introduced to Blake by his patron John Linnell, gathered with several other young painters around the aging artist. They called themselves "the Ancients," in dedication to the vision of simple pastoral life depicted in the works of Blake that they most admired, the woodcut illustrations to Thornton's Virgil. Yeats praised Palmer's etchings and the early woodcuts and etchings of Calvert which show the influence of Blake's illustrations.[18] Yeats may have first learned

[18]Yeats disregarded Palmer's early sepia drawings done under Blake's direct influence—even though his friend Charles Ricketts had praised them (*Images,* p. 105)—perhaps because they were not prints like Blake's illustrations to Virgil. In later life, Yeats specifically admired Calvert's woodcuts (Au 550), but he probably did not, in fact, distinguish between them and the engravings because, as Raymond Lister has

of Calvert from Alexander Gilchrist's *Life of William Blake* which he read around 1881 (*Images,* p. 92). He certainly encountered his work in the course of his studies for the Ellis-Yeats *Blake,* which involved visits to the home of John Linnell's children, who owned many of Blake's manuscripts and pictures. Yeats's essays of the mid-1890s show that he had read *A Memoir of Edward Calvert, Artist, by His Third Son, Samuel,* published in 1893 and illustrated with many prints from the original plates and blocks.[19] By 1901 he had apparently gained a reputation as an expert on Calvert: the Unicorn Press commissioned him to write a book on the artist for its Artists' Library of Little Engravings series,[20] and when that fell through because of financial difficulties, Pamela Coleman Smith, an artist and friend of Yeats, asked him "to do a book on *Calvert*—with reproductions of the woodcuts" to be printed on her hand press (LTWBY 133). Yeats's interest in Calvert lasted throughout his life and is apparent in later poems and letters,[21] most notably in "Under Ben Bulben" where Yeats set him with Blake, Claude, and Richard Wilson (Claude's first English follower) as preservers of the quatrocento's "greater dream":

> When that greater dream had gone
> Calvert and Wilson, Blake and Claude,
> Prepared a rest for the people of God,
> Palmer's phrase . . .
>
> [VP 639]

---

noted, "In Calvert's dextrous hands, the two techniques become almost interchangeable" (*Edward Calvert* [London: G. Bell, 1962], pp. 77–78; hereafter cited as *EC*). The slides of Blake's, Palmer's and Calvert's works which Yeats collected for a 1918 lecture on Blake and his school include Calvert's engraving *The Sheep of His Pasture* as well as woodcuts. See T. R. Henn, *The Lonely Tower: Studies in the Poetry of W. B. Yeats* (London: Methuen, 1950), pp. 347–50, for a list of the slides.

[19]Yeats owned a signed copy of this book, as well as a copy of Calvert's *Ten Spiritual Designs* (Portland, Me.: Thomas Bird Mosher, 1913), which contains enlarged reproductions of Calvert's woodcuts, etchings, and lithographs. I am grateful to Miss Anne Yeats for making her father's library available to me.

[20]*Images,* p. 106. See also the "Preface" to Calvert's *Ten Spiritual Designs* for an account of this project and Thomas Bird Mosher's unsuccessful efforts to commission an essay from Yeats for this book (p. vii).

[21]See Marion Witt, "The Making of an Elegy: Yeats's 'In Memory of Major Robert Gregory,'" *Modern Philology,* 48 (Nov. 1950), 112–21, for the influence of Palmer and Calvert on Yeats's elegy.

2. Edward Calvert, *The Bride*. By courtesy of the Library of Congress.

The Bride, which Yeats knew from *A Memoir* and possibly also through Ricketts, who owned a copy of it,[22] shows that, like Turner, Calvert developed out of the Claudian tradition, as "Under Ben Bulben" suggests. His landscapes, however, like Yeats's in the 1890s, are symbolic. In both "The Song of Wandering Aengus" and *The Bride,* the landscape is definite but not specific, and is composed of elements chosen for their symbolic significance. Neither picture nor poem (VP 149–50) provides many details to identify the peculiar qualities of this landscape. We know nothing about the hazel wood except the fact of its existence, and the flowers by the bride's feet are so generalized as to be unidentifiable.[23] The elements of the landscapes clearly exist not for the pleasures of carefully recorded detail, but for the larger meanings they represent. The inscription to *The Bride* explains its explicitly Christian symbolism: OH GOD! THY BRIDE SEEKETH THEE. A STRAY LAMB IS LED TO THY FOLDS. The bunches of grapes (so ripe that juice drips from one), the bee hives, the flowers along the bride's path signify the fullness of earthly life blessed by divine favor. The stream of life, the well-marked paths leading to the fold, the striding shepherd and bride, naked in their innocence, all resonate with meaning. Although hardly Christian, Yeats's landscape is equally symbolic. The hazel wood, the stream, the "hollow" and "hilly" lands suggest the experience of physical, objective life through which Aengus, poet and lover, pursues the antithetical, subjective life represented by the glimmering girl. The tantalizing appearance of the subjective in the objective is repeated in the elements of the landscape. "*The hazel tree,*" as Yeats explained, "*was the Irish tree of Life or of Knowledge, and in Ireland it was doubtless, as elsewhere, the tree of the heavens*" (VP 177). The tree thus features in the physical world of Life and the Fall into Knowledge through which Aengus wanders, and anticipates the consummation of his pursuit in heaven. There, the tree, transformed, bears on one branch the silver and golden apples,[24] the union of

[22]*EC,* p. 94. In 1897 Ricketts published "A Note on Original Wood Engraving" in *The Pageant* (pp. 253–66), singling out Calvert for special praise (p. 263) and reproducing two of his woodcuts.

[23]Lister comments that "Calvert did not generally depict actual scenes" (*EC,* p. 20).

[24]"In his translation of *Kabbala Unveiled,* [MacGregor] Mathers explains that the

sun and moon. The fruits and the grass dappled by their combined lights signify the final union of objective and subjective, of Aengus and the glimmering girl.

Both Yeats and Calvert achieve concentration of symbolic power by careful definition of the elements of their landscapes: Yeats by selecting only a few details; Calvert by isolating each element with the "bounding line" he had learned about from Blake. Yeats's landscape here and in the other poems of the 1890s is spare compared to that of *The Island of Statues.* The stripping down of the landscape to hazel wood, stream, hollow and hilly lands automatically concentrates the meaning as fewer elements bear more symbolic weight. Calvert's scene, while simpler and more generalized than many of, say, Claude's, contains more detail than Yeats's, perhaps by the necessity of his medium. Although a symbolist, Calvert still worked within the tradition of representation, and the elements of his symbolic landscape needed to be connected into a recognizable picture. But outline provided the means of making forms stand out from their surrounding space, of isolating tree, bride, sheep for special attention just as Yeats isolated hazel wood, stream, and hills. The purpose of this technique, Blake taught both Yeats and Calvert, was not primarily to enhance the look of the picture, but to serve its symbolic purpose. As the "great and golden rule" of symbolic art, the "bounding line" showed, Yeats explained, that the artist had distinguished "the permanent and characteristic" (E&I 120–21) in the forms he drew—had, in other words, apprehended their universal, their symbolic, significance. Forms so delineated in art impressed that significance on their viewer, just as Yeats's selection of details did.

In addition to their symbolic method, "The Song of Wandering Aengus" and *The Bride* share symbolic motifs. The stream, the hills and hollows common to both show how easily the symbols of one art can also be those of another. While we cannot attribute Yeats's streams and hills to the influence of Calvert (they are too common in art and in Ireland), the half-light which pervades "The

---

typical Kabbalistic representation of the Tree of Life is an *apple tree,* which grows from the earth to the apex of heaven and bears the sun and moon for fruit": F. A. C. Wilson, *Yeats's Iconography* (New York: Macmillan, 1960), p. 250.

Song of Wandering Aengus" and so many other Yeats poems of the 1890s derives not only from the Romantic poets, but from Calvert and Palmer and Blake in the Virgil illustrations. The twilights in Blake's illustrations had so impressed Calvert and Palmer that a full sun rarely shines in their own pictures. Palmer's praise of the illustrations to Virgil focused on the effect of their half-light, and Yeats seized on Palmer's remarks, quoting them often, seconding their identification of light as the striking quality of the pictures: Palmer, Yeats explained, "has alone praised worthily these illustrations to the first Eclogue: 'There is in all such a misty and dreamy glimmer as penetrates and kindles the inmost soul and gives complete and unreserved delight, unlike the gaudy daylight of this world.'"[25] During the 1890s Palmer's word "glimmer" became a favorite with Yeats to describe in poems and essays that region or state in which "ordinary intelligence" is put away and the hidden shapes of another world, symbols, flicker into being, providing the dim light by which man seeks that truth which will be revealed in the full light at the Last Judgment. In his essay on Shelley, for example, Yeats explained, "The poet of essences and pure ideas must seek in the half-lights that glimmer from symbol to symbol" (E&I 87). Shelley's world, like Palmer's, Calvert's, Blake's in the Virgil illustrations and Yeats's in the poems of the 1890s most often glimmers with the half-light of the symbolic morning and evening stars.[26]

In both *The Bride* and "The Song of Wandering Aengus," the half-light of the star signifies that condition in which the earthly apprehends and approaches, but does not reach, the heavenly. The bride returns to the fold of the Lord in a landscape glimmering with the light of a large evening star, as Aengus catches the fish when "moth-like stars were flickering out" and pursues it, transformed into a girl who has taken on the glimmering light of the stars. The clearly marked paths of Calvert's pictures perhaps indicate a confidence that the bride's journey will return her to the fold, but Calvert has chosen to capture her while she still

[25]E&I 125. Yeats misquotes from A. H. Palmer, *The Life and Letters of Samuel Palmer, Painter and Etcher* (London: Seeley, 1892), pp. 15–16. "Misty" should read "mystic."

[26]For a discussion of Yeats's responses to Shelley's star, see George Bornstein, *Yeats and Shelley* (Chicago: University of Chicago Press, 1970), pp. 18–19, 48.

"seeketh," as the inscription says, leaving the outcome undecided. Yeats's poem makes clear that Aengus's quest will continue as long as the world as we know it exists. Until sun and moon become one, Aengus will wander hollow and hilly lands, as the bride follows her path, under a glimmering half-light.

The half-light of the stars in "The Song of Wandering Aengus" and *The Bride* unifies the scene, the function, Kenneth Clark reminds us, of light in much landscape painting (Clark, pp. 14–15 and *passim*). The starlight, as it glints off the sheep, the trees, the hills, the stream, the bride and shepherd, visually ties together the objects in Calvert's landscape. The uniformity of texture the starlight creates, furthermore, conveys Calvert's belief that man and nature are naturally one, a belief reflected also in the companionable glance between the sheep and the bride, in the flowers around her head and in the thatched roof whose curves and hollows blend in with those of the hills. The glimmer of light through "The Song of Wandering Aengus" also creates a unity of scene as the white moths and the silver trout echo the "flickering" of the "moth-like stars." But whereas Calvert's light binds man to nature in an innocent vision of harmony, Yeats's ties nature to the supernatural which together conspire to seduce and frustrate man.[27] The "glimmering girl" takes on the flickering light of the stars, allying her to the natural world, as do the apple blossoms in her hair (like the flowers encircling the bride's head) and her assimilation by the "brightening air" of dawn. The girl's glimmering light and the flowers in her hair lure Aengus to the chase; her disappearance contrived by nature prevents its successful end.

Yeats found in Calvert the visual depiction of a symbolic region in which one might wander. Calvert's use of perspective, like Turner's, invites us into his scene. Yeats himself recognized that our world and that of Calvert's pictures seem coextensive, as he indicated when, in later life, he wrote Olivia Shakespear about his house at Rathfarnham, "This little creeper-covered farm-house might be in a Calvert woodcut" (L 799). But Yeats had difficulty during the 1890s creating in his poems a region that would similar-

[27]For a survey of the contest between man and nature in Yeats's early verse, see David Daiches, "The Earlier Poems: Some Themes and Patterns," in *In Excited Reverie*, pp. 48–67.

ly welcome his audience. Although the spatial relations in these poems are often as unclear as they had been in *The Island of Statues* ("I went out" gives little sense of direction or distance to "The Song of Wandering Aengus," and where is the floor on which Aengus lays the silver trout?), there is a greater sense of depth. The glimmering girl's fading through the brightening air suggests not only that the light of day obscures her gentler light, but that, as she runs, she disappears into the distance. And yet, as the frequently applied epithets "remote" and "vague" indicate, the poetic worlds of these poems are not places in which readers can easily wander. The problem was not that Yeats doubted, as he had when he pictured the Golden Age, that the world depicted in the poem was one man could inhabit (according to Blake, man lived his daily life in a symbolic world, and Yeats believed that, so why should the symbolic world of the poem not be a congenial place?). The problem was rather in the nature of literary symbolism as Yeats then practiced it, a problem Calvert did not encounter in his visual symbolism. In Calvert's landscapes a tree may be a symbol, but it is first a tree. Calvert included trees in his landscapes because of their symbolic meanings, yet the trees as they appear in his pictures resulted from observation of nature, especially that around Shoreham where the Ancients had gathered. In this way, Calvert's immediate personal experience always entered his art. For Yeats in the early poetry, however, a tree is first a symbol, and then a tree. Despite his vow to take his scenery from Ireland, the hazel wood in "The Song of Wandering Aengus" did not exist for Yeats first as a grove of hazel trees that he saw in Sligo. In his desire to provide a refuge "from the cares of life," he saw the symbolic value of his landscapes before (or without) seeing them as landscapes. This is the difference between the regions of the 1890s poems and those of the later poems where, for example, the tree seen from the top of the tower is first exactly that, and then—or simultaneously—a symbol. In Yeats's finest poems the landscape as symbol never takes precedence over the landscape as experienced. Readers frequently remark the greater "immediacy" of the later poems, the almost palpable quality of their images, suggesting that the poetic regions are neither vague nor remote.

Yeats learned slowly that his poetry required "self portraiture," by which he meant not just autobiography but that sense of the presence of the artist's experience of the world, a sense inherent in Calvert's art. Paradoxically, he came to that lesson and to that painterly metaphor for poetry only after rejecting the painter's art as primary model. Trying to understand the remoteness of his poetic regions, Yeats decided that picture-making was to blame for shutting out the reader. "When the tide of life sinks low," he explained in 1904, "there are pictures, as in the *Ode on a Grecian Urn* and in Virgil at the plucking of the Golden Bough. The pictures make us sorrowful. We share the poet's separation from what he describes" (Ex 163). Although Yeats implied that picture-making was necessary in some part to "the greatest works" (Ex 163), he had discovered that he had followed the painter's art as far as he could and was not satisfied. Unlike Turner and Calvert, he had failed to create regions accessible to his readers. He now looked to an art in which the world of the audience and the poetic world would be *literally* coextensive. "In Ireland, where the tide of life is rising, we turn, not to picture-making, but to the imagination of personality—to drama, gesture" (Ex 163). Practical experience with the three-dimensional art of the theater led to self portraiture—the imagination of personality—in the later poems, to the creation of regions at once symbolic and accessible.

I Have Longed for Such a Country: The Cuchulain Cycle as Peking Opera

RICHARD LONDRAVILLE

The setting of Fu-Hsing dramatic academy of Taiwan is one to reinforce the image of "youths of the pear garden," the name that has designated Chinese actors since the eighth century.[1] The school is located in the suburb of Neihu, a forty-five-minute bus ride from the center of Taipei. The buildings are comparatively new and well maintained, and there is an ample amount of open space, that most precious of commodities in Taiwan. The mountains at the academy's back and the small lake at its flank further the impression of isolation. My experiences in the Orient have been with big-city universities, and Fu-Hsing made me nostalgic for my home in northern New York.

I was going to the school for an interview with Professor Tai Chi-Hsia, one of the most important performers and teachers of Peking opera in Taiwan,[2] to discuss the possibility of staging the

[1]Chinese actors have been so called since the Emperor Ming Huang (712–755) established a college for the training of young vocalists, musicians, and dancers: Josephine Huang Hung, *Classical Chinese Plays* (Taipei: 'Mei Yai Publications, 1972), p. 4; hereafter cited as Huang.

[2]Professor Tai's career in the theatre started in mainland China when she was seven. For the next ten years she traveled extensively in Southeast Asia and played before Chinese audiences in the Philippines, Singapore, and elsewhere. She was acclaimed a "Young Phoenix," or rising star. Back in China, at the age of seventeen, she organized her own troupe and performed in Shanghai, Hankow, and other large cities, where her previous success in Southeast Asia was duplicated. In a nation-wide contest for theatrical talent she won the title "Queen of Chinese Opera." In 1948, Professor Tai came to Taiwan, where she and her troupe staged a series of island-wide performances. Later

Cuchulain plays of Yeats in the style of the Chinese drama. As I walked across the campus, I noticed students strolling on the grounds who seemed to range in age from seven or eight through the late teens. My interpreter, Fang Po, asked where Professor Tai might be found, and we were directed to the theatre building. When we arrived, we found a young man standing outside the entrance and quite uninhibitedly shouting at the top of his lungs. Fang Po waited for him to take a breath and asked again for directions. He replied graciously, took another breath, and resumed shouting, making the open-mouthed picture of Elvis on his shirt vibrate in harmony.

It was an omen. For the production I had in mind needed actors and crew who could as easily slip from one culture to another. I wanted the Chinese drama to serve as a foundation on which I could present Yeats's Cuchulain plays as a coherent cycle. That I received the cooperation I needed from individuals and institutions to realize this plan seems, in retrospect, close to impossible.

I needed Professor Tai's help to train my cast in the acting style of the Peking opera. Her students at Fu-Hsing would have been excellent for the physical requirements of the roles, but their English was not good enough. The actors whom I wished her to train were chosen from the English department of my host institution, National Taiwan Normal University, where I was spending the year as a visiting professor. These young people had little or no exposure to the theatre but demonstrated an enthusiasm for the project that compensated for their inexperience. I also needed the facilities of Fu-Hsing for costumes, properties, and a stage. (The problem of costuming appropriately in the style of the Peking opera will be appreciated when one learns that the simpler costumes take an accomplished seamstress approximately ten workdays to complete.)

When I told Professor Tai about my project, she was polite but less than enthusiastic. It was difficult for her to imagine how the

---

her interest in the screen prompted her to play a leading role in a number of films, including *The Lady General*, which was awarded a Diploma of Honor at the 1957 Third Special International Exhibition of Motion Pictures in Rome. In 1963 she visited the United States, where she produced and acted in several plays at different institutions, among them MIT and the Fashion Institute of New York.

mixing of Yeats and the Chinese drama would work, but she agreed to suspend judgment until she understood better what I had in mind. One aspect of the plan which attracted her was the opportunity to train college students in the fundamentals of her art. The least that would happen, as she saw it, was that these young people would become more appreciative of their own culture. And so, with Professor Tai at least provisionally in my corner, the work began.

In a note to *The Only Jealousy of Emer* Yeats wrote: "In writing these little plays I knew that I was creating something which could only fully succeed in a civilization very unlike ours. I think they should be written for some country where all classes share in a half-mythological, half-philosophical folk-belief which the writer and his small audience lift into a new subtlety. All my life I have longed for such a country" (VPl 566). This statement has always intrigued me, and has remained for me the focus of the problem of staging Yeats's drama. I have done considerable research concerning Yeats's debt to the Japanese *Noh,* and I have never had difficulty reconciling the aesthetic and theoretical similarities between them. But the practical problems of incorporating Noh technique into his plays are formidable.

At the Hawk's Well has nonetheless been adapted and performed as a Noh play in Japanese for Japanese audiences,[3] and it has long seemed to me that at least some of Yeats's other plays might translate as well for another culture that had a strong tradition of folk-drama. Could *A Full Moon in March,* I wondered, to use an exaggerated example, succeed in Bali staged in the style of the Balinese theatre? In 1975, during a sabbatical year in Japan, I attended several performances of the Noh in an attempt to improve upon the naive impressions I had received twenty years previously. In many ways I was fortunate that in my initial contact with the Noh I had been completely naive, so that my experience was not colored by any guidebook preconception. Although I had then understood very little of what was happening on the stage, I had been fascinated by the spectacle and mesmerized by the combination of the dance, music, and chanting.

[3]Shotaro Oshima, "Yeats and the Japanese Theatre," *Threshold,* 19 (Autumn 1965), 100.

That reaction has not altered substantially, although subsequent study has given me a greater appreciation of the form. In 1975 I also attended performances of the *Kabuki* and *Bunraku* and noted in each of them theatrical elements similar to the Noh. The Kabuki, for example, though it seemed to offer a greater range of movement for the actor, retained a stylized manner of acting which, combined with the gorgeous costumes and striking makeup, heightened the effect of otherworldliness. In short, it seemed to me that Yeats's idea of a theatre owed more to Japanese (or even Oriental) drama in general than to Noh in particular.

Had it been possible during the time I spent in Japan in 1975, I would have attempted to stage one of Yeats's plays in the style of Noh or the Kabuki. I had in mind *The Dreaming of the Bones,* which seems to me closest in feeling to the spirit of the Noh of the ghosts, the type that deals with supernatural beings.

Another special interest of mine is Yeats's treatment of the Irish hero Cuchulain. Yeats is clearly obsessed with the multiple meanings Cuchulain has for Ireland and for his own life. Cuchulain enters his consciousness in the tales he was told as a child about the great Ulster champion of the Red Branch, and appears again and again throughout Yeats's poetry and drama, finally in *The Death of Cuchulain,* written just before Yeats's death.

The five plays which constitute the Cuchulain cycle are *On Baile's Strand, The Green Helmet* (a verse revision of *The Golden Helmet*), *At the Hawk's Well, The Only Jealousy of Emer,* and *The Death of Cuchulain.* It is quite clear that Yeats intended that the plays be considered as a unit. He wrote in a note to *On Baile's Strand*: "It is one of a cycle of plays dealing with Cuchulain, with his friends and enemies. One of these plays will have Aoife as its central character, and the principal motive of another will be the power of the witches over Cuchulain's life" (VPl 526). It is also evident that he considered his Noh the means that would enable him to complete his Cuchulain plays. When he had finished *At the Hawk's Well* he wrote, "When this play and its performance run as smoothly as my skill can make them, I shall hope to write another of the same sort and so complete a dramatic celebration of the life of Cuchulain planned long ago" (E&I 221–22).

Yeats did not complete the cycle until *The Death of Cuchulain* in

1939, so the plays encompass his whole dramatic range, and seldom has a playwright demonstrated a wider range over his dramatic career. Thus the aspiring producer of Yeats's cycle is faced with a considerable problem of style. The near-Elizabethan mode of *On Baile's Strand* does not jibe with the Noh techniques of *At the Hawk's Well* and *The Only Jealousy of Emer,* and *The Death of Cuchulain* introduces new elements. The farcical elements of *The Green Helmet* do not fit well with the serious heroic atmosphere of the other plays. The usual method of production is to present the plays in their complete versions, following the chronology of Cuchulain's life. The five plays were presented this way by the Dublin University players in 1965.[4] Reg Skene presented the entire cycle in one evening in 1969 because, he wrote, he was "convinced that the major patterns of meaning in the plays become apparent only when they are considered together."[5] In 1978 Robert O'Driscoll presented these five plays, also in a single evening, at the University of Toronto. I agree that the plays need to be presented together in order that their full power be understood, but I remain uneasy that their different styles might detract from the unity of the cycle. There is also the problem of time. If all the plays are presented in a single evening, the audience must remain in a state of tension for more than four hours. In this one important element, at least, an entire evening of the Cuchulain cycle seems contrary to the effect Yeats desired, the effect of poetic intensity which can be felt at the climax of each of these plays.

In 1971 I attempted a solution to these problems in my production of *At the Hawk's Well, The Only Jealousy of Emer,* and *The Death of Cuchulain* at SUNY Potsdam. I chose these three because they roughly approximated Cuchulain's life story, and because I thought the styles similar enough to fit together. I used an auditorium which held approximately eighty people in a semicircular seating arrangement. The actors entered and exited through the audience, and the only lighting was the normal incandescent lighting of the room, switched on and off at the beginning and ending of each play, and at the black-outs in *The Death of Cuchulain.*

[4]Anthony Bradley, *William Butler Yeats* (New York: Frederick Ungar, 1979), p. 191.
[5]Reg Skene, *The Cuchulain Plays of W. B. Yeats: A Study* (New York: Columbia University Press, 1974), p. x.

The production combined the efforts of the faculty and students of several departments: the art department designed the costumes and masks, the music department wrote and performed the score, the dance department choreographed the dances, and the English department provided the actors and direction.

Although the production was well received (it was later televised), some things about it were disappointing. I especially regretted that I could find no place for the action of *On Baile's Strand*. The confrontation and battle between Cuchulain and his son seemed to me essential to a full understanding of the cycle, yet I could find no way to insert it without violating the mood of the other three plays. Also, the climactic scene in which Cuchulain fights the wave occurs offstage. I maintain that this scene demands to be danced, yet there is no dancing called for in *On Baile's Strand*.

The production also had some internal flaws. The masking and the costumes seemed effective to us, for we tried to follow Yeats's directions; but no one in the audience was able to grasp their significance until we explained them after the fact. The gold and silver motif of Fand's costume, the reasons for which were dazzlingly clear to us, did not have much meaning for the audience. They were pleased with the theatricality, but they saw little or no connection to Yeats's dramatic symbolism. Another problem was the mixture of acting styles. (Although this is in part a fault of the director, Yeats himself had difficulties with his actors on this score, as James Flannery points out.[6]) It is difficult for an actor trained in realistic techniques to accommodate the rhythms of speech and movement appropriate for Yeats's plays. What I ended with was a compromise between what I had imagined and what was possible given the resources at my disposal. Certainly every director must face this problem with nearly every production he or she attempts, but staging Yeats presents very particular difficulties. The director must create an iconography consistent with Yeats's vision and still accessible to a reasonably informed audience. No matter how carefully he has considered costuming

[6]James W. Flannery, *W. B. Yeats and the Idea of the Theatre: The Early Abbey Theatre in Theory and Practice* (New Haven: Yale University Press, 1976), pp. 191–211.

and movement, for example, the play will fail unless the audience can comprehend his ideas. And since even the most informed modern audience has little practice in viewing nonrealistic plays, there is not much hope for more than a surface appreciation. Moreover, even if a director does come up with a coherent production consistent with Yeats's dramaturgy, carrying these ideas forward from one production to another is extremely difficult, because of the differences in dramatic style from play to play. Yeats offered a partial solution to this problem when he suggested that some of the masks for *At the Hawk's Well* be used again in *The Dreaming of the Bones*: "The beautiful mask of Cuchulain may, I think, serve for Dervorgilla, and if I write plays and organize performances on any scale and with any system, I shall hope for a small number of typical masks, each capable of use in several plays. The face of the speaker should be as much a work of art as the lines that he speaks or the costume that he wears, that all may be as artificial as possible. Perhaps in the end one would write plays for certain masks" (VPl 1305).

If we still had a body of myth in our culture, known by everyone not merely through books but through oral tradition and ritual, producing these plays would be much easier. But it was the very lack of such a myth that prompted Yeats to write as he did and to go to the Noh play for his model. I do not mean here to question the central importance of the Noh to Yeats's drama. Quite the contrary; I believe that Yeats's introduction to the Noh through Pound and Fenollosa changed his drama absolutely, and that all his plays after 1916 show this change. The many variations that Yeats was able to build on the Noh form after 1916 illustrate its flexibility and suitability for his protean imagination. What have been termed his "mystery plays" and "morality" plays, for example, do not embody a new form, but are a logical extension of the Noh. Yeats needed a drama in which he could show a spiritual rather than a temporal reality, and he found it in the Noh. Leonard Nathan says: "When the supernatural order appeared on stage in *The Only Jealousy of Emer* it could not by any rationalization be passed off as a symbol for psychological or sociological realities: the supernatural, in the last plays, is the supernatural or the spiritual reality either in the self or beyond it, no more and no less. This achievement cannot be claimed for the earlier plays."[7]

Plays of the latter part of Yeats's career do not, it is true, follow the Noh model as closely as, for example, does *The Dreaming of the Bones*. It is reasonable to think that when the Noh was a fresh discovery, his work would be most like the model, and that, as Yeats continued to write, his ideas would evolve. It has been argued, however, that Yeats lacked understanding of the Japanese Noh.[8] But while it is true that without a knowledge of Japanese it would be difficult entirely to comprehend the form, Yeats's scholarship was not limited to what he learned from Pound. According to Hiro Ishibashi, he was also aware of Arthur Waley's book *The Nō Plays of Japan* (1921), and D. Suzuki's *Essays in Zen Buddhism* (first series, 1927). From the first book he expanded his technical knowledge of the Noh, and from the second he learned some of the vital elements of Japanese aesthetics.

His letters to Suzuki and Shotaro Oshima[9] also make it clear that the Noh in particular and the Japanese aesthetic in general were of interest to Yeats until the last. It seems reasonable to assume that the role of the Noh in his plays was not finished by the early twenties, but continued to be important as his dramaturgy developed. Thus the Old Man in *The Death of Cuchulain* delivers a prologue in which he reestablishes Yeats's debt to the Japanese Noh and restates the aesthetic principles that had guided Yeats's drama since 1916. The prologue does not serve to expound the action of the play, but instead constitutes a statement of dramatic theory—Yeats's last such statement.[10]

One of the most important aspects of the Japanese Noh for Yeats was its connection with tradition, with the *Spiritus Mundi*. In the slow, stately grace of the actors and the incantatory power of the verse he found qualities that had been missing from Occidental

[7]Leonard Nathan, *The Tragic Drama of William Butler Yeats: Figures in a Dance* (New York: Columbia University Press, 1965), p. 252.

[8]For the best development of this argument, see Yasuko Stucki, "Yeats's Drama and the Nō: A Comparative Study in Dramatic Theories," *Modern Drama*, 9 (1966), 101–22.

[9]Oshima's correspondence with Yeats is discussed in the former's book, *W. B. Yeats and Japan* (Tokyo: Hokuseido, 1965).

[10]See John Unterecker, "The Shaping Force in Yeats's Plays," *Modern Drama*, 7 (1964), 349.

drama for centuries. He wanted these qualities for his own plays, but realized that to make them viable he had to create a tradition. The myth that Yeats created did not spring completely from any one culture, but it contained elements that were widely familiar; Cuchulain, though grounded in Irish legend, has a universal appeal, and the spiritual doctrines that appear in his myth have a variety of antecedents and parallels.

The Japanese debt to Chinese aesthetics has been well documented, and the two dramatic traditions have substantial correspondences.[11] I am not claiming that Yeats was influenced by Chinese drama, but elements of Oriental theatre are central to his plays, and I believe one could expect, as I did, that a performance of Yeats's plays in this style would elicit the same general response from a Chinese audience as would one of their own dramas.

The history of the Chinese drama begins with the emperor Ming Huang of the T'ang dynasty, who supposedly was much impressed by a group of performers he saw on a trip he took to the palace of Jade on the moon. When he returned to earth he established a college for the training of young people as musicians, vocalists, and dancers.[12] Drama in something like its present form seems to have come into existence during the Mongol dynasty of the thirteenth century, and the dominant form today, popularly known as Peking opera, had its origins toward the middle of the Manchu or Ch'ing dynasty, and flourished under the patronage of emperor Ch'ien Lung (1736–1795) (Huang, p. 7). The Chinese drama one sees today, although it continues to evolve, has much in common with that of the nineteenth century.[13] Attending performances in the fall of 1982, I noticed many similarities between Chinese drama and Yeatsian Noh, or more precisely, correspondences between the two forms which would allow me to adapt the Cuchulain cycle to the style of the Peking opera.

[11]Faubion Bowers states that Japanese drama came originally from India through China and Korea. The lion dance is an important feature of both *Noh* and *Kabuki*, and the lion is not native to Japan: *Japanese Theatre* (New York: Hermitage House, 1952), pp. 7–8; hereafter cited as Bowers.

[12]Herbert A. Giles, *A History of Chinese Literature* (New York: D. Appleton, 1923), p. 257.

[13]Leonard C. Pronko, *Theatre East and West: Perspectives Toward a Total Theatre* (Los Angeles: University of California Press, 1967), p. 44.

Since Yeats was always aware of the power of the unadorned word, it is not remarkable that early in his dramatic career he became dissatisfied with the scenery of the theatre as he knew it, and turned from flats and paint to description for creating his scene. Even such a relatively realistic play as *The Countess Cathleen* shows this quality in its scenic directions:

> Scene I. *A room with lighted fire, and a door into the open air, through which one sees, perhaps, the trees of a wood, and these trees should be painted in a flat colour upon a gold or diapered sky. The walls are of one colour. The scene should have the effect of missal painting* [VPl 5]

In earlier versions of the play Yeats had set the scene more conventionally, with more detailed description, and a particularized wood of "*oak, pine, hazel, and quicken*" (VPl 5). He was a constant reviser, and the relatively simple setting of the last version of *The Countess Cathleen* reflects a tendency toward the elimination of specific detail which became more important as Yeats matured as a dramatist. He wanted scenery to complement the play, not dominate it. In a note to *Calvary* he demonstrated his satisfaction at having removed a considerable impediment to the full realization of his dramatic vision: "It has been a great gain to get rid of the scenery, to substitute for a crude landscape painted upon canvas three performers who, sitting before the wall or a patterned screen, describe landscape or event" (VPl 415). Instead of the particularized settings of the earlier plays, we read in *At the Hawk's Well* that "*the stage is any bare space before a wall against which stands a patterned screen*" (VPl 398). The screen represents no particular wood or room, but is literally a place before which the actors play.

Such scenery is in the mind of the audience, differing as each individual interprets it. Anyone who has listened to a radio play can appreciate this effect, even for a realistic setting. In the non-realistic Yeatsian Noh it has even greater power. By eliminating realistic scenery Yeats was able to establish the primacy of poetry and movement in his drama. If the chorus described the background for his plays, the tragedy of Cuchulain could not be diluted by a clumsy scene-painter. Once he learned the benefits of such economy Yeats never forgot it; he was always careful to maintain an abstraction and simplicity, which is still evident in the complete direction for the setting of *The Death of Cuchulain: "A bare stage of any period. A very old man looking like something out of mythology"* (VPl 1051).

The scenery of the Chinese stage is minimal, and the principal properties, a table and chairs, can represent almost anything described or mimed by the actors. Certain positions of these properties are traditional, however, and allow the audience to identify settings. A table and chairs, placed at the rear of the stage and ordinarily covered in embroidered red silk, let us know that the scene is inside a house. In other positions they represent a wall, a bed, a throne, or a mountain. "Small flags adorned with fish, surging waves, or black lines announce storms, high waves and floods. Bits of white paper tied on a stick held by a prop man are flakes of snow that harass the movements of troops as they struggle through huge drifts. . . . Four foot soldiers parading back and forth, carrying banners that represent thousands of men, may be an emperor's entire army" (Huang, p. 7).

In staging the Cuchulain cycle, I used these stage properties almost without alteration. There was a stylized picture of a hawk on the back curtain of the stage. Aoife sat on a chair at stage center, and six dancers folded and unfolded two blue cloths, each of which measured about four by twenty feet. When the play was performed on a stage that had steps leading to the audience, the dancers folded the cloths in the aisles.

The major difference between my Taiwan production and the earlier one was in the treatment of *On Baile's Strand*. As mentioned above, I found in 1971 no place for the play, yet I felt that it was needed, and that the fight between Cuchulain and his son and Cuchulain's fight with the sea present extraordinary opportunities for dance, though Yeats has both of these scenes occur offstage.

In the Taiwan production, *On Baile's Strand* opens with Musicians kneeling at the rear of the stage, gently undulating the blue cloths to suggest the sea. Another Musician enters and delivers a stylized synopsis of the play to the point at which Cuchulain, entering, encounters his son. Their ensuing dialogue culminates in a sword fight in which Cuchulain kills his son, learns his identity, then goes mad and fights the sea. He turns to the rear of the stage

The Musicians folding and unfolding the cloths at the beginning of *The Only Jealousy of Emer*. Photo by W. Hsu.

and draws his sword against the undulating blue cloths, while the Musicians envelop him. The Fool describes what is happening, and with his line, "the waves have mastered him" (VPl 524), Cuchulain falls and the Musicians gently drop the cloths and exit. It seems to me that the last lines spoken by the Blind Man about stealing the bread from the ovens are thus rendered even more effective than in the original staging.

The blue cloths are used again in *The Only Jealousy of Emer* as the Musicians open the play. As they recite their lines, the dancers move the cloths in a way which reveals Emer sitting beside the entranced Cuchulain, who is partially obscured behind a drawn drape.

In *The Death of Cuchulain* I used life-sized Chinese masks mounted on poles to represent the heads of Cuchulain's opponent. The audience was able to distinguish between his honorable opponents and those who were "of no account" by the colors used in the masks. Cuchulain's severed head repeated the pattern of his makeup. I used the Chinese traditions of costume, makeup, and masking with little alteration. Having characters immediately identified by the audience in *At the Hawk's Well* was an effect Yeats would have appreciated. Cuchulain was dressed as a *Wu-sheng,* a young, successful, beardless general. For the later plays he wore a *man-jan,* or full beard, first black to denote middle age in *On Baile's Strand* and *The Only Jealousy of Emer,* then grey in *The Death of Cuchulain.*[14] Although Cuchulain is traditionally presumed to be in his late twenties when he died, in Yeats's cycle he seems to be aging along with the poet. Bricriu is quite clearly a *Ching,* a villainous magician, and Aoife is a *Wu-tan,* or martial lady. Emer was dressed as *Cheng-tan,* a virtuous queen, and Eithne Inguba as a *Hua-tan,* a young and flirtatious woman (Arlington, p. 64). When they appear thus together at the beginning of *The Only Jealousy of Emer,* the audience knows what to expect from them.

There is traditional masklike makeup for most of the major roles in Chinese opera; that is, famous characters require particular combinations of colors and lines. But there is a general symbolism of

[14]Lewis Charles Arlington, *The Chinese Drama from the Earliest Times until Today . . .* (Shanghai: Kelly & Walsh, 1930), pp. 64, 97; hereafter cited as Arlington.

Emer and Bricriu in *The Only Jealousy of Emer*. Photo by W. Hsu.

color which is understood by the informed audience. "Red, for example, generally denotes loyalty, sacredness, or some other divine quality. Purple indicates loyalty to a lesser degree than red. Black indicates good but rather uncouth characters. Blue shows that the individual is of tiger-like ferocity, crafty, haughty, etc. Yellow shows all the qualities of blue, but to a lesser degree. Green indicates an unstable, unreliable character. Orange and pale-grey indicate old age" (Arlington, p. 107). In addition, the *Ch'ou* or comic role is identified by a roughly circular patch of white accented with black lines around the eyes. The Fool and the Blind Man are such types in the Cuchulain plays.

This tradition seems particularly appropriate, for Yeats was always fascinated by the idea of masking, especially the idea of mask in occult literature. The masking he used in his plays became, like most of his symbols, rich in associations that transcend times and cultures. In 1910 he wrote: "We shall express personal emotion through ideal form, a symbolism handled by the generations, a mask from whose eyes the disembodied looks, a style that remembers many masters that it may escape contemporary suggestion" (E&I 243). Yeats was able to use the mask in his plays to make of this early metaphor literal dramatic truth. He made some use of masks before 1916; there are "dark-faced" characters in *Deirdre,* and the Fool and the Blind Man of *On Baile's Strand* have their features "*made grotesque and extravagant by masks*" (VPl 459). But not until *At the Hawk's Well* does the mask become an integral rather than incidental part of his drama. "The immobility and austerity of the mask substitute for flesh an artifact, a dead face which is the more alive, like the golden bird of Byzantium, because it is unchanging and because it is liberated from time and the sensual music."[15]

There were practical and dramatic as well as occult and symbolic reasons for Yeats's use of the mask. The Pound-Fenollosa reactions reinforced for him some of his earlier ideas concerning the restrictions of action: "We must get rid of everything that is restless, everything that draws the attention away from the sound of the voice, or from the few moments of intense expression, whether

[15]Peter Ure, *W. B. Yeats* (New York: Grove, 1964), p. 90.

that expression is through the voice or through the hands; we must from time to time substitute for the movements that the eye sees the nobler movements that the heart sees, the rhythmical movements that seem to flow up into the imagination from some deeper life than that of the individual soul" (Ex 109).

When Yeats discovered that in the Noh masks were used to allow the audience quickly to identify the type of character represented, he no longer needed to depend upon the limitations of an actor's expression. The mask also aided in removing Yeats's art from the world of objective reality; there is no living face to remind the audience of the actor's humanity. The mask is fixed, as the player's character is fixed; there can be no development of character in "a deep," a moment of life which is essentially climax. I finally understood Yeats's insistence upon the mask while I was watching a student production of *Calvary*. Since the play was simply an acting exercise, the actors used no masks. It was especially incongruous to watch the student who played Christ; for we all have an idealized picture of Christ, and no human face will satisfy us. We may not know exactly how Christ looked, but we know he did not look like *that*.

The students who acted in my Taiwan production experienced a startling transformation when they were made up by the staff at Fu-Hsing. Even those in the simplest makeup, that of the Musicians, did not recognize one another, and the young man who played the Ching role of Bricriu seemed truly to be another order of being.

In his late plays Yeats appears to be working toward still different functions of his dramatic mask, as is evidenced by the severed head of *A Full Moon in March* and the black parallelograms of *The Death of Cuchulain*. At this point, he has clearly gone beyond the techniques he developed from his study of the Japanese Noh. One of the possibilities these disembodied heads suggest is their complete dissociation from the mask worn by the actor, which can thus still function as it did in earlier plays. Clearly, also, Yeats is moving toward the abstract: "no wood-carving can look as well as a parallelogram of painted wood" (VPl 1052). I chose to modify the black parallelograms to stylized representations of Chinese face-painting, placed on poles, for to do otherwise would have been too great a break with the tradition of the Chinese drama.

Yeats felt that most of the music he heard in the early twentieth century seemed in direct competition with the words spoken by the actors. His ideal, as he stated in *The King's Threshold,* was "to mingle words and notes together / So artfully that all the Art's but Speech / Delighted with its own music (VPl 257). Elsewhere he wrote: "The human voice can only become louder by becoming less articulate, by discovering some new musical sort of roar or scream. As poetry can do neither, the voice must be freed from this competition and find itself among little instruments" (E&I 223).

"Speech delighted with its own music" was the effect Yeats sought in his plays, but he had difficulty finding a way to produce that effect. When the music played more than a complementary role in his drama, the drama itself was changed into something different. Witness, for example, *Fighting the Waves,* an adaptation of *The Only Jealousy of Emer*: Yeats tells us that the play becomes a mere vehicle for George Antheil's music (VPl 567). In the Peking opera, although the volume is at times overwhelming for Western tastes, music is intended to complement the lyric and action.

The music I chose for the cycle represented another compromise, aimed at keeping the spirit of Chinese drama's musical accompaniment without overpowering Yeats's words. In my opinion, most of the *wen,* or civil music traditional in Peking opera, was not suited for Yeats's plays. The string and wind instruments of the wen are intended to accompany singing, and since there were to be no songs as such in the cycle, I decided to omit that type of music. I did use some *wu,* or military music: the percussion instruments used (the small and large gongs called *ta-lo* and *hsiao-lo,* the cymbals, or *shui-ch'a* and the large drums, or *t'ang-ku*) seemed appropriate accompaniment for some of the dances and for battle interludes. For the most part, both wen and wu are too overpowering for the effect Yeats wished.

The "little instruments" I chose for the production were the bamboo flute or *hsiao,* the lute, or *p'i-p'a,* and the zither, or *guu-jeng*. Through the help of my assistant, Fang Po, I learned that many Chinese folk tunes were appropriate. The dance of Fand, for example, has an almost exact counterpart in a Chinese sprite's dance with a magic wand, and Emer's dance in *The Death of Cuchulain* is matched by the song which tells of the sorrow of Queen Hsiang.

The place of dance in Yeats's plays is, of course, central. Since dance involves the whole body, since it is both pictorial and sculptural, it is the ideal medium to bridge the gap between the time and space arts. Dancing becomes not alone the quintessence of the arts, but the culmination of them all, a spontaneous manifestation of an inward emotion. The images of the dancer as a unified personality and the dance as a unified activity so permeate Yeats's work after 1916 that one finds it difficult to read far in his drama, poetry, or prose without encountering them. The dance became a major tool with which he made his thoughts "into a unity." The kind of dance that interested Yeats, however, had little in common with most Western ideas of dance.

"I have lately studied certain of these dances, with Japanese players, and I notice that their ideal of beauty, unlike that of Greece and like that of pictures from Japan and China, makes them pause at moments of muscular tension. . . . They cross the stage with a sliding movement, and one gets the impression not of undulation but of continuous straight lines" (E&I 230–31).

The person most influential in Yeats's early views on Oriental dance was Michio Ito, who danced Yeats's Guardian of the Well in *At the Hawk's Well.* Ito had no formal training in the Noh,[16] but Yeats's description of his dancing, just quoted, makes it apparent that he came very close to reproducing the spirit of Japanese dance, if not specifically the Noh. Faubion Bowers comments: "In all Japanese dancing, movements are highly attenuated and suggestive (as opposed to literal). . . . The spectator is dazzled by the controlled tension and interiorized concentration of the human body" (Bowers, p. 174). Ito probably had some idea of the postures of the Noh dance though he had never been a Noh dancer, just as a dancer in the West would know something of ballet without ever having been a member of a *corps de ballet.* In any event, it was Ito's

[16]Anthony Thwaite, "Yeats and the Noh," *Twentieth Century,* 162 (1957), 237–38.

Fand's dance in *The Only Jealousy of Emer*. Photo by W. Hsu.

dance which gave Yeats a model. "My play," he wrote, "is made possible by a Japanese dancer whom I have seen dance in a studio and in a drawing-room and on a very small stage lit by an excellent stage-light. In the studio and in the drawing-room alone, where the lighting was the light we are most accustomed to, did I see him as the tragic image that has stirred my imagination" (E&I 224).

Yeats had earlier tried to adapt his particular dramatic vision to the theatre of Ireland without much success, at least in his terms. He recognized in the Noh plays of Japan quite a different theatre from that of the Irish dramatic movement, one removed from propagandistic purposes, one concerned with the perfecting of dramatic art and little else. Once Yeats had been stirred by the tragic image of the dancer, his choice of dance as fitting center for his plays never altered substantially.

The dance in the Yeatsian Noh emerges from the logic of the play at the point when words will not suffice to express the emotion aroused. It seems there is a point at which the words the actor speaks become inadequate to express the emotion he feels, so he must move his hands, just as any of us do when we become excited. But at a further point these movements resolve themselves into dance. The emotion becomes so powerful that it dances itself into meaning. As the Old Man says in *The Death of Cuchulain,* "where there are no words there is less to spoil" (VPl 1052). There is a remarkably appropriate passage in the Japanese playwright Zeami's essay on the Noh dance. "When the spirit remains in the mind, it is called emotion; uttered in words, it is called poetry. When one cannot stop with poetry alone, he goes on to sing it out, waving his hands and stamping his feet in ecstasy."[17]

In the Chinese opera it is difficult to separate dance from the rest of the action, for the actors' movements are as highly stylized as they are in the Japanese Noh. But there are specific dances called for by specific occasions, and these, although they are not as subdued as the Noh dances, are characterized by the kind of controlled movement Yeats describes in his accounts of Ito's art. For my

[17]Quoted in Makota Ueda, *Zeami, Bashō, Yeats, Pound: A Study in Japanese and English Poetics* (The Hague: Mouton, 1965), p. 33.

production I relied upon the expertise of Professor Tai. I told her of the circumstances surrounding each of the dances which I wished performed, and she chose the appropriate dance from the repertoire of the Chinese opera. I was not surprised to learn that there was an almost perfect match in each case. Aoife's dance in *At the Hawk's Well,* for example, perfectly fitted the style of the warrior-woman, and Emer's dance in *The Death of Cuchulain* was "The Sorrow of Queen Hsiang." In my version of the cycle, I considered Cuchulain's fight with the waves to be the central dance, and accented it accordingly. It is the only dance which, except for its general style, does not have a parallel in Chinese opera.

When Cuchulain discovers that he has killed his only son, he turns to fight the sea, the archetype of life and death. Even in his madness he is able to act; he is destroyed, not conquered, by life. It seems to me that this is truly character defined in action, and one of the central images of twentieth-century literature. Everything we do is fated, but the truly heroic man acts as if he could control his own fate, and it is this acting "as if" which gives Cuchulain his power. The emotion that drives him is too powerful to be contained, and it must resolve itself in a dance. In a letter written to Lady Elizabeth Pelham on 4 January 1939, Yeats says: "It seems to me that I have found what I wanted. When I try to put all into a phrase I say, 'Man can embody truth but he cannot know it'" (L 922). The dancer can literally embody truth without knowing it, and perhaps this is the reason that the dance becomes one of Yeats's most effective symbols of man's transcendence of his mortality.

At first it appears strange that the dance in *The Death of Cuchulain* is Emer's. She has no action in the play until her dance, and no lines at all. It is not that she is the only possible dancer, for there are four other female roles, Eithne Inguba, Aoife, the Morrigu, and the Singer. Aoife might seem to be the better choice, since her sisters have danced before Cuchulain at other climatic moments of his life. Instead we see the faithful Emer enter to perform the final dance before the head of Cuchulain. (Though this dance appears restrained to Western eyes, it is actually something of a departure from the decorous dancing expected from a queen in Chinese opera. I included it—against the advice of Professor Tai—as appropriate for the powerful Irish queen.)

It is obvious in the earlier plays that the Sidhe represent some sort of spiritual union to Cuchulain. What does Emer represent at the end of his life? We learn from the Morrigu, the goddess of war, that she "arranged the dance" (VPl 1061), so there is something of godlike, fated arrangement which imbues Emer's dance. The implication of the Morrigu's claim is that not only the dance, but Cuchulain's death itself was arranged, that the men who gave Cuchulain his mortal wounds were no more than puppets.

Emer's dance, then, is as fated as everything else in this world. Everything is arranged, but the truly heroic man acts as if he could control his own fate. This refusal to admit to any power greater than his is what makes Cuchulain a tragic hero.

In other plays we have seen extensions of Cuchulain's personality in the dances of the women of the Sidhe. Emer's dance requires that she make obeisance to his severed head; and perhaps it is fitting that she does, for Emer, who has always been tied to the temporal reality of the hearth, worships that part of Cuchulain that is flesh, even when that flesh has lost its vitality. As much as she loves him, she cannot truly know him, for even as she bows before his head "*a few faint bird notes*" (VPl 1062) announce that his soul is elsewhere.

But Emer's role is not that of the mistaken mortal juxtaposed against the certainty and superiority of spiritual creatures. Here we see the dramatic presentation of Yeats's theory of opposites which contain each other. Without mortality and frailty we can have no knowledge of the spiritual. Emer, rather than Aoife, must dance in this last play of the Cuchulain cycle so that Yeats's final dramatic statement (and he certainly knew it was his last) could demonstrate that synthesis of fair and foul, flesh and spirit, which had become for him the ultimate revelation.

The stylized vocabulary of movement and gesture in the Peking opera is perhaps best understood as dance, for it is as different from our tradition of realistic stage movement as a minuet is from a casual stroll. I found it quite easy to adapt for my production, and indeed useful; it is an advantage to know that Conlaoch's determined heel-and-toe stride as he enters means he is prepared to fight, or that Eithne Inguba's walk types her as a flirtatious young woman: "A noble lady walks with grace and dignity; the flirt sways suggestively in her gaudy costume; fighters stalk; scholars pace thoughtfully; clowns scurry; and officials stride with a grand manner" (Huang, p. 24).

There are over a hundred hand gestures which carry specific meaning, and some of these enabled those in my audience who did not understand English to follow what was happening. The action of *On Baile's Strand,* for example, was almost entirely signified by means of these gestures. Cuchulain's raised and trembling hand signifies his madness after he has learned that he has killed his only son, and the audience is thus informed that he is crazed as he fights the sea. No other mode of exposition could have been any more effective.

The play took nearly four months to produce. Although four months is considerably longer than optimum for rehearsal, the special problems of this production made the additional preparation necessary. Since I was dealing with student actors, I spent a great deal of time at the beginning of our work explaining Yeats's ideas on the drama and their relevance to Oriental theatre. The students at NTNU are "the brightest and the best," selected by competitive exams, and they were eager to make the project a success. Many of them were literature majors, and their background in Occidental and Oriental literature helped to give them a feeling for the play. I talked to each actor individually about his or her part and its relationship to the whole. The actors who played the Musicians, or choric parts, had the most difficulty understanding their lines, partly because Yeats used some of his most esoteric ideas in these speeches, and partly because very little physical action, which could give clues to meaning, accompanies them. I found that the inclusion of gestures featuring the "water sleeve," or the white extension of the costume sleeve, gave the students a better sense of their lines and established early in the play the validity of traditional Peking opera gestures for the Cuchulain cycle.

Professor Tai was naturally a great help in establishing compromises between Yeats and the Chinese drama. Her extensive experi-

Cuchulain and Conlaoch in *On Baile's Strand*. The cloth used to symbolize the waves can be seen in the background. Photo by W. Hsu.

ence in the theatre had prepared her even for this barbarian intrusion, and her suggestions concerning the adaptations that I wished to make were invaluable. She was especially helpful in demonstrating movement, the aspect of the performance that made the plot comprehensible to those who had difficulty with the language.

Since this was the first acting experience for most of my cast, special and unanticipated problems arose. The girl who played the Morrigu seemed unable to get the necessary force into her speech, and repetitions and demonstrations did little good. Finally I learned that she thought a goddess should not speak so roughly. I then told her, in rather forceful terms, that she could not impose her ideas of a goddess's decorum on the play. This little show of temper on my part seemed to make its point for the rest of the cast, and I was able to be relatively gentle for the rest of the rehearsals.

Most young Chinese do not know a great deal about their own traditional drama, just as most American students know little about Shakespeare, so the experience was doubly valuable for the cast. It was exciting to see Professor Tai instill in them an appreciation for their own culture, but sometimes their well-meaning friends gave them bad advice. Our Conlaoch was told by his roommates that his walk "did not look natural," and his subsequent questions about this led to two mini-lectures on stylized movement: one in English by me, and one in Chinese by Professor Tai.

I was saved from a considerable faux pas in the instance of Fand's line to Cuchulain asking him to "kiss my mouth." I first suspected something was amiss when the actors could not hear this line delivered without bursting into laughter. It was gently explained to me that no precedent for such an action existed in Chinese drama. Not only is such affectionate display considered private by the Chinese, but until this century all roles had been played by male actors. The possibility of a stage kiss had to be treated as very remote, so I separated Cuchulain and Fand by three or four feet and had her deliver the line imperiously rather than seductively.

The characters of Cuchulain and Emer were especially fascinating to the Chinese. The brave and noble general is a popular type in Peking opera, but Cuchulain's refusal to submit to a higher lord is contrary to Confucian principles. Yet the Chinese audience found his capacity for action and for the grand gesture very attractive. Emer as loyal queen is also a familiar type, but although her sacrifice of her own happiness is exactly in character with the noble Chinese woman, the strength with which she faced Bricriu seemed almost masculine to the Chinese audience.

The production attracted a great deal of attention during its preparation, mainly because of Professor Tai's reputation, but partly because of the nature of what we were attempting. I delivered a public lecture in which I tried to explain the project, but of course it is difficult to make the details of such an unusual undertaking clear. I told the audience that what I was attempting was not Peking opera, but Irish plays done in the style of the Peking opera, and that I would use the conventions that I thought suitable and omit those that did not seem to fit. It is not surprising that some people were confused, or thought that a profanation of the Peking opera form would result. In a question period after the lecture, some reminded me that there were no formal songs in the play, and others said that the Oriental aesthetic was very unlikely to be appropriate for an Irish play. Had there been Yeatsian drama experts present, I am certain that my conflation of styles would have seemed equally sacrilegious to them.

Because of the stir which resulted from this controversy, there were overflow crowds at each performance, and the major metropolitan papers sent reviewers—a rare practice for college productions. I was prepared for an adverse reaction—not on the scale of the reaction to the *Playboy,* certainly, but at least a genteel tongue-lashing that would put the foreign professor in his place. I was therefore quite unready for the unanimously positive reaction of the audiences and the reviewers. I had started with the premise that Yeats's plays ought to succeed, as he had suggested, "in a civilization very unlike ours," but so many dire warnings had been given in the interim that I was genuinely surprised to be proved correct. An anonymous reviewer made these pertinent comments in the *Central Daily News* (31 May 1983):

> What a marvelous play. Foreign audiences were greatly amused, and Chinese audiences were enthralled. Can you imagine presenting Yeats's Cuchulain cycle in English, yet in the style of Chinese drama,

with all the gorgeous costumes, masklike makeup, graceful stage movement, the melodious *wen-chang* and the heart-thrilling *wu-chang,* together with the elegant and refined Chinese dance?

The script itself has been the weakest part of Chinese drama. The form of presentation has been perfectly refined after a long history of development. Yet the scenario itself is lagging behind. Thus it sometimes gives the impression of a gorgeous form lacking philosophical depth. If this innovative experiment is well accepted, we may also try to stage other world plays in the style of Chinese drama.

It is true that the script in a Chinese opera is itself not very important, and serves mainly as a platform for singing and spectacle. The plots are usually comparable in depth to, for example, *La Boheme* or *Madame Butterfly*. Yeats's poetry, linked to the "gorgeous form" of the Peking opera, created an effect somehow greater than the sum of the parts.

Other reviewers were as generous. In the *China Times* of 29 May 1983, Professor Dai Wei-Yang wrote: "It seems that Yeats took an imaginary trip to China. If he were still alive and saw this production, he would be glad that his ideals of the theatre have been realized through an old stage convention." On the same day the *Ming-Sheng Daily News* carried reviews by Professors Huang Tzyh-Lai and Ying Chun-Ming. The former stated: "This is the first time that a Yeats play has been staged in the style of the Chinese drama. It is an attempt to present a form of art enriched by the connection, with a cross-cultural consciousness of Eastern and Western ideas. We hope that it will attain considerable attention in literary circles, and that activities of this kind can be promoted." Ying wrote, "This innovative attempt will arouse fresh interest in and greater esteem for Chinese drama, especially among the younger generation."

Some other interesting and useful comments came from Richard Brzustowicz, Jr., an American and an instructor at National Chengchi University, who suggested half seriously that a performance of Yeats's plays be done in the style of the Taiwanese opera (a less polished form than the Peking opera) and presented to the gods of a Taoist temple, reaffirming the original ritual context of the drama.[18] How Yeats would have loved that.

[18]Letter from Richard Brzustowicz, 6 June 1983.

Professor Tai was very pleased with the production and is attempting to encourage similar work. The Cuchulain plays are now being translated by Fang Po so that they can be presented as part of the repertoire of the traditional Peking opera companies; thus "activities of this kind" are now being actively promoted. Miss Fang also wrote a long article for the *Central Daily News* of 7 August 1983, assessing the impact the production had upon experimental theater in Taiwan. The direction of experimentation, she noted, had been almost completely Western before, and our play had encouraged people to look to their own dramatic tradition with fresh eyes.

Fortunately we taped a rehearsal performance in color, so Western audiences and scholars can get some idea of the intensity and excitement of the play. The tape should have been done as a special production, with attention to the particular values of television, but time limitations did not permit us that luxury. Since the possibilities of repeating a production are minimal, I chose to have some sort of record rather than none. At a 25 November 1983 lecture-demonstration featuring the tape at the University of Toronto, I was encouraged by the positive response and support of several scholars, including experts on the Yeatsian Noh, the Japanese Noh, and the Peking opera. Several other similar lecture-demonstrations have taken place in 1984.

I started this project with the thesis that Yeats's drama needed not only a stylized form, but a stylized form with a tradition rooted in the culture and rituals of a people. (At one time I toyed with the idea of presenting some of his plays in the style of the Roman Catholic Mass, but decided such a production might be perceived as blasphemous.) In order for these plays to work in the manner in which they were written, it is important that they be presented in a culture as heterodox and inclusive as possible. The audience needs to be prepared to see strange events, and to consider these events as metaphors with which to conjure, not as literal truth. I am pleased with what has happened. Professor Tai's approval, especially after her initial reservations, is important to me, and the positive reactions of audiences and critics have been encouraging.

I have always had difficulty in reconciling my fondness for

Yeats's plays with the considerable production problems they represent. One must either concentrate on one play that will run about half an hour or try to put three or more coherently together to fill an evening. If one chooses the former course, the audience must be prepared for a short, intense experience. (The best I can remember of this type was a 1968 production in Toronto of *The Death of Cuchulain,* directed by Tomás MacAnna. The audience consisted of some of the foremost Yeatsian scholars in the world, who knew "the old epics and Mr. Yeats' plays about them" [VPl 1051–52].) Few people, however, will go to the theatre for plays lasting less than an hour. The problem of choice then arises, for the producer must decide whether to put similar plays together, or to try a kind of sampling of Yeats's art. Should they all be Noh, should they include his early style, should they concentrate on theme? I believe that a selection from the Cuchulain plays represents one solution to the problem, and I also believe that the imposition of the Peking opera form helped to make a unity of style important for demonstrating a link among these plays. I am satisfied that the two apparently disparate forms of Yeats's drama and the Peking opera fit well.

As far as any particular production is concerned, I will always find faults. The strongest elements of this one were the traditional acting style, costumes, and makeup, all of which helped the actors to compensate for their lack of experience. I could have wished for better voices, better articulation and phrasing, but such desires are unlikely to be realized short of a professional production. The Musicians, particularly, require special acting talents: they must be static yet charged with energy, and they must seem to have a kind of restrained electrical current running through their bodies.

I like the compression of *On Baile's Strand* and the dance it makes. It seems to me that all the dances of this production worked quite well, from the quiet folding and unfolding of the cloth by the Musicians to the energetic clash between Cuchulain and Conlaoch. It may be true that the best audience for Yeats's plays is a country in which people "share a half-mythological, half-philosophical folk-belief." But I choose to believe that, although the audience for his plays will never be numerous in his own culture, the community to which Yeats appeals is larger now than at any time during his lifetime; and it will continue to increase as we learn to understand and appreciate his connection with the ritual dramas of the world.

"Therefore it is natural that I go to Asia for a stage convention, for more formal faces, for a chorus that has no part in the action, and perhaps for those movements of the body copied from the marionette shows of the fourteenth century" (E&I 226). There were many times during the production of this play that these words from "Certain Noble Plays of Japan" were in my mind. Yeats never visited the Orient, and I could not help but wish that he had had my opportunity.

The Uses of Comedy and Irony in *Autobiographies* and Autobiography

JAMES OLNEY

The question that I wish to explore in this paper is a threefold one and might be expressed thus: (1) Why is comedy so largely lacking in what one might describe as classic autobiography? (2) Why, on the other hand, is comedy so prominent (as I believe it to be) in Yeats's *Autobiographies*? (3) What is the nature, and what are the motives, of comedy when it does occur in autobiography? And as a sort of fourth fold completing this threefold question I want to pose a paradox: that though there are not many humorous passages in classic autobiography yet this type, like all varieties of autobiography, might be said to be essentially and in its very nature of the comic mode.[1]

I will begin with a definition of classic autobiography, which is not my own but is as good as any other definition known to me: "A retrospective account in prose that a real person makes of his own existence stressing his own life and especially the history of

[1]Hazard Adams, almost alone among Yeats commentators, has remarked on Yeats's use of the comic mode; see his brilliant piece "Some Yeatsian Versions of Comedy," *In Excited Reverie: A Centenary Tribute to William Butler Yeats, 1865–1939,* ed. A. Norman Jeffares and K. G. W. Cross (London: Macmillan; New York: St. Martin, 1965), pp. 152–70. Adams quotes several "versions of comedy" from the *Autobiographies*; no writer on Yeats as autobiographer really deals with the subject. Quotations from *Autobiographies,* copyright 1916, 1936 by Macmillan Publishing Co., Inc., renewed 1944, 1964 by Bertha Georgie Yeats, are reprinted with permission of Macmillan Publishing Company and Macmillan London Limited.

his personality."[2] It is clear, I think, that the kind of writing performance described or defined here is not likely to produce books notable for humorous or comic effects. When a "real person" undertakes a retrospective account "of his own existence stressing his individual life and especially the history of his personality," he is more likely to be serious or perhaps solemn than he is to be comic and gay. And indeed in that long—*very* long—volume that Philippe Lejeune takes for his archetypal autobiography, the *Confessions* of Rousseau, there is only one joke as far as I can recall, and that one joke has little enough to do with Rousseau's "own existence," "his individual life," or "the history of his personality." The joke, if that is the right way to describe it, comes at the death of a woman with whom Rousseau found brief employment. "I watched her die," Rousseau says. "She had lived like a woman of talents and intelligence; she died like a philosopher. . . . She only kept her bed for the last two days, and continued to converse quietly with everyone to the last. Finally when she could no longer talk and was already in her death agony, she broke wind loudly. 'Good,' she said, turning over, 'a woman who can fart is not dead.' Those were the last words she spoke."[3] This scarcely qualifies as a great deathbed speech but at least it does provide, for Rousseau's readers, a couple of lines of levity in more than six hundred pages of very uncomic, paranoid anxiety—the anxiety of an apologist who has the desperate feeling that his audience is unmoved and unconvinced by his "apology for his own life." If Georges Gusdorf is right when he says that "autobiography appeases the more or less anguished uneasiness of an aging man who wonders if his life has not been lived in vain, frittered away haphazardly, ending now in simple failure,"[4] we can see easily enough why it should contain so few laughs—one in the case of Rousseau, none in the cases of Saint Augustine or John Bunyan or George Fox or John Stuart Mill or John Henry Newman (though I do not

[2]Philippe Lejeune, *Le pacte autobiographique* (Paris: Seuil, 1975), p. 14 (translation mine).

[3]Jean-Jacques Rousseau, *The Confessions,* tr. J. M. Cohen (Harmondsworth & New York: Penguin, 1953), pp. 85–86.

[4]Georges Gusdorf, "Conditions and Limits of Autobiography," in *Autobiography: Essays Theoretical and Critical,* ed. James Olney (Princeton: Princeton University Press, 1980), p. 39.

at all mean to say that these men wrote autobiography for the reasons specified by Gusdorf). Trying to salvage or discover meaning for a life when the life is nearly over may produce a great book but it is not likely to conduce to great risibility. Thus in what I have termed classic autobiography—and it would be easy to multiply examples—one does not find much comedy, and if one goes to such a work with the same expectations as one goes to *Joe Miller's Joke Book* one will be sadly disappointed.

I want now, however, to glance at a certain kind of irony that *is* typical of classic autobiography and indeed that is there almost by definition of the mode. Jean Starobinski concludes his essay "The Style of Autobiography" with these observations about Rousseau's *Confessions* as a sort of dramatization of his philosophy: "According to that philosophy, man originally possessed happiness and joy: in comparison with that first felicity, the present is a time of degradation and corruption. But man was originally a brute deprived of 'light,' his reason still asleep; compared to that initial obscurity, the present is a time of lucid reflection and enlarged consciousness. The past, then, is at once the object of nostalgia and the object of irony; the present is at once a state of (moral) degradation and (intellectual) superiority."[5] If, as has been claimed, classic autobiography depends for its existence on some sort of conversion in the autobiographer's life, then this great emotional and intellectual divide will almost inevitably be present in, and will indeed rule the autobiography, giving an ironic, if not always nostalgic, distancing to the past. I can clarify what I mean here by reference to Augustine's *Confessions,* which I should describe as a radically ironic but never nostalgic book: radically ironic because the "I" narrating understands every event in the narrative differently from the understanding possessed in the past by the "I" narrated (the reasons for going from Carthage to Rome for example); but never nostalgic because Augustine did not at all share Rousseau's notion of childhood as a time of innocence, happiness, and joy—quite the contrary. This variety of irony that distances the past narrated self from the present narrating self is surely what Yeats intends in a letter written to his father apropos of *Reveries*

[5]Jean Starobinski, "The Style of Autobiography," in *Autobiography: Essays Theoretical and Critical,* p. 83.

over Childhood and Youth: "While I was immature I was a different person and I can stand apart and judge" (L 589). What Yeats describes is present-tense judgement ("I can stand apart") of a past-tense condition of being ("While I was immature I was a different person"). Thus we have in the first couple of sections of *Autobiographies* fairly frequent instances of irony exercised by the mature Yeats on the immature Yeats. This, for example, in "Four Years: 1887–1891":

> [W]ith women . . . I was timid and abashed. I was sitting on a seat in front of the British Museum feeding pigeons when a couple of girls sat near and began enticing my pigeons away, laughing and whispering to one another, and I looked straight in front of me, very indignant, and presently went into the Museum without turning my head towards them. Since then I have often wondered if they were pretty or merely very young. Sometimes I told myself very adventurous love-stories with myself for hero, and at other times I planned out a life of lonely austerity, and at other times mixed the ideals and planned a life of lonely austerity mitigated by periodical lapses. [Au 153]

This kind of indulgent and semi-comic irony, exercised at the expense of a younger self, is not uncommon in autobiography. (Parenthetically, I might contrast the gentle self-irony of Yeats with the mordant self-irony of the following wonderful and justly famous passage in Augustine: "But I, wretched young man that I was—even more wretched at the beginning of my youth—had begged you for chastity and had said: 'Make me chaste and continent, but not yet.' I was afraid that you might hear me too soon and cure me too soon from the disease of a lust which I preferred to be satisfied rather than extinguished."[6] This is a very different matter from the Yeatsian self-irony, but it still results from the difference between the understanding possessed by the self then and the understanding possessed by the self now.) To return to Yeats's letter to his father: after the sentence I have been looking at—"While I was immature I was a different person and I can stand apart and judge"—a sentence that provides the logic for a

[6] *The Confessions of St. Augustine*, tr. Rex Warner (New York: New American Library, 1963), pp. 173–74.

certain gentle self-mockery early in the *Autobiographies,* Yeats goes on to say, "Later on, I should always, I feel, write of other people" (L 589), and this opens the door not to self-irony but to irony, or more exactly comedy, deployed against others, a comedy that operates according to a vastly different logic from that of self-irony. It is the logic of this other variety of irony and comedy that I want to examine now.

I call upon a couple of passages from other prose writings in Yeats to explain the comedy of the second kind. The first passage I have quoted elsewhere but it is so excellent, both in itself and as rationale for the Yeatsian practice of autobiography, that any apology I might make for repeating it would be more *pro forma* than heartfelt. It occurs in one of Yeats's annual pieces on the Irish theatre gathered together in *Explorations* as "The Irish Dramatic Movement." Speaking of what was then (in 1902) a new troupe, the National Theatrical Company, Yeats says:

> They showed plenty of inexperience, especially in the minor characters, but it was the first performance I had seen since I understood these things in which the actors kept still enough to give poetical writing its full effect upon the stage. I had imagined such acting, though I had not seen it, and had once asked a dramatic company to let me rehearse them in barrels that they might forget gesture and have their minds free to think of speech for a while. The barrels, I thought, might be on castors, so that I could shove them about with a pole when the action required it. [Ex 86–87]

When Yeats titles one of his later volumes of autobiography *Dramatis Personae: 1896–1902,* it does not take much imagination to conceive of the text as a Yeatsian drama, of the family, friends, and acquaintances therein as actors in the drama, each in his or her barrel labeled with the role to be played, and of Yeats as playwright, director, and stage manager, exercising complete control over everybody and everything, complete control over his text and his life, as he shoves the embarreled and imperiled actors about the stage with his pole of comedy and irony.

The second passage, of a somewhat more theoretical nature but still concerned with dramatic literature, comes from a short, intense piece called "The Tragic Theatre." Having remarked that in poetical drama there is supposed to be "an antithesis between character and lyric poetry," Yeats goes on: "Yet when we go back a few centuries and enter the great periods of drama, character grows less and sometimes disappears, and there is much lyric feeling. . . . Suddenly it strikes us that character is continuously present in comedy alone, and that there is much tragedy . . . where its place is taken by passions and motives." Even in Shakespeare's tragicomedy, Yeats says, "it is in the moments of comedy that character is defined, in Hamlet's gaiety, let us say; while amid the great moments, when Timon orders his tomb, when Hamlet cries to Horatio 'Absent thee from felicity awhile,' when Antony names 'Of many thousand kisses the poor last,' all is lyricism, unmixed passion, 'the integrity of fire.'" "When the tragic reverie is at its height," Yeats declares, we never say, "'How well that man is realised! I should know him were I to meet him in the street.'" Finally, Yeats writes, "I think it was while rehearsing a translation of *Les Fourberies de Scapin* in Dublin, and noticing how passionless it all was, that I saw what should have been plain from the first line I had written, that tragedy must always be a drowning and breaking of the dykes that separate man from man, and that it is upon these dykes [that] comedy keeps house" (E&I 240–41). Comedy imagines the world in terms of character, it distinguishes this individual and his folly from that individual and his folly, and it never dissolves the contours of character and social reality in the strains of that pure lyric emotion that Yeats believed specific to high tragedy. "I look upon character and personality as different things or perhaps different forms of the same thing," Yeats wrote to his father. "Juliet has personality, her Nurse has character. I look upon personality as the individual form of our passions. . . . Character belongs I think to Comedy" (L 548). And in *Autobiographies* he confirms this sense of comedy and character when he says, "Tragedy is passion alone, and rejecting character, it gets form from motives, from the wandering of passion; while comedy is the clash of character" (Au 470). It may seem somewhat paradoxical, in light of what I have said about autobiography earlier, that I should now suggest that autobiography, at least of the variety practiced by Yeats, is essentially comic rather than tragic—and indeed that all autobiography, not just that by Yeats, is in one sense always comic, never tragic. We should remark that in a tragedy like *Purgatory,* for example, there is nothing to be called character; there is only lyric passion and the keening song; while in the *Autobiographies,* on the other hand, where Yeats intends to catch character with an anecdote, we are offered a string of (as he has it in "Easter 1916") mocking tales and gibes that one imagines were first told, and probably retold many subsequent times, to please a companion around the fire at the club.

Take the character of George Moore first of all. It was apparently Moore's *Hail and Farewell,* with its consistently mocking, and often quite funny, picture of Yeats, that first induced Yeats to start on his autobiographical writings. When I say the picture is quite funny, I don't mean that Yeats found it so; on the contrary—it was largely Moore that Yeats was referring to when he wrote of himself that he had become

> *Notorious, till all my priceless things*
> *Are but a post the passing dogs defile.*
> [VP 321]

Of the first volume of *Hail and Farewell* Moore wrote to a correspondent: "The reviewers look upon my book as a book of reminiscences, whereas I took so much material and moulded it just as if I were writing a novel, and the people in my book are not personalities but human types. . . . [A]s a type of the literary fop one could not find a more perfect model than Yeats."[7] Yeats knew nothing of this letter, of course, but he knew well enough—too well, I should say—what Moore was up to, for it was very much what he was to be up to himself when he published his reminiscences of such type characters as George Bernard Shaw, Oscar Wilde—and Moore. What Yeats did not want and absolutely would not have was someone else taking over his life and his text, creating character for him when Yeats intended to be the comic playwright creating character aplenty for others: he was determined that he would control Moore and not vice versa. The interesting thing is that when Yeats reacted to *Hail and Farewell* in his journal, he did so with polemic and direct attack—"Moore . . . is

[7]Mem 269–70n. Quoted by Donoghue from National Library of Ireland, Ms. 8271.

the born demagogue. . . . He has always a passion for some crowd, is always deliberately inciting them against somebody," and so forth (Mem 270); but when he responds in a piece of autobiography intended for publication, Yeats asserts and maintains control over his life and text not through polemic but through a comic reduction of Moore and an ironic rendering of his foolishness and his pretensions.

> Moore had inherited a large Mayo estate, and no Mayo country gentleman had ever dressed the part so well. . . . Yet nature had denied to him the final touch: he had a coarse palate. Edward Martyn alone suspected it. When Moore abused the waiter or the cook, he had thought, 'I know what he is hiding'. In a London restaurant on a night when the soup was particularly good, just when Moore had the spoon at his lip, he said: 'Do you mean to say you are going to drink that?' Moore tasted the soup, then called the waiter, and ran through the usual performance. Martyn did not undeceive him, content to chuckle in solitude. [Au 443]

This, which sounds very like a mocking tale to please a companion around the fire at the club, was published after Moore's death but even had it been published during his lifetime there would have been no way for Moore to refute this sly picture of a man who pretends to culture but is undone by a coarse palate. It is as if one could hear Yeats saying to Moore, calling from the text of *Autobiographies* to the text of *Hail and Farewell,* "You imagine that you are the provider of barrels and that you have one for me titled 'literary fop.' Well, you are wrong: I'm running this show; there is your barrel—that one over there labeled 'pretentious and ill-bred fool, also coarse in palate.' Now get in there and stay in there."

"Moore's body," according to Yeats—and no doubt he thought Moore's body merely the outward form of his soul—"Moore's body was insinuating, upflowing, circulative, curvicular, pop-eyed" (Au 422).

> He had gone to Paris straight from his father's racing stables, from a house where there was no culture, as Symons and I understood that word, acquired copious inaccurate French, sat among art students, young writers about to become famous, in some café; a man carved

> out of a turnip, looking out of astonished eyes. I see him as that circle saw him, for I have in memory Manet's caricature. He spoke badly and much in a foreign tongue, read nothing, and was never to attain the discipline of style. . . . He reached to middle life ignorant even of small practical details. He said to a friend: 'How do you keep your pants from falling about your knees?' 'O', said the friend, 'I put my braces through the little tapes that are sewn there for the purpose.' A few days later, he thanked the friend with emotion. . . . He had wanted to be good as the mass of men understand goodness. In later life he wrote a long preface to prove that he had a mistress in Mayfair. [Au 404–6]

And so on, with much more to the same effect.

Yeats's treatment of Shaw and Wilde is somewhat different—they hadn't, after all, tried to make Yeats into a character actor and dispose of him in barrels of their own making as Moore had—but it is still anecdotal, devoted to drawing out character, the stuff of comedy rather than of tragedy. According to that other book of Yeats's, rich in comedy, called *A Vision,* Shaw and Wilde were contrasting types—Shaw of the twenty-first phase, Wilde of the nineteenth, the former entirely styleless, the latter nothing but style—and Yeats so creates them, so deploys them as "characters," as archetypal figures, in his *Autobiographies.* Parenthetically, I might point out here that Moore, too, along with Shaw, was assigned to the twenty-first phase in *A Vision*; and, again like Shaw, he is regularly described by Yeats in the *Autobiographies* as having no style, nor even any awareness that such a thing as style exists. The twenty-first phase is the phase of "the acquisitive man," and Yeats's description of the character of the man of phase twenty-one sounds like nothing so much as an abstraction derived from the figure particularized under Moore's name in the *Autobiographies.* One might even suppose that Yeats has in mind the fact that Moore was to be typed as "the acquisitive man" when he says that he "acquired copious inaccurate French" sitting in a Paris café. To return to Shaw: *Arms and the Man,* Yeats says,

> seemed to me inorganic, logical straightness and not the crooked road of life. . . . Shaw was right to claim Samuel Butler for his master, for Butler was the first Englishman to make the discovery

> that it is possible to write with great effect without music, without style, either good or bad, to eliminate from the mind all emotional implication and to prefer plain water to every vintage, so much metropolitan lead and solder to any tendril of the vine. Presently I had a nightmare that I was haunted by a sewing-machine, that clicked and shone, but the incredible thing was that the machine smiled, smiled perpetually. [Au 283]

Thus for Shaw. As for Wilde, Yeats speaks of his "fantasy" having "taken . . . [a] tragic turn" (Au 285), and he says that "men who belong by nature to the nights near to the full are still born, a tragic minority, and how shall they do their work when too ambitious for a private station, except as Wilde of the nineteenth Phase, as my symbolism has it, did his work?" (Au 293). But though Wilde might have been a tragic figure in his own right, in the life he lived, he is not that in Yeats's text; rather he is an archetypal figure, a man of phase nineteen, a character actor, like Ernest Dowson, assigned a humorous role in the comedy that Yeats calls "The Tragic Generation."

> A Rhymer had seen Dowson at some café in Dieppe with a particularly common harlot, and as he passed, Dowson, who was half drunk, caught him by the sleeve and whispered, 'She writes poetry—it is like Browning and Mrs. Browning'. Then there came a wonderful tale repeated by Dowson himself, whether by word of mouth or by letter I do not remember. Wilde had arrived in Dieppe, and Dowson pressed upon him the necessity of acquiring 'a more wholesome taste'. They emptied their pockets on to the café table, and though there was not much, there was enough if both heaps were put into one. Meanwhile the news had spread, and they set out accompanied by a cheering crowd. Arrived at their destination, Dowson and the crowd remained outside, and presently Wilde returned. He said in a low voice to Dowson, 'The first these ten years, and it will be the last. It was like cold mutton'—always, as Henley had said, 'a scholar and a gentleman', he now remembered that the Elizabethan dramatists used the words 'cold mutton'—and then aloud so that the crowd might hear him, 'But tell it in England, for it will entirely restore my character'. [Au 327–28]

However tragic Wilde's life may have been, however tragic Dowson's life may have been, they both assume bit parts as comic characters in *The Life of W. B. Yeats,* he the master dramatist and stage manager, in control both of his own life and of the lives of others who play minor roles, hostile or friendly, in the one grand design.

The other attempt on his life—other than George Moore's, I mean—that Yeats intended to counteract by writing his life himself was Katharine Tynan's rather awkward effort at homicide in a book she called *Twenty-five Years: Reminiscences,* which was published exactly contemporaneously with Moore's *Hail and Farewell* (Moore's three volumes were published in 1911, 1912, and 1914; *Twenty-five Years* appeared in 1913). Tynan, instead of presenting Yeats as a literary fop and a pretender to an aristocratic heritage that was never his, as Moore had done, chose instead to twit Yeats and make fun of him for his interest in the occult. Now, I think that Yeats's relationship to occult matters was much more complex and his attitude a good deal more ambivalent than Tynan recognized—indeed, he was more ambivalent and skeptical about the occult than his critics have in general recognized. This is why those who were seriously engaged in occult practices and who gave their whole heart to the occult are regularly treated with much humor by Yeats in the *Autobiographies*. Mme. Blavatsky, for example, whom Yeats describes in a wonderful phrase as "a sort of female Dr. Johnson" (Au 175), is surrounded and, as it were, held off by a string of anecdotes and comic tales designed to qualify very carefully any commitment Yeats might be supposed to have made with regard to occult practices. Likewise McGregor Mathers and the man Yeats describes as "an old white-haired Oxfordshire clergyman, the most panic-stricken person I have ever known": they are all rendered as comic figures in a way they would not have been had Yeats been a wholehearted enthusiast for the magic they engaged in. The following scene with the aged clergyman may be taken as typical. "Has your alchemical research had any success?" Yeats asks him. "Yes, I once made the elixir of life," the old gentleman responds. "A French alchemist said it had the right smell and the right colour"—then Yeats interrupts to tell the reader, "the alchemist may have been Eliphas Levi, who visited England in the 'sixties, and would have said anything"—and the clergyman again: "but the first effect of the elixir is that your nails fall out and your hair falls off. I was afraid that I might have made a mistake and that nothing else might happen, so I put it away on a shelf. I meant to drink it when I was an old man, but when I got it down the other day it had all dried up" (Au 184).

For a final example of the uses of comedy and irony in the *Autobiographies,* then, I turn to the contrasting accounts given by Katharine Tynan and Yeats of a séance the two of them attended in Dublin. Here is Katharine Tynan's account of what she calls "a spiritualistic seance in which I participated most unwillingly" (among other reasons, presumably, because she was a Roman Catholic):

> In spite of my protestations my host gently but firmly made me take a part. We sat round a table in the darkness touching each other's hands. I was quite determined to be in opposition to the whole thing, to disbelieve in it, and disapprove of it as a playing with things of life and death. Presently the table stood up slowly: the host was psychic. There were presences. The presences had communications to make and struggled to make them. Willie Yeats was banging his head on the table as though he had a fit, muttering to himself. I had a cold repulsion to the whole business. I took my hands from the table. Presently the spirits were able to speak. There was someone in the room who was hindering them. By this time I had got in a few invocations of my own. There was a tremendous deal of rapping going on. The spirits were obviously annoyed. They were asked for an indication as to who it was that was holding them back. They indicated me, and I was asked to withdraw, which I did cheerfully. The last thing I saw as the door opened to let me pass through was Willie Yeats banging his head on the table.[8]

Passing from this account to Yeats's own in *Reveries over Childhood and Youth* one seems to hear him murmur, "Oh, you want to play hard ball, do you? Right . . ." and he starts thus: "Perhaps a year before we returned to London, a Catholic friend"—Katharine Tynan, of course—"brought me to a spiritualistic séance," and then he sets the scene: half a dozen people seated around a table, the

[8]Katharine Tynan, *Twenty-five Years: Reminiscences* (New York: Devin-Adair, 1913), p. 239. Something of the intended tone of Tynan's portrait of Yeats may be gathered from the fact that this and a couple of other passages in the book are indexed under "Yeats, W. B. . . . and table-rapping."

medium asleep sitting upright in his chair, the lights turned out, and so on:

> Presently my shoulders began to twitch and my hands. I could easily have stopped them, but I had never heard of such a thing and I was curious. After a few minutes the movement became violent and I stopped it. I sat motionless for a while and then my whole body moved like a suddenly unrolled watchspring, and I was thrown backward on the wall. I again stilled the movement and sat at the table. Everybody began to say I was a medium, and that if I would not resist some wonderful thing would happen. I remembered that Balzac had once desired to take opium for the experience' sake, but would not because he dreaded the surrender of his will. We were now holding each other's hands and presently my right hand banged the knuckles of the woman next to me upon the table. She laughed, and the medium, speaking for the first time, and with difficulty, out of his mesmeric sleep, said, 'Tell her there is great danger'. He stood up and began walking round me making movements with his hands as though he were pushing something away. I was now struggling vainly with this force which compelled me to movements I had not willed, and my movements became so violent that the table was broken. I tried to pray, and because I could not remember a prayer, repeated in a loud voice-
>
> 'Of Man's first disobedience and the fruit
> Of that forbidden tree whose mortal taste
> Brought death into the world, and all our woe . . .
> Sing, Heavenly Muse.'

But the conclusion to this account, so far as Katharine Tynan is concerned, comes in the next line: "My Catholic friend had left the table and was saying a Paternoster and Ave Maria in the corner" (Au 103–4).

Briefly, I would suggest that in this very funny and quite typical passage we can see the mature Yeats directing irony at his own immature self à la Starobinski; we can see him, by the distancing effect of the comedy, holding in balance commitment and non-commitment with regard to spiritualistic phenomena; and we can see him taking his life back from Katharine Tynan by making her a minor—even unnamed—comic figure in his own drama rather than agreeing to be an actor in a play—and that play a farce—scripted by someone else.

One final remark on the tragic and the comic: Yeats, as everyone knows, calls one section of his *Autobiographies* "The Tragic Generation," and a tragic generation it no doubt was; but all is "changed, changed utterly" when the autobiographer makes it a part of his own triumphant story, transforming it into an element of his text and thus making of a figure or an event that is locally or in itself tragic a detail in a larger pattern that taken overall must play as comedy. This is the sense, mentioned earlier, in which any autobiographer, taking command of his life through inscribing it in a text, triumphs over insignificance, dead ends, and momentary tragedies by the very act of writing his autobiography. I believe that in certain sports they say that the best defense lies in offense, and one might put the matter this way: that to defend and preserve his life, Yeats adopts the strategies of comedy and irony, but he subtly transforms those defensive tactics into offensive ones, so that in the end he is triumphant, in text as in life, the actor become also the dramatist and the stage manager, and free thereby to live his life as he will.

"As Regarding Rhythm": Yeats and the Imagists

Ronald Schuchard

Over the past half century literary history has been shunned as an essential aid to textual study, but we are beginning to discover that we must revamp the histories in order to reopen literary texts. Yeats, for instance, has been given no place in the history of imagism (he was off in Ireland enmeshed in theatre business), and that history has remained unquestioned because we have not asked it to serve our understanding of his poetic rhythms and images (he was writing iambic or blank-verse lines and had a symbolist concept of the image). "Is Mr. Yeats an Imagiste?" the critics asked Pound in 1914. "No, Mr. Yeats is a symbolist, but he has written *des Images* as have many good poets before him; . . . and he has nothing against them (*les Imagistes*), at least so far as I know—except what he calls 'their devil's metres'."[1] For years the question of whether Pound or Yeats influenced the other more was bandied about with little resolution, but recently a well-known critic writing on Ezra Pound's "modernization" of Yeats revealed the effect that a complacent history can have on criticism: "While Pound favored the metronomic lines of Homer or Swinburne, Yeats's poetry was predominantly iambic, with little metrical variation and, hence, little rhythmical life. Yeats was probably one of those, to paraphrase Swinburne, who listened with his fingers instead of his

[1] "The Later Yeats," *Poetry*, 4 (May 1914), 65; rpt. in *Literary Essays of Ezra Pound*, ed. T. S. Eliot (New York: New Directions, 1968), pp. 378–81.

ears—that is, he counted syllables instead of listening to the beat or pulse of the language."[2] The failure to perceive the "rhythmical life" of Yeats's poetry on the printed page is in part the result of an ahistorical, dismissive attitude toward Yeats's theory of spoken verse, in part a failure to see that the rhythms of his poetry are founded upon the relation of cadence to metrical structure. I cannot rewrite the history of imagism in this essay, but I do propose to present, as the age demands, a new image of the movement, portraying Yeats as a pervasive presence fighting the visual paradigm of the imagists and reshaping their "devil's metres" into the third proposition of the imagist manifesto—"As regarding rhythm: to compose in the sequence of the musical phrase, not in sequence of a metronome."[3] And so I summon to the battlements once again Ezra Pound and "the forgotten school of 1909."[4]

I call first on Florence Farr (Mrs. Emery), an original member of the forgotten school, who, it will be seen, provoked her friend T. E. Hulme into an important symbolist-imagist controversy in 1908. Yeats had discovered her "exquisite recitation" at Bedford Park in 1890, and thereupon they began their twenty-two year experiment in chanting poetry with the proper cadence. By 1893 Yeats had begun to define this key element of his prosody, writing that Blake's poem "Samson" is among "the great rarity of any blank verse in English which contains cadence—the first and last of poetic virtues, within whose realm is ample room for all the rest to sleep, sing, or march, or dance, or weep—its value to literature cannot be disputed."[5] Throughout the 1890s, in poetic drama and in lyric poetry, the two worked at their auditory poetics, which were greatly furthered by their timely collaboration in 1901 with Arnold Dolmetsch, who made a psaltery for Farr and sat up many nights writing the musical notation of Yeats chanting his poems in trancelike states. In chanting with his wavering, delayed measures, shifts of pitch, unexpected gaps, intoned vowels, and passionate

[2]Thomas Rees, "Ezra Pound and the Modernization of Yeats," *Journal of Modern Literature,* 4 (Feb. 1974), 575.

[3]*Literary Essays of Ezra Pound,* p. 3.

[4]Pound so named Hulme's group in his "Prefatory Note" to "The Complete Poetical Works of T. E. Hulme," which he appended to *Ripostes* (London: Stephen Swift, 1912).

[5]*The Works of William Blake,* ed. Edwin Ellis and W. B. Yeats, I (London: Bernard Quaritch, 1893), pp. 182–83.

accents, Yeats sought to bring out of the metrical structure the "organic rhythm" of the poem—what Pound would later call "absolute rhythm"—and at the time he wanted to "fix" and preserve the pitch and cadence of that rhythm for future reader-reciters through regulated declamation, declaring that "only when declamation is regulated and recorded can it become an art perfecting itself from generation to generation."[6] This concept of fixed organic rhythm carried over into his dramaturgy, Yeats insisting that "an actor must so understand how to discriminate cadence from cadence, and so cherish the musical lineaments of verse or prose, that he delights the ear with a continually varied music" (Ex 173). By 1902 Dolmetsch felt that they had perfected what they called the "New Art," and Yeats wrote that henceforth he meant "to write all my longer poems for the stage, and all my shorter ones for the psaltery, if only some strong angel keep me to my good resolutions" (E&I 19–20). For the next three years Yeats and Farr gave scores of lecture-demonstrations on chanting and speaking to musical notes, and from 1905 to 1907 they toured the provinces of England, Scotland, and Ireland with one entitled "Literature and the Living Voice," urging a revival of the oral tradition and the restoration of an ancient "spiritual democracy"—one that would make imaginative literature accessible to all the people through the living voice.[7] In 1907 Farr even took the psaltery and their theories on American tour (leaving Yeats behind when John Quinn suggested that provincial American audiences would think their traveling together unseemly). In her absence Yeats began gathering the psaltery notations for the 1908 Collected Edition of his works, writing to Farr that "these volumes will be gone to for material & thoughts in time to come, & in our own time will consolidate our influence."[8] He told his copy editor that

[6]From the handbill advertising the Yeats-Farr lecture "Speaking to Musical Notes" on 10 June 1902 at Clifford's Inn Hall. A copy is in the National Library of Ireland, MS. 12145.

[7]For a history of their lecture tours see my "The Minstrel in the Theatre: Arnold, Chaucer, and Yeats's New Spiritual Democracy," *Yeats Annual No. 2* (London: Macmillan, 1983), pp. 3–24.

[8]Unpublished letter, 28 April 1908, Humanities Research Center, University of Texas at Austin. I am grateful to the Yeats estate for permission to quote from unpublished letters in this essay.

Farr's notations for the edition were "absolutely necessary" (L 494) and that the music "gets its meaning from the method of speaking and is a necessary record of that method. It is important to me that people whom I cannot personally teach and who may produce my work shall know my intentions" (L 492).

I call next on T. E. Hulme, at that period in 1908 when, after a maturing year of self-exile in Canada and Brussels, he returned to London intent upon rapid assimilation into the avant garde. He was soon asked to help organize the Poets' Club, and following a successful subscription of members he was elected Hon. Secretary. In that capacity he set about arranging activities and drawing up a set of rules that stipulated monthly dinner meetings at the United Arts Club, followed by "a paper on a subject connected with poetry by a member or guest of the Club."[9] What has not been known is that Farr, who met Hulme through their work on *The New Age,* was one of the club's first speakers. She wrote to Quinn on 18 June that she was going to dinner at the United Arts Club "and am to speak and read my translation of Nietzsche's dance song."[10] Most members of the Poets' Club had witnessed and indeed had for several years been indoctrinated in the Yeats-Farr chanting movement, particularly Joseph Campbell, "the mountainy singer," who had been trained as a reciter at the Abbey, and Lady Margaret Sackville, who had been an advocate of chanted verse since she first attended one of Yeats's Monday evenings in 1902. Farr's illustrated discussion of chanting before the Poets' Club and the enthusiastic endorsement it must have received actually sparked the first stage of the imagist movement—by provoking Hulme into formulating his own ideas about counterdirections in modern poetry. The confrontation of Farr's chanting and Hulme's imagism set off a dialogue on prosody that provides a wholly new context for looking at the formation of the imagist credo in 1912.

[9]Alun R. Jones, *The Life and Opinions of T. E. Hulme* (Boston: Beacon Press, 1960), p. 29.

[10]Unpublished letter, Manuscripts Divison, New York Public Library. Farr's translations of passages from *Thus Spake Zarathustra* included "A Dance Song" ("Pray you unlearn the hornblowing of affliction") from "On the Higher Man." She first chanted the song at the opening meeting of the Dancers' Society on 5 Dec. 1903 and subsequently made it a familiar part of her repertoire.

The club did not hold summer meetings, but when activity resumed in the fall Hulme had put together his "Lecture on Modern Poetry."[11] Yeats's *Collected Works* had begun to appear at the end of the summer, and Hulme must have felt that Yeats, whose poetics he implicitly addresses in the lecture, had duly shelved his career and opened the way for protomodernism. Hulme had not yet met Pound, recently arrived in London, or Edward Storer, though he had read two recent reviews of Storer's *Mirrors of Illusion,* one by F. S. Flint, the first historian of imagism. These unacquainted men, each moving independently toward visual, nonmetrical verse, were soon to become imagist allies, but at the moment Hulme seemed a single voice. The principal feature of verse at the present time, he asserted, "is this: that it is read and not chanted" (*FS,* p. 73). In contrasting the features of the outmoded poetry with the trends of the new, he noted the modern movement away from absolute toward relative truth, from heroic action to "momentary phases in the poet's mind," from regular meter to free verse, from hypnotic rhythms to an arresting and exhausting succession of visual images that "serve to suggest and evoke the state" that the poet feels (*FS,* pp. 72, 73). The character of poetry, he concluded, "has changed from the ancient art of chanting to the modern impressionist, but the mechanism of verse has remained the same. It can't go on doing so" (*FS,* p. 76). For Hulme, the image was to carry the burden of intellectual-emotional evocation, couched in a free-verse prosody that would allow the poet more delicately to arrange his pattern of images and fit the rhythm to the idea. Yeats and Farr, both of whom had often expressed their desire to adapt chanting to modern needs and common, "passion-

[11]Hulme's lecture is published in his *Further Speculations,* ed. Sam Hynes (Lincoln: University of Nebraska Press, 1962), p. 73; hereafter abbreviated *FS* in the text. The undated lecture has traditionally been dated "1908 or 1909," but internal evidence points to November 1908. In the opening paragraph Hulme refers to an article the previous week in *The Saturday Review,* where the author "spoke of poetry as the means by which it became merged into a higher kind of reality" (*FS,* p. 67). The reference appears to be to an unsigned review of five recent books of poetry, one of which is praised for springing "from a spirit most passionately bent upon the visible and invisible worlds, often upon both together, seeing them as one," while imagist poet Edward Storer's *Mirrors of Illusion* is criticized as "slag" that can only supply "a spiritual equivalent to the sucking of chocolate" (*Saturday Review,* 14 Nov. 1908, pp. 611–12).

ate" speech rhythms, held that the visual image finds its greatest evocative power in the auditory imagination and that the cadence of the living voice, which gives expression to the imagination, gives meter the semblance of freedom.

Shortly after Hulme's lecture, two splinter groups separated themselves from the Poets' Club—Hulme's "little Secessionist" group (of which more below) and an even more forgotten school of 1909, the Poetry Recital Society, founded in February 1909 by Lady Margaret Sackville in an effort to "encourage the intelligent reading of verse with due regard to emphasis and rhythm and the poet's meaning."[12] At the inaugural meeting Lady Margaret spoke on the topic "The Art of Speaking Verse," attacking the techniques of modern elocution and praising the Irish National Theatre for its "interesting attempt to break through the traditional methods and introduce a more vital and sincere way of speaking."[13] The Poetry Recital Society, independent of Yeats's involvement but heavily indebted to his inspiration, set out to create a verse-speaking renaissance, and, in an adaptation of Yeats's "spiritual democracy," its constitution expressed the plan "to bind poetry readers and lovers together throughout the English-speaking world, forming a desirable freemasonry."[14] For the next two years, as will be seen, the society was an important counterpoise to the early imagist movement.

When Hulme seceded from the Poets' Club he was joined not only by Storer and Flint, who had written that "the Poets' Club is death,"[15] but also by Farr, who diabolically led the imagists into a virtual chantry. What Flint left out of his "The History of Imagism" (1915), but preserved in manuscript, was the fact that many of the early imagist meetings took place not only in Hulme's rooms but also at the Irish Literary Society, citadel of Yeats's

[12]The society's Constitution was published in *The Poetical Gazette,* 16 (Jan. 1912) [53]. With this issue, the "Official Journal" of the society was incorporated with continuous paging into Harold Monro's *The Poetry Review,* 1 (Jan. 1912), 41–56.

[13]The lecture, read at the inaugural meeting of the Poetry Recital Society on 24 Feb. 1909, was originally published in the first number of *The Poetical Gazette* (May 1909). It was reprinted in *The Poetry Review* for Sept. 1912, pp. 454–56.

[14]*The Poetical Gazette,* 16 (Jan. 1912) [53].

[15]"Recent Verse," a review of *For Christmas MDCCCVIII* by members of the Poets' Club, *The New Age,* 11 Feb. 1909, p. 327.

theories in Hanover Square. Here Hulme carried the imagist case to Joseph Campbell, secretary of the society, and to Padraic Colum, who also learned chanting at the Abbey. To this Irish setting Farr brought two former Rhymers, Ernest Radford and Ernest Rhys, and by late March this incongruous group of poets, some writing for the eye, some for the ear, had grown into the forgotten school of 1909. Just out was Storer's book, in which he says in an appended essay: "If we wish to write music, let us use notes, not words: they are provedly superior."[16] Campbell's *The Mountainy Singer* and Flint's *In the Net of the Stars* (modeled on Yeats's *The Wind Among the Reeds*) were in proof. Farr's membership in Hulme's group prompted her into publishing *The Music of Speech*, dedicated to Yeats and Dolmetsch, which had a bold and imposing subtitle: *Containing the Words of Some Poets, Thinkers and Music-Makers Regarding the Practice of the Bardic Art Together with Fragments of Verse Set to Its Own Melody*.[17] For seven years Yeats had tried unsuccessfully to get her to bring out the book, but now she was motivated less by the competitive creative spirit than by the urgent need for an authoritative record of their achievements in musical speech. The book was a defense of chanting before the imagists, a testimonial to the place of their auditory poetics in the newly emerging mainstream of modern poetry.

Farr's maverick presence in Hulme's group was, not surprisingly, welcomed and valued, particularly by those who knew the critical respect she commanded from Yeats. Following the initial meeting at the Tour d'Eiffel restaurant on 25 March 1909, Hulme told Flint that he was delaying a second meeting until Farr could arrange to join them. "I showed your poem to Miss Farr," he added in a postscript, referring to Flint's "The Mask of Gold." "She liked the line about poppies" ("Red poppies wanton in the golden corn").[18] And while the imagists looked to her critical opinion of their work, which she judged in relation to both image and cadence, she redoubled her lectures to make herself more visi-

[16]*Mirrors of Illusion* (London: Sisley's, 1909 [1908]), p. 112.

[17]*The Music of Speech* was published in March 1909 by Elkin Mathews, Yeats's friend and publisher, who introduced Pound to the Poets' Club.

[18]Unpublished letter, 31 March 1909, Humanities Research Center, University of Texas at Austin.

bly and unmistakably the center of discussions on music and poetry. On 5 April she wrote to Quinn: "I've been frightfully active this year, giving recitals all over the place."[19] Her efforts had the desired effect, for apparently Hulme and Flint became more familiar with and sympathetic to her chanting. As Flint later wrote, "I have never yet heard verse read in any way pleasing to me except perhaps Miss Florence Farr's speaking to Psaltery of W. B. Yeats's verse."[20] Indeed, Farr appears to stand behind the radical change that took place in Flint's verse the following year, when in a group of poems called "Moods" he began the free-verse experiments that he called "unrhymed cadence."[21] The graft of the Yeatsian bell-branch on the imagist tree had begun to take.

Pound found his way through the Poets' Club to Hulme's secessionist group on 22 April, introduced, Flint recalled, "by Miss Farr and my friend T. D. Fitzgerald."[22] Flint, himself an evangelizing student of contemporary French poetry, found that Pound "could not be made to believe that there was any French poetry after Ronsard. He was very full of his *troubadours*; but I do not remember that he did more than attempt to illustrate (or refute) our theories occasionally with their example."[23] Pound likely did both, for as an imagist who would strongly come to believe that poetry should be read aloud, he soon became a bridge between the two poetries. On his first meeting at the Tour d'Eiffel, Pound as troubadour disrupted the restaurant with his emotional and sonorous chanting of "Sestina: Altaforte." It was clearly time for him to meet Yeats.

Yeats had spent the winter of 1909 in Dublin, enmeshed in burdensome theatre business. He was in London only once, for a

[19]Unpublished letter, Manuscripts Division, New York Public Library.

[20]Quoted in J. B. Harmer, *Victory in Limbo: Imagism 1908–17* (London: Secker & Warburg, 1975), p. 25, from a typescript of Flint's unpublished lecture in 1940, "The Appreciation of Poetry" (Humanities Research Center, University of Texas).

[21]Harmer, *Victory in Limbo,* p. 57. Flint subsequently published *Cadences* (London: Poetry Bookshop, 1915) and *Otherworld: Cadences* (London: Poetry Bookshop, 1920).

[22]"The History of Imagism," *The Egoist,* May 1, 1915, p. 71. Flint's manuscript notebook, containing the original draft of this essay, is in the Humanities Research Center. Fitzgerald had served as secretary of the Irish Texts Society, of which Yeats was a member.

[23]Ibid.

week in April, but he made time to see Farr and hear of her new activities and acquaintances. When he returned to Woburn Buildings in early May he wrote promptly to Pound, inviting him to join "Florence Farr with a Psaltery and some other friends" at his next Monday evening.[24] By the end of the year Yeats and Pound had talked through their independent theories on the ancient relation of music and poetry, agreeing, in Pound's words, that in Greece and in Provence poetry "attained its highest rhythmic and metrical brilliance at times when the arts of verse and music were most closely knit together, when each thing done by the poet had some definite musical urge or necessity bound up within it."[25] Pound continued to meet with the imagists and the Poets' Club through the year, and at Yeats's Monday evenings he began to espouse the dogmatic principles of prosody that inform *The Spirit of Romance* (1910), where he finds in his troubadours the needs of modern poetry, and where he argues, after Yeats, that all fine poetry "can be well judged only when heard spoken, or sung to its own measure."[26] Among those he encountered there was Sturge Moore, who had been a serious student of chanting since he first helped Yeats train speakers for the psaltery with Farr in 1902, but Pound boldly "took over" Yeats's familiar circle, as illustrated in Douglas Goldring's account of accompanying him to one of Yeats's Mondays late in 1909: "I shall never forget my surprise . . . at the way in which he dominated the room, distributed Yeat's [sic] cigarettes and Chianti, and laid down the law about poetry. Poor golden-bearded Sturge Moore, who sat in a corner with a large musical instrument by his side (on which he was never given a chance of performing) endeavoured to join in the discussion on prosody, a subject on which he believed himself not entirely ignorant, but Ezra promptly reduced him to a glum silence."[27] Much of Pound's prosody was absorbed from Yeats, but

[24]Unpublished letter, 8 May 1909, Yale University.

[25]*Literary Essays of Ezra Pound,* p. 91.

[26]*The Spirit of Romance* (Norfolk, Conn.: New Directions, 1952), p. 26. The book is based on twenty-one lectures that Pound contracted to give at the Regent Street Polytechnic beginning in the fall of 1909.

[27]*South Lodge: Reminiscences of Violet Hunt, Ford Madox Ford and the English Review Circle* (London: Constable, 1943), p. 49. Goldring served as Ford's assistant editor on *The English Review.*

Pound had his own way with Yeats, too, illustrating his own chanting techniques with some persuasiveness. On 10 December, Yeats wrote to Lady Gregory: "Which reminds me that this queer creature Ezra Pound, who has become really a great authority on the troubadours, has I think got closer to the right sort of music for poetry than Mrs. Emery—it is more definitely music with strongly marked time and yet it is effective speech. However he can't sing as he has no voice. It is like something on a very bad phonograph" (L 543).

A week later, on 18 December, Yeats, Farr, and Pound were guests at Ernest Rhys's notorious "tulip-eating" party.[28] Rhys had begun to have the imagists in for supper gatherings, "resuming the nights at the old Cheshire Cheese of the Rhymers' Club."[29] As the original nucleus of the forgotten school began to break up in the fall, the evenings were now infiltrated by poets who would form the second imagist group in 1912. Harmer asserts that "there is no evidence that discussion at Rhys's evenings ever took the more urgent tone it seems to have had for Hulme and some of his colleagues" (p. 23), but it was at Rhys's instigation that Pound undertook *The Spirit of Romance,* and by now the urgent tone had switched from Hulme's image to Yeats's cadence. On this particular night Ford Madox Hueffer brought one of his unknown discoveries from *The English Review,* D. H. Lawrence. The familiar retellings and exaggerations of the amusing evening focus on Pound, who, forced to contain himself while Yeats held forth in unbroken discourse during supper, impatiently seized a tulip from the table "and proceeded to munch it up. As Yeats, absorbed in his monologue, did not observe this strange behavior, and the rest of us were too well-bred to take any notice, Ezra, having found the tulip to his taste, did likewise with a second flower" (*ER,* p. 244). If Rhys can trust his memory, by the end of the meal Pound had consumed all the tulips.

Pound's tulip-eating has become such a favorite anecdote of the

[28]This date is satisfactorily established in Kim Herzinger, "The Night Pound Ate the Tulips: An Evening at the Ernest Rhys's," *Journal of Modern Literature,* 8 (1980), 153–55.

[29]*Everyman Remembers* (New York: Cosmopolitan Book Corp., 1931), p. 243; hereafter abbreviated *ER* in the text.

early movement that the significance of the bizarre evening has become obscured. What has been ignored is the fact that at supper Yeats "held forth at length on this new art of bringing music and poetry together" (*ER,* p. 244). Here, on one clear evening in the historical haze of 1909, Yeats directly transmitted his theories to the fluctuating imagist circle, thereby reinforcing the continuous pressure exerted by Farr and Pound. Though he had all but given up on his cultural mission of establishing a spiritual democracy, he maintained a messianic fervor for the New Art in his artistic circles. The monologue on music and poetry led to after-dinner recitations by Yeats, Radford, Hueffer, Lawrence, and Pound. Farr then brought out the psaltery, chanting in a "haunting wail" Yeats's "The Man Who Dreamed of Faeryland," her reading "suggestive of a priestess intoning a litany" (*ER,* p. 248). Yeats, Rhys confirmed, was still "bent on using the psaltery as a means of giving poetry a new musical vogue" (*ER,* p. 248), and he suggested that she chant another; she then surprised Rhys with his own "Sir Dinadan and La Belle Isoud." As the evening attests, by the end of 1909 Hulme's assertion that poetry "is read and not chanted" had been overruled. The nature of rhythm and the musical properties of prosody had become a primary topic of the group, and much of what Yeats now conveyed to them came from his recent discovery of Coventry Patmore's temporal prosody.

Yeats had come upon Patmore's work early in 1909, and on 4 March he wrote to Lady Gregory: "Patmore is I find most exciting—no poetry has excited me so much for ever so long."[30] Within days he had come across Patmore's "Essay on English Metrical Law" and wrote with equal excitement to Farr to add to her weap-

[30]Unpublished letter, National Library of Ireland, MS. 18712. See Mem 170, 189–90. When Thomas MacDonagh began his masters' thesis at University College, Dublin, on song-verse and speech-verse, later published as *Thomas Campion and the Art of English Poetry* (Dublin: Hodges, Figgis, 1913), Yeats read for him "in a chanting voice some of Coventry Patmore's poems from *The Unknown Eros*" (p. 5). "It is this chanting quality in his verse," observed MacDonagh, "joined to a wandering rhythm caught from Irish traditional music, that has informed a new species of verse. It is chant-verse, overflowing both song-verse and speech-verse. For not only does something of the word reverence of chanted speech unstress the lyric beat of this poetry, but something of the musical quality of chant lightens and changes the weight of its speech-verse" (p. 52).

onry: "I find in Patmore's book of Odes an appendix in which he states our theory of music and speech very clearly" (L 526).[31] To Yeats, Patmore provided "the support of a great authority," for in his discussion of the relation of music to language he had arrived at a strongly emphasized conclusion: "*Perfect poetry and song are, in fact, nothing more than perfect speech upon high and moving subjects*" (p. 233). Yeats pointed out the essay to members of his circle, and Sturge Moore thereafter quoted from it in his own lectures on chanting to the Poetry Recital Society. Yeats used Patmore's scholarly discussion of English prosody to support his own theory of cadence, by showing that in English meter "those qualities which, singly, or in various combination, have hitherto been declared to *be* accent, are indeed only *the conditions of accent*" (p. 231). Patmore pointed out that in modern prosody accentual division has unfortunately become "the *sole,* instead of merely the *main,* source of metre" (p. 236). To him, the true rhythm of a verse line arose not from accentual stress on certain syllables but from patterns of sound in time, units of sound and silence. For Patmore, this was time-rhythm, for Yeats, cadence. Patmore's discussion of monotone also explained Yeats's belief that "all art is, indeed, a monotony in external things for the sake of an interior variety, a sacrifice of gross effects to subtle effects, an asceticism of the imagination" (E&I 18). "There is no charm in the rhythm of monotones," Patmore explains, "unless the notion of monotone can be overcome; and, when that is the case, it is not rhythm, but rhythmical melody, whereby we are pleased" (pp. 231–32). The rhythmical value of monotones, as Yeats well knew, is that they admit of "imagined variations" (p. 232), allowing the voice to express (in quarter-tones) what the mind imagines.

Pound and others heard all of this from Yeats, who was to Pound the recognized master of rhythm, and Pound was discussing with the master the definitions of rhythm that appeared during

[31]Yeats continued: "You will find a long passage starting on page 232 which will interest you and at any rate give you the support of a great authority. I am grateful for your dedication and expect to find your book very valuable" (L 526). In its final form the "Essay on English Metrical Law" was appended to the second volume of Patmore's *Poems,* second collected edition (London: George Bell, 1886), pp. 218–67; subsequent page references are to the third collective edition (1887) and are cited parenthetically in the text. The volume was in its ninth collective edition in 1909.

the next two years, particularly "absolute rhythm" and the "inner form" of the poetic line: "it is this 'inner form,' I think, which must be preserved in music; it is only by mastery of this inner form that the great masters of rhythm—Milton, Yeats, whoever you like—are masters of it."[32]

In late December the activities of 1909 came to a close at the Poets' Club, where Joseph Campbell, attired in bardic robes, chanted Pound's "Ballad of the Goodly Fere" and Pound, who wished he had Campbell's voice, gave a lecture, "Arnaut Daniel, finest of the troubadours." Pound's and Hulme's poems appeared together in *The Book of the Poets' Club* for 1909, but thereafter, says Pound, "Hulme stopped writing poetry."[33] Pound left England for America in the early summer of 1910, leaving Hulme studying Bergson, Yeats and Farr chanting, and the Poetry Recital Society flourishing.

When Pound resettled in London in August 1911, poetry, he said, underwent "retirement to Church Walk,"[34] where "*Les Imagistes,* the descendants of the forgotten school of 1909"[35] formulated the imagist manifesto early in 1912. Accounted present in Pound's new school were Farr, Flint, H. D., Hueffer, Lawrence, J. G. Fletcher, Richard Aldington and Brigit Patmore. Lawrence, nicknamed Lorenzo by Brigit Patmore, loved to parody Farr's chanting of Yeats's poems to the psaltery. "Did any of you hear Florence Farr do her ping-wanging?" he asked the coterie. Patmore recounts:

> Lorenzo began chanting monotonously, 'You who are bent and bald and blind. . . .' Paused, then stretched his thin hands over his knees delicately, as if an instrument lay there, plucked an imaginary string and whined: 'Ping . . . wa . . . n . . . ng.' Then, three semitones

[32] *The New Age,* 8 Feb. 1912, p. 344; rpt. in *Ezra Pound and Music,* ed. R. Murray Schafer (New York: New Directions, 1977), p. 471.

[33] "This Hulme Business," *Townsman,* 2 (Jan. 1939), 15. For *Canzoni* (1911), Pound wrote "for the cenacle of 1909" a poem, "To Hulme (T. E.) and Fitzgerald," affirming his own decision to continue writing poetry, but he canceled the poem in page proof and published it later in *Des Imagistes* (1914).

[34] See Christopher Middleton, "Documents on Imagism from the Papers of F. S. Flint," *The Review,* no. 15 (April 1965), p. 50.

[35] "Prefatory Note" to "The Complete Poetical Works of T. E. Hulme," *Ripostes.*

> lower: 'Ping . . . pi . . . iing, wang.' Deepening his voice, 'With heavy heart, staccato ping-wang and a wandering mind.' And he pinged so violently to show the state of his mind that our hoots of laughter swept him with us and he couldn't look holy any longer.[36]

In spite of Lawrence's devastating mimicries, Yeats, Farr, and a growing number of allies kept the pressure on the imagists, determined never to let them substitute a visual for an aural paradigm. They had recently found an energetic proselytizer in Harold Monro, who had joined the Poetry Recital Society in March 1910 and who incorporated the society's publication, *The Poetical Gazette,* into *The Poetry Review,* where he published Pound's credo on absolute rhythm in February 1912. Yeats had taken an interest in Monro and his new periodical, and after a few numbers had appeared Monro wrote that "Yeats, Newbolt, Sturge Moore and some others have now all been expressing strong approval, which delights me."[37] But even as Monro joined the struggle against visual poetry, one of the most startling figures in Yeats's life appeared before the imagist circle—Rabindranath Tagore.

In June 1912 Yeats was "deeply moved" by his introduction to the prose translations of Tagore's poems, which he found "a great inspiration in my art."[38] He arranged for Farr to chant Tagore's poems to the imagists at Church Walk, where Pound became enraptured by the "very beautiful English prose, with mastery of cadence."[39] In Tagore, Yeats and Pound found the living example of the modern troubadour, his lyrics displaying for Yeats "in their thought a world I have dreamed of all my life long" (E&I 390). Yeats told an interviewer that "as far as literature is concerned he is still living in the fourteenth century, for the conditions for creating and holding an audience are very much like those that existed in Chaucer's time. His poetry is spoken and sung by everybody and he writes the music for his words. . . . from time to time the minstrels go to visit him and learn his new poetry. They, in turn, teach them to other minstrels, and so the songs are passed on in an

[36]Brigit Patmore, *My Friends When Young* (London: Heinemann, 1968), p. 81.

[37]John Drinkwater, *Discovery* (Boston: Houghton Mifflin, 1933), p. 224; hereafter cited as *D.*

[38]Unpublished letter, 19 Aug. 1912, to William Rothenstein, Harvard University.

[39]See the *Letters of Ezra Pound,* ed. D. D. Paige (New York: Harcourt, 1950), p. 10.

unbroken chain from village to village. His songs are hummed by travelers on the highway and caught up by those going down the rivers, until the whole country is echoing with his songs."[40] To Yeats, this was the manifestation of a "supreme culture," a true spiritual democracy wherein the common people murmured the cadences of the poet, who is positioned at the center of culture.

In August, as he prepared to write the preface to *Gitanjali,* Yeats took Tagore's poems to France, where he spent several days at Les Mouettes with Maude Gonne and James Cousins, who described Yeats as being "on fire with the fullness in them that told that the renaissance of poetry had appeared in India. . . . From poem to poem Yeats went from hour to hour, annotating, expatiating, rejoicing, till we were all afire with a new revelation of spiritual beauty."[41] The day following this rhapsodic evening, the two being left alone, Cousins observed Yeats in poetic composition, and of all the accounts of those who have heard Yeats's eerie poetic murmuring, Cousins' description is the most revealing, for it dramatizes the relation of organic rhythm to metrical rhythm and cadence.

> After a while I became aware of a queer monotonous murmur somewhere in the house. It was Yeats' voice . . . and I concluded he was engaged in some private ceremonial of worship or enchantment. The utterance . . . was not spontaneous, as it had some kind of vague architecture and design. Its constant repetition of the same sounds in similar order had the eeriness of the inaudible made audible. . . . Ultimately I got an angular and meagre glimpse through an almost closed door; . . . Yeats was sitting on a chair in a corner of the kitchen with his head bent close into the corner. For three hours the sound went on, and during the time I neither heard nor wrote a word.

When Maude and Iseult Gonne and Gretta Cousins returned from church, Yeats emerged, Cousins continues, "muttering in an undertone the same sound as I had heard all morning. 'How did you

[40]See Elsie F. Weil, "William Butler Yeats and the New Ireland," *Inter-Ocean* (Chicago), 1 Mar. 1914, Magazine, p. 1; quoted in Karin Margaret Strand, "W. B. Yeats's American Lecture Tours," Diss. Northwestern University, 1978, pp. 303–4.

[41]James H. and M. E. Cousins, *We Two Together* (Madras: Ganesh, 1950), p. 161.

get on, Willy?' Madame queried. 'I finished it.' Then I began to understand and later ascertained that such was the Yeats method of composing verse, making a sound-scheme into which words were fitted after much trial and alteration" (Cousins, p. 160).

Yeats returned to London inspired by Tagore to reactivate his plan for reviving the oral tradition by training reciters to chant and carry poetry to the people once again. But in September 1912 he discovered that Farr had decided to lay down the burden of the psaltery, hoping to find her own ideal culture in Ceylon. "Your mind and you are our Sargasso Sea," wrote Pound in his personal farewell to Farr, "Portrait d'une Femme."[42] Her final performance on the psaltery held her audience "spell-bound," and afterward Harold Monro wrote London's farewell to the mistress of cadence and rhythm: "We can but regret our loss of so fine an artist, and hope that there are others who may have learnt something from her, and who have sufficient restraint and self-surrender to submit themselves, after her manner, to the cadence and rhythms of poetry, becoming, for the time being, a sensitive medium for their conveyance to an audience, rhapsodist rather than exponent, instrument rather than representative."[43] Her last act before sailing was to return the psaltery to Yeats. He was bereft, and in a weak moment he told Sturge Moore that Mrs. Emery was "'a chalk egg he had been sitting on for years.'"[44]

Yeats nonetheless went forward with his Bengal-inspired scheme, even planning to go to India to study Tagore's minstrel culture. By November 1912 organizational plans were made, and Monro wrote enthusiastically to John Drinkwater, telling him of a meeting at the Poetry Bookshop at which his presence was indis-

[42]The poem first appeared in *Ripostes*, published in September 1912. During his confinement in St. Elizabeth's Hospital, Pound told Jayanta Padmanabha that he wrote the poem for Farr. See Josephine Johnson, *Florence Farr: Bernard Shaw's New Woman* (Gerrards Cross: Colin Smythe, 1975), p. 169. In letters of 5 July 1912, Pound asked Dorothy Shakespear if Farr, who was making plans for Ceylon, would "see her portrait before she goes," and Dorothy wrote allusively that Farr's new novel, *The Solemnization of Jacklin*, was "Such a Sargasso Sea muddle": see letters 99 and 100 in *Ezra Pound and Dorothy Shakespear: Their Letters*, ed. A. Walton Litz and Omar Pound (New York: New Directions, 1984).

[43]*Poetry Review*, 1 (Sept. 1912), 424.

[44]See T. Sturge Moore, "Yeats," *English*, 2 (Summer 1939), 277.

pensable. "Roughly the project is to read poetry in villages without formality, payment, pose, condescension, propaganda, or parson. You just give it them like the Eastern story-tellers, who gather people together at street corners. . . . When you hear the whole plan I am sure you will help, later. . . . It does not sound very much like this, but you should hear me explain it!" (*D*, pp. 224–25). Sadly, Yeats's desire to turn the London imagists into chanters in the provinces failed again, but in January 1913 Monro announced the Poetry Bookshop readings, which had their origins and found their momentum in Yeats's theory of spoken verse.[45] Ironically, when W. W. Gibson opened the readings in February with a reading of Yeats's poems, Hulme had taken rooms above the Poetry Bookshop.

Hulme gave his "Lecture on Modern Poetry" a second time at the Kensington Town Hall in April–May 1914, and perhaps the new climate for cadenced verse contributed to the abstracted and mumbled delivery that few could hear. To Yeats, the imagists still wrote "devil's metres" (Fletcher recalls Yeats's "attempt to change a line in my 'Irradiations' into something 'more Yeatsian' "[46]) but they had at least redefined *vers libre* as "a verse-form based upon cadence."[47] As the imagist poets who gathered at Church Walk split up into Georgians, Vorticists, and "Amygists," they carried with them that rhythmic principle of Yeats's and Farr's auditory poetics. Ahead lay a decade of historic readings at the Poetry Bookshop, followed in the 1920s by the Oxford Recitations, founded by John Masefield explicitly on the principles of Yeats's chanting.[48] But the ultimate reversal of Hulme's prophecy ap-

[45]Yeats first read his poems at the Poetry Bookshop on 3 July 1913, with a hundred people present and forty turned away for lack of room. He did not read again until 11 April 1916, but in the interim several readers read his poems and plays. See British Library, Add. MS. 57756. Henry Newbolt, who formally opened the Poetry Bookshop readings as a member of the Poetry Recital Society, later wrote "The new movement for the better speaking of English verse did not in the end keep to Yeats's method, which was a method of chanting rather than of reciting; but it was I believe the origin of the organised competitions and societies which now hold the field": *The Later Life and Letters of Sir Henry Newbolt*, ed. Margaret Newbolt (London: Faber & Faber, 1942), p. 5.

[46]*Life Is My Song* (New York: Farrar & Rinehart, 1937), p. 78.

[47]*Some Imagist Poets* (Boston: Houghton Mifflin, 1916), p. ix; hereafter abbreviated *SIP* in the text.

[48]See John Masefield, *So Long to Learn* (New York: Macmillan, 1952), pp. 128–37.

peared in the second volume of *Some Imagist Poets* (1916), where Amy Lowell, whom Yeats had met in August 1913, got the Church Walk imagists—Aldington, Fletcher, Flint, H. D. and Lawrence—collectively to reexplain the principles of imagism. In their preface they felt compelled to focus on "this very fact of 'cadence' which has misled so many reviewers, until some have been betrayed into saying that the Imagists discard rhythm, when rhythm is the most important quality in their technique" (*SIP,* pp. viii–ix). As though Yeats and Farr were looking over their shoulders, they concluded that "one thing must be borne in mind: a cadenced poem is written to be read aloud, in this way only will its rhythm be felt. Poetry is a spoken and not a written art" (*SIP,* p. x). Almost seventy years later, that remarkable imagist conclusion demands not only a new image of the movement, but a new hearing of the rhythmical life of Yeats's poetry.

A Note on the Scribner Archive at the Humanities Research Center

RICHARD J. FINNERAN

In the spring of 1983, the late F. S. L. Lyons told me of some materials that he had recently seen at the Humanities Research Center of the University of Texas at Austin. Although I had received copies of some manuscripts from the HRC as recently as July 1981, his description suggested that these new materials might well be relevant to *The Poems of W. B. Yeats, a New Edition*. Shortly thereafter I journeyed to the HRC and discovered that such was indeed the case.[1]

What Lyons had seen was the material that Yeats (or his agent, A. P. Watt) had submitted to Charles Scribner's Sons, New York, as copy for their unpublished "Dublin Edition." Filed in twelve blue cases numbered I–XI and Miscellaneous, the archive includes unbound pages; pages removed from books; photostats of books; page proofs; and typescripts, some with manuscript corrections. It seems clear that the material was sent to New York in two stages. The larger portion must have been submitted in the autumn of 1937. That date can be established by the fact *The Herne's Egg*, published on 21 January 1938 (Wade 194), is represented by a

[1]I am most grateful to the staff of the HRC for their kindness, both in correspondence and on my two visits there in 1983. I would like to thank especially Cathy Henderson, a veritable model of a manuscript curator. Edward Callan was unable to trace these materials when preparing his *Yeats on Yeats: The Last Introductions and the 'Dublin Edition'*, New Yeats Papers, No. 20 (Dublin: Dolmen Press, 1981); hereafter cited as Callan.

typescript, while the Cuala Press *Essays,* the printing of which was completed in the last week of October 1937 (Wade 193), is present in page proofs. As the slipcase holding the typescripts for the three Introductions to the Dublin Edition (i.e., E&I 509–30) is dated "1937," a reasonable date is September-October 1937.[2]

The tables of contents prepared by an editor at Scribner's make it certain that in 1937 a seven-volume edition was projected—in other words, one in accord with the unpublished Macmillan "Edition de Luxe," then also in progress.[3] Sometime after Yeats's death, most likely in the autumn of 1939, George Yeats or Watt submitted further materials, thereby expanding the Edition to eleven volumes, a growth identical to that of the London project, by then called "The Coole Edition" (*EYP,* p. 11). Scribner's seriously considered publishing the Dublin Edition in both 1940 and 1942, on the second occasion going so far as to print some sample pages. But by 5 January 1953, Scribner's had "abandoned" the Edition (Callan, p. 103), and the archive dropped out of sight until it surfaced in Texas.[4]

The Scribner Archive is important to the establishment of all of Yeats's major texts, but I will here confine my remarks to the poems. First, the HRC materials reinforce my conclusion about the proper arrangement of Yeats's poems: that is, having seen in print the division of his poetry into "Lyrical" and "Narrative and Dramatic" in the 1933 *Collected Poems,* Yeats preferred that scheme over the essentially chronological arrangement of all his poems planned for the Edition de Luxe. Although we have known for some time that the 8 October 1936 letter of agreement for the Dublin Edition specified that Scribner's was to follow the *Collected Poems,* it is now certain that Yeats did not have a change of heart: the table of contents for the seven-volume version of the Dublin

[2]In a letter of 9 February 1939, J. H. Wheelock of Scribner's noted that "[t]he last items of his [Yeats's] included in the copy here are 'The Vision' and 'The Great Herne's Egg'" (Callan, p. 99).

[3]See my *Editing Yeats's Poems* (London: Macmillan; New York: St. Martin's Press, 1983), pp. 5–11; hereafter cited as *EYP.* Unfortunately, the printing of that study had been completed before I learned of the materials at the HRC.

[4]The records of the HRC do not disclose when or from where the Scribner Archive was acquired or when it first became accessible to readers.

Edition shows the poems in the 1933 arrangement. Although it is true that Macmillan, London, hoping to have as much difference between the two Editions as possible, refused to let Scribner's have proofs of its Edition de Luxe, it was in no position to prevent Yeats from telling Scribner's to print his poems in whatever arrangement he chose. Considering that ever since his first lecture tour in 1903–1904, Yeats had found a large and receptive audience in the United States, and considering that only a few months before submitting the materials to Scribner's he had received a grant of £600 (with assurances of more to come) from an American "Testimonial Committee for W. B. Yeats," Yeats would hardly have offered his most devoted American readers an elaborate edition of his poems in the "wrong" order.

Second, the Scribner Archive offers further evidence that Yeats did *not* prepare corrected typescripts of *New Poems* (1938) in the winter of 1938, contrary to the implication in a letter of 17 April 1939 from George Yeats to Thomas Mark, Yeats's editor at Macmillan, London (*EYP,* p. 51). There are two sets of typescripts for *New Poems* at the HRC. The first, in elite type, must have been submitted with the first batch of material in late 1937, as can be seen, for example, in the early version of these lines from "Lapis Lazuli":

> In wooden horse or on chariot, or ship-board,
> Camel-back, horse-back, ass-back, mule-back
> They came, and multitudes put to the sword
> Old civilisations brought to rack.

These early typescripts are corrected by Yeats. A second set of carbon typescripts, in pica type, is not corrected by Yeats and was almost certainly prepared after his death. They incorporate the corrections in his own copy of *New Poems* and add a few others; moreover, they include at least one reading unique to the Macmillan *Last Poems and Plays* (1940), "Griffiths" for "Griffith" in "The Municipal Gallery Re-visited."

More important, though, the Scribner Archive provides revised texts for four poems. First, Yeats revised lines 9 and 13–14 of "Brown Penny," changing

O love is the crooked thing,
There is nobody wise enough
To find out all that is in it,
For he would be thinking of love
Till the stars had run away
And the shadows eaten the moon.
[VP 268]

to

And the penny sang up in my face,
'There is nobody wise enough
To find out all that is in it,
For he would be thinking of love
That is looped in the loops of her hair,
Till the loops of time had run.'
[P 98]

This revision eliminates the awkward image of the lunivorus shadows, and the reference to the "loops of time" suggests connections with *A Vision*.

Second, Yeats rewrote line 2 of "Ribh denounces Patrick" from

Recall that masculine Trinity. Man, woman, child (a daughter or a son) . . .
[VP 556]

to

A Trinity that is wholly masculine. Man, woman, child (daughter or son) . . . .
[P 284]

The primary reason for this change may have been the insertion of the phrase "wholly masculine," which stresses Ribh's objections to the "abstract Greek absurdity" of the Christian Trinity and perhaps also includes a cunning pun on "holy."

The other revisions were made to the plays. Yeats changed three lines in a song from *The Land of Heart's Desire* from

> The wind blows over the lonely of heart,
> And the lonely of heart is withered away.
>
> . . .
>
> The lonely of heart is withered away.'
>
> [VPl 194–95]

to

> The wind blows on the lonely heart,
> And the lonely heart is withered away.
>
> . . .
>
> The lonely heart is withered away!'
>
> [P 533]

This revision eliminates the initial confusion as to whether "the lonely of heart" is singular or plural, and the final exclamation point makes the conclusion more emphatic. Finally, in the Notes to the plays, Yeats added two new stanzas to "I was going the road one day":

> 'I know of a girl' said I
> (O the brown and the yellow beer)
> 'Who can shorten the time by the clock and the sun'
> (O my dear, O my dear).
>
> 'And one's as good as another
> (O the brown and the yellow beer),
> So get you away with your no right man'
> (O my dear, O my dear).
>
> [P 547][5]

This addition, for which Yeats had no warrant in his source, considerably alters the character of the husband in the poem, moving him toward becoming a masculine version of Crazy Jane.[6]

[5]Cf. VPl 645. Yeats made the changes in holograph on a printed page of the Notes. With minor variants, the changes were typed onto a slip of paper and pasted onto the page. It is likely that the typing was done at Scribner's, as there is an indication that the new stanzas should be placed between the first and second stanzas of the printed text. Such a placement would make the poem incoherent.

[6]His source was Lady Gregory's translation of "The Noble Enchanter," published in the 1901 Christmas issue of *The Irish Homestead* (rpt. *EYP*, pp. 136–37).

A skeptic might suggest that Yeats made these revisions for the sole purpose of introducing some differences between the Scribner Dublin Edition and the Macmillan Edition de Luxe, both of which—had fate been kinder to him—might have been published in 1938. Yet I do not believe that he ever treated his texts so cavalierly, and in my judgment all four changes are improvements. In any event, the Scribner Archive at the University of Texas remains an important source for all future editors of Yeats.

Yeats made one other revision to his poems in the Scribner Archive, changing the opening line of the first of "Two Songs Rewritten for the Tune's Sake" from "That blonde there is my heart's desire," the text of *A Full Moon in March* (London: Macmillan 1935), p. 56, to "A bright haired slut is my heart's desire." That reading was not used in the new *Poems* (P 281), however, because the text was subject to even further revision by Yeats (*EYP*, pp. 45–47).

A Yeats Bibliography for 1982

K. P. S. JOCHUM

The following checklist contains all the 1982 publications that came to my notice before 1 November 1983. It also includes several 1981 items that I found too late for inclusion in the previous checklist and, in an appendix, some additions to entries in the 1981 compilation (which are referred to by 81– plus serial numbers). Items I have not seen are marked°. For further explanations see the prefatory note to the 1981 checklist.

I should add that I do not include master's theses and items written completely (i.e. without an abstract in a European language) in languages that I cannot read, such as Arabic or Japanese. Japanese items can be found by consulting the *Japanese Periodical Index: Humanities and Social Sciences,* published in Tokyo since 1948 and still current.

My thanks to James Lovic Allen, Birgit Bramsbäck, Norbert K. Buchta, Eleonore Engelhardt, Richard J. Finneran, Warwick Gould, Colin McDowell, Colin Smythe, the Department of Russian of the University of Dublin, and my observant proof reader, Ursula Lindner.

82–1. ALBU, RODICA: "W. B. Yeats and Romanian Poetry: Suggestions for a Tentative Comparative Approach," *Analele ştiinţifice ale Universităţii "Al. I. Cuza" din Iasi. Serie nouă: Secţiunea IIIf. Literatură,* 27 (1981), 95–106.

Compares Yeats's poetry with that of Mihail Eminescu and Lucian Blaga.

82–2. ALCORN, MARSHALL WISE: "'Still Razor-Keen, Still like a Looking-Glass': Literary Studies in Narcissistic Sublimation and Lyric Volition," °Ph.D. thesis, University of Texas at Austin, 1981. 338 pp. (*DAI,* 42:11 [May 1981], 4829A.)

On *Purgatory,* according to abstract.

82–3. ALLEN, JAMES LOVIC: "House, Horse, and Hound: Emblems of Nobility in Yeats's 'The Curse of Cromwell,'" *Yeats Eliot Review,* 7:1&2 (June 1982), 69–77.

82–4. ——: *Yeats's Epitaph: A Key to Symbolic Unity in His Life and Work.* Washington, D.C.: University Press of America, 1982. xi, 270 pp.

Incorporates 81–1. Contains chapters on the relationship of the epitaph in "Under Ben Bulben" to Yeats's reading of an essay on Rilke and to Swift's epitaph, on the image of the horseman and the horse in the epitaph and in Yeats's other works, on the relevance of Yeats's burial in Drumcliff Churchyard, and on the "two eternities."

82–5. AMIRTHANAYAGAM, GUY, ED.: *Writers in East-West Encounter: New Cultural Bearings.* London: Macmillan, 1982. xii, 218 pp.

G. Amirthanayagam: "Pontifex and Scapegoat: The Poet in Twentieth-Century Culture," 150–201; *passim* on Yeats, especially pp. 181–90.

82–6. ATTRIDGE, DEREK: *The Rhythms of English Poetry.* London: Longman, 1982. xiv, 395 pp. (English Language Series, 14.)

See pp. 326–29 for an analysis of a section from "Easter 1916."

82–7. AVERILL, DEBORAH M.: *The Irish Short Story from George Moore to Frank O'Connor.* Washington, D.C.: University Press of America, 1982. x, 328 pp.

Mainly on Moore, Joyce, O'Kelly, Corkery, O'Flaherty, O'Faolain, and O'Connor; Yeats is referred to *passim* (see index).

82–8. BALLIET, CONRAD A.: "Maud Gonne MacBride: Violent Pacifist," *Irish Renaissance Annual,* 3 (1982), 93–105.

82–9. ——: "Maud Gonne's Favorite Poem," *American Notes and Queries,* 21:1&2 (Sept./Oct. 1982), 14–16.

The poem is "Red Hanrahan's Song about Ireland" and not "The Two Trees." This note was previously published in the same periodical, 17:7 (March 1979), 102–3.

82–10. BARRICELLI, JEAN-PIERRE, AND JOSEPH GIBALDI, EDS.: *Interrelations of Literature.* New York: MLA, 1982. vi, 339 pp.

Jonathan Culler: "Literature and Linguistics," 1–24, comments on Halliday's interpretation of "Leda and the Swan" (J3106); Ulrich Weisstein: "Literature and the Visual Arts," 251–77, includes a note on "Sailing to Byzantium."

82–11. BAWER, BRUCE: "Two on a Tower: Hardy and Yeats," *Yeats Eliot Review*, 7:1&2 (June 1982), 91–108.

Discusses the similarities rather than differences between the two poets.

82–12. BECKER, EDWARD LINDLEY: "The Moment of Vision in W. B. Yeats, Wallace Stevens, T. S. Eliot, and Robinson Jeffers," Ph.D. thesis, University of California, Berkeley, 1980. iv, 323 pp. (*DAI*, 41:7 [Jan. 1981], 3101A).

"The moment of vision is an instant of supreme awareness in which reality is perceived whole" (p. 1). On Yeats's poetry *passim*.

82–13. BELL, GLORIA JEAN: "Imitation, Freedom, and the Triadic Model in the Early Dramatic and Narrative Works of W. B. Yeats," Ph.D. thesis, University of Colorado at Boulder, 1982. vii, 251 pp. (*DAI*, 43:4 [Oct. 1982], 1149A.)

82–14. BENSON, EUGENE: *J. M. Synge*. London: Macmillan, 1982. xii, 167 pp. (Macmillan Modern Dramatists.)

Numerous references to Yeats (see index), especially in the chapter "Synge and the Theatre," 34–50.

82–15. °BERTHA, CSILLA: "Yeats nó drámái: Nemzeti gondolat és egyetemes jelentés," *Hevesi szemle*, 9:2 (1981), 45–50.

"Yeats's nō plays; the national idea and general meaning."

82–16. BERTHOLF, ROBERT J., AND ANNETTE S. LEVITT, EDS.: *William Blake and the Moderns*. Albany, N.Y.: State University of New York Press, 1982. xv, 294 pp.

Hazard Adams: "The Seven Eyes of Yeats," 3–14; Robert F. Gleckner: "Joyce's Blake: Paths of Influence," 135–63 (Yeats is referred to *passim*).

82–17. BILLIGHEIMER, RACHEL VICTORIA: "Wheels of Eternity: Circle Symbolism in the Works of W. B. Yeats and W. Blake," °Ph.D. thesis, York University (Downsview, Ont.), 1980. (*DAI*, 42:7 [Jan. 1982], 3143A.)

82–18. BLACKFORD, RUSSELL: "Withheld Meaning in Yeats's 'Cuchulain Comforted,'" *Aumla*, 57 (May 1982), 24–30.

82–19. BLAMIRES, HARRY: *Twentieth-Century English Literature*. London: Macmillan, 1982. xii, 304 pp. (Macmillan History of Literature.)

"The Irish Movement," 32–36; "W. B. Yeats," 90–93; and *passim* (see index).

82–20. BOHLMANN, OTTO: *Yeats and Nietzsche: An Exploration of Major Nietzschean Echoes in the Writings of William Butler Yeats*. London: Macmillan, 1982. xviii, 222 pp.

An investigation arranged under such topics as "Conflict, Will,

Power," "The Tragic Disposition," "Realism, Aesthetics, Art," "The Hero," and "Cyclical History." It seems to me, however, that Bohlmann sees too many Nietzschean echoes and that he does not fix their place in relation to other "influences."

Reviews:

F. S. L. Lyons: "Strong Enchantment," *TLS,* 31 Dec. 1982, 1438.

82–21. BOLAND, EAVAN: "Yeats as a Critic," *Irish Times,* 8 May 1982, 12.

A review of *The Secret Rose* (82–213).

82–22. BONACCORSO, RICHARD: Review of *The Secret Rose* (81–145), *Éire-Ireland,* 17:2 (Summer 1982), 155–56.

82–23. BONNEFOY, YVES: *Entretiens sur la poésie.* Neuchatel: Baconnière, 1981. 170 pp.

"La traduction de la poésie (1976)," 95–102; on the problems confronting the translator of "Sailing to Byzantium." Bonnefoy's translation was published in *Modern Poetry in Translation,* 16 (Spring 1973), 11–12.

82–24. BORNSTEIN, GEORGE: "Last Romantic or Last Victorian: Yeats, Tennyson, and Browning," *Yeats Annual,* 1 (1982), 114–32.

82–25. ——: "Victorians and Volumes, Foreigners and First Drafts: Four Gaps in Postromantic Influence Study," *Romanticism Past and Present,* 6:2 (1982), 1–9.

Contains some notes on Yeats.

82–26. BOWERS, NEAL: *Theodore Roethke: The Journey from I to Otherwise.* Columbia: University of Missouri Press, 1982. xi, 228 pp.

On Yeats's influence *passim* (see index).

82–27. BOYCE, DAVID GEORGE: *Nationalism in Ireland.* London: Croom Helm / Dublin: Gill & Macmillan, 1982. 441 pp.

Several remarks on Yeats (see index).

82–28. BRASCH, CHARLES: *The Universal Dance: A Selection from the Critical Prose Writings of Charles Brasch.* Edited by J. L. Watson. Dunedin: University of Otago Press, 1981. 232 pp.

Several references to Yeats (see index), especially in "Writer and Reader" (pp. 126–29, a comparison with Eliot) and "Poetry and Politics" (pp. 186–200, comments on "Easter 1916").

82–29. BRONSON, EDWARD FULTON: "The Dance of Apocalypse: Yeats and Michael Robartes," °Ph.D. thesis, University of Maryland, 1982. 241 pp. (*DAI,* 43:5 [Nov. 1982], 1550A–51A.)

82–30. BUCHTA, NORBERT K.: *Rezeption and ästhetische Verarbeitung romantischer Poetologie im lyrischen Werk William Butler Yeats'.* Königstein: Forum Academicum, 1982. v, 276 pp. (Hochschulschriften Literaturwissenschaft, 52.)

Originally a Dr. phil. thesis, University of Frankfurt. Buchta argues that Yeats's reaction to Romantic poetics in selected prose pieces and poems shows that he believed in concepts which were essentially outmoded. This accounts for unrelieved tensions in Yeats's later works.

82–31. BUCKLEY, VINCENT: "Poetry and the Avoidance of Nationalism," *Threshold,* 32 (Winter 1982), 8–34.

Contains a few references to Yeats.

82–32. BURZYŃSKA, JOANNA: "Yeatsian Methods of Expressing an Archetypal Situation in *A Full Moon in March,*" *Linguistica et Anglica Gedaniensia,* 2 (1981), 109–24.

82–33. BUSHRUI, SUHEIL: "Yeats: The Poet as Hero," *Essays and Studies,* 35 (1982), 101–23.

The poet's responsibility to society as shown in *The King's Threshold.*

82–34. ——, AND BERNARD BENSTOCK, EDS.: *James Joyce: An International Perspective.* Gerrards Cross: Colin Smythe / Totowa, N.J.: Barnes & Noble, 1982. xiii, 301 pp. (Irish Literary Studies, 10.)

Vivian Mercier: "John Eglinton as Socrates: A Study of 'Scylla and Charybdis,'" 65–81, and Ann Saddlemyer: "James Joyce and the Irish Dramatic Movement," 190–212, contain some notes on Yeats. See also the index for further Yeats references.

82–35. BYNNER, WITTER: *The Works of Witter Bynner: Selected Letters.* Edited and with an introduction by James Kraft. New York: Farrar, Straus, Giroux, 1981. xxv, 275 pp.

Some references to Yeats (see index). Apparently Yeats and Bynner knew each other and exchanged letters, none of them included in this selection.

82–36. CAVE, RICHARD ALLEN: "Vision and Revision," *Times Higher Education Supplement,* 6 Nov. 1981, 14.

A review of *The Secret Rose* (81–145).

82–37. CLARK, DAVID: "The Secrets of the Rose," *Irish Literary Supplement,* 1:1 (Spring 1982), 13.

A Review of *The Secret Rose* (81–145).

82–38. CLARKE, BRENNA KATZ: *The Emergence of the Irish Peasant Play at the Abbey Theatre.* Ann Arbor: UMI Research Press, 1982. xii, 223 pp. (Theater and Dramatic Studies, 12.)

Frequent references to Yeats (see index).

82–39. CLARKE, R. DARDIS: "Half a Century of the Irish Academy of Letters," *Irish Times,* 14 Sept. 1982, 8.

82–40. ——: "In Quest of an Abbey Managing Director," *Irish Times,* 12 Jan. 1982, 8.

On Yeats and F. R. Higgins.

82–41. CLAUSEN, CHRISTOPHER: "Did You Once See Willy Plain?" *Virginia Quarterly Review,* 58:2 (Spring 1982), 327–32.

Describes an encounter with an old man in 1965 who said that he had had Yeats as a lodger in Hampstead.

82–42. CONNOLLY, PETER, ED.: *Literature and the Changing Ireland.* Gerrards Cross: Colin Smythe / Totowa, N.J.: Barnes & Noble, 1982. ix, 230 pp. (Irish Literary Studies, 9.)

With one exception (Kiberd), these are the papers delivered at the IASAIL conference in Maynooth, July 1979. On Yeats: Declan Kiberd: "The Perils of Nostalgia: A Critique of the Revival," 1–24.

Vivian Mercier: "Victorian Evangelicalism and the Anglo-Irish Literary Revival," 59–101.

Suheil B. Bushrui: "Images of a Changing Ireland in the Works of W. B. Yeats," 103–32; on the manifestations of Yeats's "ideal nationalism" throughout his poetic career.

Stan Smith: "Historians and Magicians: Ireland between Fantasy and History," 133–56.

D. E. S. Maxwell: "Semantic Scruples: A Rhetoric for Politics in the North," 157–74; includes a section on Yeats's political poetry.

82–43. CONOLLY, LEONARD W., ED.: *Theatrical Touring and Founding in North America.* Westport, Conn.: Greenwood Press, 1982. xiv, 245 pp. (Contributions in Drama and Theatre Studies, 5.)

Ann Saddlemyer: "National Drama and the Founding of Theatres," 193–211. Suggests "some tentative, exploratory comparisons between Canadian and Irish theatre." On Yeats *passim.*

82–44. CORSE, LARRY B., AND SANDRA CORSE: *Articles on American and British Literature: An Index to Selected Periodicals, 1950–1977.* Chicago: Swallow Press / Ohio University Press, 1981. xii, 413 pp.

Yeats, pp. 407–10; about 170 items.

82–45. CRAIG, [ROBERT] CAIRNS: *Yeats, Eliot, Pound, and the Politics of Poetry: Richest to the Richest.* London: Croom Helm, 1982. ix, 323 pp.

Based on °"W. B. Yeats, T. S. Eliot, and the Associationist Aesthetic," Ph.D. thesis, University of Edinburgh, 1978. Includes "The Continuity of Associationist Aesthetic: From Archibald Alison to T. S. Eliot (and Beyond)," *Dalhousie Review,* 60:1 (Spring 1980), 20–37. Analyzes "the dynamics of the process that led Yeats, Eliot and Pound from a 'pure' poetry to a poetry of social involvement." This is done with the help of associationist psychology which "is entirely dependent on the power of memory" (p. 24). The reification of memory leads the three poets to a "justification for repressive political doctrines" (p. 289). Refers specifically to the Byzantium poems, "Easter 1916," "In Memory of Major Robert Gregory," "Leda and the Swan," "The Madness of King Goll," and "Nineteen Hundred and Nineteen."

Reviews:

Edward Hirsch, *Criticism,* 24:4 (Fall 1982), 398–400.

Laurence Lerner: "The Illiberal Imagination," *New Statesman,* 5 March 1982, 23–24.

82–46. CRONIN, ANTHONY: *Heritage Now: Irish Literature in the English Language.* Dingle, Co. Kerry: Brandon, 1982. 215 pp.

"William Butler Yeats: Containing Contradictions," 87–93.

82–47. DARRAS, JACQUES: "Comme je la vois," *Critique* [Paris], 38:421–422 (June–July 1982), 603–11.

The author's view of Irish literature, including Yeats.

82–48. DAVIE, DONALD: "Poets on Stilts: Yeats and Some Contemporaries," *PN Review,* 30 [9:4] (1982), 14–17.

A discussion of "High Talk," leading to statements about Yeats's insecure place among the best poets of the century.

82–49. DAVIES, ALISTAIR: *An Annotated Critical Bibliography of Modernism.* Brighton: Harvester Press / Totowa, N.J.: Barnes & Noble, 1982. xiii, 261 pp. (Harvester Annotated Critical Bibliographies, 1.)

"William Butler Yeats," 69–111 (about 100 entries); see also the indexes for further references.

82–50. DAVIES, JOAN MARY: "The Prose Style of W. B. Yeats's *Autobiography,*" °Ph.D. thesis, University of Maryland, 1981. 170 pp. (*DAI,* 42:8 [Feb. 1982], 3609A.)

82–51. DAVIS, WILLIAM V.: "'The Coming among Us of the Dead': Yeats's 'After Long Silence,'" *McNeese Review,* 27 (1980–81), 45–49.

82–52. DELETIĆ, MIRJANA: "Magijsko i okultno u teorijskim radovima i poeziji V. B. Jejtsa," *Književnost,* yr. 37 / vol. 73:1–2 (1982), 210–29.

"Magic and occultism in the theoretical works and the poetry of W. B. Yeats."

82–53. DOWGUN, RICHARD: "Responses to Tragedy: Hazlitt to T. S. Eliot," °Ph.D. thesis, University of Pennsylvania, 1982. 267 pp. (*DAI,* 43:3 [Sept. 1982], 807A–8A.)

Includes a discussion of Yeats.

82–54. EDEL, LEON: *Stuff of Sleep and Dreams: Experiments in Literary Psychology.* London: Chatto & Windus, 1982. xiii, 353 pp.

"Portrait of the Artist as an Old Man," 138–63; revised from an article in *American Scholar,* 47:1 (Winter 1977/78), 52–68; also in David Dirck

VanTassel, ed.: *Aging, Death, and the Completion of Being*. Philadelphia: University of Pennsylvania Press, 1979, pp. 193–214. On Tolstoy, Henry James, and Yeats.

82–55. Ellmann, Richard: *James Joyce*. New and revised edition. New York: Oxford University Press, 1982. xviii, 887 pp.

New edition of J97 and 7001.

82–56. Empson, William: "Yeats and Byzantium," *Grand Street*, 1:4 (Summer 1982), 67–95.

On both Byzantium poems.

82–57. Engelberg, Edward: "Absence and Presence in Yeats's Poetry," *Yeats Annual*, 1 (1982), 48–67.

82–58. Engelking, Leszek: "Yeats sztuka dla tancerzy" [Yeats's plays for dancers], *Literatura na świecie*, no. 124 (Aug. 1981), 208–19.

82–59. Farrell, James Thomas: *On Irish Themes*. Edited with an introduction by Dennis Flynn; foreword by William V. Shannon. Philadelphia: University of Pennsylvania Press, 1982. xiii, 201 pp.

"Observations on the First Period of the Irish Renaissance," 40–44; reprint of J6030. For other references to Yeats, see index.

82–60. Finkelstein, Norman Mark: "The Utopian Invariant: Interiority and Exteriority in Twentieth-Century Poetic Consciousness," °Ph.D. thesis, Emory University, 1980. 333 pp. (*DAI*, 41:7 [Jan. 1981], 3104A–5A.)

Discusses Yeats, Pound, W. C. Williams, George Oppen, Charles Olson, Robert Duncan, and Jack Spicer.

82–61. FitzGerald, Mary: "How the Abbey Said No: Readers' Reports and the Rejection of *The Silver Tassie*," *O'Casey Annual*, 1 (1982), 73–87.

Discusses the involvement of Yeats and Lady Gregory; quotes from unpublished material.

82–62. Flannery, James W.: "High Ideals and the Reality of the Marketplace: A Financial Record of the Early Abbey Theatre," *Studies*, 71:283 (Autumn 1982), 246–69.

82–63. ——: "Poetry and Politics in Revolutionary Belfast," *George Spelvin's Theatre Book*, 4:3 (Fall 1982), 69–78.

On staging *Cathleen ni Houlihan* and *The Unicorn from the Stars* and on Yeats's "dramatic legacy" in general.

82–64. ——: "Yeats's Cuchulain," *Irish Literary Supplement*, 1:2 (Fall 1982), 20.

Review of *The Death of Cuchulain* (82–206).

82–65. Fletcher, Ian: "'Leda and the Swan' as Iconic Poem," *Yeats Annual*, 1 (1982), 82–113; illustrations between pp. 114 and 115.

82–66. FOSTER, JOHN WILSON: "*The Aran Islands* Revisited," *University of Toronto Quarterly,* 51:3 (Spring 1982), 248–63.

82–67. ——: "Yeats and the Folklore of the Irish Revival," *Éire-Ireland,* 17:2 (Summer 1982), 6–18.

Cultural nationalists such as Yeats believed that "Irish folklore could be reborn as literature," but this is questionable.

82–68. FRANCHI, FLORENCE: "Ulick O'Connor, W. B. Yeats et le nô japonais," *Cahiers du Centre d'études irlandaises,* 7 (1982), 43–53.

82–69. FRASER, GEORGE SUTHERLAND: *Poems of G. S. Fraser.* Edited by Ian Fletcher and John Lucas. Leicester: Leicester University Press, 1981. 209 pp.

"For Yeats," 34–55; "Elegy for Freud and Yeats," 44–45; "Home Thoughts on Ireland," 174–76.

82–70. FRÉCHET, RENÉ: Review of *Per Amica Silentia Lunae,* French translation (1979), *Études anglaises,* 35:1 (Jan.–March 1982), 99.

82–71. FREYER, GRATTAN: "The Poet and the Intriguers," *Books Ireland,* 69 (Dec. 1982), 217, 219.

Review of *The Death of Cuchulain* (82–206).

82–72. GALLAGHER, MICHAEL PAUL: "Yeats, the Mountain and the Temple," *Month,* 244:1382 / n.s. 15:11 (Nov. 1982), 388.

Evensong address at Drumcliffe Church on the opening of the Yeats International Summer School, August 1982.

82–73. GARAB, ARRA M.: "Two American Sources of W. B. Yeats's 'The Second Coming,'" *Yeats Eliot Review,* 7:1&2 (June 1982), 117–19.

A sonnet by Percy MacKaye, entitled "Christmas 1915," and a fable by Edward J. O'Brien, entitled "The Fool."

82–74. GENET, JACQUELINE: Review of *The Secret Rose* (81–145), *Études irlandaises,* 7 (Dec. 1982), 268–69.

82–75. GIFFORD, DON: *Joyce Annotated: Notes for "Dubliners" and "A Portrait of the Artist as a Young Man."* Second edition, revised and enlarged. Berkeley: University of California Press, 1982. ix, 308 pp.

Numerous references to Yeats (see index). The first edition was published in 1967 as *Notes for Joyce.*

82–76. GORE, JEANNE GUERRERO: "William Butler Yeats's *Purgatory*: Tragedy or Its Mirror-Image?" °Ph.D. thesis, George Peabody College for Teachers at Vanderbilt University, 1981. 96 pp. (*DAI,* 42:11 [May 1982], 4832A).

82–77. GRAVES, ROBERT: *In Broken Images: Selected Letters of Robert Graves 1914–1946.* Edited, with commentary, by Paul O'Prey. London: Hutchinson, 1982. 372 pp.

Deprecatory notes on pp. 171, 262, 305–6. See also 82–171.

82–78. GRENE, NICHOLAS, AND ANN SADDLEMYER: "Stephen MacKenna on Synge: A Lost Memoir," *Irish University Review,* 12:2 (Autumn 1982), 141–51.

82–79. GRENNAN, EAMON: "Mastery and Beyond: Speech and Silence in *The Tower,*" *Études irlandaises,* 7 (Dec. 1982), 55–70.

82–80. GRIGSON, GEOFFREY: *The Private Art: A Poetry Notebook.* London: Allison & Busby, 1982. iv, 231 pp.

Several short references to Yeats (see index).

82–81. GUHA, NARESH: "W. B. Yeats and Japan (A Select Bibliography)," *Jadavpur Journal of Comparative Literature,* 18–19 (1980–81), 125–29.

Very select.

82–82. GUINNESS, BRYAN: *Potpourri from the Thirties.* Burford, Oxfordshire: Cygnet Press, 1982. xi, 174 pp.

Lord Moyne's reminiscences of Yeats, pp. 30, 33–35, 64–65.

82–83. GUTIÉRREZ DE LA SOLANA, ALBERTO, AND ELIO ALBA-BUFFILL, EDS.: *Festschrift José Cid Pérez.* New York: Senda Nueva de Ediciones, 1981. 369 pp.

William J. Duffy: "Deirdre, Yeats and Synge," 181–84.

82–84. HAFFENDEN, JOHN: *The Life of John Berryman.* Boston: Routledge & Kegan Paul, 1982. xiii, 451 pp.

Several notes on Yeats and Berryman, including the account of a meeting in 1937 (see index).

82–85. HARRIS, DANIEL A.: "The 'Figured Page': Dramatic Epistle in Browning and Yeats," *Yeats Annual,* 1 (1982), 133–94.

Compares "The Gift of Harun Al-Rashid" with its source, Browning's "An Epistle, Containing the Strange Medical Experience of Karshish, the Arab Physician."

82–86. HASSETT, JOSEPH M.: "Slouching towards Intimacy," *Harvard Magazine,* 84:4 (March/April 1982), 7–8.

On "the lumbering pace at which W. B. Yeats and Lady Dorothy Wellesley achieved intimacy of address in their correspondence."

82–87. HENKE, SUZETTE A.: "Yeats's *John Sherman*: A Portal of Discovery," *Canadian Journal of Irish Studies,* 8:1 (June 1982), 25–35.

82–88. HEWITT, JERENE: "The Epigram in English," Ph.D. thesis, University of California, Irvine, 1981. xv, 689 pp. (*DAI,* 42:11 [May 1982], 4819A.)

On Yeats's epigrams, pp. 304–13.

82–89. HIRSCH, EDWARD: "Yeats's Apocalyptic Horsemen," *Irish Renaissance Annual,* 3 (1982), 71–92.

82–90. HIRSCHBERG, STUART: "Art as the Looking Glass of Civilization in W. B. Yeats's 'Under Ben Bulben,'" *Studies,* 71:284 (Winter 1982), 399–404.

82–91. HOLDSWORTH, CAROLYN, COMP.: "Dissertation Abstracts, 1980," *Yeats Annual,* 1 (1982), 207–20.

Reprints the abstracts of 14 Ph.D. theses on Yeats.

82–92. INGRAM, ALISON: *Index to the Archives of Grant Richards 1897–1948.* Cambridge: Chadwyck-Healey, 1981. Unpaged.

Printed index to the microfilm of the archives; contains some Yeats material.

82–93. IRISH TIMES: "James Joyce: A Special Supplement . . . ," *Irish Times,* 2 Feb. 1982. 8 pp.

See particularly Micheál Ó hAodha: "The Would-Be Playwright," 8.

82–94. ISLAM, SYED MANZOORUL: "Gyres and Spirits: An Exploration of Some Parallels between W. B. Yeats and Emanuel Swedenborg," °Ph.D. thesis, Queen's University (Kingston, Ont.), 1981. (*DAI,* 42:8 [Feb. 1982], 3610A.)

82–95. IZUBUCHI, HIROSHI: "Faulkner and Yeats—An Essay," *William Faulkner: Materials, Studies and Criticism,* 4:1 (Dec. 1981), 1–14.

In Japanese with an English summary, pp. 15–16. Points out the similarities in both writers' views of history.

82–96. JEFFARES, ALEXANDER NORMAN: *Anglo-Irish Literature.* London: Macmillan, 1982. x, 349 pp. (Macmillan History of Literature.)

"William Butler Yeats," 148–60, and *passim* (see index).

82–97. ——: "Three Plays by W. B. Yeats: *The Land of Heart's Desire* (1894), *The Words upon the Window-Pane* (1930), *The Herne's Egg* (1938)," *Gaéliana,* 4 (1982), 57–74.

82–98. ——: Review of *Explorations* (81–144), *Irish University Review,* 12:1 (Spring 1982), 121–22.

82–99. JEFFERSON, GEORGE: *Edward Garnett: A Life in Literature.* London: Cape, 1982. x, 350 pp.

On Yeats, pp. 18, 28–29, 45–46.

82–100. °JOHN, ALAN ARTHUR: "Yeats and Dante," Ph.D. thesis, University of Chicago, 1981.

82–101. JOHNSON, JOSEPHINE A.: "The Music of Speech: Florence Farr and W. B. Yeats," *Literature in Performance,* 2:1 (Nov. 1981), 56–65.

82–102. JOHNSON, LIONEL: *The Collected Poems of Lionel Johnson.* Second and revised edition, edited by Ian Fletcher. New York: Garland, 1982. lxxvi, 381 pp. (Garland English Texts, 3.)

New edition of J5775.

82–103. JOHNSON, PAUL: *Ireland: A History from the Twelfth Century to the Present Day.* London: Granada, 1981. 272 pp.

First published as °*Ireland: Land of Troubles*. London: Eyre Methuen, 1980. On Yeats, pp. 124–26, 157–59, 180–81.

82–104. JOHNSON, TONI O'BRIEN: *Synge: The Medieval and the Grotesque*. Gerrards Cross: Colin Smythe / Totowa, N.J.: Barnes & Noble, 1982. viii, 209 pp. (Irish Literary Studies, 11.)

Several references to Yeats (see index).

82–105. JOHNSON, WALTER RALPH: *The Idea of Lyric: Lyric Modes in Ancient and Modern Poetry*. Berkeley: University of California Press, 1982. xi, 214 pp.

Note on Yeats as lyric performer before an imagined audience, pp. 15–17.

82–106. JOUBERT, JOHN: "On Setting Yeats's 'Byzantium,'" *Musical Times*, 123:1670 (April 1982), 249–50.

Describes his composition "Gong-tormented Sea," for symphony orchestra and chorus, based on "Byzantium."

82–107. JUSSIM, ESTELLE: *Slave to Beauty: The Eccentric Life and Controversial Career of F. Holland Day, Photographer, Publisher, Aesthete*. Boston: Godine, 1981. ix, 310 pp.

On Yeats, pp. 48–51, and *passim* (see index).

82–108. KEANE, PATRICK J.: "The Human Entrails and the Starry Heavens: Some Instances of Visual Art as Patterns for Yeats's Mingling of Heaven and Earth," *Bulletin of Research in the Humanities*, 84:3 (Autumn 1981), 366–91.

On the "role played by visual art in Yeats's attempts to make intelligible his own central theme: the interpenetration of the human and the spiritual." Discusses the influence of Blake.

82–109. KHOROL'SKII, V. V.: "Simbolizm U. B. Ietsa (Evoliutsiia tvorcheskogo metoda)," *Problemy metoda i zhanra v zarubezhnoi literature*, 6 (1981), 146–59.

"The symbolism of WBY (The evolution of the creative method)."

82–110. KIDDER, RUSHWORTH M.: "Exploring an Inner Landscape: William Butler Yeats," *Christian Science Monitor*, 23 Aug. 1982, 20–21.

82–111. KISHEL, JOSEPH: "Yeats's Elegies," *Yeats Eliot Review*, 7:1&2 (June 1982), 78–90.

82–112. KLEIMAN, CAROL: *Sean O'Casey's Bridge of Vision: Four Essays on Structure and Perspective*. Toronto: University of Toronto Press, 1982. xiv, 148 pp.

Several references to the *Silver Tassie* affair (see index).

82–113. KLINKENBORG, VERLYN, AND HERBERT CAHOON: *British Literary Manuscripts*. New York: Pierpont Morgan Library in association with Dover Publications, 1981. 2 vols.

Autograph manuscript of "Aodh to Dectora" and note in vol. 2, item 115; see also the index to vol. 2 for Yeats MSS. in the library.

82–114. KOCH, KENNETH, AND KATE FARRELL: *Sleeping on the Wing: An Anthology of Modern Poetry with Essays on Reading and Writing*. New York: Random House, 1981. xvii, 315 pp.

"William Butler Yeats," 77–81.

82–115. KONSTANTINOVIĆ, ZORAN, STEVEN P. SCHER, AND ULRICH WEISSTEIN, EDS.: *Literature and the Other Arts*. Proceedings of the IXth Congress of the International Comparative Literature Association, Innsbruck 1979, part 3. Innsbruck: Verlag des Instituts für Sprachwissenschaft der Universität, 1981. 354 pp. (Innsbrucker Beiträge zur Literaturwissenschaft: Sonderheft, 51.)

Sylvia M. Patsch: "*The Countess Cathleen:* The Irish Legend of Sin, Redemption, and Vicarious Self-Sacrifice as Interpreted by William Butler Yeats, Werner Egk, and Oskar Kokoschka," 269–72.

82–116.KOSOK, HEINZ, ED.: *Studies in Anglo-Irish Literature*. Bonn: Bouvier, 1982. viii, 496 pp. (Wuppertaler Schriftenreihe Literatur, 19.)

The papers written for the Wuppertal symposium on Anglo-Irish literature in July 1981. The following are on Yeats:

Hans Walter Gabler: "James Joyce and Ireland," 65–73.

John Wilson Foster: "The Revival of Saga and Historical Romance during the Irish Renaissance: The Ideology of Cultural Nationalism," 126–36.

Mary FitzGerald: "Some Problems of Nationality in the Early Irish Theatre," 148–54 (on Yeats and Lady Gregory).

Paul F. Botheroyd: "The Years of the Travellers: Tinkers, Tramps, and Travellers in Early Twentieth-Century Irish Drama and Society," 167–75.

S. N. R. Kazmi: "Poetry and Politics: A Case Study of W. B. Yeats," 198–204.

Fahmy F. Farag: "The Ireland That Sings: Yeats and the Heresy of Universal Education," 205–13.

Conrad A. Balliet: "Yeats and His Bloody Repetition," 214–26 (blood imagery in the poetry, especially in "Blood and the Moon").

Robert Welch: "Yeats's Crazy Jane Poems and Gaelic Love Song," 227–35.

Joseph T. Swann: "'Where All the Ladders Start': Language and Experience in Yeats's Later Poetry," 236–45.

Ronald Marken: "'The Strange Heart Beating': Prosodic Considerations of Yeats's Poetry," 246–53.

Andrew Parkin: "W. B. Yeats's Stage Diction," 254–61.

Christina Hunt Mahony: "The Influence of John Todhunter on the Plays of W. B. Yeats," 262–68.

Siga Asanga: "The Playwright in the Theatre: Dramatic Theory and Practice since W. B. Yeats," 455–65 (mainly on Nigerian playwrights John Pepper Clark and Wole Soyinka).

Robert Mahony: "Some Problems in Editing Anglo-Irish Dramatic Texts," 490–96.

82–117. KOVALEV, IURI VITALEVICH, AND ANNA FUKSON: *Current Soviet Bibliography of Studies in Anglo-Irish Literature, 1972–1975*. [Dublin: University of Dublin, Department of Russian, 1981]. 20 pp.

A mimeographed list.

82–118. KRAUSE, DAVID: *The Profane Book of Irish Comedy*. Ithaca: Cornell University Press, 1982. 341 pp.

Incorporates "The Ironic Victory of Defeat in Irish Comedy," *O'Casey Annual,* 1 (1982), 33–63; and other previously published articles. On Yeats *passim* (see index).

82–119. KUITI, CHITTARANJAN: "Beaconlight to the Modern Poet," *Journal of the Department of English, University of Calcutta,* 16:2 (1980–81), 20–34.

Donne's influence on Yeats's poetry.

82–120. LEAMON, WARREN: "The Romantic as Playwright," *Western Humanities Review,* 36:2 (Summer 1982), 97–108.

82–121. LICKINDORF, ELIZABETH T.: "W. B. Yeats's *Per Amica Silentia Lunae,*" *English Studies in Africa,* 25:1 (1982), 39–53.

Includes a discussion of related poems.

82–122. LOWERY, ROBERT G.: "The Autobiographies: An Historical Approach," *O'Casey Annual,* 1 (1982), 97–140.

On references to and quotations from Yeats in O'Casey's autobiographies.

82–123. LUCAS, JAMES L.: *The Religious Dimensions of Twentieth-Century British and American Literature: A Textbook in the Analysis of Types*. Washington, D.C.: University Press of America, 1982. x, 295 pp.

"William Butler Yeats: The Heterodox Platonist," 65–82; on Christianity in some of the poems and in *Calvary* and *The Resurrection*.

82–124. LUCAS, JOHN: *Romantic to Modern Literature: Essays and Ideas of Culture 1750–1900*. Brighton: Harvester Press, 1982. vii, 231 pp.

"From Naturalism to Symbolism," 188–205; first published in *Renaissance and Modern Studies,* 21 (1977), 124–39. Includes notes on Yeats's view of symbolism.

82–125. MCCORMACK, WILLIAM J., AND ALISTAIR STEAD, EDS.: *James Joyce and Modern Literature*. London: Routledge & Kegan Paul, 1982. xiii, 222 pp.

W. J. McCormack: "Nightmares of History: James Joyce and the Phenomenon of Anglo-Irish Literature," 77–107.

82–126. MACDONOGH, CAROLINE: "Notes on MacDonogh and Yeats," *Gaéliana,* 4 (1982), 205–15.

Yeats echoes in MacDonogh's poetry.

82–127. MCHUGH, ROGER, AND MAURICE HARMON: *Short History of Anglo-Irish Literature: From Its Origins to the Present Day.* Dublin: Wolfhound Press, 1982. 377 pp.

See especially the chapters "The Irish Literary Revival" and "After the Revival," pp. 125–325.

82–128. MACINNES, MAIRI: "Marvell in Yorkshire, Yeats in Sligo," *PN Review,* 28 [9:2] (1982), 29–33.

The garden metaphor in Marvell's and Yeats's poetry.

82–129. MCIVOR, PETER: "Forrest Reid, *Uladh,* and the Ulster Literary Theatre," *Éire-Ireland,* 17:2 (Summer 1982), 134–41.

82–130. MCKENNA, DAVID: "The Word and the Flesh—A View of Theatre as Performance," *Crane Bag,* 6:1 (1982), 90–91.

Contains some deprecatory remarks on Yeats.

82–131. MCNALLY, JAMES: "A Brief Confluence: Yeats and Anatole France," *Humanities in the South,* 54 (Fall 1981), 6–7.

Some images in "Sailing to Byzantium" seem to be indebted to ch. X of Anatole France's novel *Penguin Island.*

82–132. MACWEENEY, ALEN: "Yeats—MacWeeney—Ireland: Conjuring the Magic in a Great Bardic Vision. A Photographic Essay by Alen MacWeeney, Text by Artelia Court," *American Photographer,* 6:3 (March 1981), 56–67.

Photographs with captions from Yeats's poetry.

82–133. MAGILL, FRANK N., ED.: *Critical Survey of Poetry.* Englewood Cliffs: Salem Press, 1982. 8 vols.

James Lovic Allen: "William Butler Yeats," 7:3181–3209; a survey of life and works plus extended analyses of "Leda and the Swan," "The Second Coming," "Among School Children," and "Sailing to Byzantium."

82–134. MANNING, DALE: "Beyond Colonus: Tragic Vision and the Transfigured Imagination in the Late Works of Henry James, William Butler Yeats, and T. S. Eliot," °Ph.D. thesis, George Peabody College for Teachers at Vanderbilt University, 1982. 247 pp. (*DAI,* 43:6 [Dec. 1982], 1968A.)

82–135. MARCUS, PHILLIP L.: "Incarnation in 'Middle Yeats,'" *Yeats Annual,* 1 (1982), 68–81.

"Middle Yeats" is defined as the period c. 1900–1917.

82–136. MARTIN, AUGUSTINE: Review of *The Secret Rose* (81–145) and

The Celtic Twilight (81–143), *Irish University Review*, 12:1 (Spring 1982), 113–16.

82–137. MARTIN, STODDARD: *Wagner to "The Waste Land": A Study of the Relationship of Wagner to English Literature*. London: Macmillan, 1982. xi, 277 pp.

"Yeats," 121–34, and *passim* (see index).

82–138. MEIR, COLIN: "Narrative Verse in Yeats, Clarke, and Kavanagh," *Gaéliana*, 4 (1982), 219–36.

82–139. MIKHAIL, EDWARD HALIM: *Lady Gregory: An Annotated Bibliography of Criticism*. Troy, N.Y.: Whitston, 1982. xi, 258 pp.

Includes many items relevant to Yeats studies.

82–140. MISRA, K. S.: *Twentieth Century English Poetic Drama: A Revaluation*. New Delhi: Vikas, 1981. vii, 367 pp.

"Poetic Drama before T. S. Eliot: The Irish Phase," 16–49, and *passim* on Yeats's plays (see index).

82–141. MOFFETT, CAROLYN: "Through the Looking Glass: An Analysis of the Mirror Imagery in the Poetry of William Butler Yeats," *McNeese Review*, 27 (1980–81), 80–92.

82–142. MONTGOMERY, BENILDE: "The Presence of Parnell in Three Plays by Lady Gregory," *Irish Renaissance Annual*, 3 (1982), 106–23.

Includes some notes on Yeats.

82–143. MORGAN, KEITH: "Yeats and Thompson," *New Society*, 25 Nov. 1982, 359.

Criticizes E. P. Thompson who said that "The Second Coming" is "one of the most necessary, and full-throated, political statements of this century" (*New Society*, 11 Nov. 1982, 244).

82–144. NEUMAN, SHIRLEY C.: *Some One Myth: Yeats's Autobiographical Prose*. Mountrath, Portlaoise: Dolmen Press, 1982. 160 pp. (New Yeats Papers, 19.)

Discusses the individual books of *Autobiographies* as well as *A Vision* and *On the Boiler*, and "demonstrates and attempts to evaluate Yeats's exploitation of the possibilities of autobiography in the service of his conviction that biography is but the dramatic embodiment of myth. . . . The analysis emphasizes Yeats's attempt to create a biographical equivalent of myth through his manipulation of the autobiographical form and through the implications of his style" (back cover).

82–145. NORDIC REJOYCINGS 1982—IN COMMEMORATION OF THE CENTENARY OF THE BIRTH OF JAMES JOYCE. N.p.: James Joyce Society of Sweden and Finland, [1982]. 148 pp.

Birgit Bramsbäck: "Allusions to Yeats in *Stephen Hero* and *A Portrait of the Artist as a Young Man*," 9–25.

82–146. North, Michael: "The Paradox of the Mausoleum: Public Monuments and the Early Aesthetics of W. B. Yeats," *Centennial Review,* 26:3 (Summer 1982), 221–38.

82–147. O'Brien, Joseph Valentine: *"Dear Dirty Dublin": A City in Distress, 1899–1916.* Berkeley: University of California Press, 1982. xiv, 338 pp.

Note on Yeats and the Abbey Theatre, pp. 50–53, 56.

82–148. O'Donnell, William H.: "The Art of Yeats's 'Lapis Lazuli,'" *Massachusetts Review,* 23:2 (Summer 1982), 353–67.

82–149. O'Driscoll, Robert, ed.: *The Celtic Consciousness.* Mountrath, Portlaoise: Dolmen Press / Edinburgh: Cannongate, 1982. xxxi, 642 pp.

First published °Toronto: McClelland & Stewart, 1981. Yeats is referred to *passim,* particularly in Lorna Reynolds: "The Irish Literary Revival: Preparation and Personalities," 383–99; R. O'Driscoll: "The Aesthetic and Intellectual Foundations of the Celtic Literary Revival in Ireland," 401–25; and "Epilogue: The Celtic Hero," 610–19 (on the production of *The Celtic Hero,* a conflation of four of Yeats's Cuchulain plays, with photographs).

82–150. O'Hara, Daniel T.: Review of *The Secret Rose* (81–145), *Victorian Studies,* 26:1 (Autumn 1982), 99–101.

82–151. Ó Muirithe, Diarmaid: "'There's Broth in the Pot,'" *Éigse,* 18:2 (1981), 305–8.

The source of the song in *The Pot of Broth.*

82–152. Pall, Santosh: "The Soul Must Dance: Yeats's 'Byzantium,'" *Temenos,* no. 2 (1982), 25–44.

Extract from a doctorate thesis, °"Yeats and the Sacred Dance" (University of Delhi); the author is herself a performer of Indian traditional dance.

82–153. Parkinson, Thomas: "This Extraordinary Book," *Yeats Annual,* 1 (1982), 195–206.

A Vision (1925).

82–154. Pearce, Donald: "Ghostly Paradigms of Things in 'Among School Children,'" *Yeats Eliot Review,* 7:1&2 (June 1982), 51–68.

82–155. Pérez Romero, Carmen: *Juan Ramón Jiménez y la poesía anglosajona.* Cáceres: Universidad de Extremadura, Seminario da Crítica Literaria, 1981. 176 pp. (Colección El Criticón, 1.)

"El simbolismo de W. B. Yeats y su incidencia en la poesía juanramoniana," 119–22; "Cotejo de 'A Coat' y 'Vino, primero, pura,'" 123–39; "'La Rosa' en W. B. Yeats y en Juan Ramón Jiménez," 141–63 (the rose image); "Traducciones de Yeats," 165–70.

82–156. PETERSON, RICHARD F.: *William Butler Yeats.* Boston: Twayne, 1982. 228 pp. (Twayne's English Authors Series, 328.)

Written along the usual lines of the series, with chronology, short biography, and chronological assessment of the major works, ending with a chapter on Yeats's "modernity." One of the better introductory studies.

82–157. PETILLON, PIERRE-YVES: "En étrange pays, fragments d'une île (1891–1916)," *Critique* [Paris], 38:421–422 (June–July 1982), 537–60.

82–158. PIPER, DAVID: *The Image of the Poet: British Poets and Their Portraits.* Oxford: Clarendon Press, 1982. xxi, 219 pp.

On Yeats, pp. 184–91.

82–159. POUND, EZRA, AND FORD MADOX FORD: *Pound/Ford: The Story of a Literary Friendship.* The correspondence between Ezra Pound and Ford Madox Ford and their writings about each other; edited with an introduction and narrative commentary and notes by Brita Lindberg-Seyersted. London: Faber & Faber, 1982. xxiv, 222 pp.

Several short references to Yeats (see index).

82–160. PROFFITT, EDWARD: *Poetry: An Introduction & Anthology.* Boston: Houghton Mifflin, 1981. xv, 463 pp.

Note on "The Dolls," pp. 74–75.

82–161. °PRUITT, VIRGINIA D.: "Yeats, the Mask, and the Poetry of Old Age," *Journal of Geriatric Psychiatry,* 15:1 (1982), 99–112.

82–162. PUTZEL, STEVEN D.: "The Black Pig: Yeats's Early Apocalyptic Beast," *Éire-Ireland,* 17:3 (Fall 1982), 86–102.

The sources of the image in Irish folklore and mythology.

82–163. RAINE, KATHLEEN: *The Inner Journey of the Poet and Other Papers.* Edited by Brian Keeble. London: Allen & Unwin, 1982. xi, 208 pp.

Extended references to Yeats in "The Inner Journey of the Poet," 25–39; "Poetic Symbols as a Vehicle of Tradition," 40–79; "Waste Land, Holy Land," 80–98.

82–164. RAJAN, TILOTTAMA: "The Romantic Backgrounds of Yeats's Use of Dante in 'Ego Dominus Tuus,'" *Yeats Eliot Review,* 7:1&2 (June 1982), 120–22.

Carlyle as a link between Yeats and Dante.

82–165. REIMAN, DONALD H.: "Wordsworth, Shelley, and the Romantic Inheritance," *Romanticism Past and Present,* 5:2 (1981), 1–22.

Contains some notes on Yeats.

82–166. ROSEMERGY, JANET MARY CRAMER: "Kathleen Raine, Poet of Eden: Her Poetry and Criticism," °Ph.D. thesis, University of Michigan, 1981. 305 pp. (*DAI,* 42:9 [March 1982], 3995A.)

Includes a comparison with Yeats.

82–167. SALVATI, JULIANNE MIA: "W. B. Yeats and His 'Sweet Dancer,'" °Ph.D. thesis, University of Rhode Island, 1981. 158 pp. (*DAI*, 43:2 [Aug. 1982], 307A–8A.)

Explores the dancer's impact on the dance plays.

82–168. SCHRICKER, GALE C.: *A New Species of Man: The Poetic Persona of W. B. Yeats*. Lewisburg, Pa.: Bucknell University Press, 1982. 214 pp.

Persona is defined as the synthesis of character and personality which Yeats sought to establish in his prose and poetry.

82–169. SENA, VINOD: *W. B. Yeats: The Poet as Critic*. London: Macmillan, 1981. xv, 232 pp.

Identical with *The Poet as Critic: W. B. Yeats on Poetry, Drama, and Tradition*. Delhi: Macmillan of India, 1980; includes much previously published material. A book arising out of the author's feeling that Yeats the critic has been unduly neglected.

Reviews:

Eavan Boland: "Yeats as a Critic," *Irish Times*, 8 May 1982, 12.

Ragini Ramachandra, *Literary Criterion*, 16:2 (1981), 90–93.

Rajiva Verma: "Yeats as a Critic," *Humanities Review*, 3:1 (Jan.–June 1981), 38–40.

82–170. °SEPEDA, T.: "Yeats and Women: The Nineteenth Century," Ph.D. thesis, University of Reading, 1981.

82–171. SEYMOUR-SMITH, MARTIN: *Robert Graves: His Life and Work*. London: Hutchinson, 1982. xiv, 608 pp.

Discusses Graves's aversion to Yeats on pp. 250–52, 324–25 and *passim* (see index). See also 82–77.

82–172. SILVER, ARNOLD: *Bernard Shaw: The Darker Side*. Stanford: Stanford University Press, 1982. xiii, 353 pp.

On Shaw's reaction to *The Land of Heart's Desire* and on *Candida* as a parody of Yeats's play, pp. 88–96.

82–173. SIRIUS: *Running to Paradise*. Brutkasten Records 85 R 030, 1982. 12″ long play record.

The group Sirius consists of four German musicians who play various kinds of mostly electrical instruments. The compositions are by Stefan Neubauer, who also sings the lyrics. The following Yeats poems are included: "The Sad Shepherd," "The Fiddler of Dooney," "Why Should Not Old Men Be Mad?" "Running to Paradise," "September, 1913," "Three Songs to the One Burden, III," and "The Happy Townland." The short text on the slip case is silly.

82–174. SMITH, PETER ALDERSON: "*The Countess Cathleen* and the Otherworld," *Éire-Ireland*, 17:2 (Summer 1982), 141–46.

On the roots of the names and the imagery in Gaelic tradition.

82–175. SMITH, ROBERT JEROME: "Thou Shalt Be Irish: A Study of the Influence of German Romantic Folk-Ideology on the Irish Literary Revival," *Kansas Quarterly*, 13:2 (Spring 1981), 103–13.

82–176. SMYTHE, COLIN, ED.: *Robert Gregory 1881–1918: A Centenary Tribute with a Foreword by His Children*. Gerrards Cross: Colin Smythe, 1981. 40 pp.

82–177. SOTHEBY PARKE BERNET: *Valuable Autograph Letters, Literary Manuscripts, and Historical Documents Including Sections of Continental and Music Manuscripts*. Sale of 29 and 30 June 1982. London: Sotheby, 1982.

Lists several letters by Yeats to various correspondents and the Lennox Robinson papers (which include Yeats material). See index under Robinson and Yeats.

82–178. ——: *English Literature Comprising Printed Books, Autograph Letters, and Manuscripts*. Sale of 15 December 1982. London: Sotheby, 1982.

Lists letters by and to Yeats, including a letter from Henry James (dated 25 Aug. 1915), an autograph draft of "His Dream," letters to Sean O'Casey, some letters about Swift, and several letters to Oliver Edwards.

82–179. SPALTRO, KATHLEEN AGNES: "As Though God's Death Were But a Play: Literature and Dogma in Crisis," °Ph.D. thesis, Northwestern University, 1981. 209 pp. (*DAI*, 42:9 [March 1982], 3689A.)

Includes a discussion of *The Resurrection*.

82–180. STALLWORTHY, JON: "The Poet as Archaeologist: W. B. Yeats and Seamus Heaney," *Review of English Studies*, 33:130 (May 1982), 158–74.

82–181. STUART, FRANCIS: "Remembering Yeats," *Irish Times*, 12 June 1982, 12.

A poem.

82–182. SULLIVAN, KEVIN: "James Joyce and Anglo-Ireland," *Recorder*, 43 (1982), 24–34.

82–183. SUTTON, DOROTHY MOSELEY: "Soul Clap Its Hands and Sing: Yeats's Debt to Blake," °Ph.D. thesis, University of Kentucky, 1981. 214 pp. (*DAI*, 42:7 [Jan. 1982], 3157A.)

82–184. SYNGE, JOHN MILLINGTON, LADY ISABELLA AUGUSTA GREGORY, AND W. B. YEATS: *Theatre Business*. The correspondence of the first Abbey Theatre directors. . . . selected and edited by Ann Saddlemyer. Gerrards Cross: Colin Smythe, 1982. 330 pp.

Incorporates *Some Letters of John M. Synge* (J849). Includes 42 letters etc. from Yeats to Synge, 54 from Lady Gregory to Synge, 75 from Synge to Lady Gregory, 23 from Synge to Yeats, and one letter from Lady Gregory to Yeats (on Synge's death), plus associated material, a chronology of events, pronouncements and productions, and a reprint of the Wareing pamphlet (J6312). The editor (who has done a thorough job) also provides an introduction (pp. 9–18).

Reviews:

Grattan Freyer: "The Poet and the Intriguers," *Books Ireland,* 69 (Dec. 1982), 217, 219.

Nicholas Grene, *Hermathena,* 133 (Winter 1982), 74–76.

Michael O hAodha: "Plays and Controversies," *Irish Times,* 5 June 1982, 12.

Katharine Worth: "Manoeuvres of Management," *TLS,* 22 Oct. 1982, 1158.

82–185. SYNGE, JOHN MILLINGTON: *The Well of the Saints.* Edited with an introduction and notes by Nicholas Grene. Washington, D.C.: Catholic University of America Press / Gerrards Cross: Colin Smythe, 1982. ix, 80 pp. (Irish Dramatic Texts.)

Notes on Yeats in the "Introduction," especially pp. 1–5.

82–186. THOMPSON, WILLIAM IRWIN: *The Imagination of an Insurrection: Dublin, Easter 1916. A Study of an Ideological Movement.* West Stockbridge, Mass.: Lindisfarne Press, 1982. xv, 262 pp.

Reprint of J5951 with a new two-page preface.

82–187. TRILLING, LIONEL: *Speaking of Literature and Society.* Edited by Diana Trilling. Oxford: Oxford University Press, 1982. xv, 429 pp. (The Works of Lionel Trilling: Uniform Edition.)

"Yeats as Critic," 381–86; reprinted from *Mid-Century,* no. 27 (Summer 1961), 3–8. A review of *Essays and Introductions* (W211U).

82–188. UNGER, LEONARD. *Eliot's Compound Ghost: Influence and Confluence.* University Park: Pennsylvania State University Press, 1981. vii, 131 pp.

Yeats echoes in "Little Gidding," pp. 112–13.

82–189. VIERECK, PETER: "Context for George's 'Gleaning' and Yeats Parallels," *Literary Review,* 26:1 (Autumn 1982), 95–99.

Stefan George's poem "Nach der Lese" ("After the gleaning") is the German equivalent of "The Lake Isle of Innisfree."

82–190. VON BUCHAU, STEPHANIE: "San Francisco/Bay Area," *Opera News,* 47:1 (July 1982), 34–35.

Review of a performance of John Harbison's opera *Full Moon in March,* based on Yeats's play: "In many ways typical of modern opera—emotionally dry, philosophically pretentious, physically static."

82–191. WALKER, DOROTHY: *Louis le Brocquy.* With an introduction by John Russell, Dublin: Ward River Press, 1981. 167 pp.

See pp. 56–58 and 146–50 for notes on le Brocquy's Yeats images, including his own comments.

82–192. WALL, MERVYN: "An Interview with Mervyn Wall. Conducted by Gordon Henderson," *Journal of Irish Literature,* 11:1&2 (Jan.–May 1982), 3–18.

Includes a few comments on Yeats.

82–193. WANG, AN-YAN TANG: "Subjectivity and Objectivity in the Poetic Mind: A Comparative Study of the Poetry of William Butler Yeats and Tu Fu," °Ph.D. thesis, Indiana University, 1981. 63 pp. (*DAI,* 42:7 [Jan. 1982], 3152A.)

Tu Fu lived from 712 to 770.

82–194. WARD, DAVID: "Yeats's Conflicts with His Audience, 1897–1917," *ELH,* 49:1 (Spring 1982), 143–63.

Attempts to show "how Yeats's poems carry the stamp of historical forces in the sociological and psychological processes which he experienced as he produced them."

82–195. WATANABE, HISAYOSHI: "An Inquiry into Yeats's 'Terrible Beauty,'" *Studies in English Literature* [Tokyo], 58:2 (Dec. 1981), 143–53.

In Japanese; English synopsis in English Number, 1982, 150–51. On "Easter 1916."

82–196. WATKINS, VERNON: "For Whom Does a Poet Write?" *Temenos,* no. 1 (1981), 93–96.

Previously unpublished lecture of 1957, partly on Yeats, followed by texts of some of the poems which Watkins read on the occasion, including his "A Photograph of Yeats," pp. 99–100.

82–197. WEINTRAUB, STANLEY, ED.: *Modern British Dramatists, 1900–1945.* Detroit: Gale, 1982. 2 vols. (Dictionary of Literary Biography, 10.)

S. Weintraub: "William Butler Yeats," 2:227–37; William H. O'Donnell: "The Abbey Theatre and Irish Drama, 1900–1945," 2:309–18.

82–198. WEISS, THEODORE: *The Man from Porlock: Engagements 1944–1981.* Princeton: Princeton University Press, 1982. vii, 321 pp.

"The Many-Sidedness of Modernism," 131–44; a review of M. L. Rosenthal's *Sailing into the Unknown* (1978), reprinted from *TLS,* 1 Feb. 1980, 124–25.

82–199. WELTE, WERNER, ED.: *Sprachtheorie und angewandte Linguistik: Festschrift für Alfred Wollmann zum 60. Geburtstag.* Tübingen: Narr, 1982. xiii, 275 pp. (Tübinger Beiträge zur Linguistik, 195.)

Manfred Pfister: "Sailing to Innisfree: Stilwandel und ideologische Entwicklung in der Lyrik von W. B. Yeats," 113–30. Compares "The White Birds" and "Sailing to Byzantium" and finds that Yeats early and late, exhibits "transcendental irrationality, an elitist hero cult, and dreams of authoritarian hierarchies," while rejecting critical observation and democratic pluralism.

82–200. WHITTINGTON, JENNIFER: *Literary Recordings: A Checklist of the Archive of Recorded Poetry and Literature in the Library of Congress.* Revised, enlarged edition. Washington, D.C.: Library of Congress, 1981. vi, 299 pp.

New edition of J529. See index for recordings of Yeats's works by Yeats and others.

82–201. WILSON, BRUCE M.: "'From Mirror after Mirror': Yeats and Eastern Thought," *Comparative Literature,* 34:1 (Winter 1982), 28–46.

82–202. WILSON, ROBERT ANTON: *Masks of the Illuminati.* London: Sphere Books, 1981. vii, 294 pp.

A kind of fantastic novel, partly on the Golden Dawn, with Yeats figuring in it along with Joyce, Pound, Einstein, and others.

82–203. WRIGHT, GEORGE T.: "Yeats's Expressive Style," *Yeats Eliot Review,* 7:1&2 (June 1982), 109–16.

An analysis of "Crazy Jane on God."

82–204. YEATS, W. B.: *The Collected Plays of W. B. Yeats.* London: Macmillan, 1982. vi, 705 pp. (Papermac.)

First paperback edition.

82–205. ——: *The Collected Poems of W. B. Yeats.* London: Macmillan, 1982. xviii, 565 pp. (Papermac.)

First paperback edition.

82–206. ——: *The Death of Cuchulain.* Manuscript materials including the author's final text. Edited by Phillip L. Marcus. Ithaca: Cornell University Press, 1982. x, 182 pp. (The Cornell Yeats.)

Photographic facsimiles of the manuscript and a late typescript versions, facing the editor's transcriptions. The introduction (pp. 3–16) traces the evolution of the play and evaluates the changes made by Yeats while he composed it. For reviews see 82–64, 71.

82–207. °——: *Ich hatte die Weisheit, die Liebe uns gibt.* Herausgegeben mit einem Nachwort und Anmerkungen versehen von Karl Heinz Bergner. Translations by Stefan Andres and others. Berlin: Volk und Welt, 1981. 229 pp.

82–208. °——: *John Sherman; Dhoya.* Introduzione de Pietro De Logu, traduzione e note di Dario Calimani. Turin: Einaudi, 1982. xxx, 115 pp.

Reviewed by F[ernando] Ferrara, *Istituto universitario orientale: Annali. Anglistica,* 25:1 (1982), 167–69.

82–209. ——: "The Manuscript of 'Leo Africanus.' Edited by Steve L. Adams and George Mills Harper," *Yeats Annual,* 1 (1982), 3–47.

The "Editorial Introduction" (pp. 3–17) surveys Yeats's involvement with Leo Africanus and his psychical experiments from 1909 to 1919.

82–210. ——: "Navigînd spre Bizant," translated by Mircea Ivănescu, *Transilvania,* n.s. 10:12 (Dec. 1981), 27.

82–211. ——: "Odjazd da Bizancjum," translated by Czeslaw Miłosz, *Literatura na świecie,* no. 122 (June 1981), 82–83.

82–212. ——: "Późne wiersce" [Late poems], translated by Stanisław Barańczak; "Przy źródle jastrzębia" [At the Hawk's Well], translated by Leszek Engelking; "Wiersze" [Poems], translated by L. Engelking, *Literatura na świecie,* no. 124 (Aug. 1981), 188–207, 220–21.

82–213. ——: *The Secret Rose and Other Stories: The Celtic Twilight. The Secret Rose. Stories of Red Hanrahan.* London: Macmillan, 1982. vii, 3–261 pp. (Papermac.)

A selection from *Mythologies* (W211P). For a review see 82–21.

82–214. YEATS ANNUAL NO. 1. Edited by Richard J. Finneran. London: Macmillan, 1982. xiii, 259 pp.

Contains 82–24, 57, 65, 85, 91, 135, 153, 209, and 8 reviews.

82–215. YOSHINO, MASAAKI: "'Easter 1916': A Poet's Witness," *Studies in English Language and Literature* [Kyushu University], 32 (Jan. 1982), 13–26.

In Japanese; English summary on p. 98.

Additions to Entries in the 1981 Bibliography

81–16. CALLAN: *Yeats on Yeats.*

Reviews:

Richard J. Finneran, *Irish Literary Supplement,* 1:1 (Spring 1982), 13.

Jacqueline Genet, *Études irlandaises,* 7 (Dec. 1982), 269–71.

81–31. CULLINGFORD: *Yeats, Ireland, and Fascism.*

Reviews:

Reed Way Dasenbrock, *Modern Language Notes,* 97:5 (Dec. 1982), 1262–65.

Brian John: "Yeats's Politics," *University of Toronto Quarterly,* 51:3 (Spring 1982), 303–6.

Declan Kiberd, *Irish University Review,* 12:1 (Spring 1982), 122–23.

81–38. DYSON: *Yeats, Eliot, and R. S. Thomas.*

Reviews:

Felicity Currie, *Critical Quarterly,* 24:3 (Autumn 1982), 65–71.

81–52. FREYER: *W. B. Yeats and the Anti-Democratic Tradition.*

Reviews:

Eavan Boland: "Last Romantic," *Irish Times,* 13 Feb. 1982, 12.

Janet Madden-Simpson: "That Man's Scope," *Books Ireland,* 62 (April 1982), 59–60.

Brian Martin: "Madly Elitist," *TLS,* 6 Aug. 1982, 867.

Tom Paulin, *New Statesman,* 5 Feb. 1982, 24.

81–56. GENET: *William Butler Yeats.*

Reviews:

Michel Le Bris: "L'Irlande à la vie à la mort: Les résistants de la première heure," *Nouvel Observateur,* 31 July 1982, 44–46.

81–77. KRIMM: *W. B. Yeats and the Emergence of the Irish Free State.*

Reviews:

Declan Kiberd, *Irish University Review,* 12:1 (Spring 1982), 122–23.

Janet Madden-Simpson: "That Man's Scope," *Books Ireland,* 62 (April 1982), 59–60.

81–100. O'HARA: *Tragic Knowledge.*

Reviews:

Hazard Adams, *Journal of Aesthetics and Art Criticism,* 40:4 (Summer 1982), 434.

Wallace Martin: "William Butler Yeats," *Contemporary Literature,* 23:2 (Spring 1982), 239–43.

Dissertation Abstracts, 1983

Compiled by DEBORAH MARTIN

The dissertation abstracts included here are published with permission of University Microfilms International, publisher of *Dissertation Abstracts International* (copyright © 1983 by University Microfilms International), and may not be reproduced without their prior permission.[1] Full-text copies of the dissertations are available upon request, for a fee, from University Microfilms International, 300 North Zeeb Road, Ann Arbor, Michigan 48106.

Modern Verse Defined by W. B. Yeats: A Comparative Study of Romance, Tragedy, and the Lyric, with an Introduction to Tu Fu and His Antithetical Tradition
So, Susan Suk-Ning, Ph.D., Princeton University, 1982)
493 pp. Order No. DA8301421.

This is a comparative study of the modern lyric. The theoretical issues raised are those of the lyric and modernity, of cultural and generic differences, of poetic influence and poetic knowledge, of Romantic philosophy and tragic vision. The central issue is the modern poet's "calling" in relation to his audience, real and imagined.

Its approach is derived from what Keats calls the "allegorical lives" of poets, what Eliot calls his "perfection of pattern," or what Yeats calls his "perfection of form," the rhythmic body. Its method is derived from a study of Yeats's antithetical theory of poetry and personalities, his "double vision," and his two minds, the critical and the creative, in dialogue.

[1]Minor corrections have been made.

In terms of craft and technique it is a study of freedom and control. In terms of literary criticism it is a defense of "workshop criticism" and of the "lyrical" approach via Yeats's prose and traditional Chinese criticism. It argues against analytic attitudes and scientific pretensions and calls for the cooperation of the brain and the belly in the comprehension of the poetic process. Ultimately it is a defense of poetry against the separation of art from life, of what Yeats calls "the personal factor" and "the moral element" in literature.

Chapter I sets up the premise of arguments and introduces the "Asiatic" aspect of Yeats's "double vision" via the turn-of-the-century "Cathay," the Chinese antithetical mind, and its sense of tragedy and of romance. Chapters II to V follow Yeats from the years of "Discoveries" through *Per Amica Silentia Lunae* to *A Vision*. These discoveries are then applied to the reading of Yeats's assessment of *Modern Verse: 1892–1935* in Chapter VI, and to Tu Fu's poetry in particular and "Modern Verse" in general in Chapter VII.

Due to the complexities of these poets' enterprise and the "modern" and therefore learned traditions in which they wrote, this study of their "allegorical lives" is necessarily complicated by the questions of inheritance and intent. These last will be guided by the description of their journeys to the "Mountain-Top." Yeats's journey is described through his dialogue "of generations for generations" in his "*one* poem of a lifetime." Tu Fu's journey is described through a selection of his poems (translated by this author) from "Gazing on Mount T'ai" to the 766 song cycles, ending with "From a Height."

(*DAI*, 43: 8 [Feb. 1983] 2660-A.)

Poetry and Magic: A Study of Yeats's Poems of Meditation
Gerety, Jane, Ph.D., The University of Michigan, 1982.
250 pp. Chairman: George Bornstein. Order No. DA8304494.

Many scholars have noted the influence of Yeats's occult interests on themes and symbols in his poetry while others have pointed to the convergence of magical philosophy and Romantic aesthetics in his poetic theory. Less attention has been paid, however, to the debt Yeats owes to magic for the structures of his poems, particularly his meditative poems. This study explores the influence of his magical studies on his development as a poet and traces the relationship of certain methods of meditation learned in the practice of magic to his poetry of meditation.

In his early view, Yeats relates poetry to magic by showing the reliance each has on the visionary power of the mind and on symbols. His search for a national tradition on which to found his art leads him to ascribe the beginnings of poetry to magic and to advocate a return to the magical view of the world. Yeats sees Blake and Shelley as visionary artists and follows the example of his Romantic mentors in populating his own early verse with seekers after hidden wisdom.

In Yeats's later writing about the alliance of poetry and magic, he works toward a definition of vision that includes antipathy and confrontation as well as unity and merging. He continues to create visionary personae in his fiction and verse and also to construct poems of meditation in which the speakers, by a complex process of interaction with images, attain vision. The structures of these meditative poems show the influence of the methods of meditation Yeats learned in the Golden Dawn: contemplation of images and symbols; Tarot meditation; and symbolic ritual meditation. By means of these structures, Yeats was able to expand the traditional Romantic form, the greater Romantic lyric, and increase its dramatic potential. In the most fully developed poetry of meditation, that based on re-creation of initiation ceremonies, acts of will complement those of imagination in the speaker's quest of a moment of vision.

(*DAI*, 43:10 [April 1983] 3324-A.)

Knowledge and Sweeter Ignorance:
The Strategies of Yeats's Poetic Structures

Krogfus, Miles Edward, Ph.D., University of Minnesota, 1982. 257 pp. Order No. DA8308077.

The many studies of Yeats's poetry tend to explicate it in relationship to his ideas at the expense of any extended analysis of the poetic structures which embody these ideas. I reverse this familiar pattern, and offer detailed commentaries on some of the important elements of his poetic structures in chapters I through III of my thesis, leading in turn to an examination in chapter IV of heretofore neglected Yeatsian metaphors: lightning and the threshold.

Yeats uses his poetic structures to create magical charms that will have the power to transform reality into what he would desire it to be. The first element of these structures, which I discuss in chapter I, is Yeats's use of sentence and line in his poetry. Another element of his structures, his use of refrains and repeated phrases, I discuss in chapter II. The next element of Yeats's structures, his use of poetic dialogues, which I discuss in chapter III, is the clearest embodiment of drama in his verse.

The title of my final chapter, as well as that of the entire thesis, comes from Yeats's poem "Shepherd and Goatherd." His vacillation between what his head and heart tell him is forcibly expressed in this phrase. His poetic structures at first seem to allow poet and reader to attain greater knowledge of the world, but the knowledge attained develops more from the heart than the head. The latter is used to skillfully create elaborate structures that seem logical and intellectually comprehensive, but which are more significantly dramatic, and emotionally comprehensive.

Drama is what serves as truth for Yeats. His is a poetry of power, an attempt to so charge diction and syntax that they will embody drama as the central truth of human experience. Through his poetic structures, Yeats attempts to convince himself and the reader that his *dramatis personae* have importance and their words and actions significance. When he accomplishes his intentions, his verse is charged with enough drama so that the merest inflection or slightest change in gesture is rendered dramatic. Drama becomes the final means and end of his verbal magic.

(*DAI*, 43:11 [May 1983] 3604-A.)

Yeatsian Talk: The Critical Theory of W. B. Yeats and the Victorian Background

Sherman, Debora Anne, Ph.D., Brown University, 1982. 432 pp. Order No. DA8228336.

Yeats's critical and aesthetic theories, often ignored as largely idiosyncratic and immaterial to the poetry, significantly influence the shape of that work. Such words as "reverie," "mood," and "emotion of multitude," with their 'nintyish cast, reflect deeply held beliefs about the nature of the poetic vision and poetic method. Moreover, these beliefs were derived from Yeats's early exposure to a Victorian aesthetic which revolved around the issues of mood and reverie, an aesthetic shared in and influenced by Tennyson, Ruskin, Rossetti, Pater, Swinburne, and the Pre-Raphaelites. This nexus of Victorian theories of reverie and mood accounts, in fact, for the particularity of Yeats's poetry. Reverie describes a Victorian adumbration of Romantic theories of poetic perception which incorporate psychological theories of the mind prevalent in the nineteenth century to the immanent teleology of Romanticism. Reverie thus represents an attempt to overcome the problem of Romantic subjectivity through critical theory. Reverie, as a version of the epiphanic moment, became a unique poetic ethos which Yeats defined as "tragic gaiety." Mood, on the other hand, refers to the Victorian tendency to regard aesthetic emotion as fundamentally significant to aesthetic experience because it was both individually observed and universal in quality. These theories of mood characterize a Victorian aesthetic which justified the symbol as both universal and self-created, thus suggesting a median point in critical theory between the transcendent symbols of the Romantics and the self-enclosed poetic worlds of the Symbolists. Yeats developed his theory of "the moods" into a poetic methodology he called "the emotion of multitude" which formed the basis of his later elaborate mythology of the mask. Finally, the symbolic prefiguration and fulfillment which dominate the later poetry suggest the influence of Victorian typological symbolism upon his work. In these several ways, Yeats's aesthetic permutations upon Victorian theory become an important adjunct to the poetry.

(*DAI*, 43:11 [May 1983] 3606-A.)

A Search for Authority: Prolegomena to a Definitive Critical Edition of W. B. Yeats's A Vision *(1937)*
Hood, Connie Kelly, Ph.D., The University of Tennessee, 1983.
289 pp. Order No. DA8319325.
Major Professor: Dr. Norman J. Sanders

The groundwork is laid in this project for the text of a definitive critical edition of *A Vision* (1937). Some twenty-one thousand pages of unpublished materials have been examined in order to chart Yeats's process of creating the book, its publishing history, the critical reception, and the interrelationships of the various manuscripts and texts from the automatic writing of 1917 to the 1962 state of the printed text. Instead of a new text of *A Vision,* a list of emendations to the London 1937 copy-text is given. All known marginalia written in copies of the first edition and various states of the second edition in the hands of Yeats, his wife, and Thomas Mark (his editor at Macmillan) are listed. Textual notes explain the sources of the emendations and point out cruces and interesting manuscript variants. A chapter on the "Manuscript" discusses in detail the materials which Yeats sent to the printers. The variants in the printed texts of 1937 (London), 1938 (New York), 1956 (New York), 1961 (London), and 1962 (London) are listed in a chapter of historical collations. A final chapter on word division lists endline hyphenation. The bibliography contains four separate lists: published and unpublished primary and secondary materials which were consulted for this project.

(*DAI,* 44:4 [October 1983] 1082-A.)

Apocalyptic Imagery in Four Twentieth-Century Poets: W. B. Yeats, T. S. Eliot, Robert Lowell and Allen Ginsberg
Sarwar, Selim, Ph.D., McGill University (Canada), 1983.

In twentieth-century poets such as W. B. Yeats, T. S. Eliot, Robert Lowell, and Allen Ginsberg, the literary apocalyptic—identifiable by its homology with the major elements of the biblical Apocalypse—undergoes progressively complex transmutations. While in the early Yeats the apocalyptic is evocative of earnest Romantic moods, in his later work it is complicated by irony, yoked to the cycles of Yeatsian history, and counteracted by exaggerated postures of defiance. In Eliot, a reductive juxtaposition of the apocalyptic and the contemporary foreshortens the traditional paradigms to a diminutive modern-day scale. In Lowell, the apocalyptic is manifested variously as a bitter inversion of American Puritan eschatology, the telescoping of the personal and the cosmic, and a catastrophe in slow motion. The climactic point of distortion, however, is reached in Ginsberg's poetry in which apocalyptic horrors form a bizarre combination with humor and bathos. While their treatment of the eschatological is widely divergent, an element common to all four poets is their ambivalence toward the paradigms of an apocalyptic new world.

(*DAI,* 44:5 [November 1983] 1082-A.)

Reviews

James Lovic Allen. *Yeats's Epitaph: A Key to Symbolic Unity in His Life and Work.*
Washington, D. C.: University Press of America, 1982. xi + 270 pp.
Reviewed by Donald T. Torchiana

James Lovic Allen's *Yeats's Epitaph* is a concentrated yet sustained speculation on the important and final meaning of the famous lines on Yeats's gravestone:

Cast a cold eye
On life, on death.
Horseman, pass by!
[VP 640]

As the meticulously explained subtitle claims, this epitaph is "a key to his life and work." The book itself bristles with footnotes and constant references to the shortcomings of previous scholars in this preciously limited yet expansive domain. In the face of much of this earlier commentary, Allen counters with the powerfully novel conclusion that Yeats identifies himself with the horseman of the epitaph and thus is primarily addressing himself in these lines. The book is rigorously (and tendentiously) argued, the evidence a mass of relevant and farfetched details, and the implications far more wide-ranging than the short title might suggest. My job, consequently, must be to pursue Allen's argument chapter by chapter and then, finally, to gauge its convincingness.

After a short "Preface" of explanation and acknowledgments, five chapters follow, each with endnotes, and a Special Bibliography and Index complete the book. The first chapter, "Rilke and the Epitaph," asserts that the earlier version of the epitaph (a quatrain) had preceded Yeats's reading of William Rose's essay on Rilke. Hence, "Yeats did not *create* the quatrain in reaction to Rilke's thought, but rather simply *used* what had already been shaped during some considerable period of previous time into an astonishingly compact and richly symbolic poetic statement of his own views on the relationships between life and death" (p. 9). To back up his thesis, Allen produces five pieces of evidence that point to the impossibility that Yeats might have arrived at the final form of his epitaph in but twelve days or less after reading Rose's essay. In general, this is the most convincing chapter of the book, though the point made seems, at least at first reading, very nearly trivial. Moreover, some of the argument is at best circumstantial, for instance the closing observation that Yeats could not have made such an important decision on the use of his quatrain in but twelve days or less after his reading.

The second chapter, "Swift and the Epitaph," is at once more pedestrian and at the same time less convincing. We begin, of course, with the usual ragging of other critics who have also sensed a connection between Yeats's and Swift's epitaphs. But even Allen's arguments for the likeness can also lapse, when, for example, he would have us believe that "world-besotted" and "blood-sodden" are "metaphorical equivalents" (p. 27). Still more doubtful, however, rings Allen's claim that, unlike Swift, Yeats broke with the traditions and conventions of epitaph writing by addressing not the passerby but "himself—as well as perhaps . . . a select group of others like himself" (p. 35). As we shall see, this insubstantial argument will become absolutely essential to Allen's thesis.

The third chapter, by far the longest, is entitled "How Many Kinds of Horseman?" Allen's primary proposition in the chapter is forced by the conclusion of his previous chapter, for he is basically saying that horseman is equivalent to swordsman, and that swordsman is of course equivalent to Yeats. So we arrive at his central thesis near the beginning of the chapter: "Yeats identified himself with the horseman of the epitaph and . . . the imperative in that inscription is addressed primarily to himself" (p. 74). Acknowledging, virtually from the first, that "to some, the analysis which follows may seem overly subtle at times, perhaps even totally implausible and unacceptable in places" (p. 50), Allen goes right on analyzing in this overlong and certainly cluttered chapter. We are regaled with all the possible horsemen in Yeats's work: aristocrats, riders of the Sidhe, warriors, travelers, riders of the apocalypse, and so forth. All are meant to underscore the theme of life-as-journey where horse and horseman represent body and soul.

But why then Drumcliff Churchyard? This is the question the next chapter addresses. Allen offers four reasons for Yeats's choice. For one thing, Sligo was his home and family locale. For another, Drumcliff was especially blessed with supernatural lore and associations. It and Ben Bulben were also identified with ancient heroic life. The link with Columcille—man of action, poet, and defender of poets—was also important, especially since he seems to have combined druidism and early non-Roman Irish Christianity, a Christianity supposedly Asiatic in its origins. Finally, Yeats's paternal grandfather, he who had placed the Celtic cross by the road, was perhaps reason enough to choose Drumcliff.

The final chapter, "The Two Eternities," seems even less relevant to the epitaph, if not to the poem "Under Ben Bulben," than was the fourth. Allen's chore here is to show how Yeats reconciled the two eternities of race and soul. To cast a cold eye, then, is to merge them and continue on to a third eternity. By his usual sleight of hand, Allen equates "cold" with "indifferent" (p. 222), the word Yeats had used in an earlier version of the poem. We are also made acquainted yet one more time with all the mistakes of previous commentators. In the end, Yeats's grandfather, Yeats's namesake, the redheaded rector, appears to have embodied all the important elements of these eternities—church (soul) and Ireland (race), something of a saint, sage, and horseman: "a good man on a horse" (p. 239).

Allen's book certainly deserves to be read. It is dense, overstrenuously argued, sometimes farfetched, and brave in its attempt to sum up an attitude toward life and art in an epitaph. Much of what Allen writes is extraneous, strictly speaking, to the actual epitaph itself, which is required to carry far too much weight. Although readers may be impressed by the range of Allen's argument, they will probably not agree after all that Yeats was addressing himself from his own tombstone. Instead, to address another horseman, as the epitaph really seems to do, need not be taken as falling into a mere conventional phrase. On page 52, while agreeing with one of F. A. C. Wilson's conclusions, Allen castigates that critic for his "somewhat irritatingly self-conscious manner and verbal style." That charge might all too well be laid at James Lovic Allen's own feet.

Douglas N. Archibald. *Yeats*.
Syracuse: Syracuse University Press,
1983. xiv + 280 pp.
Reviewed by William H. O'Donnell

Douglas Archibald's book *Yeats* is filled with evidence that its author is an excellent teacher. He sees his subject with a wide-ranging, insightful eye, and he enriches his consideration of literature and of history with a strongly felt sense of cultural and personal values. He laces his expression with spritely touches that will amuse a reader and would, in a lecture hall, capture the attention of even a drowsy student in the back row. Archibald's central interest, within a sweeping survey of Yeats's entire career as a poet, is nothing less than the history of Yeats's imagination. The book draws upon Archibald's extensive and thoughtful study of the uses that Yeats's imagination made of his Irish philosophical forebears, especially Swift, Berkeley, and Burke, and also of Yeats's immediate domestic and political environment.

The one-word title, while it has the apparent virtue of economy, does little to help a reader who seeks to discover the book's specific subject matter. The introduction wisely acknowledges that some selectivity will be necessary, although an approach that is more nearly encyclopedic is implied by the lengthy list of topics to be covered:

> Yeats's interaction with the Romantic and modernist traditions in literature; his relationships with his family, especially his father, and his friends, especially Maud Gonne and Lady Gregory; the burden of his Anglo-Irish heritage and his celebrations of its major exemplars; his involvement with the occult, spiritism, and magic; his eclectic and willful historiography; his response to the turbulence of contemporary Irish and European culture and politics; his ardent desire to embody his belief that consciousness is conflict, to define and confront the antinomies of human experience, and occasionally to resolve them; and his need, at the end, to gather all the strands, to ready the achieved self for a new plunge into the void. [P. xiv]

And, for all practical purposes, that list is a table of contents for the volume.

The opening chapter—a tour de force in which Archibald usefully compares and contrasts "A Prayer for My Daughter" with Coleridge's "Frost at Midnight"—and the next chapter's excellent study of Yeats's important links and conflicts with John Butler Yeats suggest that the book will focus specifically on Yeats's imaginative "encounters" and that the intended audience are specialists who do not have to be told, for example, that "Robert's death in 1873" refers to Yeats's brother, that "York Street" refers to John Butler Yeats's Dublin studio, or that "the self-portrait" could only refer to the last and best known of John Butler Yeats's several self-portraits (pp. 15, 18). Archibald wrote the John Butler Yeats volume in the Bucknell University Press Irish series and thus might be expected to champion John Butler Yeats here. In fact, the artist's presence is felt both directly, in this chapter, and in some valuable comparisons later in the book, as when Archibald observes that many of the short poems in *Words for Music Perhaps* and *A Woman Young and Old* "contain an extraordinary compression of Yeats's ideas" and "bear the same relationship to his philosophical poetry as JBY's sketches do to his portraits: not notes or practice, but instantly, gaily rendered miniatures" (p. 215). Archibald also remembers the limits as well as the wealth of the contacts between father and son: "There are important matters that WBY does not discuss with his father, and there are moments when one feels that JBY does not quite understand what is happening in his son's mind, and how exciting it is" (p. 21).

The third chapter is a lengthy review and analysis of Yeats's contacts with Mabel Beardsley, Maud Gonne, and Lady Gregory. The discussion of Maud Gonne is well handled, if sometimes a bit harder on the old girl than might be necessary and if perhaps sometimes willing to downplay her masses of gold-brown hair and other physical attributes that would have held considerable interest for a young bachelor, no matter how literary his other instincts might have been. The extensive attention given to straightforward biography in this chapter begins to suggest that nonspecialist readers are also part of the book's audience. And certainly all categories of readers are likely to be pleased with interesting observations such as the linking of the stone imagery in "Easter 1916" with Maud Gonne's dream of herself as a stone statue; specialist readers will be less pleased with the several minor errors of fact, here and elsewhere. For example, Parnell's coffin arrived in 1891 at Kingstown, not 1889 at Kingston; the bridegroom in *Cathleen ni Houlihan,* set in 1798, joins the United Irishmen, not the Fenians (a broad usage that was not established until after 1858); the Gaelic poet Raftery is mentioned in an essay and in the novel *The Speckled Bird,* but not in any of Yeats's short stories; Maud Gonne married in February, not June 1903; the codicil to Hugh Lane's will was unwitnessed, not unsigned (he signed both of its pages); and the strange old man, not Hanrahan, bewitches the cards into a pack of hounds and a hare in the story "Red Hanrahan" (pp. 48, 44, 72, 43, 97, 139). One wishes too that the book had been better served in its system of annotation, which encourages a compression of reference, sometimes at the risk of obscurity. Perhaps not all readers could easily recognize, with no clues in the text or notes, the author of "Of what the Bard! / Who present, past and future sees" and "Experience is in love with the productions of Time" (p. 202)—the first is a misquotation ("Hear the voice of the Bard! / . . .") of the "Introduction" to "Songs of Experience," and the second is a prose proverb from "The Marriage of Heaven and Hell." Similarly, when Archibald mentions "the reconstituted Heracles walking among the gods, something intended and complete, a truth that cannot be known and must be embodied" (p. 225), I think most readers would welcome a citation of the pertinent passages (AV-B 226, 302) that explain Yeats's use of Heracles.

The middle third of the book, on Yeats's Irish cultural and political encounters, clearly displays the strengths and the limitations of the plan of the book and of Archibald's approach to the history of Yeats's imagination. These two chapters, which cover Yeats's entire lifetime, provide an effective summary of his cultural and political involvements, although a few of the sections, for example a lengthy study of "The Wanderings of Oisin," pay little attention to imaginative encounters and thus suggest that they were included principally to allow the book to meet its (unstated) secondary goal of providing a comprehensive introduction to Yeats's career as a poet. To a considerable extent it does meet that secondary aim of serving inexperienced readers of the poetry, and often does so very ably, as in the sure-handed sketch of Crazy Jane and in the careful studies of many of the major poems—a key element in the book's value. But the pages spent in achieving comprehensiveness here, as in a later compilation of *A Vision*'s technical vocabulary and in shorter segments elsewhere, have perhaps forced a too compressed handling of the principal topic, the history of Yeats's imagination. For example, in an earlier, long essay on Yeats's encounters with Burke, Archibald's graceful and carefully detailed account had permitted him the luxury of a fervent peroration that yet did not overwhelm the essay. In the shorter scope provided in the book, however, the same arguments, even if highly principled, sometimes sit less comfortably. The ferocity of his political and philosophical indictments of "In Memory of Eva Gore-Booth and Con Markiewicz" and *Purgatory* is startling, although deeply felt, and is explained thus: "Failures and accomplishments in political thought and expression, for a poet, are also failures and accomplishments of the imagination" (p. 162). Archibald regrets these episodes in the history of Yeats's imagination. In the poem he finds "Friendship and the imagination's apprehension of public events are equally betrayed by reactionary pique." The play, which he finds "so good" in purely dramatic terms, he considers "deeply repellent" (p. 155).

Readers who prefer a less intrusive tone in literary discussions of Yeats's late politics, however, will still recognize in this section the same richly resonant literary and philosophical appreciation that so productively informs Archibald's readings of the poems for which he has sympathy—and luckily that is usually the case. I applaud Archibald's willingness to give careful readings of many poems, especially since his usually adroit sense of pace allows ample detail without pausing so long at an individual line that he might bore a reader who lacks keen interest in the particular poem being discussed. I can recommend to beginning readers and to more experienced readers alike the analyses of "Upon a Dying Lady," "A Prayer for My Daughter," "Meditations in Time of Civil War," "Nineteen Hundred and Nineteen," "The Tower," "Among School Children," and "Vacillation." Also of interest are "The Wanderings of Oisin," "Easter 1916" (but why insist on using the term "Uprising" when referring to the Rising?), "Sailing to Byzantium," and "Byzantium."

Archibald is extraordinarily impressive in his keen sensitivity to the great poems in which Yeats faces the anguish of mortality and in which the poet achieves, in Archibald's moving description, "moments when Yeats passes beyond time, when he achieves a stance, vision, and language that are remarkable equally for their scope and their intensity. For him such moments are costly, fleeting, and ecstatic; for us they are chastening and sustaining" (p. 254).

David R. Clark. *Yeats at Songs and Choruses.*
Amherst: University of Massachusetts Press, 1983. xxiv + 283 pp.
Reviewed by THOMAS PARKINSON

This book treats several poems written between 1926 and 1931, making use of the manuscripts and typescripts and printed versions that Clark is editing for the series of editions of the individual volumes of Yeats's works forthcoming from Cornell University Press. Clark has been working on these matters for some time, and several of his commentaries have already been published.

The commentaries in this book, however, are very extensive and full, and they are heavily documented with reproductions of the manuscripts and with illustrations of paintings that were in the background of Yeats's "Her Triumph." The book is richly illustrated, the illustrations adding up to a formidable fifty-six. It is also thoroughly documented in other ways, and it is a relief to see a book on Yeats that is thoroughly responsible in its use of secondary works. Clark is not at all pedantic about this; in citing others' work he is graceful as well as responsible. He writes with clarity and verve.

The strategy of the book is to take work by Yeats that is largely objective and set apart from the "personal" Yeats, stressing the songs of Crazy Jane and the songs in *Words for Music Perhaps,* as well as the choruses from *Oedipus at Colonus* and *Antigone* that close *A Man Young and Old* and *A Woman Young and Old.* The only poem that comes from Yeats the man speaking to a person living in his life that Clark treats is "After Long Silence." That seems to me to have been a prudent gesture to those who might complain that his book is simply not related to the characteristic Yeats *oeuvre.*

The chapters of the book tend to take a single form. They begin with an identification of the poem to be discussed, followed by a sensitive and reasonable interpretation of the poem that reveals problems that are not completely soluble within the printed text. These problems are then considered in relation to the ancillary evidence, mainly that of the manuscripts and the multiple versions through which the poems go, leading in turn to other source material, in one case—"Her Triumph"—to various paintings and drawings of Saint George or Perseus and related works. Clark then comes to the best resolution he can of the problems posed by the poem, both in its final printed text and in the commentaries promoted by that text.

Working with the Yeats manuscripts is an exasperation, but the greater the exasperation the greater the rewards. Yeats himself could not always read his own handwriting, at least in his later years, and he frequently had to consult his wife to determine what he had written earlier, sometimes only the day before. Those who had the privilege of working with Mrs. Yeats will remember moments when even her expertise faltered. I for one am extremely sympathetic to Clark when he describes his difficulties in deciding whether Crivelli or Bellini is the name that Yeats might have written, only to settle finally on Carpaccio. The book spends substantial time on the problems of dealing with the material, and there are times when the auxiliary labor becomes the main subject of the writing. Then the text seems like a parallel to *The Road to Xanadu,* and like that book it sometimes leads the reader to ask Clark to get on with it. The tone becomes one of nit-picking.

My own reaction, for example, to the prolonged study of Yeats's dragons and "Her Triumph" is that, yes, the result is illumination of the way that Yeats's mind probably worked, and there is pleasure in seeing the range of his interests and concerns. Clark's transcriptions are admirable, as they generally are, and the process of composition is, as it usually is with Yeats, surprising and revealing about the poem and about the nature of poetry. The difficulty I have, that I have always had both in reading other critics' studies of the manuscripts and in making my own, is that I find a point of diminishing returns in such studies.

Clark, for instance, makes what I think is an important revelation about "Three Things"—that is, his interpretation of "stretching and yawning"—but I do not share his sense of having nailed down the proper reading. I still don't see, granted the tone and structure of the final version, why the meaning has to be identified with that of Pound in his rendering of Daniel. What Clark's reading does is to enrich the possibilities of the reading. In that respect, it shows a danger that Yeats studies will have to face increasingly as the manuscripts get thoroughly transcribed, and that is the danger of becoming too bemused with data. Modern literature generally poses that danger, and while my own view is that (*pace* Stanley Fish) there is a text in this class and that one can come more or less close to its nature and reference, finality is not always possible or advisable.

Another problem that Clark's book poses is the danger of trying to see how many angelic commentators can dance on the manuscript of a very small poem. Here one can get into all sorts of troubles and interpretations of a poem such as "After Long Silence" that seems to me at least reasonably clear. There is one line in the manuscript that Ellmann, Stallworthy, and Clark all read in the same way: "And there fore ignorant." Since I cannot imagine Yeats writing that line, and because the "there fore" is not at all clear, I read it "And then were ignorant." Wild horses won't change that reading. In the future we may find many such disagreements, and I hope we can all keep our sense of balance and reasonable judgment. In Clark's book, I find the lengthy analysis of "After Long Silence" perhaps excessive, merely in length, and I wonder if "Her Triumph" is a poem that warrants so much interpretation, fascinating as much of it is.

This is a book that I admire and respect. There is no sense in acting as if any admirer of Yeats would not profit from reading and studying it. It is also immediately enjoyable, written with clarity and enthusiasm, and produced with elegance and generosity by the University of Massachusetts Press. It is a genuinely distinguished book. I can imagine, however, that the materials of Yeats's manuscripts might, in less tactful and reasonable hands, result in obfuscation. Even so fine a critic as Clark becomes at times the captive of the data and the beguilements of the search for origins.

This book is indispensable to the study of Yeats. If I seem to have been grudging in my treatment of it, I do so out of the sense that it is an important work that poses certain problems that students of Yeats should keep in mind. Nobody will, after this book, read the poems treated by Clark as they were read before these bright, clear, and fully documented analyses.

Terence Diggory. *Yeats & American Poetry: The Tradition of the Self.*
Princeton: Princeton University Press, 1983. xix + 262 pp.
Reviewed by George Bornstein

Yeats's relation to American poetry may strike many scholars as a forced topic. They will not think so after reading this capacious yet careful study. After an introductory chapter explaining what he means by a "tradition of the self" and another on Yeats's response to four nineteenth-century American writers (Emerson, Poe, Thoreau, and especially Whitman), Terence Diggory appropriately begins his exploration of Yeats's impact on American poets with a long discussion of his complicated relation to Pound. In four subsequent chapters organized by decade, Diggory then focuses on Yeats's contribution to natural speech in the 1910s (Lindsay, Frost, and Williams), to creation of a poetic self in the 1920s (Stevens, Eliot, and Jeffers), to public speech in the 1930s (the Fugitives, Horace Gregory, and MacLeish), and, posthumously, to confessional poetry in the 1940s and after (Roethke, Berryman, and Lowell). Despite the artificial tidiness of those divisions, Diggory manages sensitive appraisals which combine precise documentation with a flair for incisive comparison. The study succeeds best in its literary history and practical criticism, but runs into trouble in some of its theorizing.

Rightly arguing against the elevation of Emerson by recent theorists of influence, Diggory instead establishes Whitman as the central figure of nineteenth-century American letters both for Yeats and for subsequent poets. While associating Emerson with theosophy, Poe with personality, and Thoreau with a rustic ideal balancing the metaphysical with the concrete, Yeats saw above all in Whitman a poet creating himself and then placing that fictional self among historical circumstances. That act, combined with Whitman's exaltation of human passion and brazen embrace of a non-English nationalism and regionalism, made him the central American figure for the early Yeats. Whitman, in turn, became one of Yeats's earliest American admirers, as the discussion of his approval of the early article "The Poetry of Sir Samuel Ferguson" shows. A consistent strength of Diggory's method is his perceptive attention to the stages of one poet's reaction to another, so that influence emerges as diachronic rather than static. In the case of Whitman, Diggory accurately plots the later Yeats's disenchantment with Whitman's apparent lack of a "Vision of Evil" and fascination with mass democratic sentiment, which in *A Vision* appeared as a "half-civilised" leveling down verging on poetic demagogy. Diggory provocatively argues that Yeats's characteristic catalogues, for example, enumerate individuals by name to distinguish them from the anonymous mass, and hence to distinguish the poet as well, whereas Whitman's catalogues tend to be anonymous and to assimilate the poet into that anonymity.

Yeats & American Poetry offers fewer surprises with major writers, or with those whose relation to Yeats has been well studied, than it does with minor ones. The chapter on Pound, for example, adds to the many extant studies chiefly a synoptic though thorough overview, together with observations on fugitive poems like the "Laudantes Decem" sequence. Interest picks up with T. S. Eliot, where Diggory shows the unexpected importance of Yeats's drama to Eliot, particularly the first performance of *At the Hawk's Well* in 1916 (Pound made sure Eliot saw it). Yeats's drama mattered as well to Stevens, Jeffers, MacLeish, and particularly Frost, for whom the line "The butter's at your elbow, Father Hart," from *The Land of Heart's Desire,* became an unexpected touchstone of natural speech in poetry. Diggory is particularly good on Jeffers's lifelong encounter with Yeats's work, from his first volume to his last. Jeffers emerges as one of the many poets for whom *The Wind Among the Reeds* assumed an early importance succeeded by that of the major work from *Responsibilities* onward; the line "I pace upon the battlements and stare" from "The Tower" finds an echo in "I lean on the broad worn stones of the parapet top" of Jeffers's "Margrave." The better-known impact on Roethke (who characterized his attitude toward Yeats as "One dares to stand up to a great style, to compete with Papa" [p. 196]) and Berryman (who wrote that he "didn't so much wish to resemble as *to be*" Yeats [p. 197]) receives here a superb retelling. Diggory documents his argument so well that one only occasionally demurs. Not all references to cabins in Stevens's poetry need derive from "The Lake Isle of Innisfree," and Berryman's description of Henry in *Dream Songs* as "an imaginary character (not the poet, not me)" (p. 206) owes less to Yeats than to Browning's description of his *Dramatic Lyrics* as "so many utterances of so many imaginary persons, not mine."

The book's subtitle, "The Tradition of the Self," portends difficulties in the theoretical underpinning of Diggory's careful historical work. A fascination with that gnomic phrase in the 1909 diary leads him to elevate it to a master principle which both ignores its own inherently oxymoronic quality and scants Yeats's concern with tradition elsewhere. Diggory rightly insists that Yeats had in some ways to create his own tradition, but he did so partly by fusing already extant ingredients; to ignore the role of Anglo-Irish, Romantic, or esoteric traditions (to name but three) leads to misrepresentation. Part of the problem comes from the skewed presentation of the one of those components which the book discusses most fully, the Romantic. Though he shrewdly contrasts Wordsworth viewing himself in terms of past stages of his life in "Tintern Abbey" to Yeats viewing himself in terms of his own past creations in "The Circus Animals' Desertion," Diggory goes astray in centering his discussion on Wordsworth, whom Yeats always viewed ambivalently, and in mentioning only cursorily Blake and Shelley, whom he engaged more deeply as both models and antagonists. Diggory's strange notion that a Romantic poet "in expressing a self that already exists, merely records preexisting experience" (p. 6) hardly fits the author of *Milton*; there the poet both creates himself in the act of writing (a central component of Diggory's "tradition") and displays more insight into the process than any author discussed in the book except Yeats himself.

Alignment with the wrong Romantic tradition undercuts Diggory's interesting "Conclusion." There he speculates that after a Classical phase in which a poet-son seeks to emulate his father in the craft and a Romantic phase in which the son seeks to rival the father by distorting him, we are in a third, postmodern stage in which the son places himself in the role of his own father so that the very idea of tradition dissipates. In that phase Yeats's influence as defined by *Yeats & American Poetry* disappears. Here an anecdote recorded elsewhere in this book is pertinent. Frost claimed to remember Pound saying to Yeats, "You're too full of adjectives and expletives. Let's wring you dry" (p. 67). Against both Pound and Diggory, I would maintain that poets have not yet succeeded in wringing Yeats dry. He is likely to remain a fountain for the foreseeable future.

A. E. Dyson. *Yeats, Eliot and R. S. Thomas: Riding the Echo.* Atlantic Highlands, N.J.: Humanities Press, 1981. xx + 339 pp. *Reviewed by* DONALD E. STANFORD

The greater part of Dyson's book is devoted to highly personalized and usually highly appreciative discussions of the poems of Yeats's "major phase—1916–1939" (184 pages), Eliot's *Four Quartets* (100 pages), and highlights of the career of the Welsh poet R. S. Thomas (42 pages). Every reader will learn something from this book, for the author, during the last three decades, has thoroughly immersed himself in his subject. He has read the most important poems of the three poets many times, and he has taught them for years to his graduate and undergraduate students. He brings his teaching experience into the discussions of the poems. His book is *useful* criticism. Before conducting another seminar on Eliot, I shall certainly reread his chapter on *Four Quartets,* with special attention to his critique of "Little Gidding."

In his introduction, entitled "Riding the Echo," and from time to time elsewhere in his discussions, Dyson lays down the principles by which he reads, evaluates, and teaches poetry. The phrase "riding the echo" comes from a poem by R. S. Thomas. Dyson means by it that "the works of major creators set up resonances and echoes among themselves" (p. xiii). By riding these resonances we can enter the world of Yeats or Eliot, push language "beyond . . . the boundaries of discursive English" (p. xiii), and extend our own consciousness. This notion has close affinities with the basic symbolist doctrine that "all art aspires to the condition of music"—a statement that Dyson quotes with approval more than once (pp. xv, 208). It is, he says, "a precept that underlies most of the best modern criticism, as well as most of the best modern art" (p. xv). "We are indeed fortunate that our greatest poets in English have been rooted in this tradition with whatever slight reservations at times ever since. What then can the critic do? Point to this and that—not trying to explain, except maybe in questions" (p. 208).

Well, I think the critic should be expected to do much more than this—and fortunately Dyson himself does so. But let me return for a moment to the statement that "all art aspires to the condition of music." It has been repeated frequently in our literature for about a century. I believe that the great Paul Valéry himself, in what I would like to think was momentary irresponsibility, reiterated it. Nevertheless, the idea should be reexamined. Why should all art aspire to the condition of music? The media of painting are paint and canvas or something similar, the media of sculpture are marble, bronze, etc. None of these has any similarity to music, the medium of which is pure sound. The medium of poetry is language, which when spoken—actually or imaginatively in the mind's ear, is also sound, and Dyson quite rightly emphasizes the importance of sound (he advocates reading all poetry aloud) in contributing to the total effect of a poem. But the effectiveness of words as pure sound is extremely limited. As pure sound what poem can challenge a Mozart concerto? The power of poetry resides in its rational content (the denotative meaning of words), reinforced by the appropriate connotative effects and meanings (including sound) that language has accumulated over the centuries. This combination of sound and sense elevates the art of poetry to a region above that of music and quite different from it. It is this complex interrelation of sound and sense that, in my opinion, makes poetry the most important of all the arts. Do serious students of literature really believe that the authors of, for example, *The Canterbury Tales, Hamlet,* and *Paradise Lost* were aspiring to achieve in their works the condition of music? This symbolist attempt to devalue the rational content of the language of poetry has tended to degrade poetry as an art. If one wishes to express experiences (mystical or otherwise) that are ineffable, one would do well to practice an art other than poetry.

The notion that all art should aspire to the condition of music has been frequently employed by poets of our time as a method of structuring a poem along musical lines with particular emphasis on theme and variation of theme, and on recurrent imagery and motif. *The Waste Land* has been called "a music of ideas." In *Four Quartets* Eliot employed musical devices from beginning to end, and a good deal of scholarly energy has been spent in attempting to demonstrate which Beethoven quartet or quartets Eliot had in mind—or perhaps it was a quartet by Bartok? But methods that are effective in structuring music are not necessarily the most effective or economical means of organizing a poem. Repetition of phrase, image, and motif without substantial development in thought may become tedious. Dyson, however, finds in this kind of repetition, as in the opening of "Burnt Norton," "a symphony of echoes" (p. 194).

Dyson defines and employs other critical principles about which this reviewer has reservations. He appears to believe that ambiguity and lack of clarity are poetic virtues. He praises Yeats for his "unsolved ambivalence, conflicting directions, [and] opposed possibilities" (p. 3). He finds in *Four Quartets* a "'meaning' . . . manifestly not of a kind that can even tempt toward paraphrase" (p. 194). He apparently accepts Eliot's doctrine that a poem means what it means to the individual reader, that if necessary the reader himself should at least partially write the poem. Of "Burnt Norton" he says, "Literary and musical themes will crowd in, for each one of us is different" (p. 188); "We may each provide a different gloss for the rose garden. . . . No way to evade the concreteness, the elusiveness, the resonance, unless we retreat into idiocy" (p. 189). Of a passage from "The Dry Salvages" he writes, "Any reader who does not supply his own images will not be reading the poem" (p. 189). We seem to have a theory that states that a poem not only means what it means to the individual reader, but that the appropriate response to a poem may be for the reader to write his or her own poem. The possibility that some readers may be more intelligent and perceptive than others is not considered, for there is no "right" reading of a poem. The poem means what it means to the individual.

In one of his rare negative comments on Eliot, Dyson faults the fourth section of "East Coker" for being too explicit in its Christian references: "it is sad that Eliot's habitual subtlety should falter at such a point" (p. 232). Dyson fears dogmatism in both the artist and the critic: "No artist worthy of respect . . . will be dogmatic" (p. 192); "criticism of too dogmatic a kind makes me uneasy" (p. 9). And, finally, Dyson asserts that "the doctrines announced by Blake, Wordsworth, and other early nineteenth-century prophets, based on belief in individual uniqueness and celebration of individual creativity, are doctrines by which man's future will be shaped" (p. xv). This is a prospect that I find disturbing. My reservations about certain aspects of Dyson's critical position are fundamental. But more to the purpose of this review, I have mentioned them because they have caused his critiques of Yeats and Eliot to be frequently too tentative, cautious and noncommittal. And in the case of R. S. Thomas, I think they have led to a critical misjudgment of some importance.

When Dyson gets down to detailed examination of certain poems by Yeats—where he is at his best—and by Eliot, he frequently rewards the reader with fresh insights and challenging interpretations. He begins his discussion of Yeats's major phase with penetrating remarks about "The Wild Swans at Coole," a poem in which "a new dimension of greatness appears in Yeats's art" (p. 7). This quiet, beautifully controlled poem on one of Yeats's major themes, youth versus age, deserves perhaps even more praise than Dyson gives it. In his good examination of "The Tower," Dyson makes the convincing point that, in the opening lines, Aristotle and Locke should have been substituted for Plato and Plotinus as dealers in "abstract things" (VP 409; p. 38). "A Prayer for My Daughter" he describes, correctly I think, as an expression of "escapist hopes" (p. 32), and he appears to be as baffled as I am by the paradoxical phrases "murderous innocence" and "radical innocence" (VP 403, 405) in the same poem. He explains the difficult phrase "twenty centuries of stony sleep" (VP 402) in "The Second Coming" as referring to the sleep of the beast during the Christian cycle. His analyses of "Long-legged Fly," "Sailing to Byzantium," and "Lapis Lazuli" are especially helpful, as are his examinations of the flaws in the often too highly praised "In Memory of Major Robert Gregory" and of the difficulties of "Byzantium." (In this last poem he cannot explain the difference Yeats intended between "shade" and "image" [VP 497]. I think a look at *The Egyptian Book of the Dead* would solve the problem. According to Egyptian belief, after death the human personality splits into several entities, including *Ka,* image or double, and *Khaibit,* shade or shadow.) He refers to the shortcoming (usually overlooked) of "All Souls' Night"—that Yeats never tells us his "mummy truths" (VP 474). All we have in this poem are character sketches of three occultists and a spooky atmosphere. He considers "In Memory of Eva Gore-Booth and Con Markiewicz" one of Yeats's most noble poems and "among the most liquidly beautiful poems in the language" (p. 104), praise a bit too high perhaps, but he correctly points to Yeats's "warm humanity" and his "exhilirating [sic] power to celebrate friendship and eroticism equally" (p. 113). It is a good point, and although Dyson doesn't say so, it is precisely this "warm humanity" that is one reason for claiming Yeats to be a greater poet than Eliot. In his detailed, careful analysis of "Among School Children," he finds an unsolved ambiguity in the fifth stanza—whether it is the mother or child who is doomed to "sleep, shriek, struggle to escape" (VP 444), and he makes the interesting observation that perhaps Yeats had in mind Blake's infant who says of his birth:

> My mother groaned, my father wept;
> Into the dangerous world I leapt,
> Helpless, naked, piping loud.
> [P. 92]

Dyson has two puzzling comments on "Among School Children." In the fourth stanza Yeats contrasts the child Maud Gonne with Gonne's "present image"—"Hollow of cheek as though it drank the wind" (VP 444). Of Gonne's "present image" Dyson says, "For a moment, a Leonardo da Vinci beauty confronts him" (p. 91). Gonne, like Yeats, was in her sixties at the time Yeats wrote the poem. It seems clear that Yeats is contrasting Gonne's present faded state with her former beauty, an interpretation consistent with one of the major themes of the poem, the superiority of youth over age. Also, in the final stanza Dyson refers to two dancers "their eyes lit with love" (p. 97), whereas in Yeats's poem there is only one dancer.

From time to time, incidentally, Dyson mentions affinities between the thought of Yeats and Jung, although the two probably never met and it is difficult to establish a direct mutual influence. The reader may wish to know that this subject is more thoroughly explored in James Olney's *The Rhizome and the Flower: The Perennial Philosophy—Yeats and Jung* (Berkeley: University of California Press, 1980), published a year before Dyson's book, but evidently not available to him. (His preface date is January 1980.)

Dyson's treatment of *Four Quartets* is on the whole less successful than his discussion of Yeats, perhaps because he pushes his method of "riding the echo" further than he does in his study of Yeats, and perhaps also because he is dealing with poetry that is at times deliberately obscurantist. But there are puzzling moments when Dyson seems to be trying *not* to understand. Of the famous stanza in part three of "Burnt Norton" beginning "Descend lower, descend only / Into the world of perpetual solitude," which it is generally agreed derives from Saint John of the Cross's concept of the dark night of the soul, Dyson merely says, "Perhaps Eliot is having a bad moment; perhaps he feels that bad moments must be recalled again before we can rest in the rose garden" (p. 207). With reference to a similar passage (also probably influenced by Saint John) in part three of "East Coker," beginning "I said to my soul be still," Dyson comments that the "quiet beauty is appealing to listen to but impossible to gloss" (p. 227). Saint John, whose influence on *Four Quartets* is obvious, gets very short notice: there are only two fleeting references to him. Still more remarkable is Dyson's bewilderment concerning the final two lines of "Burnt Norton":

> Ridiculous the waste sad time
> Stretching before and after.

He says, "Perhaps we should do best to let the last two lines rest as a riddle, a challenge to discernment" (p. 211). Yet they seem to be among the clearest in meaning of all Eliot. Eliot has just defined what Dyson has called a "numinous moment"—"Sudden in a shaft of sunlight." These moments occur throughout Eliot's poetry in both its pre-Christian and Christian phases. They are moments of fullness of being: as a Christian, Eliot would consider them to be moments of mystical illumination. In *Four Quartets* they are the highest experiences of which the human soul in its earthly life is capable. Human life between these infrequent mystical moments is "Ridiculous . . . waste," or as he expressed it earlier in his career, a *waste land*. It is this downgrading of normal human secular experience that will, I believe, eventually exclude Eliot from the category of major poets.

Nonetheless, there are helpful and illuminating passages in Dyson's discussion of Eliot. I quote in abbreviated form his comment on a single image in "Little Gidding" that has deepened my own appreciation of that poem:

> The lines
>
> Dust in the air suspended
> Marks the place where a story ended
>
> take me back vividly to a moment in the summer of 1944. A flying-bomb had stopped almost overhead; . . . there was an almighty crash . . . I have an ineffaceable memory of the great cloud of dust which rose from a neighbouring street, climbed above the housetops and, for what seemed like eternity, stayed quite still. . . . Within it, one knew, was the transformed dust of houses, furniture, people—transformed in a moment. [Pp. 267–68].

In his interesting final evaluation of *Four Quartets,* Dyson sees the poem as less Christian, less dogmatic than its author. He thinks "Burnt Norton" the greatest of all Eliot's poems, he admires especially the haunting slow movement of "The Dry Salvages," and he considers "Little Gidding" as "perhaps the most teasing . . . enigma that the poet left" (p. 283).

In his discussion of R. S. Thomas, Dyson says of the Welsh poet that he "in time will be seen as the outstanding poet, to date, of the second half of this century" (p. xix). And he argues that Thomas's poems, "Pietà," "Belfry," "In Church," *Laboratories of the Spirit, H'm,* and *Frequencies,* establish him "now without doubt, in my view, among the five or six greatest poets to have written in English in this century" (p. 303). I cannot concur in these very high evaluations, nor do I have space here to enter into an extended evaluation of my own, and in fact Dyson devotes only a small part of his book to Thomas. He seems to me a minor poet working in a free verse prosody resembling that of the minor imagists but lacking the rhythm and resonance of the more important writers of free verse, such as Stevens, Pound, Williams, and H. D., and most certainly deficient in their sparkling, intense imagery. His subject matter is usually religious. Dyson considers "Pietà" to be one of his best poems. I quote the entire poem:

Always the same hills
Crowd the horizon,
Remote witnesses
Of the still scene.

And in the foreground
The tall Cross,
Sombre, untenanted,
Aches for the Body
That is back in the cradle
Of a maid's arms.
[P. 285]

Dyson devotes three pages of explication to this poem, admiring especially the image of the Cross aching to take the body of Christ once more into its arms.

In a perceptive comment on Eliot, Dyson refers to "the ubiquitous echo-chambers of *The Waste Land*" (p. 224). The poem or the fragment of a poem as echo-chamber is an excellent metaphor to represent the dead end of the symbolist tradition, the autonomous poem resounding with internal resonances that are ultimately meaningless because sealed off from life. Villiers de l'Isle-Adam said that as for living, our servants can do that for us. Dyson's critical method of "riding the echo" could, if carried to its ultimate conclusion, lead to a similar dead end. Fortunately, Dyson usually does not carry his method too far, and hence there is much of value in his book, especially in his chapter on Yeats. And fortunately too, for Yeats's eventual reputation, Yeats himself was only somewhat influenced from time to time by symbolist theory. He was not a pure symbolist poet.

Hugh Kenner. *A Colder Eye: The Modern Irish Writers.* New York: Alfred A. Knopf, 1983. xiv + 301 pp.
Reviewed by GEORGE MILLS HARPER

Almost any thoughtful reader will have a difficult time deciding what audience *A Colder Eye* is intended for. Only those who are saturated with Irish literature will make much sense of it, and they will find little they didn't already know, though they will be pleased and shocked in turn by Kenner's forthright critical opinions, as well as by the style in which they are projected.

Those who know his earlier books will not, of course, be surprised at the language and syntax, which sometimes sound like a strange melange of James Joyce and Flann O'Brien. I am reminded of a recent observation—not quite fair I think—about a new book by another distinguished critic. In "Professor Frye and the Bible" (*South Atlantic Quarterly,* 82, no. 2 [1983], 163), Charles Wheeler says, "The book is not devious or dishonest. But it is thoroughly self-indulgent." If that were said of Kenner, he might reply, in the words of Oscar Wilde to the editor of the *St. James's Gazette,* "I wrote this book entirely for my own pleasure, and it gave me very great pleasure to write it" (*The Letters of Oscar Wilde,* ed. Rupert Hart-Davis [New York: Harcourt, Brace & World, 1962], p. 257. The book in question was *The Picture of Dorian Gray.*)

Kenner is both wary and wise. Anticipating critical dissent, he notes in the "Acknowledgments" that he has been "encouraged . . . to persist in my stubborn courses," and he cautions his readers to "study the chapter called 'Warning'" (p. xiv). Beginning with an explanation of "[w]hat an Irish Bull is," that chapter is designed to impress upon the unwary that "the Irish Facts [read 'nonfacts'] which infest all talk and all written memoirs have demonstrably effected some permeation into all areas of sober scholarship" (p. 110), including, of course, Kenner's own: "Do not regard what you read here as resting on any final authority save my own sense of what fits" (p. xiv). (There are, in fact, several nonfacts in *A Colder Eye.*)

Although Kenner insists that his book "tries, within reasonable limits of space, to tell a coherent story, which could be subtitled *Yeats and His Shadow*" (p. xi), all but thoroughly indoctrinated readers will find it difficult to find or follow the story. (I am reminded of Blake's offering "the end of a golden string" to the readers of *Jerusalem.*) And Kenner would surely be disappointed if they accepted such statements as more than "Irish Facts." Half in jest, half in earnest, he cannot resist catchy phrases, outlandish diction, and unidentified (often twisted) literary allusions. The irony is deep and pervasive.

Even the chapter headings are puzzles: "Warning," "Points to

Ponder," "A Bag of Cats," "A Tale of a Pot," "More Points to Ponder," "A Dwindling Gyre," "The Terminator," etc. The two chapters on "points to ponder" consist entirely of selected quotations (five pages in all) to illustrate, perhaps, Patrick Kavanagh's quoted observation that "Irishness is a form of anti-art" (p. 12). These chapters, like Sterne's famous chapter on digressions, do not further the "coherent story." But they reveal a great deal about the writer, and sophisticated readers will enjoy the revelation.

Most of the time, also, they will enjoy the studied eccentricity of Kenner's style. A professor himself, he gets a mildly masochistic pleasure from mocking gibes at the profession—from a "nonfact" in Richard Ellmann's biography of Joyce (p. 4), to the curricula of the "exalted company" of Yale and Harvard professors who assigned *The Playboy of the Western World* because of its notoriety: "It was the rioting had launched John Synge into seminar immortality, like, as the man said of someone else altogether, a shot off a shovel" (p. 41). Kenner enjoys the subtle irony of pointing out in a footnote (p. 277) that he borrowed "shot off a shovel" from Joyce, but not that Joyce had taken it from folklore, where it differs by one key letter.

Much more pervasive, however, is the irony directed at the "Irishness of a thing" (p. 12, quoting Kavanagh again)—that is, at the Irish themselves. Although Kenner obviously loves the country and its people, he seems unable to resist one caustic thrust after another, many at Yeats, who is, as Kenner suggests, the shadowy subject of his book. Alluding to Ceres, in a discussion of *The Pot of Broth* ("A Tale of a Pot"), he writes: "But she stopped short of Ireland, where the Irishman does as he does, and might as well do otherwise, except that otherwise is not just now the way it is being done, by him" (p. 46). Speaking of Irish history ("A nightmare from which no one can awake and salient with the discontinuities of nightmare" [p. 47]), but indirectly of Ballylee, he summarizes several centuries: "Ruined castles, ruined houses, ruined towers round or square, mark achievement that flared briefly and flamed out, whereupon a few more stragglers shifted their ground" (p. 47). Compare the following extension, the sarcasm of which he defends by quoting a note from *The Wind Among the Reeds*: "The land *is* alive, yes, but with malicious ancient people, the *Sidhe* (say

'Shee') who steal wits and whose gold proves a bag of leaves, whose stone a stone" (pp. 47–48). And there is more on the subject: "Somewhere, somewhere, somewhere there needed to be an abounding glittering life" (p. 114). In 1894 Yeats "had located such a life no nearer than faeryland" (p. 114), Kenner observes, adding "So intent an alienation might be called derangement of a sort" (p. 115). Although *A Vision* (Yeats's "esoteric testament" [p. 213]) is mentioned only twice, it too is about "the experience of living in two temporal processes at once. Its complications are like those of Ptolemaic astronomy, which out of fidelity to data that seemed intractable had multiplied eccentric and tilted wheels till the heavens clanked" (p. 92). Any careful reader of *A Colder Eye* could multiply examples of this kind of eccentric and oversimplified, if not tilted, criticism.

Though I squirmed as I read, I found a kind of inverted pleasure in observing the art of my favorite writers being scrutinized with Kenner's colder and often jaundiced eye. Because most students and critics of modern Irish literature are likely to share my feelings, and because Kenner makes no concessions to the onion-sellers, many readers will not stay to the end. But they should. Although the book adds little to the sum of common critical knowledge about Irish literature, its author is a man of great learning whose slanted vision frequently offers startling insights into well-known passages and accepted motivations. And he knows quite well that "the rocky little country was adequately stocked with genius" (p. 112).

Gloria C. Kline. *The Last Courtly Lover: Yeats and the Idea of Woman.*
Ann Arbor: UMI Research Press, 1983. xiii + 199 pp.
Reviewed by David R. Clark

O do not love too long,
Or you will grow out of fashion
Like an old song.
[VP 212]

This is the epigraph of Gloria C. Kline's book, and "[t]he issues of [her] reading of Yeats are . . . to discover what he meant by 'the old high way of love' (VP 206), how his meaning functioned toward the cohesiveness of his entire work, and what he foresaw as the result of change or loss of this meaning" (p. 2). Her plan is to "trace Yeats's mythopoesis of courtly love," following "the course of his works in the courtly mode, . . . those poems and plays which present the woman as an elevated figure who has a spiritual influence on the man, can provide him a unifying image, and for that reason is reverently, sometimes fearfully, pursued or 'courted' by him" (p. 4).

Inevitably, a second, though unstated, aim or effect of the book is to assess the work and life of this "Last Courtly Lover" in the light of the liberated feminism of the latter half of the twentieth century. Both undertakings are of great interest to readers of Yeats today. The full story of Yeats's use of the courtly love tradition will vastly enrich our understanding of the poetry, and to see how Yeats stands up in the contemporary enlightenment about women will test the greatness, in the sense of scope and permanence, of that poetry. Therefore one picks up *The Last Courtly Lover* with eager expectation.

The organization of the book follows "the elements of [Harry] Slochower's definition of mythopoesis [in *Mythopoesis: Mythic Patterns in the Literary Classics* (Detroit: Wayne State University Press, 1970)]" (p. 4). Yeats is a mythopoet "who, coming at the close of an era, re-creates the ideals of its decaying social structures so that 'the hero's quest becomes *a critique* of the existing social norms and points to a futuristic order which is envisaged as integrating the valuable residues of the past and present'" (p. 1 [Slochower, p. 34]).

There are an "Introduction" and four chapters. Most of the introduction is taken up with a highly entertaining summary of Yeats's long pursuit of Maud Gonne. Chapter 1, "The Myth," gives an account of "the myth of courtly love as it appeared in the nineteenth century" (p. 4). Chapter 2, "The Personal Quest," concerns Yeats's application in life and works of courtly love attitudes to women, principally the first love, Laura Armstrong; the "woman lost," Maud Gonne; and the "woman won," Mrs. Yeats.

(An "Album of Illustrations" at the end of the book gives us all Yeats's ladies gathered between pictures of the courtly lover in youth and age.) *The Island of Statues,* poems from *The Wind Among the Reeds, The Countess Cathleen,* "The Cap and Bells," and some of the Solomon poems are the principal texts here.

Chapter 3, "The Cultural Quest," turns from Unity of Being to Unity of Culture: it associates, in a very convincing discussion, Lady Gregory with Castiglione's Duchess of Urbino and goes on quite interestingly to show the masculine and feminine principles at work in Yeats's system in *A Vision.* Chapter 4, "Recapitulation and Critique," deals suggestively with the later Yeats and his discovery of

> the potency of the negative aspects of the feminine. He had tried to make woman the emblem of perfect stasis in the *antithetical* garden, but he found that as *primary* nature, she was the image of disintegration and Chaos. He had finally learned that the pose of the courtly lover is a double denial. First, the Lover denies the femininity of his own psyche to project those qualities on his Lady and then to possess them again through possession of her. Second, the Lover denies his Lady the wholeness of her nature, rejecting in her those things which he would for whatever subjective reason not want to make part of himself. [P. 125]

In Yeats's "period of recapitulation and critique" a new view of the myth appears, and "[t]he Lover and his Rose are replaced by the Mother goddess and the slain god. Yeats's youthful romantic poses become poses of madness, extreme asceticism, and what he understood of femininity itself" (p. 126). This chapter deals with the unsavory Margot Ruddock episode, with Crazy Jane, with *A Woman Young and Old,* "Supernatural Songs," *The King of the Great Clock Tower, A Full Moon in March, The Herne's Egg,* "The Three Bushes," and Dorothy Wellesley. Kline is a bit humorless about Crazy Jane, taking too seriously Yeats's exorcism of "that slut" (p. 133).

Looking at Yeats's achievement, Kline finds that

> Yeats ends his mythopoesis of courtly love far from being the patriarchal chauvinist who wants to enclose a bird-brained woman

> behind garden walls, praising her the more for the more of her mind that she gives up. He ends instead by praising her for using her mind, analytically and intuitively. . . . [H]is course took him for a time into a feminine underworld. There, seeing through the eyes of his female personae, he comprehended that a woman cannot have Unity of Being without her own intellect and that a man cannot have Unity of Being without recognizing the feminine principle at work in himself. [P. 163]

I am tempted here to insert, sardonically, the most male chauvinist stanza of Yeats that I know, a mercifully rejected third stanza of "Three Things" in which a woman persona, "a bone upon the shore" (not "a rag, a bone, and a hank of hair"!) cites her dearest memories:

> The third thing is & I think of it yet
> Cried a bone washed up on the shore
> A man has fetched his deepest thought
> His finest fancies for my blind
> Ignorant & foolish mind
> A bone wave whitened & dried in the sun.
> [Copyright © 1977 Anne Yeats
> and Michael Butler Yeats]

Everything about this stanza is chauvinist except its rejection.

Kline gives Yeats the benefit of the doubt in her hopeful concluding question:

> In Yeats's system of the Great Years and their phases, the new revelation from the feminine principle was always rough, distressing to the antithetical culture it was replacing and, in the passage of time, destined to be refined and reshaped by the masculine principle. When Yeats asks at the close of this poem ["What Magic Drum?"], "What beast has licked its young?" could he possibly be understood as suggesting a union of natures or principles . . . a union that would not violate the femininity of the Lady of the old culture but complement the masculinity of the new male and allow the feminine, through him, to be formative of the coming culture? [Pp. 163–64]

Possibly.

Kline's book is certainly interesting. She has a brisk, sprightly style and is very clever in concocting "curious adjacencies" (p. 171), to borrow a fine phrase that she quotes from Monk Gibbon, startling juxtapositions. Often these juxtapositions are brilliant and illuminating, as when she relates the "quiet feet" (VP 207) of Cathleen ni Houlihan to foot binding in China and high heels in Hollywood (p. 32).

The book is based on a dissertation and is, so far as I know, a first book. One should therefore be grateful for its positive qualities and not be harsh with its faults. It is not, however, the wise and thorough study that one would like to see on this subject. In Chapter 1, "The Myth," Kline relies heavily on one scholar, D. W. Robertson, Jr., who "says that the courtly love of Yeats's era is the only one that ever existed" (p. 2). He "insists that the very idea is a cultural artifact of the nineteenth and early twentieth centuries and, therefore, an impediment to the understanding of medieval life and literature" (p. 23). Robertson's view has been influential, but it is hardly the only view. A more balanced judgment is that of Roger Boase in *The Origin and Meaning of Courtly Love: A Critical Study of European Scholarship* (Manchester: Manchester University Press; Totowa, N.J.: Rowman & Littlefield, 1977). His book includes a critique of Robertson's views and a summation: "Courtly Love was, we may conclude, a comprehensive cultural phenomenon: a literary movement, an ideology, an ethical system, a style of life, and an expression of the play element in culture, which arose in an aristocratic Christian environment exposed to Hispano-Arabic influences. This phenomenon occurred in the south of France and was first studied in Renaissance Italy, but Spain provides the key to its origins and to the origins of troubadour scholarship" (pp. 129–30). This seems to be the scholarly consensus at the moment, and Kline's ignoring this view is symptomatic of her rather erratic scholarship.

Kline's scholarly manner can be dashing, but she is sometimes tripped up by loose ends. For example, she seems greatly preoccupied with Yeats's assertion in *The Trembling of the Veil,* "We begin to live when we have conceived life as tragedy" (Au 189). Kline finds this passage operational thirty-two years before it was first published in 1921: "Yeats refers to January 30, 1889, when he met Maud [Gonne], as the day that 'the troubling of my life began' (Mem 40). He was ready to welcome trouble. Under the influence of the romantics, he declared, 'We begin to live when we have conceived life as tragedy'" (p. 9).

Later, Kline decides that by 1908 Yeats "had moved out of his Celtic Twilight of dim-haired goddesses and had published stringent criticism of those poets who had been his early guides in romantic love. . . . He had read Nietzsche; he no longer conceived of life as tragedy" (p. 15). So by 1908 Yeats had abandoned an attitude that he expressed in 1921! Later we read that "Yeats, who had early adopted the romantic attitude that 'We begin to live [etc.]' . . . became over the years realistic enough to end his disappointed personal quest in the comedy of *The Player Queen*" (p. 25). But the tragedy quotation and the play were published only a year apart. Moreover, Yeats had changed the play from tragedy to comedy very soon after beginning it around 1907 and into a farce in 1915. So here the "realistic" attitude precedes the "romantic" after all.

Again Kline refers to "Yeats's declaration that acceptance of life as tragic is basic to the romantic attitude" (p. 39). But Yeats says nothing about the romantic attitude and asks us to conceive life, not as "tragic" but as "tragedy." Tragedy is a form of drama.

Other confusions occur, many of them too complex to trace here. Here are some brief examples of the kind of thing that disturbs one's confidence in Kline's pronouncements. Writing of Yeats's youth, she says, "In an early poem ("The Sorrow of Love" (CP 40) [VP 119]), he celebrates the function of the feminine image in the artist's imposition of order on the chaos of nature" (p. 2). But the "imposition of order" enters this 1892 poem in its 1925 revision with the line "Could but compose man's image and his cry." The version that she cites is no longer an early poem.

Kline says that the "second period [of Yeats's attitude toward Maud Gonne] ended with a quarrel in summer 1893, and Yeats took a lover, Mrs. Olivia Shakespear" (p. 12). This sounds as if the Yeats-Shakespear liaison began in 1893, which is misleading. Yeats was introduced to Mrs. Shakespear in late spring 1894 (Mem 74), came to an understanding with her sometime in the summer or early autumn of 1895 (Mem 85–86), and in March 1896 took Woburn Buildings, where they conducted their liaison for about a year (Mem 88).

Kline says that the epitaph that ends "Dream of Death"

She was more beautiful than thy first love,
But now lies under boards
[VP 123]

compares Maud Gonne to Laura Armstrong (p. 59). This seems to me to take "first love" too literally. Yeats means that anyone's "first love" is remembered as of great beauty. Does Yeats's poem "First Love" (VP 451) also refer to Laura Armstrong? Obviously not.

Kline believes that Yeats saw Laura Armstrong as "pure Witch" and "chose his name for her—Vivien—from the legend of Merlin and his Witch Vivien that he had known from childhood in the *Mabinogion* and later in Chrétien de Troyes, whose version of it Yeats includes in the mysteries of courtly love that mark the 15th phase of the current era in *A Vision*" (p. 64). But I do not find this legend in the *Mabinogion*. Thomas L. Dume pointed out in 1950 that the passage mistakenly attributed by Yeats to Chrétien comes from the Huth-Merlin (Thomas Leslie Dume, "William Butler Yeats: A Survey of His Reading." Unpublished dissertation, Temple University, 1950, p. 276, note 298).

According to Kline, "[c]harges of heresy were leveled at *The Countess Cathleen*. . . . It remained for Yeats's friend George Moore to publish a pamphlet called *Souls for Gold!* (London, 1899) attacking Yeats for suggesting that Irish women would barter their souls. Yeats responded that the pamphlet was either 'sheer dishonesty' or else the product of delirium in Moore, who was undergoing some religious trauma of his own at the time" (pp. 81–82). But *Souls for Gold!* was written by F. Hugh O'Donnell: see Robert Hogan and James Kilroy, *The Irish Literary Theatre, 1899–1901* (Dublin: Dolmen Press; Atlantic Highlands, N.J.: Humanities Press, 1975), pp. 30–33. George Moore had nothing to do with it. Yeats refers to the "Mad Rogue" O'Donnell, not to Moore (Mem 120).

In *The Player Queen*, says Kline, the real queen, emulating Saint Octema, "allows only the unicorn to make love to her" (p. 91). Here Kline accepts the wild fantasy of Strolling Michael about the

Queen's coupling with a white unicorn. Septimus rejects the story, defending the chastity, not of the Queen, but of the unicorn! Kline says that in *The Player Queen,* Nona's "loyalty and her humor reflect the personality of George Yeats, whom the poet married during his struggle to write the play" (p. 92). But Yeats met Georgie Hyde-Lees in 1912. Nona is a well-developed character by 7 August 1910 (*W. B. Yeats: The Writing of* The Player Queen, ed. Curtis B. Bradford [DeKalb: Northern Illinois University Press, 1977], p. 249). The lines about Septimus's tapping on Nona's spine the rhythm of love poems to Dectora, quoted by Kline to demonstrate Nona's and Mrs. Yeats's loyalty and humor, appear in the manuscripts in 1915, two years before Yeats's marriage (Bradford, pp. 269, 329).

Kline speaks of "Yeats's system . . . published as *A Vision* first in 1927, then revised in 1938" (p. 93). Actually the first edition of *A Vision* was published on 15 January 1926, the revised edition on 7 October 1937.

Kline says that if a woman "had a beautiful body, as did Maud Gonne and Florence Farr, she could be a visual and physical inspiration to man the creator; if not, she could like Lady Gregory achieve that beauty which is the spoil of the victory of the soul and become his intellectual inspiration" (p. 111). But it is specifically "the physical beauty of woman" that Yeats and Castiglione say is "the spoil or monument of the victory of the soul, for physical beauty, only possible to subjective natures, is described as the result of emotional toil in past lives" (VPl 566). This note to *The Only Jealousy of Emer* reminds me to object that this play, the one probably most relevant to Kline's thesis, is, so far as I can find, never discussed or cited by her.

Of the lines "As trips the scared moon / Away must she trip" in "He and She" (VP 559) Kline writes: "[t]he Definitive Edition, here referred to as CP, says the 'scared moon,' which agrees with fear of blindness, but the Variorum says 'sacred moon,' . . . as does the *Collected Poems* of London, 1961" (pp. 139–40). But actually the *Variorum* gives "scared moon" in the copy text and "sacred moon" as a variant in *Collected Poems* (1956), Kline's "CP," so she has reversed these. The manuscripts show that "scared" is correct.

Of the lines in "Chosen" "Where—wrote a learned astrologer— / The Zodiac is changed into a sphere" (VP 535), Kline says, "Yeats's reference to himself as 'a learned astrologer' is coy" (p. 141). Does she not know Yeats's note to *The Winding Stair and Other Poems*? "The 'learned astrologer' in *Chosen* was Macrobius, and the particular passage . . . is from Macrobius's comment upon 'Scipio's Dream' (Lib. I. Cap. XII. Sec. 5) . . ." (VP 831). Or is Kline being coy?

According to Kline, "[t]he lyric Yeats wrote for the head [i.e., the severed head in "The Binding of the Hair" (VP 157)] compares the effortless art of the body of the woman with the labor of the poet, a recapitulation of the idea of 'Adam's Curse,' . . . omitting the earlier parallel that women, too, must 'labor to be beautiful' . . ." (p. 146). But the "earlier parallel" was first published in 1902, the "recapitulation" in 1896 (VP 204, 157).

I have spoken of Kline's use of "curious adjacencies." Here is one of the more curious. Lolly Yeats recorded that on Maud Gonne's first visit to the Yeatses, she had come "'in a hansom all the way from Belgravia and kept the hansom waiting while she was here.'" Maud's "descent from the two-wheeled hansom," says Kline, "has been foreshadowed and will receive a final echo." In the foreshadowing, Yeats's "cousin Laura Armstrong . . . came upon him when he was eighteen . . . , driving a pony-cart with her red hair blowing loose in the wind, and invited him to get in for a ride." The final echo occurs when "[i]n Crazy Jane's vision of the departure of Cuchulain, the hero rides away with his wife Emer in a two-wheeled carriage [see VP 628]. The incitement to action in the episode of Maud derives from her failure to invite him, figuratively, to ride off in the hansom that she kept waiting" (p. 50). This is clever—perhaps brilliant—but it adds to neither our understanding nor our appreciation of Yeats. The connection is quite mechanical. And note that Yeats himself does not mention the hansom's waiting (Au 123, Mem 40). There can be no significant connection.

Kline's book is full of ideas and valuable suggestions. Many of her readings are fresh and perceptive. But one must know Yeats and his work well to avoid the pitfalls on the road on which she leads us. A solid study of her fascinating subject still remains to be done.

Herbert J. Levine. *Yeats's Daimonic Renewal.* Ann Arbor: UMI Research Press, 1983. vii + 169 pp. *Reviewed by* EDWARD ENGELBERG

This is precisely the kind of specialized study about Yeats that is welcome. Rather than retracing well-worn paths, undertaking yet another all-embracing volume, or focusing on some new methodology that will yield an arresting reading, Herbert Levine sets himself a workmanlike task: a careful and sequential reading of *Per Amica Silentia Lunae.* That small work, critics have long ago agreed, marks an important step in Yeats's journey toward defining, and to some extent resolving, his poetic directions. It appeared in 1918 (eight years before the more elaborate and more contrived first version of *A Vision*), and it still stands as a testament of faith and as a roadmap to the "mature" Yeats (he was fifty-two). Levine correctly says in his introductory chapter that *Per Amica* "seeks to account for . . . adversities of the poet's fate and to articulate the possibilities of creative renewal in mid-career" (p. 2). "Mid-career" might seem generous, until we recall what lay ahead: *The Wild Swans at Coole, The Tower,* and *Last Poems; Four Plays for Dancers, Autobiographies,* and the later plays—and more. Yeats was married in 1917, and that this event coincided with the writing of *Per Amica* has not been overlooked as a fortuitous moment, for both the man and the poet. From the beginning, Yeats sharpened the dualistic perspective that so pervaded the nineteenth century; eventually he outlined elaborately conceived series of antinomies. Levine demonstrates—quite ably I believe—that the attempt was a success.

The whole machinery of self, anti-self, mask, and daimon is systematically constructed in *Per Amica,* each section manifesting and objectifying some portion of a personal and poetic crisis in the process of healing and being placed, so to speak, into a workable paradigm. We are reminded that all these matters were already implicit in the earlier poems and stories. Clearly the mystical Yeats did not emerge on the scene with a sudden spring: he had already served a long, if somewhat uneven, apprenticeship. By 1917, however, the aim became nothing less than a critical reexamination and reformulation, the failure of which, Yeats was convinced, would mean the end of his poetic growth—and indeed the end of his career.

Levine is himself systematic, beginning with the proem to *Per Amica,* "Ego Dominus Tuus," and carefully guiding us through the two major parts—*Anima Hominis* and *Anima Mundi*—and their numerous subsections. There is some danger in this method of sliding into a routine, and Levine does not altogether avoid it: chronological analysis runs the risk of interpretive evenness. Nevertheless, there are everywhere interesting reminders: for example, how much Nietzsche lurks in Yeats, or to what extent *Per Amica* served him as a place in which to make some wider use of his Romantic inheritance and to accommodate it to the new "modernism" to which Yeats became increasingly—if selectively—attracted. Levine does not ignore some of the discomfiture he shares with most readers when confronted with Yeats's "caricature or racism" (p. 76), though I do not know whether the term "racism," with all its attendant current connotations, really fits the case. Yeats was seduced by certain notions of strength and decadence (Nietzsche was reinforcement, and the harrowing experience of the "decadent" 1890s haunted him), which sometimes led him to embarrassing rhetoric. But he always managed to recover (or to cover up), and never went as far as, say, Wyndham Lewis or D. H. Lawrence. "Eternal recurrence is one of the central doctrines in Yeats's tradition" (p. 77), and that very promise of *Wiederkehr* is a reassuring antithesis to Yeats's occasionally cosmic rages.

Levine devotes one chapter to the *Plays for Dancers* and links them to the general doctrines of *Per Amica.* His reiteration that these plays were often intensely autobiographical is comfortably linked to the preceding explication of *Per Amica*: "Yeats needed to imagine himself in his play [*At the Hawk's Well*] as an utterly dessicated scarecrow of a man, in order to set off the antithetical splendor of Cuchulain" (p. 91). One certainly ought to be well aware of Yeats's repeated pattern of setting up a self that is overshadowed by anti-self, and often we do not quite know which he wished us to favor. Is the old man who sails to Byzantium not meant to remind us all the more vividly of the "fish, flesh, or fowl" (VP 407)—the energy of life—that he is forced to abandon?

Levine concludes with a chapter on Yeats's "Poetic Renewal

through Lyric Debate: 1910–21," and an intriguingly titled epilogue, "On Reading Yeats without *A Vision*." The penultimate chapter is somewhat too schematic, chronicling the "lyric debate" with boundaries that are perhaps too rigid and with manifestations that are perhaps too simplified. Hindsight gives us too much power as critics, and the anticipatory as seen from a later perspective might not have been nearly so much anticipation as the evidence of a creatively confused toiler. In the epilogue Levine seems to suggest that the personal (and preferable) stance of *Per Amica* is, in *A Vision,* dismembered—to its disadvantage—for the sake of a "cosmological emphasis" (p. 134). The individual Daimon becomes something of a cultural mechanism, which in *A Vision* is overburdened by a difficult style and a cumbersome machinery. If we think especially of the second edition of *A Vision* (1937), that charge has merit—"prose horribly burdened with . . . terminology" and "abstruse" categories (p. 135). *A Vision* cannot be ignored, but it need not always be enjoyed.

Finally, we may question Levine's repeated reference to *Per Amica* as a "theory of poetic creation" (p. 2 and *passim*). I believe, rather, that *Per Amica* provided a quasi-philosophical framework within which a poetic theory took shape. Disentangling Yeats's poetic from his mystic (and mythic) structures is not easy, but to equate them may be a disservice to both. *Per Amica,* as Levine suggests, plays out the quarrels Yeats had with himself around that crucial year, 1917; the "theory of poetic creation" will be found in the poems, plays, and prose that form part of the resolution of those quarrels. Levine's book provides an accessible guide both to the nature of those poetic challenges and to their resolutions.

Shirley Neuman. *Some One Myth: Yeats's Autobiographical Prose* [New Yeats Papers XIX].
Dublin: Dolmen Press:
Atlantic Highlands, N.J.: Humanities Press, 1982. 160 pp.
Reviewed by JAMES OLNEY

In *Some One Myth* Shirley Neuman has written the best book we have thus far on Yeats as autobiographer. This is so whether we wish to consider *Autobiographies* within the taxonomic space occupied by autobiography—autobiography as a distinct, distinguishable literary mode—or whether we wish to think of *Autobiographies* as a peculiarly Yeatsian production, to be understood within the context of Yeats's entire *oeuvre* but without any particular reference to other autobiographies or to the autobiographical mode in general. (I should say in passing that I believe the latter to be the better, more fruitful way to take hold of *Autobiographies*. To put it another way, it has never occurred to me to include *Autobiographies* in any course I have taught on autobiography, but I would always include it, as a more or less central text, in a seminar on Yeats. Indeed, if *Autobiographies* were thrown together with what I take to be the landmark works in the autobiographical tradition—Augustine's *Confessions,* Montaigne's *Essays,* Rousseau's *Confessions,* Mill's *Autobiography,* Newman's *Apologia,* Wright's *Black Boy,*, to cite a handful—we should have to see it as not a great autobiography, in fact as hardly even a distinguished one; in the context of Yeats's collected works, however, it takes its equal and needful place—perhaps a preeminent place, since the other volumes are also exercises in autobiography but hidden behind half-deceptive titles—alongside *Collected Poems, Collected Plays, A Vision, Essays and Introductions, Explorations,* the *Letters,* etc.) But to return to the point: Shirley Neuman, thanks to study and thought that she has earlier given to autobiography and thanks to her command of the autobiographical impetus behind all of Yeats's diverse but peculiarly unified volumes, has produced an excellent study of *Autobiographies* as autobiography and an equally excellent study of the Yeats who believed that "all sound philosophy is but biography" (*Ex* 235) and that "man can embody truth but he cannot know it" (*L* 922).

When I say that Shirley Neuman had already devoted thought and study to the subject of autobiography before she took up Yeats as autobiographer, I have in mind primarily a superb monograph called *Gertrude Stein: Autobiography and the Problem of Narration*. In this brief but intense volume, Neuman outlines the strategies of what she terms "literary autobiography," and the theory that she there develops of the poet-as-autobiographer—one for whom the referential world is no more (but also no less) a constraining contingency in autobiography than in poetry or fiction—serves her very well in her treatment of Yeats. Yeats, like Stein, wrote autobiography and nothing but, and in *Autobiographies* as in all his other works, his *modus operandi* implies "that there is an equivalence between self and not-self, between art and life, and that art is a deliberately shaped and publicly projected version of one's autobiography" (p. 41). But the life that Yeats or Stein was concerned with, as we can see in the narrative persona of *The Autobiography of Alice B. Toklas,* was hardly the exciting jumble and chaos that might be taken for life by your ordinary, everyday naive autobiographer. "Yeats concerned himself in *Autobiographies* not with the man, with what he termed 'the bundle of accident and incoherence that sits down to breakfast,' [E&I 509] but with the author; he knew very well what critics of the genre have just begun to take into account, that the reader is interested in the literary autobiographer as a man consistent with his previous works" (p. 54). This is very well said, both of Yeats in particular and of the literary autobiographer in general, and it leads on to what is the guiding thesis of *Some One Myth*: "When the writer simultaneously creates literature and is created by that literature, his autobiography becomes a reversible garment: it remains the expected portrait of the artist and, therefore, of the genesis of his works, but turned, it reveals the author shaping himself through his works and in their image" (p. 55). This, of course, is the reciprocal, circular "one myth" of the title, which comes from a passage that I have always thought as richly suggestive and explanatory as any in Yeats: "The Greeks, a certain scholar has told me, considered that myths are the activities of the Daimons, and that the Daimons shape our characters and our lives. I have often had the fancy that there is some one myth for every man, which, if we but knew it, would make us understand all he did and thought" (E&I 107). Yeats's one myth was the myth of the poet, created in the life and inscribed in the art, where "I, the poet William Yeats" (VP 406) is "reborn as an idea, something intended, complete . . . ; more type than man, more passion than type" (E&I 509), and this creation, this inscription, this rebirth takes place as much in *Autobiographies* as in any of the other Yeatsian volumes.

The non-Yeatsian quotations in the foregoing paragraph are all taken from the first chapter of *Some One Myth,* entitled "Personal Utterance and The Lunar Parable: Early Prose and *A Vision*." In this brilliant chapter Neuman develops her notion of literary autobiography in general, that is to say, of autobiography as artifact rather than record, autobiography as thematic/dramatic enactment rather than historical exposition; and she also demonstrates how Yeats in particular set about figuring his own life as myth with himself and his friends as actors in that cosmic parable of *A Vision* that he scripted but always, he maintained, under the guidance of those tutelary Daimons that "shape our characters and our lives." This ground-laying chapter is followed by five chapters that treat in detail the varying strategies of each of the separate and disparate volumes that compose *Autobiographies* (*Estrangement* and *The Death of Synge* are taken together as they resemble each other in their pseudodiaristic strategy while differing markedly from the other volumes). Neuman concludes with a fine chapter, "*On the Boiler*: The Fanatic Heart," that discovers for that rather wild performance a variant way of realizing the invariant autobiographical impetus and the unchanging "one myth." Each of the chapters has its own angle of approach, determined by the shifting modes adopted by Yeats, and what I would like to do, but haven't the room for, is to demonstrate, through extensive quotations, the subtle adjustments in Neuman's perspective and terminology designed to accord with the altering strategies Yeats adopts for *Reveries over Childhood and Youth, The Trembling of the Veil, Dramatis Personae, Estrangement* and *The Death of Synge, The Bounty of Sweden,* and *On the Boiler.* As I cannot allow myself to illustrate all of these, I shall content myself with the treatment in what I take to be an exemplary chapter, the one on *Estrangement* and *The Death of Synge*.

In each of the volumes of *Autobiographies* Yeats is, as it were, testing the limits of the autobiographical form, experimenting with narrative and nonnarrative techniques, with retrospective recall and present-time rumination, with anecdotal presentation and preacherly denunciation. He begins *Estrangement* and *The Death of Synge* (composed of carefully arranged selections from a journal that he kept in 1909 and later) with a sort of Statement of First Principles, claiming to be writing in the tradition of the *journal intime*: "To keep these notes natural and useful to me I must keep one note from leading on to another, that I may not surrender myself to literature. Every note must come as a casual thought, then it will be my life. Neither Christ nor Buddha nor Socrates wrote a book, for to do that is to exchange life for a logical process" (Au 461). Whether Yeats was serious or not in implying that his journal-keeping had much in common with the saintly and nonliterary activities of Christ, Buddha, and Socrates, the real truth is, as Neuman argues, that the rest of this *intimiste* claim has very little to do with his actual performance in *Estrangement* and *The Death of Synge*. The reader who imagines that Yeats will really offer up a transparent view of his life, without ever surrendering himself to literature, has been misled—deliberately misled, moreover—and is destined to be sorely disappointed. On the contrary, Yeats omits "large sections of the original *Journal*," Neuman says, and he reorders "many of those remaining, considerably intensifies certain concerns of the original documents and gives them a thematic and stylistic coherence they had not previously possessed" (p. 102). So much for Yeats's brief attempt at being Christ-like, Buddhistic, and Socratic. Yeats "actively intervenes as writer," according to Neuman, "to emphasize and structure the latent thematic possibilities of the *Journal*, to transform life into literature. His *intimiste* statement is not only unveracious as a declaration of intention for *Estrangement*, it functions as a deliberately misleading signpost. It enables Yeats to juxtapose certain thematic and cultural concerns, gaining for them an intensity born of a cumulative effect, without using the more connected discourse of the philosophical essay or novel. . . . They accumulate their force of conviction by reverberating one against the other, by suggesting equivalencies, and not by closely reasoned connections" (p. 102).

That *Estrangement* and *The Death of Synge* are not only very different modally from the other volumes in *Autobiographies* but also quite unlike what one might expect in a typical autobiography—the retrospective, connected, narrative account of a life—must have occurred to many readers. Yet, as Neuman argues, Yeats was working within a particular, and in many ways central, tradition of autobiography even in the carefully rearranged journal entries of these two volumes: "[B]y presenting himself as a poet with a correlative political Mask instead of displaying 'the bundle of accident and incoherence that sits down to breakfast,' he does write a form of autobiography which his own literary aesthetic permits. And while he abandons the mimetic form towards which autobiography had tended throughout the Victorian period, Yeats adapts an equally influential autobiographical tradition, that of Montaigne's *Essays*. . . . The interest of the passages as autobiography lies in their revealing, as Montaigne claimed of his writings, not only the man making his work, but the work shaping the man. . . . The autobiography becomes 'consubstantial' with its author" (p. 109). Here we have a nice example of Neuman's expert treatment of *Autobiographies* as autobiography and as Yeatsian document. Other chapters of *Some One Myth* vary the approach, as other volumes of *Autobiographies* vary the strategy for transforming life into literature, but it is this carefully balanced, dual treatment of the subject that makes Shirley Neuman's study the best we have on the *Autobiographies* and a very fine and thoughtful piece of work indeed.

William H. O'Donnell. *A Guide to the Prose Fiction of W. B. Yeats*. Ann Arbor: UMI Research Press, 1983. viii + 182 pp.
Reviewed by MARY HELEN THUENTE

This book, a new title in the "Studies in Modern Literature" series, which aims to publish the best of recent doctoral dissertations, fulfills the criteria for selection that A. Walton Litz, the general editor of the series, announced: careful scholarship, a readable style, and critical analysis of lasting value. *A Guide to the Prose Fiction of W. B. Yeats* illuminates an important but hitherto neglected area of Yeats's development as a writer—the twenty-three stories and two novels he wrote between 1887 and 1905. O'Donnell, in succinct discussions of each work, reviews past critical interpretations, offers some new insights, and considers Yeats's revisions and the relationships between various stories. His book certainly fills a gap in Yeats studies and provides a good detailed introduction to the individual stories and novels. O'Donnell's work suffers, however, from a narrowness of perspective that should have been corrected before it was published as a book.

O'Donnell's attempt to identify the factors that led Yeats to write fiction is disappointing. He argues that the popularity of the short story in the London literary circles that Yeats frequented "was a major factor in Yeats's decision to try prose fiction, and he did not begin writing short stories until just after his family moved to London in 1887" (p. 7). O'Donnell mentions the influence of Yeats's father and sister—also writing short stories at this time—but he completely ignores the significance of Irish literary tradition. Yeats's decision to become an "Irish" writer during the late 1880s was also a factor of large significance in his decision to write prose fiction, because the short fictional tale had been an important genre in nineteenth-century Irish fiction and folklore. Yeats read all the major Irish fiction writers when assembling materials for his anthology of short fiction, *Representative Irish Tales* (1891), a work O'Donnell mentions only once. His anthologies of Irish folklore, *Fairy and Folk Tales of the Irish Peasantry* (1888) and *Irish Fairy Tales* (1892), had included tales by William Carleton, Samuel Lover, and Gerald Griffin.

O'Donnell identifies two "major" elements in Yeats's prose fiction: Irish folklore and the occult. Rather inconsistently, however, he argues that these should not be too deeply explored: "our understanding of the stories is not much enhanced by detailed study of occult lore" (p. 94). Earlier detailed examinations of the occult in the *Secret Rose* stories contradict this. Similarly, although O'Donnell is correct that it is not necessary to find exact precedents for the legendary details Yeats uses, his superficial treatment of Irish folklore and Yeats's involvement with it certainly limits his analysis in many places. O'Donnell argues that the passion and spiritual energy that characterize most of Yeats's fictional heroes had a Blakean precedent. Nonetheless, *The Celtic Twilight* and many of Yeats's prose articles demonstrate that his extensive reading in Irish fiction and folklore also helped convince him that the quintessential Irish personality epitomized passion and spiritual energy. Likewise, Yeats's highly subjective use of motifs from Irish folklore was very much in the tradition of earlier folklorists. O'Donnell argues that the combination of ferocity and gentleness in Dhoya's personality is inconsistent, and thus a weakness in characterization. Yeats, however, was not attempting psychological realism in "Dhoya": Dhoya's character reflects the antithetical personalities of the legendary heroes that Yeats admired and that he included in his never-published anthology entitled *Irish Adventurers*. O'Donnell does not recognize any distinction between the folklore of the nineteenth-century Irish peasantry and ancient Irish mythology, and consequently he is unaware that Yeats's revisions in his prose fiction frequently involve the deletion of folklore motifs and their replacement by mythological ones.

The limits of O'Donnell's analysis of Irish folklore are illustrated by his discussion of "The Death of Hanrahan." In the original version of the story, the eagle, yew, and pike become the instruments of Hanrahan's death when he attacks them in his search for food. O'Donnell, who prefers tightly structured plots, calls Yeats's subsequent deletion of the eagle, tree, and pike a "loss" of a "clever . . . unifying device" (p. 84). Yeats, however, had used them for much more than structure. The eagle, yew, and pike were prominent motifs in popular Irish legends concerning ancient animals and trees that possessed visionary knowledge. O'Donnell, who also ignores the significance that these motifs had in earlier versions of other Hanrahan stories, overlooks the fact that Yeats knew such motifs from his own collecting of oral traditions and from Douglas Hyde, and that he used Hanrahan's assault on them for food rather than for the legendary knowledge and wisdom they possessed to symbolize ironically his inadequacies as a visionary. He similarly dismisses the symbolic significance of the legendary and occult details of the cauldron, the stone, the sword, and the spear, which Yeats later added to the story, as "the use of an unmotivated and arbitrary clutter of Arthurian and Celtic machinery" (p. 84). But Richard Ellmann's discussion of these four motifs makes a strong case for their major symbolic importance to Yeats (*The Identity of Yeats* [New York: Oxford University Press, 1964], p. 29). Likewise, Yeats's intentions in his characterization of Hanrahan would have been clarified by a discussion of how he changed the legendary conception of Hanrahan's model, Owen Roe O'Sullivan. For example, in deleting O'Sullivan's bitter anti-English sentiments, Yeats was skirting the political issues that animated much nineteenth-century Irish fiction.

O'Donnell presumes that Irish folklore provided Yeats with

subject matter, but he does not consider or appreciate the stylistic repercussions it had in Yeats's writings. He has, further, a rather confused sense of the genres of traditional narrative: the terms "legend," "folktale" and "fairy tale" are used randomly and often inaccurately throughout the book. For example, he calls "The Cradles of Gold" a folktale, when in fact it is a legend based on fairy lore. Yeats understood the generic differences between a legend, with its fragmentary structure and pseudohistorical basis, and a folktale, with its stylized plot structure and timeless setting. Moreover, the narrative techniques of legends and folktales that Yeats used in his short fiction vary considerably from those of the modern short story, the primary context of O'Donnell's discussion.

The faults that O'Donnell finds in "Dhoya"—which he calls "a clumsy tale" and "mere apprentice work" for which "massive alterations would have been necessary to bring it up to the level of even the weakest of the *Secret Rose* stories" (pp. 31, 33)—are strengths if one recognizes that Yeats was creating a local legend, a fact that Richard Finneran makes clear in his edition of "Dhoya." Yet O'Donnell, using the modern short story as his norm, criticizes the "completely extraneous" and "gratuitous" remarks by the narrator and the plot's lack of organic structure (p. 31). The 1892 reviewer who praised "Dhoya" as a "very skilfully told" and "wild imaginative legend" assessed it more accurately within the literary tradition in which Yeats wrote it (JSD 11).

O'Donnell repeatedly faults Yeats's use of anecdotal, episodic narrative structures and symbolic actions and details as deviations from the organic structure and psychological realism of the modern short story. He dismisses "The Rose of Shadows" and "The Cradles of Gold" as "merely . . . adaptation[s] of local folklore" (p. 70), although he praises "Costello the Proud" for being "extremely close to the folk original that Douglas Hyde had published in 1893" (p. 87). He considers "Out of the Rose" to be superior to all of Yeats's earlier prose fiction because of its economical exposition of plot and because of its originality. He suggests that Yeats used traditional plots extensively simply because he had trouble inventing plots. But Yeats had a serious commitment to folklore, as his appraisal of 1893 attests: "Folk-lore is at once the Bible, the

Thirty-nine Articles, and the Book of Common Prayer, and well-nigh all the great poets have lived by its light. Homer, Aeschylus, Sophocles, Shakespeare, and even Dante, Goethe, and Keats, were little more than folk-lorists with musical tongues" (UP1 284).

Yeats's use of the plots and narrative techniques of the folktale fares no better with O'Donnell than his use of legends. Yeats's achievement in recreating one of the most popular Irish folktales in "Michael Clancy, the Great Dhoul, and Death" is judged by O'Donnell's standard of the modern short story and thus deemed to demonstrate the "trite conventionality" and "the limits of [a] popular genre" of folklore (p. 55). The recent translation into English of Max Luthi's classic 1947 study *Das europäische Volksmärchen: Form und Wesen* should encourage literary critics to evaluate some of the narrative techniques in Yeats's prose fiction within the highly sophisticated narrative tradition of the European folktale. Indeed, several of the stylistic traits of the folktale that Luthi discusses foreshadow elements in Yeats's drama.

This short book of only one hundred and forty-six pages of text ends abruptly with a discussion of "Stories of Michael Robartes." A concluding chapter synthesizing O'Donnell's analysis of Yeats's individual works would certainly have strengthened it. This valuable introduction and guide to Yeats's prose fiction could have been very good indeed, had it more adequately explored the backgrounds and larger issues.

M. L. Rosenthal and Sally M. Gall. *The Modern Poetic Sequence: The Genius of Modern Poetry*.
New York and Oxford: Oxford University Press, 1983. ix + 508 pp.
Reviewed by RAEBURN MILLER

This is a very long book—important yet exasperating. Its two purposes are suggested by the title and subtitle: the authors define the "crucial" but "hardly yet even recognized" (p. vii) genre of the modern poetic sequence, then go on to argue that the analysis of such sequences is "the most fruitful evaluative approach to poetry as a whole and to modern poetry in particular" (p. vii). Their definition of the form is welcome, their analysis of various examples useful and generally convincing. But by applying the term so inclusively and making such exaggerated claims for the overriding importance of their approach, they lessen the total effectiveness of the book.

That poets have frequently arranged individual poems into groups is obvious enough in most periods of literary history and especially so in the twentieth century. Even a device so slight as numbering the poems within such collections can demonstrate an intended unity, and such intentions are also sometimes indicated by external assertions of coherence. Wallace Stevens, for example, wanted to call his collected poetry *The Whole of Harmonium*. But Rosenthal and Gall focus their attention on a concept of sequence more organically defined, with little consistent or direct reference to the poet's intent. Beginning with the famous passage in which Poe denies the possibility of a long poem, they paraphrase him to say, "A poem depends for its life . . . on a progression of specific qualities and intensities of emotionally and sensuously charged awareness" (p. 6). The identified modern sequence, then, is one whose parts compose such a progression: "a grouping of poems in dynamically coherent relationship" (p. 231), "a pure flow of lyrical affects, feeding into one another, exploding into contrasting states, and interacting organically" (p. 277). The character of such a sequence is "its balancings of stress and interplay among its centers of passionate preoccupation" (p. 9). As the authors suggest in discussing one variety of sequence, the confessional, "[t]he whole direction of modern poetry, with its cultivation of intense subjectivity and radiant centers of affect, has been toward becoming a poetry of psychological pressure and its attempted encompassment" (p. 477). The form of the modern sequence as this work defines it has served well to encompass the social and psychological pressures of the time.

Yet is the sequence, for all its success, truly "like . . . an epic poem" (p. 3) and the genre "most suitable for epic and heroic undertakings" (p. 494)? Well, perhaps. Has it really "dominated the ambition of every great modern poet" (p. 5)? Of Robert Frost?

Marianne Moore? Richard Wilbur? The authors are as troubling as Poe himself was in dismissing large areas of traditional poetic value. They speak of the "clankingly restrictive armor of plot" (p. 20). "[W]e have come to need immediacy of presentation above all," they say, "and are soon impatient with exposition, explanation, or moralizing that drains away a work's presentative energy and mobility of alertness and feeling" (p. 173). They are especially suspicious of formal consistency: this aspect disqualifies *The Dream Songs* (*The Dream Songs*!) from full acceptance as a modern sequence because it forgoes "one of the great advantages of the *true* sequence: its playing off of significantly varied metrical, rhythmic, and even visual patterns against one another" (p. 421; my italics). Readers may agree that the modern sequence exists and deserves analysis without seeing it as "*the* modern poetic form" (p. vii)—as, indeed, the essential nature of poetry now at last "suddenly and beautifully revealed" (p. vii).

The bulk of the volume is devoted to the consideration of a number of specific sequences, some in elaborate detail, others more briefly. On the whole, these readings are successful, rooted in the work and in good sense, unlike so much other contemporary criticism. After a nod to Shakespeare's sonnets ("formal redundancy" [p. 18]) and Tennyson's *In Memoriam* ("weighed down by its endless succession of uniform stanzas" [pp. 22–23]), the authors examine *Maud* with approval, then discuss at length *Song of Myself* and two of Dickinson's sad little hand-sewn "fascicles" (numbers 15 and 16) as early and full-fledged examples of the genre. After a substantial (and especially persuasive) treatment of Hardy's *Poems of 1912–13,* they turn to Yeats, on whom they spend two chapters—fifty pages. (He and Pound are the poets who "wrote more sequences than anyone else" [p. 97], "rivals in inventive prolificacy" [p. viii].) They list no fewer than ten sequences by Yeats, including "the nineteen poems of *Last Poems and Two Plays* . . . in their original order" (p. 97), and three of these sequences they see as part of a larger sequence, *The Tower,* already introduced as such in Rosenthal's *Sailing into the Unknown: Yeats, Pound, and Eliot* (1978). Other groups "come close" (p. 110 and *passim*). In dealing with individual poems the authors are at their best on selections from *Words for Music Perhaps,* but their rather arbitrary inclination to divide that work into shorter sequences makes their discussions of "Meditations in Time of Civil War" and *A Man Young and Old* more useful to the development of their argument.

The next examples treated in detail are those of Eliot (yes, *The Waste Land* is here a sequence), Pound, and Williams. By this point they have said pretty much what they have to say about the definition of the form and their discussions grow more predictable, though their attempts to deal with the frustrations of the *Cantos* are entertaining. Finally, in less detail, they introduce a large number of other sequences—*The Bridge* and *The Maximus Poems,* of course, and odder selections by MacDiarmid, Stevens, Auden, Lowell, Plath, and many, many more. Of these, the most interesting analysis is that of Ramon Guthrie's *Maximum Security Ward,* a "somewhat neglected" work (p. 445), in behalf of which their enthusiasm is compelling.

It is true, as the authors say, that "a huge volume—an encyclopaedia—would be needed to take proper note" of all the modern sequences of value (p. 477). Yet questions of inclusion and exclusion must trouble any reader of this study. The purpose of the book is sometimes obscured by the welter of poems described, and at times the thesis comes to seem only a hook on which to hang an explication. Beyond admittedly inappropriate quibbling about why some works are here (Henley's *In Hospital*?!) and why others are not (my own choice for the greatest modern sequence, Gertrude Stein's *Stanzas in Meditation,* is ignored), a more important concern is with the elastic definition of the sequence itself. To treat the shored fragments of *The Waste Land* as discrete units in a sequence, while asserting, at the opposite extreme, that the independent poems of *Life Studies* and *Ariel* are rightly understood only as sections in sequences, is to stretch the concept of the form almost beyond meaning. I do not propose to offer a more restrictive definition, but one is surely needed for this "genre in process" (p. 155). A reader begins to feel that these authors possess the ingenuity to read anything they admire as a sequence, indeed that it is essential for them to do so if they are to maintain their belief that lyrical structure is the essence of poetic achievement. I doubt they are right in the effort or the belief that inspires that effort. To read the *Iliad,* say, or *De rerum natura* or the *Commedia* as achieving significance through "the balance of affects—radiant tonal centers of . . . emotionally and sensuously charged awareness" (p. 15) might be possible and even illuminating, but surely not final or central, and surely not a form of analysis available directly or indirectly to the original authors or their original audiences; yet can there be any doubt that these are greater works, as poems, than any of the sequences analyzed here, or indeed any modern poem? (And how, one wonders, could an author, benighted enough to value the short lyric for itself, *prevent* a group of poems from being read as a sequence? Rosenthal and Gall may have inadvertently suggested a way when they dismiss Auden's *Collected Poetry* for being arranged alphabetically by first lines—one recalls that Vassar Miller's first book was alphabetized by titles—but such a device seems an extreme solution!)

Three other minor objections. The style of these authors is never very engaging and sometimes falls into critical pomposity at its worst: "Clearly, the sequence suffers from its overloading, occasioned by a desire to hammer in the allegorical implications of its Laurentian primitivism" (p. 466). And a vice similarly familiar in this sort of criticism is their self-indicting tone of condescension toward such poets as Housman and Masters, even, more surprisingly, toward *The Bridge* and "Notes Toward a Supreme Fiction." Finally, unless I am mistaken, the allusion in the Sexton poem quoted on page 441 is not to Kipling but rather to a remark Freud is reported to have made about his own cigar.

Let me conclude in a more positive vein. Whatever dissatisfaction a reader may feel about some of the ways this book goes about its work, the importance of the modern poetic sequence is unquestionable, and we owe much to these authors for the effort they have made in asserting and defining that importance. They have provided a new foundation for the analysis of much of the poetry of our century.

There is, by the way, an index, but its utility is suggested by its headnote: "Books and sequences are indexed by title, not author. Individual poems are listed by sequence; otherwise (with the exception of anonymous works), by author" (p. 495).

Gale C. Schricker. *A New Species of Man: The Poetic Persona of W. B. Yeats.*
Lewisburg, Pa.: Bucknell University Press; London and Toronto: Associated University Presses, 1982. 214 pp.
Reviewed by RICHARD FALLIS

Of the making of dissertations on Yeats there is no end, and sometimes they come into print as books too quickly. That seems to be what has happened here. Based on a Bryn Mawr dissertation of 1980, *A New Species of Man* takes up an important topic and seeks to treat it in a fresh and serious way. As a dissertation, this would be a promising work; as a book, it is interesting in some specifics and informed by a thesis worth further development, but it feels too much like a dissertation not given time to mature.

Schricker's purpose is "to achieve an intensive and *inclusive* understanding of how Yeats's concept of 'unity of being' becomes manifest over time in his prose and poetry through the development of the device I call the 'poetic persona'" (p. 9). Deriving her basic position from Giovanni Gentile, a philosopher Yeats certainly admired, she argues that the Yeatsian "poetic persona" consists of "transcendent and empirical aspects of the one self in a dynamic poetic interplay that explores and reveals the potentials and limitations of the compound self—once the persona is accepted as one continuous identity rather than a succession of masks" (p. 18).

As that last phrase suggests, Schricker is at pains to distinguish her position from those of other critics. Richard Ellmann's emphasis on masks and Thomas Parkinson's on "modes" of the speaker's identity seem to her to undercut Yeats's drive towards "unity of being." Likewise, she argues that George Wright errs by asserting that it is in single poems—not in the totality of his work—that Yeats achieves his persona: "In the majority of Yeats's poems, he speaks through the poetic 'I,' and that speaking, thinking 'I' is the persona, the manifestation of Yeats's identity in the act of uniting empirical and transcendent, or object and subject, aspects of self. . . . No one poem embodies this unity; rather it occurs, as Gentile stresses it must, in the persona's act of development through the poetic canon" (p. 44).

One could well argue with these presentations of earlier critics, and this first chapter, in fact, raises a good many questions for this reader. Some have to do with the richness and even the validity of the theoretical model in relation to Yeats. Does asserting an "interplay" of "empirical" and "transcendent" aspects of the persona oversimplify? Are "empirical" and "transcendent" quite right for many of the poems or for what Yeats argues in "A General Introduction for My Work," the essay around which Schricker centers her book? Is the only "poetic persona" Yeats creates the one who speaks as "I"? On the one hand, the model seems too reminiscent of the notion of a "divided self" that has become a cliché in interpreting the Victorian poets; on the other, it seems to deny Yeats's powers of self-dramatization. The idea of a continuous persona in the prose and the poems is interesting, but the structure of the book—earlier chapters on the prose, a long later one on the poems—works against the unity Schricker wants to demonstrate.

Beyond these matters, the general treatment of "persona" as a concept seems thin, especially in comparison with Robert Elliott's in *The Literary Persona*. In discussing the term, Schricker relies heavily on scholars of more than one generation back: Gentile, Adolf Trendelenburg, and Leo Spitzer. Elliott's range of reference is much wider. Schricker ignores, as he does not, how Maynard Mack and Alvin Kernan used the idea to move toward new ways of reading satire and how Lionel Trilling and Donald Davie warned that *persona* may not be an especially meaningful term for poetry written after the eighteenth century. Schricker does not mention Joan Webber's argument that the Romantics and Victorians were the heirs of the seventeenth-century Puritans in their sense of what "I" can mean, nor does she refer to Elizabeth Bruss's influential discussions of the form and nature of autobiographical writing. In terms of a specifically literary persona, it would be interesting to know where Schricker would place Yeats's in relation to the "I" of some Augustan satire or the "I" of American confessional poetry. More broadly, she does not refer to many of the recent anthropological and psychological studies of the idea of persona or the debate about such issues in contemporary literary theory. In sum, the theoretical model has some fundamental merit, but it seems too narrow in its expression and application and thus runs the risk of limiting Yeats.

The second and third chapters—on the fiction, autobiographical writings, and *A Vision*—do not fully satisfy on this last matter. The fiction is assumed to be "a projection of self within fictional contexts" which records Yeats's "discovery that the created self, the persona, must operate from the context of empirical life and not a fictional plot, if the emphasis is to be on the unification of the self rather than the story." In contrast, "*The Autobiography* [sic] records the development of the empirical self to see what form it takes, and *A Vision* projects abstract life structures to see how particular empirical lives evolve and fit together into composite wholes" (p. 83). The sense of the experimental nature of all these works is to be welcomed: the open-ended approach to the *Autobiographies* and the discussion of point of view in *Per Amica Silentia Lunae* are both helpful. But the interpretations of *A Vision* and the earlier fiction tend to force both into inappropriate categories which almost seem predicated on seeing them as artistic or intellectual failures.

The longest chapter deals with the poems, particularly those in the first person singular, arguing that "[t]he empirical poet . . . does not achieve unity of being in his life, but his poetic double does achieve this unity in that the persona of the lyric canon embodies the process of becoming within the whole structure of being, which is the quest archetype" (p. 127). Basing her understanding of this archetypal pattern on Northrop Frye's, Schricker sees four distinct phases in the development of Yeats's persona. In the poems of up to about 1900, the persona deals with "the lonely experience of the first confrontation of the transcendent and empirical aspects of identity" (p. 129). A second phase, represented by poems of about 1900 to 1917, shows the "confrontation in the persona of idealistic hero and empirical world" (p. 129). Later, in poems of about 1917 to 1922, the persona "withdraws from conflict to meditate on the opposing natures of his internal ideals and social reality" (p. 129). In the last phase, represented by poems from *The Tower* onward, the persona moves into his "ideal real world" so that "the quest for unity of being is completed with the persona's realization, at the end of the poetic canon, of the form his life has taken" (p. 130).

This model is worked out in detail, with commentaries on scores of poems and much argument with earlier critics. As a generalization the model has value, but it seems to yield rather few fresh insights into specifics. It is most helpful, I think, on the poems informed by a self-conscious double vision and on some of the dialogue poems. But too often the readings slip toward paraphrase, and there is too much dissertation-like worrying about other critics. It is, certainly, a plausible way of thinking about Yeats's development, but, in its specifics, it does not seem very different from several others. Would not, for example, even a pattern of adult development so readily available as Erik Erikson's offer more interpretively rich possibilities?

Yeatsians may also feel that Schricker is not fully aware of current work; most of the standard books are cited in the bibliography, but rather few journal articles are included and none after 1975. Given the emphasis on "A General Introduction for My Work," it is unfortunate that she apparently did not have access to Edward Callan's *Yeats on Yeats* for its discussion of the essay's background. Likewise, a rather superficial sense of Yeats's life weakens some of the arguments about the persona's "empirical aspect." The discussions of the influence of Edward Dowden, Oscar Wilde, and J. B. Yeats all seem naive. The handling of this last could have been much enriched by careful attention to William Murphy's biography, as the discussion of how Yeats presents his relationship with Maud Gonne could have been strengthened by reference to Curtis Bradford's essay on the subject. Moreover, Yeats's occult interests—surely crucial to both his "empirical" and "transcendent" aspects and his entire understanding of his "persona"—are given little attention. Virginia Moore, but neither Kathleen Raine nor George Mills Harper, appears in her bibliography, and the Order of the Golden Dawn is mentioned merely as "a mystical society to which Yeats belonged in early adulthood" (p. 28).

Finally, there is the issue of what is—and is not—included in the discussion of Yeats's own work. The largest omissions are of any extended analyses of the plays and critical prose. Admittedly, the plays pose difficulties if we identify "poetic persona" simply with "I" (but one thinks immediately of the Old Man in *The Death of Cuchulain*). Still, such poet figures as Aleel and Seanchan seem as relevant to Schricker's argument as the narrators of the *Celtic Twi-*

light and the *Secret Rose* stories. And, on the matter of Yeats's fiction, why no mention of *The Speckled Bird*? There are references to the critical essays, but they are rarely more than references. Surely many of them, especially some in *Ideas of Good and Evil* or "J. M. Synge and the Ireland of his Time," are important evidence about Yeats's persona. Discussion of them would have challenged and enriched Schricker's argument.

To return to where I began, *A New Species of Man* has the strengths and also the weaknesses of a good dissertation. It makes some interesting general points, offers some useful specific insights. But the book as it stands does not offer the intellectual challenges of the best work on its general topic, and one eventually grows tired of the insistence on a theoretical model that seems too closed a system and too rigidly applied to provoke much intensive response from the reader. A few more years, more reading, more testing of ideas, and a means of expression freer of the belaborings of dissertations would have made this a much stronger book.

Passim: Brief Notices

MARY FITZGERALD

This section contains brief notices of publications which refer to the life and work of W. B. Yeats only briefly or in passing. Although these items are not sufficiently Yeats-oriented to warrant extended review in this annual, they may well be of interest to our readers.

Valuable Autograph Letters & Historical Documents.
[Christie's sale catalog for 20 July 1983.]
London: Christie's, Manson and Woods, Ltd., 1983. 67 pp.

Items 396 and 397 in this catalog (pp. 56–59) are of special interest to Yeatsians. The first is a substantial portion of the W. B. Yeats–Dorothy Wellesley correspondence, published and unpublished, and the second consists of twelve letters from Yeats to Douglas Hyde, dating from 1888 to 1889. Both sets are described in detail, with quotation from letters. On page 57, several published letters are noted as missing from the collection offered for sale: most of these are in the Humanities Research Center at the University of Texas at Austin.

English Literature, Comprising Printed Books, Autograph Letters, and Manuscripts.
[Sotheby's sale catalog for 21–22 July 1983.]
London: Sotheby Parke Bernet & Co., 1983. 231 pp.

This sale catalog contains eighteen pages of detailed descriptions of many Yeats items of great interest to Yeats scholars (pp. 202–20), some of them from the personal library of our late colleague Oliver Edwards, others from the estates of Lennox Robinson and the heirs of Lady Gregory. Letters are quoted in excerpted form, and black and white reproductions of a John Butler Yeats sketch of W. B. Yeats, "probably drawn at Coole in about 1899," and a pastel drawing of the river and lake at Coole Park by the poet himself are offered (pp. 202–3).

British Poets, 1880–1914. Donald Stanford, ed.
Dictionary of Literary Biography, 19.
Detroit: Gale Research, 1983. 486 pp.

This reference volume, which follows the standard format for the Dictionary of Literary Biography—bibliography, photographs, and brief critical essays—contains a fifty-three page entry on Yeats (by far the longest in the volume), written by B. L. Reid (pp. 399–452). In accordance with the DLB formula, the essay is primarily biographical in structure, and well over half of it is given to explicating major poems. Reid has risen admirably to the challenge of compressing Yeats's entire poetic career into less than fifty pages (good photographs of the poet and of several of his manuscripts take up some of the pages), though he seems simply to stop after offering a reading of "The Circus Animals' Desertion," instead of making some concluding summation. Very occasionally he lapses into misstatement, as when he gives Mrs. Yeats's name as Georgiana or conflates Yeats's two harangues of the Abbey audience into one (The phrase, "You have disgraced yourselves again," was uttered to the audience rioting at Sean O'Casey's *The Plough and the Stars,* not to those who hated *The Playboy of the*

Western World), but on the whole the essay does what it is meant to do: be helpful to students. The prose style is lively and usefully anecdotal, and the reproductions of Yeats's manuscripts prove very handy indeed.

Edward Callan. *Auden: A Carnival of Intellect.*
New York and Oxford: Oxford University Press, 1983. 299 pp.

Yeats appears sporadically throughout this fine critical biography of W. H. Auden. He is, moreover, the subject of an entire chapter, "Disenchantment with Yeats: *From Singing-Master to Ogre*" (pp. 143–62). Callan notes that "much of the story of Auden's development as a poet after 1940 is also the story of his struggle to exorcise the persistent spirit of Yeats. The stages of his growing disenchantment with Yeats mark the hardening of his conviction that the greatest threats to individual freedom in the modern world—the Utopias of both left and right—were a direct legacy of the Romantic outlook on which Yeats prided himself" (pp. 145–46). He traces this growing disenchantment in Auden's several revisions of "In Memory of W. B. Yeats," in his repudiation of "September 1, 1939," and in his opera *Elegy for Young Lovers,* whose main character clearly derives from and parodies Yeats. Callan has much to offer his fellow Yeatsians in this chapter and in the book as a whole.

The Celtic Consciousness. Robert O'Driscoll, ed.
Dublin: Dolmen Press, 1982. xxxi + 642 pp.

For sheer heft, nothing quite matches this weighty volume, done with characteristic elegance and finesse by Liam Miller's Dolmen Press. Since it is physically likely to last forever, one wishes that its contents were uniformly up to the standard of excellence exhibited by its form. But given its genesis—it is a collection of essays and poems inspired by and submitted to the conference

"Canada and the Celtic Consciousness" held in February 1978—variety in scholarly quality was unavoidable. The fifty-three individual items (not counting foreword, introduction, and epilogue) ably assembled and edited by Robert O'Driscoll constitute a smorgasbord of topics by various scholars, ranging from "Celtic Calligraphy: From Penstroke to Print" to "David Jones." Some are to be tasted, others to be swallowed, and some few to be chewed and digested. Yeats is directly concerned in essays by O'Driscoll and by Lorna Reynolds; Yeatsians will find much that they already know in both, as Yeats is discussed in terms of the conference theme and so is used to shed light rather than to have light shed upon him; and they may well wish to browse through the other essays, some of them controversial.

Anthony Cronin. *Heritage Now; Irish Literature in the English Language.*
Dingle, Co. Kerry: Brandon, 1982. 214 pp.

The relatively new Brandon Book Publishers present this collection of nineteen vigorous essays by Anthony Cronin, dealing with major Irish writers from the dawn of Anglo-Irish literature to the present. He covers Maria Edgeworth, Thomas Moore, William Carleton, James Clarence Mangan, Charles Lever, William Allingham, George Moore, Edith Somerville and Martin Ross, John Millington Synge, James Joyce (two chapters), James Stephens, Thomas MacGreevy, Francis Stuart, Samuel Beckett, Patrick Kavanagh, Louis MacNeice, Flann O'Brien, and of course W. B. Yeats.

The essays have diverse origins—some as radio talks or book reviews—but all are revised thoughtfully and well for this collection. (There are no footnotes, although occasionally a scholarly work is cited in the text.) These essays, moreover, do more than merely record the author's personal response to the writers under discussion. The insights offered on many writers are thought-provoking, and the point of view—that of a contemporary Irish poet considering the present state of the Irish reputations of those concerned—provides a consistent perspective.

Most of the chapters attempt to define and to assess the writer's "place" in the Anglo-Irish canon, and the one on Yeats is no exception. Although it is only seven pages long (pp. 87–93), most of it in the nature of intelligent and well-read appreciation rather than analysis, it offers something worthwhile. There is nothing especially new in it for readers of this annual, except perhaps the observation that the poets who began to write immediately after Yeats's death were perhaps less dominated by him than is commonly believed, largely because of Macmillan's "strange policy with their paper ration during the war years and after which meant that his *Collected Poems* did not appear again until 1950; and if verbal and technical influences do not take early enough they do not take at all" (p. 88).

Christopher Fitz-Simon. *The Arts in Ireland: A Chronology*. Dublin: Gill and Macmillan; Atlantic Highlands, N.J.: Humanities Press, 1982. 257 pp.

This book-length time-line of Irish literary and artistic history covers major events from 7000 B.C. to 1970 A.D. Dates of landmark occurrences outside Ireland are supplied as pointers from time to time, but the focus is primarily and narrowly on the range implied in the title of the volume.

Handsomely produced, it is easy on the eye, with bold lettering and no stinting of white space, and it is sumptuously illustrated throughout with black and white photographs and sketches of art and artists. Yeats is represented by his plays and poems and a full-page reproduction of his father's 1900 portrait, appearing at appropriate and familiar intervals.

The Arts in Ireland is a handy and worthwhile reference tool that should prove especially useful in keeping Yeats's achievements in their historical context among the other literary and artistic milestones in Irish affairs. For those whose knowledge of Ireland is less than thorough, the book is bound to seem a necessity, but even for those Yeatsians whose grasp of Irish literature and history is quite firm it will likely prove a pleasant browsing experience time and time again.

Robert G. Lowery. *Sean O'Casey's Autobiographies: An Annotated Index.*
London; Westport, Conn.: Greenwood Press, 1983. xxxi + 487 pp.

Yeatsians will find this book useful to the extent that Sean O'Casey's life and career as recorded in his six volumes of autobiography intertwine with Yeats's life and career—which is to say, quite a bit—not only for the obviously easier reference to the Yeats passages in O'Casey that it makes possible, but also for its wealth of information on people, places, and events that shaped the lives of both writers. For all entries, Robert Lowery gives identification and context, supplying page references to the American edition of the autobiographies and, for the United Kingdom, the PAN paperback edition, because "it was the latest larger printing (from 1971), and if it is not in print when this appears, it should still be easier to obtain than the first British editions or the two-volume Macmillan paperback (1963)" and because "it incorporates all the changes for the first printings" (p. xxvi).

Lowery has also drawn attention to the many variants—though he does not cite them all here—and has suggested the need for a new, more scholarly edition of the autobiographies. He has, with this volume, certainly provided a very helpful reference tool for all who work in modern Irish literature.

Roger McHugh and Maurice Harmon. *Short History of Anglo-Irish Literature from Its Origins to the Present Day.*
Totowa, N.J.: Barnes & Noble, 1982. 377 pp.

In six chapters, from "The Older Civilization and Its Literature" to "Contemporary Writing," with an appendix on Synge's dialect, McHugh and Harmon trace at almost breakneck speed the outline of the history of Irish literature in the English language. As befits his stature, Yeats appears *passim* throughout the book, from page 28 to page 208. He is treated most fully in the chapters entitled "The Irish Literary Revival" and "After the Revival," but given the scope of this enterprise and the space limitations, he is accorded a necessarily superficial treatment. Nonetheless, the book certainly places Yeats in his Irish literary context, and for that reason it should be welcomed and read by many students—and even some more advanced Yeats scholars.

Recent Research on Anglo-Irish Writers: A Supplement to Anglo-Irish Literature: A Review of Research. Richard J. Finneran, ed.
New York: Modern Language Association, 1983. xvi + 361 pp.

As the subtitle suggests, this volume updates the 1976 edition of the MLA review of research in Anglo-Irish literature, bringing commentary on the published criticism about leading Irish writers up to 1981 (and in some cases 1982). The Yeats chapter is once again the work of Richard Finneran. In addition, chapters on modern fiction and modern poetry now complement the updated coverage of modern drama. The range is comprehensive, and commentary is brief and pointed. An index is provided.

Vale: F. S. L. Lyons

F. S. L. Lyons died in Dublin on 21 September 1983, after a sudden illness. He was only fifty-nine. Scarcely a few months earlier, after years of research, he had begun writing the preliminary draft of his authorized biography of W. B. Yeats.

Of Lyons's standing as the leading Irish historian of his generation we need not speak: the books remain, the record of honors and awards is too lengthy to recite. Yet when his appointment to take up the biography was announced early in 1974, many Yeatsians were skeptical: would a historian—even one of his undoubted stature—have the literary sensitivity necessary to do justice to the biography of so complex a writer? All such fears were quickly dispelled when Lyons began to lecture and to publish on Yeats. It was immediately evident that here was a superb scholar who had mastered the methodology of a discipline not his own, and who had immersed himself in both the primary and secondary materials to such a degree that we could turn to him, as he had initially turned to us, for opinions and advice. At the time of his death, no one had any thought but that the biography would be a masterpiece, the equal of anything he had done, a cornerstone of Yeats studies for the remainder of this century and beyond.

He was a joy to work with. The anonymous obituary in *The Times* (24 September 1983), in the midst of much well-deserved praise, noted oddly that something in Lyons's manner "precluded intimacy." We are confident that all Yeatsians fortunate enough to meet and to get to know the man in the last several years would join us in finding that judgment utterly wrong. Indeed, it was precisely his human qualities that first impressed one, quite apart from his scholarly reputation or his stature as Yeats's biographer. His letters were marvelously witty and warm—as well as prompt and helpful—and each of us has a favorite personal memory of him. Those of us who attended the Yeats Symposium last year, where he heard much of what appears in this volume, share a memory that we cherish especially, his speech at the closing banquet. Recounting his adventures as the authorized biographer, he ended, too generously, with thanks to his fellow Yeatsians: "I was a stranger and you took me in."

Yeats once suggested that

> Not what it leaves behind it in the light
> But what it carries with it to the dark
> Exalts the soul. . . .

We would not debate that concept, but we would add in commentary that what Leland Lyons has left to us is a shining legacy indeed: an image not only of the true scholar but also of the "perfection of mankind."